HOW THE WEST WON

HOW THE WEST
WON

The Neglected Story of
the Triumph of Modernity

Rodney Stark

ISI
BOOKS

Wilmington, Delaware

Library of Congress Cataloging-in-Publication Data

Stark, Rodney.

How the West won : the neglected story of the triumph of modernity / Rodney Stark.
— 1st edition. pages ; cm
Includes bibliographical references and index.
ISBN 978-1-61017-085-7
  1. Civilization, Western—History. 2. Civilization, Modern—History. 3. Science—History. 4. Technology—History. 5. Intellectual life--History. I. Title.
CB245.S715 2014
909'.09821—dc23
                     2013047815

Published in the United States by

ISI Books
Intercollegiate Studies Institute
3901 Centerville Road
Wilmington, Delaware 19807-1938
www.isibooks.org

Manufactured in the United States of America

Contents

Contents

Introduction

What You *Don't* Know about the Rise of the West

This is a remarkably unfashionable book.

Forty years ago the most important and popular freshman course at the best American colleges and universities was "Western Civilization." It not only covered the general history of the West but also included historical surveys of art, music, literature, philosophy, and science. But this course has long since disappeared from most college catalogues on grounds that Western civilization is but one of many civilizations and it is ethnocentric and arrogant for us to study ours.[1]

It is widely claimed that to offer a course in "Western Civilization" is to become an apologist "for Western hegemony and oppression" (as the classicist Bruce Thornton aptly put it).[2] Thus, Stanford dropped its widely admired "Western Civilization" course just months after the Reverend Jesse Jackson came on campus and led members of the Black Student Union in chants of "Hey-hey, ho-ho, Western Civ has got to go."[3] More recently, faculty at the University of Texas condemned "Western Civilization" courses as inherently right wing, and Yale even returned a $20 million contribution rather than reinstate the course.

To the extent that this policy prevails, Americans will become increasingly ignorant of how the modern world came to be. Worse yet, they are in danger of being badly misled by a flood of absurd, politically correct fabrications, all of them popular on college campuses: That the Greeks copied their whole culture from black Egyptians.[4] That European science originated in Islam.[5] That Western affluence was stolen from non-Western societies.[6] That Western modernity was really produced in China, and not so very long ago.[7] The truth is that, although the West wisely adopted bits and pieces of technology from Asia, modernity is *entirely* the product of Western civilization.

I use the term *modernity* to identify that fundamental store of scientific knowledge and procedures, powerful technologies, artistic achievements, political freedoms, economic arrangements, moral sensibilities, and improved standards of living that characterize Western nations and are now revolutionizing life in the rest of the world. For there is another truth: to the extent that other cultures have failed to adopt at least major aspects of Western ways, they remain backward and impoverished.

Ideas Matter

This book is not, however, simply a summary of the standard lessons of the old "Western Civilization" classes. Despite their value, these courses usually were far too enamored of philosophy and art, far too reluctant to acknowledge the positive effects of Christianity, and amazingly oblivious to advances in technology, especially those transforming mundane activities such as farming and banking.

In addition, while writing this volume I frequently found it necessary to challenge the received wisdom about Western history. To mention only a few examples:

- Rather than a great tragedy, the fall of Rome was the single most *beneficial* event in the rise of Western civilization. The many stultifying centuries of Roman rule saw only two significant instances of progress: the invention of concrete and the rise of Christianity, the latter taking place despite Roman attempts to prevent it.
- The "Dark Ages" never happened—that was an era of remarkable progress and innovation that included the invention of capitalism.
- The crusaders did not march east in pursuit of land and loot. They went deeply into debt to finance their participation in what they regarded as a religious mission. Most thought it unlikely that they would live to return (and most didn't).

- Although still ignored by most historians, dramatic changes in climate played a major role in the rise of the West—a period of unusually warm weather (from about 800 to about 1250) was followed by centuries of extreme cold, now known as the Little Ice Age (from about 1300 to about 1850).
- There was no "Scientific Revolution" during the seventeenth century—these brilliant achievements were the culmination of normal scientific progress stretching back to the founding of universities in the twelfth century by Scholastic natural philosophers.
- The Reformations did not result in religious freedom but merely replaced repressive Catholic monopoly churches with equally repressive Protestant monopoly churches (it became a serious criminal offense to celebrate the Mass in most of Protestant Europe).
- Europe did not grow rich by draining wealth from its worldwide colonies; in fact, the colonies drained wealth from Europe—and meanwhile gained the benefits of modernity.

Also, both the textbooks and the instructors involved in the old "Western Civ" courses were content merely to describe the rise of Western civilization. They usually avoided any comparisons with Islam or Asia and ignored the issue of *why* modernity happened only in the West. That is the neglected story I aim to tell.

To explore that question is not ethnocentric; it is the only way to develop an informed understanding of how and why the modern world emerged as it did.

In early times China was far ahead of Europe in terms of many vital technologies. But when Portuguese voyagers reached China in 1517, they found a backward society in which the privileged classes were far more concerned with crippling young girls by binding their feet than with developing more productive agriculture—despite frequent famines. Why?

Or why did the powerful Ottoman Empire depend on Western foreigners to provide it with fleets and arms?[8]

Or how was it possible for a relative handful of British officials, aided by a few regular army officers and noncommissioned officers, to rule the enormous Indian subcontinent?

Or, to change the focus, why did science and democracy originate in the West, along with representational art, chimneys, soap, pipe organs, and a system of musical notation? Why was it that for several hundred years beginning in the thirteenth century only Europeans had eyeglasses and mechanical clocks? And what about telescopes, microscopes, and periscopes?

There have been many attempts to answer these questions. Several recent authors attribute it all to favorable geography—that Europe benefited from a benign climate, more fertile fields, and abundant natural resources, especially iron and coal.[9] But, as Victor Davis Hanson pointed out in his book *Carnage and Culture*, "China, India, and Africa are especially blessed in natural ores, and enjoy growing seasons superior to those of northern Europe."[10] Moreover, much of Europe was covered with dense hardwood forests that could not readily be cleared to permit farming or grazing until iron tools became available. Little wonder that Europe was long occupied by cultures far behind those of the Middle East and Asia.

Other scholars have attributed the success of the West to guns and steel, to sailing ships, or to superior agriculture.[11] The problem here is that these "causes" are part of what needs to be explained: why did Europeans excel at metallurgy, shipbuilding, and farming? The same objection arises to the claim that science holds the secret to "Western domination,"[12] as well as to the Marxist thesis that it was all due to capitalism.[13] Why did science and capitalism develop only in Europe?

In attempting to explain this remarkable cultural singularity, I will, of course, pay attention to material factors—obviously history would have been quite different had Europe lacked iron and coal or been landlocked. Even so, my explanations will not rest primarily on material conditions and forces. Instead I give primacy to *ideas*, even though this is quite unfashionable in contemporary scholarly circles. I do so because I fully agree with the distinguished economist and historian Deirdre McCloskey that "material, economic forces . . . were not the original and sustaining causes of the modern rise." Or, as she put it in the subtitle of her fine book: "Why economics can't explain the modern world." Quietly mocking Karl Marx, McCloskey asserted that Europe achieved modernity because of "ideology."[14]

If Marx was sincere when he dismissed the possibility of ideas being causative agents as "ideological humbug,"[15] one must wonder why he labored so long to communicate his socialist ideas rather than just relaxing and letting "economic determinism" run its "inevitable" course. In fact, Marx's beloved material causes exist mainly as humans *perceive* them—as people pursue goals guided by their ideas about what is desirable and possible. Indeed, to explain why working-class people so often did not embrace the socialist revolution, Marx and Friedrich Engels had to invent the concept of "false consciousness"—an entirely *ideological* cause.

Similarly, it is ideas that explain why science arose only in the West. Only Westerners thought that science was possible, that the universe functioned according to rational rules that could be discovered. We owe this belief partly to the ancient Greeks and partly to the unique Judeo-Christian conception of God as a rational creator. Clearly, then, the French historian Daniel Mornet had it right when he said that the French Revolution would not have occurred had there not been widespread poverty, but neither would it have occurred without revolutionary philosophies, for it was "ideas that set men in motion."[16]

Once we recognize the primacy of ideas, we realize the irrelevance of long-running scholarly debates about whether certain inventions were developed independently in Europe or imported from the East. The act of invention is obviously crucial, but just as important, societies must value innovations enough to *use* them. The Chinese, for example, developed gunpowder very early on—but centuries later they still lacked artillery and firearms. An iron industry flourished in northern China in the eleventh century—but then Mandarins at the imperial court declared a state monopoly on iron and seized everything, destroying China's iron production.

This book explains why such setbacks occurred—and why they did *not* occur in the West.

Turning Points

Finally, I will be equally out of fashion by giving weight to specific events. It has become the received wisdom that events such as battles are mere decorations on the great flow of history, that the triumph of the Greeks over the immense Persian host at Marathon (490 BC) or their sinking of the Persian fleet at Salamis (480 BC) merely reflected (as one popular historian put it) "something deeper . . . a shift in economic power from the

Fertile Crescent to the Mediterranean."[17] Rot! Had the very badly out-numbered Greeks lost either battle, that "shift" would not have occurred and we probably never would have heard of Plato or Aristotle.

Of course, the Greeks won, Plato and Aristotle lived, and Western civilization flourished. That is the story I shall tell.

Part I

Classical Beginnings
(500 BC–AD 500)

1

Stagnant Empires and the Greek "Miracle"

One easily supposes that large societies are a modern phenomenon. Not so. At the dawn of history most people lived lives of misery and exploitation in tyrannical empires that covered huge areas.[1]

The first empire arose in Mesopotamia more than six thousand years ago.[2] Then came the Egyptian, Chinese, Persian, and Indian empires. All these empires suffered from chronic power struggles among the ruling elites, but aside from those, some border wars, and immense public-works projects, very little happened. Change, whether technological or cultural, was so slow as to go nearly unnoticed. As the centuries passed most people lived as they always had, "just a notch above barest subsistence . . . little better off than their oxen," in the words of the anthropologist Marvin Harris.[3] This was not because they lacked the potential to achieve a much higher standard of living but because a predatory ruling elite extracted every ounce of "surplus" production. All signs of resistance were brutally crushed.

In the midst of all this misery and repression, a "miracle" of progress and freedom took place in Greece among people who lived not in an empire but in hundreds of small, independent city-states. It was here that the formation of Western civilization began. Sad to say, this beacon of human potential eventually was extinguished by the rise of new empires. But its legacies survived.

The Poverty of Ancient Empires

We remain fascinated by accounts of the opulent splendor of ancient imperial courts, of gigantic palaces with golden fixtures and silk-lined walls, of bejeweled wives and concubines served by countless slaves and servants. Imagine the wealth of the great Egyptian pharaohs in light of the staggering treasures buried with King Tutankhamun (1341–1323 BC), a minor and short-lived pharaoh. Even though Tut's coffin was made of solid gold, his treasures are mere trinkets compared with what must have been buried with Ramesses II (ca. 1303–1213 BC), who probably was the wealthiest and most powerful of all the pharaohs. But it wasn't only treasure that was buried with the early pharaohs; many of their retainers, wives, concubines, and even pet dogs were slaughtered and placed in their tombs. One First Dynasty royal Egyptian tomb included 318 sacrificed humans; their average age was estimated to have been twenty-five.[4] In Mesopotamia an emperor's entire court, including not only wives and servants but also senior officials and confidants, was buried with the sovereign. And late in the second millennium BC, each Chinese royal funeral saw *thousands* put to death.[5]

In all the ancient empires, monumentalism was rife. Pharaohs built pyramids, huge statues such as the Sphinx, immense shrines, and even whole personal cities. The rulers of Mesopotamia built enormous ziggurats, shrines consisting of a set of huge square blocks (or floors) of decreasing size set atop one another, often having five levels or more. The setbacks surrounding each block were often landscaped with trees and shrubs (hence the "Hanging Gardens" of Babylon). The largest surviving ziggurat, near Susa in southern Iran, is 336 feet per side at the base and is estimated to have been about seventeen stories high.[6]

But despite such monuments and fabulous royal wealth, the great empires were very poor. As the historian E. L. Jones noted, "Emperors amassed vast wealth but received incomes that were nevertheless small relative to the immensity of the territories and populations governed."[7] Indeed, because of imperial opulence, "century after century the standard of living in China, northern India, Mesopotamia, and Egypt hovered slightly above or below what might be called the threshold of pauperization," as Marvin Harris put it.[8] Too often historians have noted the immense wealth of rulers without grasping the sacrifices this imposed on the populace. The Wikipedia article on the Maurya Empire, which ruled most of India from 321 to 185 BC, praises it for generating prosperity, while innocently noting a report from the time that the Indians "all live frugally . . . and their food is principally a rice-pottage," as though this were merely a matter of preference. To quote Jones once again, "The splendours of Asian courts . . . merely testify that political organization could squeeze blood out of stones if the stones were numerous enough."[9]

A review of tax rates imposed by the ancient empires reveals just how hard the nobility squeezed. In Mesopotamia the official tax rate was 10 percent of all crops, but in fact the collectors often demanded as much as half. In Egypt the pharaoh took at least a fifth of all harvests and required peasants to work on "public" projects in the off-season. In India the ruler was entitled to one-fourth of the crop and could take a third in "emergencies."[10] Local elites and landlords usually took even more. With taxes claiming half or more of a harvest, and about a third of a grain crop kept to provide seeds for the next planting, the peasants had very little left for their own subsistence. In addition to taxes were outright confiscations of individuals' entire wealth, which often required no justification. Hence, as Ricardo Caminos put it about the ancient Egyptians, "peasant families always wavered between abject poverty and utter destitution."[11]

If the elite seizes all production above the minimum needed for survival, people have no motivation to produce more. In despotic states where rulers concentrate on exacting the maximum amount from those they control, subjects become notably avaricious too. They consume, hoard, and hide the fruits of their labor, and they fail to produce nearly as much as they might. Even when some people do manage to be productive, chances are that their efforts will merely enrich their rulers. The result is a standard of living far below the society's potential productive capacities. The average free citizen did not live much better than did the huge numbers held in slavery by the ancient empires.

The economic system of ancient empires and of all despotic states has come to be known as the *command economy*,[12] since the state commands and coerces markets and labor—to exact wealth for itself—rather than allowing them to function freely. The people are usually subject not only to confiscatory taxation but also to forced labor, which accounts for the monumentalism of empires. Pharaohs did not hire tens of thousands of peasants to build pyramids; they forced them to do so—and fed them so poorly and exposed them to such dangerous working conditions that many did not survive.[13] It is estimated that nearly six million Chinese peasants were forced to build the Grand Canal in China, and perhaps as many as two million of them died.[14] Another million probably died to build the Great Wall of China.[15]

Command economies began with the earliest empires and have lasted in many parts of the modern world—they still attract ardent advocates. But command economies neglect the most basic economic fact of life: *All wealth derives from production.* It must be grown, dug up, cut down, hunted, herded, fabricated, or otherwise created. The amount of wealth produced within any society depends not only on the number involved in production but also on their motivation and the effectiveness of their productive technology. When wealth is subject to devastating taxes and the constant threat of usurpation, the challenge is to *keep* one's wealth, not to make it productive. This principle applies not merely to the wealthy but with even greater force to those with very little—which accounts for the substantial underproduction of command economies.

An example will clarify these points.

Late in the tenth century an iron industry began to develop in parts of northern China.[16] By 1018 the smelters were producing an estimated 35,000 tons a year, an incredible achievement for the time, and sixty years later they may have been producing more than 100,000 tons. This was not a government operation. Private individuals had seized the opportunity presented by a strong demand for iron and the supplies of easily mined ore and coal. With the smelters and foundries located along a network of canals and navigable rivers, the iron could be easily brought to distant markets. Soon these new Chinese iron industrialists were reaping huge profits and reinvesting heavily in the expansion of their smelters and foundries. The availability of large supplies of iron led to the introduction of iron agricultural tools, which in turn began to increase food production. In short, China began to enter an "industrial revolution."

But then it all stopped as suddenly as it had begun. By the end of the eleventh century, only tiny amounts of iron were produced, and soon after that the smelters and foundries were abandoned ruins. What had happened?

Eventually, Mandarins at the imperial court had noticed that some commoners were getting rich by manufacturing and were hiring peasant laborers at high wages. They deemed such activities to be threats to Confucian values and social tranquility. Commoners must know their place; only the elite should be wealthy. So they declared a state monopoly on iron and seized everything. And that was that. As the nineteenth-century historian Winwood Reade summed up, the reason for China's many centuries of economic and social stagnation is plain: *"Property is insecure. In this one phrase the whole history of Asia is contained."*[17]

No wonder that progress was so slow within the ancient empires. Anything of value—land, crops, livestock, buildings, even children—could be arbitrarily seized, and as the Chinese iron magnates learned, it often was. Worse yet, the tyrannical empires invested little of the wealth they extracted to increase production. They consumed it instead—often in various forms of display. The Egyptian pyramids, the Hanging Gardens of Babylon, and the Taj Mahal were all built as beautiful monuments to repressive rule; they were without productive value and were paid for by misery and want.

The ancient empires inherited a considerable level of civilization from the societies they combined and ruled, and technological progress may have continued as an empire consolidated its grasp. But then improvements effectively stopped.[18] For example, in 1900 Chinese peasants were using essentially the same tools and techniques they had been using for more than three thousand years. The same was true in Egypt. Despite their dependence on agriculture, in none of the ancient empires (including Rome) was there any selective breeding of plants or animals.[19]

Stagnation occurred because the ruling elites had no need for innovations and usually neither rewarded innovators nor adopted their innovations. Worse, the ruling elites often destroyed, outlawed, or made little use of innovations that did occur, whether of domestic or foreign origin. For example, the Romans knew of the watermill but made nearly no use of it, continuing to rely on muscle power to grind their flour.[20] The Ottoman Empire prohibited the mechanical clock, and so did the Chinese.[21] (Imperial opposition to progress is pursued at greater length in chapter 2.)

The Greek "Miracle"

Amid these long centuries of exploitation and stagnation, suddenly there burst forth the Greek "miracle," an era of prodigious progress: intellectual and artistic as well as technological.[22] In her famous book *The Greek Way*, the great classicist Edith Hamilton noted that what most set the

Greeks apart from all prior societies was joyful living. This way of life was "something quite new," she wrote:

> The Greeks were the first people in the world to play, and they played on a great scale. All over Greece there were games, all sorts of games; athletic contests of every description . . . contests in music, where one side outsung the other; in dancing . . . games so many that one grows weary with the list of them. . . . Wretched people, toiling people, do not play. Nothing like the Greek games is conceivable in Egypt or Mesopotamia. . . . Play died when Greece died and many a century passed before it was resurrected.[23]

Greek play reflected the exuberance of life in small societies of free citizens. In this era, freedom too was unique to Greece (despite the multitudes of slaves). And out of this freedom grew not only joy and play but also the first flood of innovations leading to modernity.

Historians date the beginning of ancient Greek civilization to around 750 BC, but the brilliant era of Greek achievement began about 600 BC and ended in about 338 BC, when Philip of Macedon (father of Alexander the Great) conquered the Greeks. Even in these golden days, there really wasn't an ancient "Greece." What existed were Greeks—a single people, united, as Herodotus (484–425 BC) noted, by common blood, customs, language, and religion but who lived in about a thousand city-states.[24] Initially these city-states were politically independent.[25] Over time, some conquered others and many entered into alliances and unions, but overall there remained a diverse and independent set of small Greek societies.

The Greek city-states were located throughout what is today Greece and also in Sicily and southern Italy, around the Black Sea, and along the coast of Asia Minor (most of which is now Turkey)—"like frogs around a pond," as Plato put it. Many city-states were tiny, having no more than 1,000 residents,[26] and even the largest were small when compared with the populations of the empires of this era. In 430 BC Athens may have had a population of 155,000, Corinth was estimated to have 70,000 residents, and there were about 40,000 Spartans.[27] In contrast, there were about 40 million Persians.[28]

The independence of the city-states was aided by geography. Greece is crisscrossed with mountain ranges that occupy about 80 percent of the land area,[29] and each of the valleys scattered among the mountains (most of them coastal) sustained a city-state, and sometimes two. In addition, many islands in the nearby waters became city-states. Of course, the geography of Greece is quite contrary to claims that Europe's eventual supremacy rested on natural advantages. Even the best agricultural land in Greece is rocky and "its productivity is mediocre," as Leopold Migeotte notes in *The Economy of the Greek Cities*.[30] Moreover, observes Victor Davis Hanson in *Carnage and Culture*, Greece is "without a single large navigable river, cursed with almost no abundance of natural resources."[31] In contrast, the great empires of the time—including Egypt, Persia, and China—occupied huge, fertile plains well served by major rivers. This facilitated control from a central capital.[32] Thus, having an "unfavorable" geography contributed to the greatness of Greece, for disunity and competition were fundamental to everything else.

Michael Grant spoke for all classical historians when he wrote, "The achievement of the . . . Greeks, in a wide variety of fields, was stupendous."[33] Here the focus will be on six areas. First comes warfare, because only the Greeks' remarkable military superiority allowed them to survive as independent city-states rather than to have been submerged by the Persian Empire. Next is the great Greek achievement of democracy, followed by economic progress, literacy, the arts, and technology. Then the chapter turns to a seventh field, the most lasting of all the Greek achievements: speculative philosophy and formal logic.

Warfare

Given constant wars among the many Greek city-states, the Greeks developed weapons and tactics far superior to those of contemporary empires, especially the nearby Persians. Perhaps the most important factor distinguishing Greek armies from those of the surrounding empires is that the men in the ranks were neither mercenaries nor slaves but citizen soldiers (known as hoplites). The self-interest of Greek fighters was, therefore, not merely to survive a battle but to win it, thus defending their homes, possessions, and families. Despite being civilians, Greek soldiers were far better trained and disciplined than their opponents, which was essential for fulfilling the tactics that made Greek formations devastatingly superior to their enemies.

It is obvious that, all else being equal, victory will go to the side that outnumbers the other. What is less obvious is that where outnumbering really counts is not across the whole field of battle but at the points of contact. And by use of the phalanx—a dense, highly coordinated formation—the Greeks greatly outnumbered their enemies where the two sides actually met.

The phalanx consisted of closely packed infantry, four to eight rows deep, wearing bronze helmets with cheek plates, breast plates, and greaves, or leg armor. (Because of the weight of their armor, they were called heavy infantry.) Each Greek soldier also carried a large shield that protected his left side and the right side of the man next to him. From this wall of shields were projected sharp pikes (seven to nine feet long) that could stab opponents, often before they could reach the Greeks with their weapons.[34] Intensive practice allowed the phalanx to maneuver as a single unit, in response to commands. Of particular significance when fighting non-Greek foes, the phalanx was nearly impervious to cavalry charges, the horses being impaled on the pikes. As military historian Jim Lacey explained, "When it comes to cavalry charging a phalanx, human bravery counts for nothing. It was the courage of the horse that mattered, and in this case [the Battle of Marathon] Persia's fabled Nesaian mounts proved to be no braver than any other horse."[35]

Greek opponents, often Persians, usually wore little or no armor, and most of them used a weapon such as a sword or an axe that was swung, not jabbed, and therefore required "elbow room." Because of the compactness of the phalanx and the looseness of non-Greek formations, Greeks outnumbered their opponents by as many as three to one when the two groups collided—and suffered many fewer casualties. Herodotus described Persian tactics against the Spartans in the Battle of Plataea (479 BC): "They were dashing out beyond the front lines individually or in groups of ten . . . charging right into the Spartan ranks where they perished."[36] According to Herodotus, at the famous Battle of Marathon (490 BC) about 10,000 Athenians confronted about 50,000 Persians, with the loss of only 192 Greeks but more than 6,000 Persians.[37]

The Greeks were able to drive a huge Persian force from the battlefield by exhibiting a style of warfare that has remained the basic Western model ever after—*well-organized, well-armed, highly trained and disciplined infantry having high morale and tactical flexibility.*[38] Morale cannot be overlooked. When the renowned Greek dramatist Aeschylus (525–456 BC) died, his epitaph (which he wrote himself) made no mention of his plays but noted only that he had fought at Marathon—"of his noble prowess, the grove of Marathon can speak, or the long-haired Persians who know it well."[39]

There is no better summation of Greek military superiority than the stirring adventures of a Greek army in Persia as reported by the Greek general and remarkable writer-historian Xenophon (430–354 BC). His *The Persian Expedition* (also known as *The March Up Country*) is one of the great reads in Western literature.

Xenophon was born in Athens to an aristocratic family and studied for several years with the philosopher Socrates (ca. 470–399 BC), about whom he eventually wrote a book. (That a student of Socrates became a famous soldier is not so strange given the rarely mentioned fact that Socrates himself took part as an ordinary soldier in three military campaigns and distinguished himself for his bravery.) At around age thirty, Xenophon joined a Greek mercenary army being recruited by Cyrus the Younger to seize the Persian throne from his brother Artaxerxes II.[40] Although Greek armies consisted of citizen volunteers, there always were some adventuresome souls who, during peacetime, were willing to fight elsewhere for pay. In 401 BC an army of 10,000 Greek mercenaries set forth into Persia, where they were joined by an army of Persians and marched about 1,500 miles to confront Artaxerxes's imperial army at Cunaxa, north of Babylon. During the battle the Greek phalanxes smashed an entire wing of the huge imperial army while suffering only one casualty. Their superb performance was in vain, however, because Prince Cyrus was killed when he rashly charged across the battle line in pursuit of his brother. Subsequently, the Greek commander Clearchus was invited to a peace conference along with his other senior officers. They were betrayed and beheaded by Artaxerxes II. Left without leaders, deep in hostile Mesopotamia, the Greeks, known ever after as the Ten Thousand, had to consider their options. In a series of democratic votes they decided not to surrender but to fight their way home. They elected new officers, including Xenophon as a general, and set out on a long march along a dangerous route. Pursued all the way by a far larger Persian force that they had to defeat again and again, challenged by savage local tribes all along the way, caught in snow drifts in the high mountain passes, and afflicted with outbreaks of illness, the Ten Thousand reached safety after a yearlong journey covering several thousand miles. "Five out of six made it out alive," Victor Davis Hanson reports, "the majority of the dead lost not in battle, but in the high snows of Armenia."[41]

The performance of the Ten Thousand anticipated the results of foreign intrusions by Western forces over the next several millennia. Most Western expeditionary forces, from Alexander the Great to the British redcoats in Africa and India, were greatly outnumbered and often far from home. Nevertheless, they consistently routed their opponents because of the superiority of Western arms, tactics, and organization dating from the days of the ancient Greeks. For example, in 1879 at the Battle of Rorke's Drift in Africa, 139 British regulars, only 80 of them actual riflemen, were attacked by an army of more than 4,000 Zulus, by far Africa's most celebrated fighters, hundreds of them armed with captured British rifles. When it was over after ten hours of shooting, the tiny band of redcoats still stood firm in their disciplined formation surrounded by more than a thousand dead Zulus. The British suffered 15 dead and 12 wounded.[42]

This British victory was based on a fundamental principle of Western warfare as expressed by Plato: that true courage is the ability of a soldier to fight and stay in rank even when he knows the odds are against him.[43] The oath taken by young recruits to the Athenian army included: "I will not desert the man at my side wherever I am positioned in line."[44] A Roman army manual stressed that victory is achieved not "by mere numbers and innate courage, but by skill and training."[45] Indeed, intensive and realistic training has long been central to Western military might. As the great Jewish historian and Roman commander Josephus (AD 35–100) explained, the Roman army's "maneuvers are like bloodless battles, and their battles bloody maneuvers."[46]

That Plato concerned himself with military matters underlines what is the most fundamental aspect of Western military affairs: that war is too important to leave to brave hotheads. Rather, it is a matter requiring reflection and reason. Thus, beginning with the Greeks, the West has always possessed clearly articulated principles of warfare, culminating in such institutions as the U.S. Army War College, the Prussian *Kriegsakademie*, and the French *École Supérieure de Guerre*—institutions devoted to military *science*.

Democracy

The existence of so many close-by, independent communities had many consequences for Greek governance. For one thing, should citizens become too disaffected, they could pick up and move elsewhere. Many historical figures, such as philosophers, are known to have moved a number of times. Moreover, it was impossible for the elite to become distant, unapproachable rulers. Even Athens was so small that officials had to deal with the public face-to-face, which greatly limited their control and power.

When freedom is combined with groups too large to rely on informal decision making, experiments with political organization are inevitable. Consequently, the Greeks were among the first to systematically explore and develop various systems of democracy. In fact, they coined the word: *demos* is Greek for people, and *kratos* means power; hence democracy means people power. Democracy may have been first instituted in Athens, but it soon was widely adopted. In most city-states, as in Athens, *direct* democracy was practiced. That is, most important issues were decided by the votes of all male citizens. There were no class distinctions involved in Athenian citizenship (and in that of most city-states); men in manual occupations enjoyed full rights of citizenship, as did the wealthiest landowners. Indeed, since most officials were selected by drawing lots and all voters were eligible, "artisans, shopkeepers, workers, and traders" were always among those serving.[47] A major innovation was the written constitution spelling out the rules for governance—Aristotle summarized 157 different Greek city-state constitutions.[48]

Keep in mind that democracy merely gives power to the people; it does not ensure that power will be used wisely or humanely. That is, Athens did not have what came to be known as a "liberal" democracy— one committed to the rule of law and basic human rights. For example, Athenians several times voted to slaughter all the men and enslave all the women and children of a conquered city-state. They also voted to convict Socrates of heresy and to impose the death sentence.

In recent times it has become fashionable to scoff at Greek "democracy" on grounds that it excluded women and slaves. That seems excessively anachronistic, especially considering that the alternative was various forms of authoritarian rule, none of which freed the slaves or empowered women. Of course, Greek democracy was somewhat unstable, there being interludes of rule by tyrants. But somehow democracy was reinstated time and again—until the Macedonian invasion and the subsequent rule by Rome.

The major benefit of Greek democracy was sufficient freedom so that individuals could benefit from innovations making them more productive, with the collective result of economic progress.

Economic Progress

Although the study of ancient economics is inexact for want of reliable facts,[49] scholars agree that the ancient Greeks enjoyed centuries of economic growth, slow by modern standards but substantial for the time.[50]

As a consequence of democratic rule, taxes were much lower in the Greek city-states than in any empire of the era, and property was not subject to arbitrary seizure. It follows that increased productivity was profitable. The more that Greek farmers grew, for example, the higher their standard of living. We can assume, therefore, that they were inclined to seek and adopt more productive crops, methods, and equipment. The same ought to have applied to other producers. If so, the Greek city-states should have experienced long-term economic growth.

Evidence suggests that they did. For instance, archaeological evidence indicates significant improvement in the average diet. Measurements of skeletons of Greek men buried in ancient cemeteries reveal them to have been taller, on average, than Greek military recruits in 1949.[51] In addition, even as the leading Greek city-states experienced substantial population growth over the centuries,[52] the average level of consumption among peasants is estimated to have increased by about 50 percent.[53] An additional indication of economic growth in ancient Greece comes from the major increases in the average size of Greek houses: in the eighth century BC it was 53 square meters; by the sixth century BC it had grown to 122 square meters; and by the fifth century BC it was 325 square meters.[54]

The Greeks also developed a far more sophisticated economy with several modern aspects. First came a shift from commerce based on commodities to one based on finances—in *Politics*, Aristotle described this as the pursuit of "monetary acquisition." In keeping with that transition, the Greeks invented banks—which Edward Cohen, an expert on the ancient economy, described as "private businesses ('banks,' *trapezai*), which accepted from various sources funds ('deposits') for which they had an absolute obligation of repayment while being free to profit from, or even lose, these monies in their own loan and investment activities."[55] Many ancient societies had institutions that safeguarded deposits; very often temples had this function. But these were not banks. It was the lending and investment of deposits that defined these Greek entities as the first banks. Strangely enough, because the Greeks deemed it demeaning for a free man to work under someone else's control, even the banks consisted of an owner (and perhaps his wife) and a staff of slaves.[56] In any event, these developments not only reflected economic progress but also facilitated it.

At the height of the Greek "miracle," then, ordinary free Greeks lived far better than both their ancestors and their neighbors (such as the Persians) who suffered under imperial rule.

Literacy

Writing probably predated the rise of classical Greece by several thousand years, but elsewhere literacy was limited to a small set of scribes who wrote whatever communications and records were required by the elite. Everyone else lived in a purely oral culture. There were no books; if there were playwrights or philosophers, they left no trace.

Thus it was a cultural revolution when literacy became widespread in Greece—when as many as a third or more of freeborn men were able to read and write, as probably was the case in Athens and some other ancient Greek cities.[57] Greek literacy owed its initial debt to the development of a phonetic alphabet of only twenty-four letters, which made it far easier to read and to write, since words could be "sounded out."[58] Ideographic writing systems such as Chinese or ancient Egyptian required mastery of about three thousand different characters for elementary literacy—and as many as *fifty thousand* for full literacy.[59] The Greeks also founded schools where large numbers of boys (but not girls) learned to read.[60]

Widespread literacy resulted in books and the accumulation of learning. Books such as those by Herodotus and Xenophon preserved important historical knowledge. Great works of literature that had long existed only in oral form survived because they were written down. And philosophers were able to build their work on that of their predecessors—"unrolling the treasures . . . they have written down in books and left behind them," as Plato reported.[61] Of course, Greek philosophers have lived on to shape Western civilization only because so many of their books survived. Literacy also greatly facilitated the spread of accurate knowledge of new technology among the ancient Greeks. For all these reasons, the Greeks referred to writing as "the mother of memory."[62]

Arts

Greek sculpture was a revolution of realism (even if the focus was on ideally beautiful men and women). Whereas earlier artists had sculpted stylized humans and animals, the Greeks sculpted humans and animals so real as to seem alive.[63] The Greeks also began the tradition of "the art-ist," in the sense that individual sculptors were (and are) known. The art in the ancient empires was produced by anonymous craftsmen within a traditional style. Greek sculptors were free to pursue personal expressions of the prevailing style and therefore engraved their names on the bases of their work. Many became sufficiently famous to have been written about at the time.[64] Praxiteles (ca. 370–330 BC) is well remembered for having made statues of the female nude respectable—his famous Aphrodite of Knidos was said by the Roman scholar Pliny (AD 23–79) to be the great-est statue in the world (which reflected the Roman belief in the superior-ity of Greek culture). Greek painting was similarly admired by Romans, but, sad to say, none of it has survived.

The Greeks did not invent theater, but they advanced it far beyond the religious ceremonies and pageants of ancient times. They were prob-ably the first to stage dramas with spoken dialogue rather than chant-ing, and likewise they probably invented tragedies and comedies. As with sculpture, Greek theater was not an enactment of timeless traditions but the work of celebrated playwrights. Greek theater was performed in out-door bowls carved into hillsides, having superb acoustics and often able to seat up to fourteen thousand. Some of the plays that have survived in manuscript, such as *Medea* by Euripides (ca. 484–406 BC), continue to be performed.[65]

The Greeks were especially inventive in music.[66] They stressed sound over form—music was best that sounded best. Thus did they establish the basis for "tempering" the scale. The ancient Greeks also developed the first system of musical notation, although it was a sketchy shorthand that fell well short of the notation system in use today (which was developed by medieval Europeans). Greeks pursued the physics of how strings cre-ated sound, establishing the fundamental equations involved, and devel-oped or perfected many instruments, the water organ being the most remarkable. This was a forerunner of the modern pipe organ, using water pressure to drive the air over the pipes. Like the modern organ, the Greek water organ was played on a keyboard.[67]

Finally, the Greeks set the models for major forms of literature that have flourished ever since.[68] Of particular importance were epic and lyric poetry. Two monumental works of epic poetry—the *Iliad* and the *Odyssey*, attributed to the mysterious Homer—remain pillars of West-ern literature. Herodotus is often called the father of history in that the

Greeks were the first to write general accounts of events. And, of course, the Greeks invented philosophical dialogues.

Technology

Our knowledge of Greek inventions and technological innovations suffers badly from what might be called learned neglect.[69] Both in ancient times and today, those of literary inclinations tend to be little interested in, and badly informed about, practical matters such as plowing, plumbing, pumping, and propelling. Ancient Greek authors noted little about technology, new or old, and clearly were incorrect in some of what they did report. Hence our knowledge of Greek technology is scanty.[70]

It was the Greeks who invented waterwheels and used them to turn mills to grind flour. They facilitated this process by developing systems of gears that transformed the vertical motion of the waterwheel into a horizontal motion. The great mathematician and engineer Archimedes (287–212 BC) invented the hydraulic screw, a form of water pump still in use in some parts of the Middle East. The screw greatly facilitated irrigation by making it possible to raise water from lower to higher ground. The Greeks used the first known winches during a war with Persia to tighten cables supporting a pontoon bridge across the Hellespont in 480 BC. Around 515 BC they developed the crane, a structure using winches and pulleys to lift heavy loads, to replace ramps as the means for lifting stones into place on construction projects. About the same time they developed the wheelbarrow for use on construction projects and in agriculture.

Similarly, the Greeks perfected the water clock (or clepsydra), a great improvement on sundials (since they were more accurate and worked in the dark). The water clock measured time by releasing a flow of water at a carefully calibrated rate. Earlier water clocks in China, Egypt, and Babylon saw their accuracy suffer as the water level declined in the vessel of origin. The Greeks introduced a method for regulating the flow. They also devised water clocks that propelled a dial indicator to show the time, and even clocks that set off noisemakers to serve as alarms. These Greek water clocks were the most accurate timekeepers in the world until replaced by mechanical clocks in medieval Europe. It also was the Greeks who invented the astrolabe, an astronomical instrument used to locate and predict the location of the sun, moon, planets, and stars. In addition to being useful for astrologers, the astrolabe was of immense value for navigation.

Often overlooked is the Greek invention of maps. The first maps probably were produced by Anaximander (610–546 BC), but it was Dikaiarch of Messina (350–285 BC) who introduced longitude and latitude to mapmaking. Related to maps is the Greek invention of calipers, the earliest example having been found in the wreck of a Greek ship dating from the sixth century BC.

Of major importance was the Greek development of the catapult (from the Greek word *katapeltes*, "to throw into"). Invented in the city-state of Syracuse, catapults were used to shoot large arrows or stones with great force. They revolutionized siege warfare; missiles could be hurled long distances and over walls, and breeches could be knocked into walls.[71]

There were many other Greek technological innovations, including new techniques for creating and casting bronze, new mining methods, even a steam engine (although it was embodied only in a toy). But in the end what counted most in the Greek heritage were thoughts, not things.

Greek Rationalism

The Greeks were not the first to wonder about the meaning of life and the causes of natural phenomena. But they were the first to do so in systematic ways. In the words of the eminent scholar Martin West, "they taught themselves to reason."[72]

The ancients believed that the fundamental feature of the universe was *chaos*, a state of disorder and confusion. One may meditate on such a universe, one may attribute phenomena to the whims of various gods, but one may not usefully attempt to reason about why things happen as they do. So long as this assumption prevailed, natural explanations of nature seemed utterly absurd, "being too naive for the subtlety and complexity of the universe," as the Chinese Taoists put it.[73] Thus, as Herodotus noted after a trip to Egypt, it never occurred to "the priests or anyone else" to investigate "why [the Nile] floods every year."[74] It was enough to attribute it to the goddess Isis. Herodotus went on to summarize three naturalistic explanations of why the Nile floods that Greek visitors to Egypt had formulated. He correctly dismissed all three as false, but the point is that Greek visitors had addressed the question of why, whereas the Egyptians had sought no natural explanation even though their entire civilization depended on the Nile's annual flooding.

As Herodotus's example illustrates, the ancient Greeks took the single most significant step toward the rise of Western science when they proposed that the universe is orderly and governed by underlying principles that the human mind could discern through observation and reason.[75] It is uncertain who first took this step, or when. But the assumption that the universe is orderly and predictable was given an immense boost by Thales (ca. 624–546 BC) when he correctly predicted a solar eclipse on May 28, 585 BC. Thales was born into the nobility in the Greek city-state of Miletus in Asia Minor (now Turkey). Early on he began to speculate about natural causes as opposed to supernatural explanations of worldly phenomena. We know that Thales was an early geometrician, that he tried to explain earthquakes, and that he believed that all matter must consist of a single, basic component. But since none of his writings survived, we know few details about his work.

Pythagoras (ca. 570–ca. 500–490 BC) powerfully reinforced the claim that the universe is orderly. He and his followers taught that the universe is a *cosmos*, that term originally meaning orderly and harmonious (it soon was equated with *universe*, thus blending the object with its fundamental property). Pythagoras was born on the island of Samos off the coast of modern Turkey. At the age of forty he emigrated to the Greek city-state of Croton in southern Italy, where he gathered followers and spent the rest of his life. Today, Pythagoras is known as the father of numbers because he stressed the importance of mathematics in explaining the cosmos. He is also celebrated for the theorem in geometry named after him and for inventing the term *philosopher* (lover of wisdom) to describe himself. In ancient Greece, however, Pythagoras was best known for his religious doctrines—that all living creatures have souls, that souls are immortal, and that after death each soul enters a new body.

The next Greek philosopher of lasting importance was Anaxagoras (ca. 500–428 BC). Born and trained in the Greek city-state of Clazomenae in Asia Minor, he is credited with bringing philosophy to Athens. Anaxagoras was remarkably perceptive about cosmology, proposing that the sun and stars are red-hot stones, that the moon does not produce its own light but merely reflects light from the sun, and that eclipses of the moon occur when the earth comes between it and the sun. But perhaps his most original contribution was the one that almost cost him his life: that behind the entire cosmos was a Mind (*Nous*). It was this Mind that made all things and put them in motion. "Mind is unlimited and self-ruled and is mixed with no thing, but is alone and by itself. . . . It is the finest of all things and the purest, and it has all judgment about everything and the greatest power."[76] In this way Anaxagoras articulated an early form of monotheism, attributing divinity only to Mind and ignoring the traditional gods. For this, an Athenian court sentenced him to death for impiety, but Pericles was able to secure his release if he left Athens. So Anaxagoras retired to Lampsacus in Asia Minor, where he died the year Plato was born.

The magisterial British mathematician and philosopher Alfred North Whitehead (1861–1947) was not being entirely whimsical when he remarked that Western philosophy is but "a series of footnotes to Plato."[77] Plato (ca. 428–348 BC) is one of the two most famous and influential figures in Western philosophy—the other being his student Aristotle (384–322 BC). Because Plato used the dialogue form in his writings and, for many years, used Socrates (who had been his teacher) as the spokesman for the "correct" views, there is some disagreement as to which ideas were Plato's own and which ones should be attributed to Socrates. This is a valid concern for intellectual historians, but the more important point is that we know of these ideas only because Plato wrote about them. Thus it is correct to identify these ideas as Platonic.

Early in his career, Plato devoted himself to explaining natural phenomena. As he put it: "I thought it was a glorious thing to know the causes of everything."[78] Eventually, however, he became convinced that the causes he was seeking lay not in the natural world but rather "that all things are ordered by a mind or minds"—that is, by divinity.[79] Plato argued that the existence of divinity is implicit in the order of the universe, for this order "cannot be explained without an intelligent ordering cause."[80]

Pursuing his new approach, Plato proposed that the universe is divided into two realms, the *visible* and the *invisible*. He asserted (through the mouth of Socrates) that the invisible is real, the visible being merely a fuzzy, reflected shadow of the invisible. This is known as the Theory of Forms.

According to Plato, every object in the visible universe is an imprecise and inferior manifestation of an ideal object, a pure *Form*. He held that only the ideal Forms are truly real—illusion being involved in all visible things. Thus all circular objects reflect a pure and perfect circle; all trees reflect the ideal, perfect tree; all horses represent the perfect horse.

Human emotions and even virtues also reflect perfect Forms that exist only as "ideals" in the invisible world.

Plato also noted that the cosmos is filled with motion and activity. What causes this? Plato's answer drew on Pythagoras: everything, both animate and inanimate, is inhabited by a *soul*. It is its soul that causes the sun to move; it is the human soul that is capable of thoughts such as philosophy. Plato further distinguished the soul as consisting of three aspects: *logos* (the mind, reason), *thymos* (emotion), and *eros* (desire). Souls existed before anything else and are immortal. In fact, Plato believed in reincarnation: that after death souls pass into new beings or things. And, of course, there must be a soul of all souls, and a Pure Form of absolute goodness. These conclusions carried Plato back to his conception of divinity, earning him the designation as the founder of rational theology (the application of reason to expand the understanding of religious questions such as the nature of God).[81]

Plato claimed in *Laws* that gods exist and, indeed, are the cause of all things; they have perfect knowledge and perfect goodness.[82] They are moral rulers of the universe and cannot be influenced by sacrifices or gifts. Echoing Anaxagoras's concept of Mind, Plato concluded that there is one supreme god who is "in every way perfect."[83] He deduced that God is immutable, for if he changed it could necessarily only be to become less perfect. God is all-knowing and all-powerful.[84] God is timeless; he has always existed and always will. But Plato conceived of this supreme God as so remote and impersonal that he took no part in anything. Even the creation of the universe was the work of a lesser divinity, whom Plato designated the *demiurge*—the personification of reason. Here Plato differed from most other Greek philosophers, who believed that the universe was uncreated and eternal, locked in a never-ending cycle of being. Aristotle, for example, condemned the idea "that the universe came into being at some point in time . . . as unthinkable."[85] Plato also accepted the existence of the traditional Greek gods as a species of lower godlings.

Aristotle was not only Plato's student but also the tutor of Alexander the Great (356–323 BC). He was born in Macedon and at eighteen went to Athens to study under Plato. After Plato's death he traveled in Asia Minor and then returned to Macedon to tutor Alexander and two other future kings: Ptolemy, who became the first Greek king of Egypt, and Cassander, who succeeded Alexander as king of Macedon.

Unlike Plato, Aristotle never lost interest in explaining the natural world. His reflections led him to the conclusion that there must be an "unmoved mover," a first cause of all motion. He defined the first mover as God.[86] In his conception, God was as remote and impersonal as Plato's supreme divinity. Once having put the universe in motion, according to Aristotle, God can contemplate only the perfect—that is, his own contemplation. From this Aristotle deduced that God must be unaware of the existence of the world.[87] Hence, God compels our wonder, but worship of him is pointless.[88] Aristotle also had no time for the traditional Greek pantheon and was openly contemptuous of Alexander's claims to divinity. Following Alexander's death, there was a movement in Athens to bring Aristotle to trial for not honoring the gods, so he fled Athens for the family estate in Chalcis, on the island of Euboea, where he died the next year.

Aristotle's major impact on Western civilization came neither from his metaphysics nor from his many observations of natural phenomena. Most important was his recognition that philosophical debates typically turned on one or more of the participants' being guilty of faulty reasoning. This led him to develop rules for correct reasoning, whereby formal logic was born. It is unnecessary to pause here to outline what came to be called Aristotelian logic—the syllogism being the primary example. It is enough to recognize that an emphasis on logical reasoning, as opposed to mysticism and meditation, became the defining hallmark of Christianity.[89]

The final touches on the Greek heritage came from the Stoics, a school of philosophers founded by Zeno (334–262 BC). The name *Stoic* derived from the fact that Zeno met with his followers at the Stoa Poecile (painted porch) in Athens. The son of a Phoenician merchant, Zeno came to Athens at the age of twenty-two in search of an education in philosophy. He divided philosophy into three parts: logic, physics (including especially metaphysics), and ethics (right living). But he and the Stoics are best remembered for their ethics, which stressed self-control and correct reasoning as the keys to a satisfying and virtuous life. Zeno held that because God is the cause of everything that happens—indeed, the universe *is* God—humans ought to calmly accept life as it comes and avoid emotional responses, whether joy or sorrow. The emphasis on self-control turned out to have great appeal to the Romans, especially the elite. Stoicism became the leading pagan philosophy, moral shortcomings included.

Ancient Morality

A common failure in assessments of ancient Greece's immense contributions to Western civilization is to notice only its gleaming marble buildings, magnificent statues, brilliant philosophy, and commitment to democracy. As the German philosopher Wilhelm von Humboldt (1767–1835) put it: "In the Greeks alone we find the ideal of that which we should like to be."[90] But there was a darker side that eventually played a substantial role in the downfall of Greek civilization: for all the brilliance of the Greek philosophers, they did not rise above the moral limitations of the ancient world.

The economies of all the Greek city-states rested on extensive slavery. In many, including Athens, slaves probably outnumbered the free citizens.[91] Even modest households often owned two or three slaves; Aristotle owned thirteen and Plato owned six.[92] The presence of such an overwhelming number of slaves, with few limits on their mistreatment, resulted in an increasingly idle citizenry and coarsened Greek sensibilities. Incredibly, many authors have shrugged off the massive slavery supporting ancient Greece as merely the price that had to be paid for the splendor of Greek culture.[93] For example, the influential twentieth-century historian Joseph Vogt accepted Greek slavery as a necessary evil: "Slavery was essential to the [Greek] . . . devotion to spiritual considerations. . . . Slavery and its attendant loss of humanity were part of the sacrifice which had to be paid for this achievement."[94] But it seems far more likely that the Greek "miracle" happened *despite* the impediment of slavery. As the ratio of slaves to free citizens grew, Greek progress declined proportionately. No Greek philosopher was sufficiently "enlightened" to have condemned slavery. That awaited the rise of Christianity: the first known instance of the general abolition of slavery anywhere in the world lay a millennium in the future, in medieval Europe.

In addition, war was endemic among the Greek city-states. As historian Charles Freeman notes, "there was hardly a year in the fifth century that Athens was not fighting someone somewhere."[95] Brutality dominated, especially in the aftermath of defeat. In 416 BC Athens demanded that the island city-state of Melos become its colony. When the Melians refused, Athens laid siege, and when Melos surrendered the Athenians murdered all the men and sold all the women and children into slavery. Later, when the citizens of Mytilene revolted against Athenian rule,

Athens's democratic assembly voted that its population be treated as the Melians had been.

Thus did Greek democracy embrace a self-destructive tyranny.

New Empires

If the Greek "miracle" was based on the existence of many independent city-states, Greek progress stagnated as the city-states were submerged beneath new empires.

The first to arise was the Athenian Empire. In 478 BC various Greek city-states formed a military alliance, known as the Delian League, in response to repeated Persian attempts to conquer Greece. From the start, Athens exploited the league to its own advantage. It gradually increased its control over the league's resources and the internal affairs of other member city-states, until eventually Athens ruled an empire. According to Aristotle, "After the Athenians had gained their empire, they treated their allies rather dictatorially."[96] This resulted in festering conflicts, especially with Sparta, and led to the Peloponnesian War in 431 BC. It was a long war, pitting the Athenian Empire against the Peloponnesian League headed by Sparta. The first phase of the war ended in 421 BC with the signing of a peace treaty. Hostilities resumed in 415 BC when Athens sent an expeditionary force to attack Syracuse, a Greek city-state in Sicily. The attempt to conquer Syracuse was a disastrous failure; the entire Athenian fleet was lost. The war ended in 405 BC when the Spartan navy under Lysander cut off Athens's supply of grain by blockading the Hellespont; in the ensuing battle, 168 of 180 Athenian ships were sunk. After a year's occupation by Spartans, Athens recovered its freedom and restored its democracy.

In 378 BC Athens rebuilt a semblance of empire by organizing a confederation of city-states for self-defense against Sparta. Even after Thebes defeated Sparta in 371 BC, Athens attempted to exert its power over the other members, which led to the Social War (or War of the Allies) in 357 BC. Once again the Athenian fleet was destroyed, thus ending forever any semblance of an Athenian Empire. But it also marked the end of an independent Greece.

While the Greeks continued to war with one another, a new power was growing to their north. The small kingdom of Macedon was occupied by people who spoke a dialect of Greek and even claimed to be Greeks. Most other Greeks, and especially the Athenians, rejected that claim and dismissed the Macedonians as uncouth, in part because they were ruled by a hereditary king rather than an elected assembly and because some of the nobility, including the king, had multiple wives. But soon after Philip II became king of Macedon, the Greeks became concerned about a Macedonian threat.

One of Philip's first actions was to redesign his army. He lengthened the pikes with which his traditional heavy-infantry phalanxes were armed and created a well-armored heavy cavalry. These innovations soon proved their worth when Philip took control of most of Thessaly while Athens was busy with the Social War. As the Greeks became increasingly concerned about Philip's inroads, Demosthenes raised an Athenian coalition that included Thebes, by then the strongest of the Greek city-states. When these allies confronted the Macedonians at the Battle of Chaeronea in 338 BC, they were overwhelmed, leaving Philip as the master of all Greece.

But not for long. Two years later Philip was assassinated. (To this day there is debate over who may have been involved in the conspiracy.) Philip was, of course, succeeded by his son Alexander, soon to be called the Great. Although Aristotle had been his tutor, Alexander was no philosopher. He was, instead, a military genius. When he died after thirteen years of rule, the Macedonian Empire stretched from Greece to the Indus River, including all of Persia, as well as Egypt to the South. The eastern end of the Macedonian Empire was soon lost, but the Hellenic portion remained a Macedonian kingdom for several centuries, and the Egyptian portion was ruled by the Greek dynasty founded by Alexander the Great's general Ptolemy until the death of Cleopatra in 30 BC.

The rise of Rome sealed the Macedonian Empire's fate. Rome initially took over the many Greek city-states in Italy. Then, during Rome's second war with Carthage (218–207 BC), King Philip V of Macedon allied himself with Hannibal, the Carthaginian commander, and helped him protect his supply lines from North Africa. Soon after Hannibal's defeat, Rome launched an expeditionary army against Macedon. It defeated Philip's forces in 197 BC and then his son's army in 168 BC. This placed most of Greece under Roman control. Then the entire Hellenic world came under Roman rule after the defeat of Marc Antony and Cleopatra's forces at Actium in 31 BC and again at Alexandria in 30 BC.

Gone but Not Forgotten

Although the Romans retained most Greek culture, the era of innovation had ended. In fact, the end of the Greek "miracle" had begun centuries before as the hundreds of independent city-states coalesced into the Athenian Empire and the Peloponnesian League. This is confirmed by a remarkable but forgotten study by the great American anthropologist Alfred L. Kroeber. In *Configurations of Culture Growth* (1944), he presented data on when distinguished contributors to philosophy, science, and the arts have appeared through history; he looked at the period 900 BC through the present. For ancient Greece, Kroeber's data showed a towering peak for the century 450 to 350 BC, followed by a steep and rapid decline.[97] This is consistent with the geography of Greek philosophers: prior to the ascendency of Athens, famous philosophers had lived in many different city-states. But by the fourth century all the important philosophers lived in Athens—Socrates, Plato, Aristotle, and Zeno. The last, of course, did not measure up to the other three, and after Zeno, Greek philosophy declined into mediocrity. Meanwhile, Greek artists ceased to innovate, no new technology appeared, and democracy never returned. It was over.

But not forgotten. As the twentieth-century British historian J. M. Roberts put it so well: "Once the political and military structure protecting it had gone, ancient Egyptian civilization ceased to be significant except to scholars and cranks. Greece went on as a world influence long after Greek cities were themselves only ruins."[98]

2

Jerusalem's Rational God

T he intellectual revolution that took place in Greece had no
impact on most of its neighboring societies—the Persians were
no more interested than were the Egyptians. But Greek philosophy had profound impact among the Jews. Unlike priests of the religions
that dominated most of the world, from early days Jewish theologians
were struck by the fact that what their scripture said about God was
quite compatible with some aspects of Greek conceptions of a supreme
god. In addition, since they were committed to reasoning about God, the
Jews were quick to embrace the Greek concern for valid reasoning. What
emerged was an image of God as not only eternal and immutable but also
as conscious, concerned, and *rational*. The early Christians fully accepted
this image of God. They also added and emphasized the proposition that
our knowledge of God and of his creation is *progressive*. Faith in both
reason and progress were essential to the rise of the West.

Hellenism and Judaism

At present there is bitter and misguided debate over whether or not Greek
thought influenced Jewish theology. On one side are obvious examples of
an extensive intermingling of the two traditions. On the other side are
a host of Jewish scholars who claim that the rabbis who produced the
Talmud had very little knowledge of Greek philosophy and despised it:

"Cursed be the man who would breed swine and cursed be the man who would teach his son Greek wisdom."[1]

Whatever the Talmudic rabbis did or didn't know about Greek philosophy seems irrelevant. Their writings did not begin until the third century AD, and it is certain that in earlier times there was extensive Hellenic influence on Jewish life and theology. As the twentieth-century historian Morton Smith put it, "The Hellenization extended even to the basic structure of Rabbinic thought."[2] It was this Hellenized Judaism that influenced early Christian theologians; they had virtually no contact with the Talmudic rabbis, nor any interest in their teachings.

It is important to realize that as early as 200 BC, most Jews lived not in Palestine but in Roman cities—especially the cities dominated by Greek culture. These communities are known as the Jewish Diaspora (literally: dispersion), and they were home to at least six million Jews, compared with only a million Jews still living in Palestine.[3] (Several million more Jews lived to the east of Palestine, including a substantial community in Babylon, but little record of them survives and they played little or no role in the rise of the West.) The majority of Jews living in the Hellenized western cities were quite assimilated. Intermarriage with Gentiles was widespread.[4] Moreover, the Diasporan Jews read, wrote, spoke, thought, and worshiped in Greek. Of inscriptions found in the Jewish catacombs in Rome, fewer than 2 percent are in Hebrew or Aramaic, while 74 percent are in Greek and the remainder in Latin.[5] Most of the Diasporan Jews had Greek names; many of them, Israeli scholar Victor Tcherikover noted, "did not even hesitate to [adopt] names derived from those of Greek deities, such as Apollonius."[6] As early as the third century BC the religious services held in Diasporan synagogues were conducted in Greek, and so few Diasporan Jews could read Hebrew that it was necessary to translate the Torah into Greek—the Septuagint.

The Hellenization of the Jews was not limited to the Diaspora.[7] Beginning with Alexander the Great's conquest of the Middle East, Palestine came under the control of Ptolemaic (Greek) Egypt. This soon led to the founding of twenty-nine Greek cities in Palestine—some of them in Galilee, the two largest of these being Tiberius (on the Sea of Galilee) and Sepphoris, which was only about four miles from Nazareth.[8] By early in the second century BC, Jerusalem was so transformed into a Greek city that it was known as Antioch-at-Jerusalem.[9] According to the eminent scholar-theologian Sir Henry Chadwick, "Greek influence reached its height under King Herod (73–04 BC) . . . who built a Greek theatre, amphitheatre, and hippodrome in or near Jerusalem."[10]

In these highly Hellenized social settings it was inevitable that Greek philosophy would influence religious perspectives. As Chadwick put it: "As early as Philo, we see that the current intellectual coin of the more literate classes of society is this blend of Stoic ethics with Platonic metaphysics and some Aristotelian logic. Like the form of Greek spoken in the hellenistic world . . . Philo simply takes it for granted. "[11] Thus, the most revered and influential Jewish leader and writer of the era, Philo of Alexandria (20 BC–AD 50), attempted to interpret the law "through the mirror of Greek philosophy,"[12] and he described God in ways that Plato would have found familiar: "the perfectly pure unsullied Mind of the universe, transcending virtue, transcending knowledge, transcending good itself and the beautiful itself."[13] According to scholar Erwin R. Goodenough, Philo "read Plato in terms of Moses, and Moses in terms of Plato, to the point he was convinced that each said essentially the same things."[14]

But Philo was wrong. Although it is true that the Jewish conception of God is consistent with some aspects of the supreme God proposed by Plato, Aristotle, and the other Greek philosophers, the Jewish God is different in important ways. Like Plato and Aristotle's God, *Yahweh* is believed to be perfect, eternal, and immutable. But he is no remote ideal. He is the loving Creator who is intensely conscious of humankind. He sees and hears; he communicates; he *intervenes*. And it was the fully developed Jewish conception of God, not the remote and inert God of the Greeks or even the God of Philo, that shaped Christian theology and underlay the rise of the West.

Early Christianity and Greek Philosophy

From the start, the early Christian fathers were familiar with Greek philosophy—Paul correctly quoted the Stoic Greek poet Aratus (ca. 315–240 BC) in his impromptu sermon to local philosophers on Mars Hill in Athens (Acts 17:28). In fact, some early and influential Christian theologians had been trained as philosophers before they converted to Christianity. And as their conversions testified, the many points of agreement between the philosophers and Christian theology were widely acknowledged. Clement of Alexandria (ca. 150–ca. 215), who probably was born in Athens and who studied with several philosophical masters before converting, wrote:

> Before the advent of the Lord, philosophy was necessary to the Greeks for righteousness . . . being a kind of preparatory training. . . . Perchance, too, philosophy was given to the Greeks directly and primarily, till the Lord should call the Greeks. For this was a schoolmaster to bring "the Hellenic mind," as the law, the Hebrews, "to Christ." Philosophy, therefore, was a preparation, paving the way for him who is perfected in Christ.[15]

Perhaps no early church father held Greek philosophy in higher regard than did Justin Martyr (ca. 100–165). Justin was born into a Greek-speaking pagan family in Samaria, was formally trained in philosophy, and continued to wear his philosopher's cloak even after his conversion to Christianity in about 130. Eventually he opened a school in Rome where two future church fathers, Irenaeus and Tatian, may have been his students. Justin was given the surname "Martyr" for having been flogged and beheaded during an outbreak of anti-Christian persecution during the reign of Marcus Aurelius.

Justin held that "the gospel and the best elements in Plato and the Stoics are almost identical ways of apprehending the same truth."[16] One reason for this close correspondence, according to Justin, was that the Greeks depended immensely on Moses—a view ratified by Philo as well as by Neoplatonist contemporaries of Justin, including Plotinus, who asked, "What is Plato, but Moses in Attic Greek?"[17] In this sense, Justin identified the Jewish prophets and Greek philosophers as "Christians before Christ."[18] Of course, he and other early Christian thinkers were wrong about the early Greeks having learned from Moses, as Saint Augustine wryly admitted in his *City of God*.[19] But that doesn't alter the fact of extensive similarities between Christianity and Platonism.

Justin gave a second reason for the great similarity between Christian theology and Greek philosophy: both rested on the divine gift of reason, which, he said, "has sown the seeds of truth in all men as beings created in God's image."[20] And since God's greatest gift to humanity was the power to reason, Christian revelation must be entirely compatible with "the highest Reason."[21] Consequently, Justin viewed Jesus as a philosopher as well as the son of God, as the personification of "right reason."[22]

To Justin, then, Plato was correct when he conceived of God as outside the universe, timeless, and immutable, and when he said that humans possessed free will. But Justin, Clement, and other early Christian writers also pointed out many shortcomings in Greek philosophy. For example, they denied Greek claims that God was remote and impersonal, that souls took up life in a new body, and that lesser gods existed. And where Greek philosophy and Christianity disagreed, according to Justin, the latter was authoritative, for philosophy was merely human, whereas Christianity was divine—revelation was the ultimate basis of truth.

One problem early Christian writers identified was that none of the numerous divinities in the Greek pantheon was adequate to serve as a conscious creator of a lawful universe, not even Zeus. Like humans, the Greek gods were subject to the inexorable workings of the natural cycles of all things. Some Greek scholars, including Aristotle, did posit a god of infinite scope having charge of the universe, but they conceived of this god as essentially an impersonal essence, much like the Chinese Tao. Such a god lent a certain spiritual aura to a cyclical universe and its ideal, abstract properties, but being an essence, "God" *did* nothing and never had.

Even when Plato posited a demiurge—an inferior god who served as creator of the world, the supreme God being too remote and spiritual for such an enterprise—this creator paled in contrast with an omnipotent God who made the universe out of nothing.[23] Moreover, for Plato the universe had been created in accord not with firm operating principles but with ideals. These primarily consisted of ideal shapes. Thus the universe must be a sphere because that is the symmetrical and perfect shape, and heavenly bodies must rotate in a circle because that is the motion that is most perfect.[24] As a priori assumptions, Platonic idealism long impeded discovery: many centuries later, Copernicus's unshakable belief in ideal shapes prevented him from entertaining the thought that planetary orbits might be elliptical, not circular.

A second problem in Greek philosophy, according to early Christian writers, related to the Greek conception of the universe as not only eternal and uncreated but also locked into endless cycles of progress and decay. In *On the Heavens*, Aristotle noted that "the same ideas recur to men not once or twice but over and over again," and in his *Politics* he pointed out that everything has "been invented several times over in the course of ages, or rather times without number." Since he was living in a Golden Age, he concluded, the levels of technology of his time were at the maximum attainable level, precluding further progress. As for inventions, so too for individuals—the same persons would be born again and again as the blind cycles of the universe rolled along. According to Chrysippus in his now-lost *On the Cosmos*, the Stoics taught that the "difference between former and actual existences of the same people will be only extrinsic and accidental; such differences do not produce another man as contrasted with his counterpart from a previous world-age."[25] As for the universe itself, Parmenides held that all perceptions of change are illusions, for the universe is in a static state of perfection, "uncreated and indestructible; for it is complete, immovable, and without end."[26] Other influential Greeks, such as the Ionians, taught that although the universe is infinite and eternal, it also is subject to endless cycles of succession. Although Plato saw things a bit differently, he too firmly believed in cycles, that eternal laws caused each Golden Age to be followed by chaos and collapse.

Finally, the early Christians saw that the Greeks insisted on turning the cosmos, and inanimate objects more generally, into *living things*. Plato taught that the demiurge had created the cosmos as "a single visible living creature." Hence the world had a soul, and although "solitary," it was "able by reason of its excellence to bear itself company, needing no other acquaintance or friend but sufficient to itself."[27] The problem with transforming inanimate objects into living creatures capable of aims, emotions, and desires was that it short-circuited the search for physical theories. The causes of the motion of objects, for example, were ascribed to *motives*, not to natural forces. According to Aristotle, celestial bodies moved in circles because of their affection for this action, and objects fell to the ground "because of their innate love for the centre of the world."[28]

For these reasons, the early Christian fathers did not fully embrace Greek philosophy. They were content to demonstrate where it supported Christian doctrines and, where there was disagreement, to show how much more rational and satisfying were the Christian views.[29] Thus the primary effect of Greek philosophy on Christianity had far less to do with doctrines per se than with the commitment of even the earliest Christian theologians to reason and logic.[30]

The Rational Creator of the Cosmos

Justin Martyr was not alone in stressing the authority of reason.[31] That has been the most fundamental assumption of influential Christian theologians from earliest times. From the very start the church fathers were forced to reason out the implications of Jesus's teachings, which Jesus did not leave as written scripture. The precedent for a theology of deduction and inference began with Paul: "For our knowledge is imperfect and our prophesy is imperfect."[32]

As Tertullian (ca. 160–ca. 225) put it, "Reason is a thing of God, inasmuch as there is nothing which God the Maker of all has not provided, disposed, ordained by reason—nothing which he has not willed should be handled and understood by reason."[33] This was echoed in *The Recognitions*, which tradition attributed to Clement of Rome: "Do not think that we say that these things are only to be received by faith, but also that they are to be asserted by reason. For indeed it is not safe to commit these things to bare faith without reason, since assuredly truth cannot be without reason."[34]

Hence the immensely influential Saint Augustine (354–430) merely expressed the prevailing wisdom when he held that reason was indispensable to faith: "Heaven forbid that God should hate in us that by which he made us superior to the animals! Heaven forbid that we should believe in such a way as not to accept or seek reasons, since we could not even believe if we did not possess rational souls." Augustine added that although it was necessary "for faith to precede reason in certain matters of great moment that cannot yet be grasped, surely the very small portion of reason that persuades us of this must precede faith."[35]

Augustine devoted all of book 8 in his *City of God* to explicating and assessing the bonds between Greek philosophy and Christianity, placing the primary emphasis on reason as a basis of truth. He noted that Plato "perfected philosophy" by using reason to prove the existence of God and to deduce many of his aspects from the many observations of order in the universe—such as the predictable movements of the heavenly bodies, the succession of the seasons, and the rise and fall of the tides.[36]

But Augustine recognized something else inherent in Plato's commitment to reason: Socrates had surpassed his predecessors, Plato had advanced knowledge beyond Socrates, and Christianity was far advanced beyond all the Greeks—clearly philosophy was *progressive*. Indeed, some Greek philosophers were inclined to think that history was itself a progressive phenomenon.[37] Augustine shared that view, stressing that the general trajectory of history is progressive as knowledge accumulates and technology improves. Scholars have identified this belief as *the idea of progress*.

By this I do not mean that human progress is *inevitable*, as Gottfried Leibniz (1646–1716) may have believed, but merely that, at least in the West, there has been a progressive trend, especially in the sphere of technology, and in the widespread agreement that things can be and ought to be made better. Because humans lead their lives "under the spell of ideas,"[38] the idea of progress has marked the path to modernity.

Faith in Progress

A remarkable amount of nonsense has been taught about the idea of progress. The prolific Cambridge professor J. B. Bury's 1920 book *The Idea of Progress* dominated opinion for several generations with the message that belief in progress is a recent development, having originated during the eighteenth-century era sometimes called the Enlightenment. This claim is as mistaken as the notion that science developed despite the barriers religion erected. The truth is that science arose only because the doctrine of the rational creator of a rational universe made scientific inquiry plausible. Similarly, the idea of progress was inherent in Jewish conceptions of history and was central to Christian thought from very early days.

The Jews believed that history was progressing toward a golden Messianic Age, when, in the words of the distinguished historian Marjorie Reeves, "a Holy People was expected to reign in Palestine in an era of peace, justice, and plenty, in which the earth would flower in unheard of abundance. . . . The Messianic age is conceived as within history, not beyond it."[39] Early Christianity fully incorporated Jewish millenarianism and hence a progressive view of history. There was another aspect to Christian faith in progress as well: almost without exception, Christian theologians have assumed that the application of reason can yield an *increasingly more accurate* understanding of God's will.[40]

Augustine noted that there were "certain matters pertaining to the doctrine of salvation that we cannot yet grasp"—but "one day," he added, "we shall be able to do so."[41] Progress in general was inevitable as well, he supposed. Augustine wrote: "Has not the genius of man invented and applied countless astonishing arts, partly the result of necessity, partly the result of exuberant invention, so that this vigour of mind . . . betokens an inexhaustible wealth in the nature which can invent, learn, or employ such arts. What wonderful—one might say stupefying—advances has human industry made in the arts of weaving and building, of agriculture and navigation!" He likewise celebrated the "skill [that] has been attained in measures and numbers! With what sagacity have the movements and connections of the stars been discovered!" Augustine concluded that all of these advances resulted from the "unspeakable boon" that God conferred on his creation—a "rational nature."[42]

Many other Christian thinkers echoed Augustine's optimism about progress. In the thirteenth century Gilbert de Tournai wrote, "Never will we find truth if we content ourselves with what is already known. . . . Those things that have been written before us are not laws but guides. The truth is open to all, for it is not yet totally possessed."[43] In 1306 Fra Giordano preached in Florence: "Not all the arts have been found; we shall never see an end to finding them. Every day one could discover a new art."[44] But the most notable statement came from Saint Thomas Aquinas (1225–1274) in the *Summa Theologica*, which stands as a monument to the theology of reason and set the standard for all subsequent Christian theologians. Because humans could not see into the very essence of things, Aquinas argued, they must reason their way to knowledge, step by step—using the tools of philosophy, especially the principles of logic, to construct theology.[45]

For Augustine, Aquinas, and the others, such views reflected the fundamental Christian premise that *God's revelations are always limited to the capacity of humans at that time to comprehend.*[46] In the fourth century Saint John Chrysostom stated that even the seraphim do not see God as he is. Instead, they see "a condescension accommodated to their nature. What is this condescension? It is when God appears and makes himself known, not as he is, but in the way one incapable of beholding him is able to look upon him. In this way God reveals himself proportionately to the weakness of those who behold him."[47]

In addition, with all these thinkers we see the Christian belief in man's rational nature—what Augustine called that "unspeakable boon"— and also in God himself as the epitome of reason.[48] Had they seen God as an inexplicable essence, as had the Greek philosophers, the very idea of rational theology—and, more broadly, of progress itself—would have been unthinkable.

The twentieth-century classical scholar Moses I. Finley was quite aware that the European embrace of progress was "unique in human history."[49] But he seems not to have realized that the idea of progress is profoundly Christian. The philosopher John Macmurray put it best when he said, "That we think of progress at all shows the extent of the influence of Christianity upon us."[50]

The West and the Rest

To this discussion a qualification must be added: faith in progress was fundamental to *western* Christianity. As for Orthodox Christianity in the Byzantine East, it prohibited both clocks and pipe organs from its churches.[51]

Nor was it only the Orthodox Church that did not embrace the idea of progress. By looking at other major traditions from the East, we can appreciate the uniqueness of the Western approach.

Consider life under Islam, which arose as a religion and cultural force several centuries after Christianity did. In 1485 Bayezid II, sultan of the Ottoman Empire and caliph of Islam, outlawed the printing press. That ban remained in effect throughout the Muslim world for at least the next three centuries.

The sultan's action represented far more than the power of tyrants. It reflected Muslim commitment to the *idea of decline* in contrast to the idea of progress. In addition to the Qur'an, Muslims give great authority to a collection of writings known as Hadith. These consist of sayings attributed to Muhammad and accounts of his actions. In the first Hadith Muhammad is quoted as saying: "Time has come full circle back to where it was on the day when first the heavens and earth were created." The second Hadith quotes the prophet thus: "The best generation is my generation, then the ones who follow and then those who follow them." The Palestinian historian Tarif Khalidi interpreted these passages—which were "both frequently cited and commented upon" by Muslim scholars—to "suggest a universe running down, an imminent end to man and all his works."[52] They also imply the superior virtue of the past. In this context, prohibiting the printing press was not surprising, for books written by hand—the standard from the past—would seem inherently better.

Even more important, Islam holds that the universe is inherently irrational—that there is no cause and effect—because everything happens as the direct result of Allah's will at that particular time. Anything is possible. Attempts at science, then, are not only foolish but also blasphemous, in that they imply limits to Allah's power and authority.[53] Therefore, Muslim scholars study law (what does Allah require?), not science.

But what of the "Golden Era" of Muslim science and learning that flourished while Europe languished in the "Dark Ages"? Chapter 4 makes it clear that the "Dark Ages" are a myth. The "Golden Era" of Islamic science and learning is too. Some Muslim-occupied societies gave the appearance of sophistication only because of the culture sustained by their subject peoples—Jews and various brands of Christianity (see chapter 14).

Islam's conception of the universe and its resulting opposition to reason, science, and philosophical inquiry have had a profound impact down to the present day. Muslim societies today are manifestly backward in comparison with those of the West. As Robert Reilly points out in *The Closing of the Muslim Mind*, "The Arab world stands near the bottom of every measure of human development; . . . scientific inquiry is nearly moribund in the Islamic world; . . . Spain translates more books in a single year than the entire Arab world has in the past *thousand* years; . . . some people in Saudi Arabia still refuse to believe man has been to the moon; and . . . some Muslim media present natural disasters like Hurricane Katrina as God's direct retribution."[54]

It is also useful to look at China. Many historians claim that, until modern times, almost every significant invention was first made in China. If so, then it also must be admitted that nearly every one of these Chinese inventions was either disregarded or very little exploited; some even were prohibited. As Jean Gimpel, the French historian of medieval inventions, put it: "it is a feature of Chinese technology that its great inventions . . . never played a major evolutionary role in Chinese history."[55]

Consider the case of gunpowder. Whether gunpowder was independently invented in Europe or imported from China is irrelevant. It is well known that the Chinese had gunpowder by the thirteenth century and even cast a few cannons. But when Western voyagers reached China in the sixteenth century the Chinese lacked both artillery and firearms, whereas the Europeans had an abundance of both. The Chinese also invented a mechanical clock, but the court Mandarins soon ordered all of them destroyed. As a result, when Westerners arrived, nobody in China really knew what time it was.[56]

The reason so many innovations and inventions were abandoned or even outlawed in China had to do with Confucian opposition to change on grounds that the past was greatly superior. The twelfth-century Mandarin Li Yen-chang captured this viewpoint when he said, "If scholars are made to concentrate their attention solely on the classics and are prevented from slipping into study of the vulgar practices of later generations, then the empire will be fortunate indeed!"[57]

Nothing sums up the importance of the idea of progress better than the story of the great Chinese admiral Zheng He (also Cheng Ho).[58] In 1405 Zheng He commanded a large Chinese fleet that sailed across the Indian Ocean and reached the coast of East Africa. His purpose was to display the power of China and to collect exotica—especially unusual animals—for the imperial court. The voyage was entirely successful, making its way to and from Africa without major mishaps and bringing back a cargo of exotic goods and strange animals, including several giraffes. In all, Zheng He led seven of these voyages, each of them successfully completed, the last one in 1433 (during which he may have died and been buried at sea). It is believed that Zheng He's Chinese fleet included several hundred ships and that the major ships dwarfed anything being sailed in the West at this time.[59]

The Chinese flotilla must have awed the occupants of the Indian and African ports it visited, and had the Chinese been so inclined, they could easily have imposed their rule over coastal areas all along their route, just as Westerners were soon to do following Vasco da Gama's Portuguese expedition that reached India in 1498. Moreover, had Chinese voyaging continued, they might well have sailed around Africa to Europe or across the Pacific to the "New World."

But after 1433 the voyages ceased. What happened?

The death of Zheng He would not have been enough to halt the voyages completely, given the obvious successes of the previous expeditions and the opportunities at hand. Instead, a decree came down from the emperor forbidding the construction of any oceangoing ships. The emperor also had Zheng He's fleet dragged ashore and stripped of useful timbers; the remains were allowed to rot. Even the plans for such ships were destroyed, and the Chinese attempted to erase all records of Zheng He's voyages. Soon it was a capital offense to build a seagoing ship (as opposed to junks for sailing along the coast and on the inland waterways). For good measure, all the exotic animals Zheng He had brought back to the imperial zoo were killed.

Why? The court Mandarins believed that there was nothing in the outer world of value to China and that any contacts were potentially unsettling to the Confucian social order. Progress be damned.

Contrast this with the medieval West's eager adoption of technologies that had been invented elsewhere. As Samuel Lilley wrote in his history of technological progress, "The European Middle Ages collected innovations from all over the world, especially from China, and built them into a new unity which formed the basis of our modern civilization."[60]

These counterexamples to the history of the West expose the weakness of the widely accepted claim that technological progress is pretty much an inevitable product of the times—that, for example, when conditions were right the incandescent bulb and the phonograph would have been invented whether or not Thomas Edison ever existed. Inventions don't just happen. *Someone* has to bring them about, and the likelihood that anyone will attempt to do so is influenced by the extent to which they believe that inventions are possible—that is, the extent to which the culture accepts the idea of progress.

Perhaps of even greater significance is that inventions not only must be made but also must be sufficiently valued to be used. That is not inevitable either. What if the phonograph had been outlawed, as the printing press was in the Ottoman Empire? What if the state had declared a monopoly on the incandescent lightbulb and destroyed all privately produced bulbs, as the Chinese did with iron production in the eleventh century?

The Road to Modernity

Throughout the remainder of the book, we shall see how the Christian conception of God as the rational creator of a comprehensible universe, who therefore expects that humans will become increasingly sophisticated and informed, continually prodded the West along the road to modernity.

3

⚭

The Roman Interlude

I n many ways Rome was the Athenian Empire writ large. Like Athens, Rome began its rise to power as a city-state, one of the many scattered up and down the Italian peninsula, most of which were Greek—Rome's culture was so influenced by its Greek neighbors that it often is referred to as Greco-Roman. Also like Athens, Rome was almost constantly at war. As did Athenians, Romans enjoyed a long era of relative freedom, having been governed as a republic, although both Rome and Athens abounded in slaves. Like the Athenian Empire, Roman rule suppressed cultural and technological progress. Eventually both Athens and Rome were Christianized. And even though the Roman Empire endured far longer than did that of Athens, in the end Rome, too, was unable to fend off enemies from the north.

Readers may wonder why I refer to the Roman Interlude rather than the Roman Era. I do so because I regard the Roman Empire as at best a pause in the rise of the West, and more plausibly as a setback.

Building an Empire

What was to become the famous city on seven hills began in the eighth century BC as a village on one hill above the Tiber River, about fourteen miles from the Mediterranean. Unfortunately, there is no contemporary history of Rome prior to about 200 BC, when centuries of oral traditions were first committed to writing. According to these accounts, a series of seven kings ruled Rome prior to the founding of a republican form of government in about 500 BC. Republican Rome was militantly expansionist, and Roman forces slowly exerted their rule over Italy. First, they forced the submission of the other Latin-speaking city-states, subduing the last two in 393 BC. Next, after the Gauls sacked Rome in 387 BC, the Romans responded by taking the Gaulic areas of northern Italy and then turned south, gradually annexing all the Greek city-states in Italy— Tarentum was the last to fall in 272 BC. At this point Roman expansionism moved beyond Italy, which brought it into conflict with Carthage and resulted in the three Punic Wars (264–146 BC).

The city of Carthage was located on the coast of North Africa (near modern Tunis) and possessed an extensive maritime empire. Conflict began when the Romans expanded into Sicily, then ruled by Carthage. After losing several naval battles, the Carthaginians ceded Sicily and signed a peace treaty with Rome. Shortly thereafter, Carthage invaded Spain and took control of lucrative silver mines. Although Spain was not then part of Rome's empire, continuing conflict led Rome to declare war on Carthage. In response, in 218 BC the Carthaginian commander in Spain, Hannibal Barca (247–182 BC), led an army of veteran troops accompanied by thirty-six elephants over the Alps in the dead of winter and into Italy. Remembered as one of the greatest generals in history, Hannibal won every battle against the Romans in Italy—the most famous being at Cannae in 216 BC, when his brilliant maneuvering of a smaller force allowed him to annihilate a Roman army, killing at least fifty thousand.[1]

But Hannibal lacked siege engines and could not conquer well-fortified cities such as Rome. In addition, Carthage made few effective efforts to resupply him, so Hannibal's army had to live off the land. Eventually, after roving undefeated up and down Italy for sixteen years, Hannibal was forced to rush home to defend Carthage from a Roman naval assault. Back in Africa, without most of his well-trained veterans (most of whom had by then become middle-aged), Hannibal was defeated in the Battle of Zama in 202 BC.

Finally, in 149 BC the Romans decided to eliminate all competition from a once-again-flourishing Carthage and sent an army to lay siege to the city. After three years, the Romans breached the walls and utterly destroyed Carthage. Its buildings were leveled and all its residents were killed or sold into slavery.

Once Carthage was smashed, Greece quickly succumbed to Roman rule, while Roman conquerors drove north into Gaul; overran Spain; seized much of Persia, Palestine, and Egypt; and, after several setbacks, acquired Britain. Now another large and repressive empire stood in the way of progress.

Unlike the empires of the East, all of which were ruled by tyrants, for centuries Rome was governed as a republic, although this did not offer nearly so much individual freedom as did the Greek democracies. Legislative power was exercised by the Senate, a small body formed in 509 BC and made up of very wealthy men born into the patrician class and owning land worth at least 100,000 dinarii (professional Roman soldiers were paid one dinari a day). New senators were elected by those already members of the Senate, and executive power was vested in two consuls who were selected by the Senate, each for a one-year term. Eventually, in 367 BC, men not qualified for the Senate forced the creation of the Plebeian Council, which also had the power to pass laws. Soon Plebeians were being elected to the Senate as well.

Meanwhile, the Roman elite grew fabulously wealthy as a result of military victories that brought home huge amounts of booty and enormous numbers of slaves. Plutarch (AD 46–120) estimated that Julius Caesar's campaign in Gaul yielded at least a million slaves.[2] The constant flood of cheap slaves destroyed the population of independent farmers, their land being bought up (and sometimes usurped) to form huge *latifundia*— agricultural estates based on slave laborers (Latin: *latus* = spacious; *fundus* = farm or estate). The displaced farmers poured into Rome and other Italian cities, forming a dependent population that created political instability and that needed to be pacified with free "bread and circuses." In fact, in every Roman city large numbers "qualified for free daily donations of bread, olive oil, and wine," as Peter Heather pointed out in his history of the Roman Empire.[3] Seats in the arenas were free, although the better ones cost money. The destruction of the independent farmers also deprived Rome of its most important source of citizen-soldiers: farmers' sons.

Finally, after nearly a century of pretending that the Senate still ruled, Rome ceased to be a republic. The Roman "mob" helped bring an end to the republic, as did the new long-service, professional army: both groups were always ready to back a tyrant who promised them immediate rewards. The assassination of Julius Caesar in 44 BC set off a power struggle that ended in 31 BC with the ascension of Octavian as Caesar Augustus, the first emperor of Rome. Ruled by emperors, Rome lasted for another five centuries.

Greco-Roman Culture

It is no accident that the first history of Rome was written in Greek—by the Roman senator Fabius Pictor in about 200 BC. The Roman upper classes more often spoke Greek than they did Latin, which revealed that Romans acknowledged the superiority of Grecian culture. There arose an obsession with things Greek following the Roman defeat of the Macedonians in 167 BC, after which Rome was flooded with Greek musicians, chefs, hairdressers, artists, philosophers, and even skilled prostitutes.[4] Wealthy Romans sent their sons to be educated in Greece.[5] Even from very early times, Roman culture had been greatly shaped by its neighboring Greek city-states. Nowhere was this more obvious than in the Romanization of the entire Greek pantheon.

Gods

The religious life of the earliest Romans is unknown because they soon adopted all the gods of Mount Olympus as their own; only the names were changed. (See table 3–1.)

A major difference was that in Greek city-states the temples were supported by taxes and staffed by full-time, professional priests, while the Roman temples were supported by voluntary donations and staffed by unpaid, part-time priests. The lifestyle of Greek priests did not depend on attracting enthusiastic worshipers, whereas competition among the Roman temples for support helps explain why the Romans were far more religious than the Greeks, Persians, Egyptians, and other pagans of their era.[6] Nothing of any significance was done in Rome without the performance of the proper rituals. The Senate did not meet, armies did not march, and decisions, both major and minor, were postponed if the signs and portents were not favorable. Such importance was placed on divination that, for example, if lightning was observed during the meeting of some public body, "the assembly would be dismissed, and even after the vote had been taken the college of augurs might declare it void," in the words of the historian J. H. W. G. Liebeschuetz.[7]

Table 3–1: Greco-Roman Gods

Greek Name	Roman Name
Zeus	Jupiter/Jove
Hera	Juno
Poseidon	Neptune
Demeter	Ceres
Athena	Minerva
Apollo	Apollo
Artemis	Diana
Aphrodite	Venus
Ares	Mars
Hermes	Mercury
Hephaetus	Vulcan
Dionysus	Bacchus
Cronus	Saturn
Hades	Hades/ Pluto
Tyche	Fortuna
Pan	Faunus
Helios	Sol
Selene	Luna
Eros	Cupid

In contrast with other pagan societies, where only the elite had full access to the temples, the temples were not closed to ordinary Romans, nor were the idols hidden from public view. Everyone was welcome and their patronage was solicited. Consequently, even many poor people and slaves contributed funds to the construction of temples—as is attested by temple inscriptions listing donors.[8] But if the Romans were more involved in religion, the fact remains that it was Greek religion that they pursued, at least until the arrival of Judaism, Christianity, and various Eastern faiths.

Arts and Letters

Not only were Roman arts and letters consciously modeled on Greek examples; Romans regarded their own products as quite inferior to those of Greece. Rich Romans preferred to purchase Greek sculptures, thousands of which were plundered by Roman commanders to display in their triumphal processions back in Rome following victories over the Greeks. Roman copies of Greek sculptures also were produced by the thousands. In many instances, molds were made from Greek originals and then bronze copies were cast. Often, too, marble copies were carved using careful measurements of the original—many famous "Greek" sculptures currently in museums are actually Roman copies. Oddly, Roman copyists usually could not match the Greeks' ability to create statues able to stand unsupported—Roman copies almost invariably used a post, typically disguised as a bush or tree, to support them.[9] It long was stressed that Greek sculptors also benefited from an ample local supply of beautiful white marble, but then it was discovered that both Greeks and Romans painted all their sculptures (the paint long ago wore off). Until the unearthing of Pompeii, buried in AD 79 by the eruption of Mount Vesuvius, little was known about either Greek or Roman painting; most paintings were murals and are long lost. But murals surviving in Pompeii reveal that it was common for Romans to hire painters to decorate their walls with lifelike paintings—some of them of couples engaged in a variety of sexual acts.[10]

Like art, so too Roman literature was fundamentally Greek. In fact, it was written in Greek until a Greek introduced Latin translations of Greek works. Livius Andronicus (284–204 BC), who launched the Roman stage with an adapted Greek comedy in 240 BC, was a Greek brought to Rome as a slave. Having gained his freedom, he produced a series of plays and is said to have been the first Roman to write in Latin. Perhaps Andronicus's major achievement was a Latin translation of the *Odyssey*. Long after Andronicus's death, Roman theater continued to be dominated by Greek plays. Titus Plautus (254–184 BC) is credited with more than forty popular plays, all adapted from Greek originals. The well-known Terence (195–159 BC) came to Rome as a slave and is still famous for his comedies, all of which were translated from Greek originals and set in Greece. Similarly, the celebrated Lucius Accius (170–ca. 86 BC) is credited with more than fifty plays, most (if not all) of them translated from the Greek, some of them concerned with the Trojan War.[11] As for philosophy, the Romans were content to pursue Stoicism (see chapter 1) and Neoplatonism, both of them primarily Grecian.[12]

Technology

The Romans have long been celebrated as engineers but not as inventors. As Samuel Lilley put it, "The Romans could do no more . . . than exploit . . . the techniques they had learned from the Greeks. . . . Perhaps the only important invention that the Romans gave the world was that of concrete—and its applications in building."[13] Moreover, the great Roman engineering achievements mainly involved the construction of monumental public works, something at which empires always excel. The Romans built huge arenas, constructed elevated aqueducts to bring water quite long distances to many cities, and are regularly praised for the elaborate network of roads that crisscrossed the empire. They even built a few sewers. But none of these constructions employed any principles or techniques not well known to the Greeks.[14] "For example," Lilley wrote, "to drain their mines in Spain and Portugal they used large and elaborate machinery based on the water-raising wheel and the screw of [the Greek] Archimedes, but drove them by slaves in treadmills instead of by animal or water power."[15]

As for the Roman roads, nothing more was involved than being able to shape and lay paving stones. The undue admiration for the Roman road system originated with classicists who either never actually inspected one of the many surviving examples or were so lacking in practical experience that they failed to notice obvious shortcomings. The Roman roads were very narrow—usually less than ten feet wide[16]—and in many places were far too steep for anything but foot traffic. In addition, the Romans often did not build bridges, relying on fords that could be crossed on foot but that frequently were too deep and steep for carts and wagons.[17] These inadequacies existed because the sole purpose of Roman roads was to permit soldiers to march quickly from one part of the empire to another. But even the soldiers preferred to walk along the side of the roads whenever possible, and that's where nearly all civilian travelers walked or led their beasts. Why? Because paving stones were hard on legs and feet when dry, and very slippery when wet.

In addition to a lack of technological innovations, the Romans made little or no use of some known technologies. For example, they were entirely familiar with water power but preferred to use slave labor to grind their flour or, as noted above, to pump out their mine shafts. As Lilley explained, "The supply of captured slaves was apparently inexhaustible. Slavery was a more convenient way than machinery of dealing with heavy power problems. The wealthy Roman invested his capital in slaves, not machines."[18]

Sports and Entertainment

Romans loved to watch and bet on chariot races, as did the Greeks. But the Romans departed from the Greeks in their other preferences for spectator sports. As dangerous as chariot races could be, the purpose was to win by coming in first, not to kill the other competitors. Not so with the other major Roman spectator sports. A few public entertainments involved wild animals killing one another. Many more involved wild animals killing men and women who had been sentenced to death for various offenses, including for being Christians. Besides being fed to wild animals, people were executed in the arenas in a variety of sadistic ways—flogging, burning, skinning, impaling, dismemberment, and even crucifixion.

Many exhibitions involved the torture and slaughter of prisoners taken in battle. In 306 Emperor Constantine celebrated his victory over intruders on the Rhine frontier by having two captured Germanic Frankish kings fed to wild beasts in the arena at Trier. In 383 Emperor Valentinian II had a group of captured Persian soldiers slaughtered in the Colosseum. This event prompted the leading Roman statesman Quintus Aurelius Symmachus (AD 345–402) to write a note of praise to the emperor:

> A column of chained prisoners . . . led in procession and faces once so fierce now changed to pitiable pallor. A name which once was terrifying to us [is] now the object of our delight, and hands trained to wield outlandish weapons afraid to meet the equipment of gladiators. May you enjoy the laurels of victory often and easily. . . . Let our brave soldiers take [the barbarians] prisoner and the arena in the city finish them off.[19]

And, of course, slaves were always fair game to be killed in various ways. But anyone could become a victim—once, when the supply of condemned criminals to be killed by wild animals ran out, the Emperor Caligula ordered that the first several rows of spectators be thrown to the beasts, and so they were.[20]

And then there were the gladiators. Gladiators were trained in various forms of combat in special schools—great emphasis was placed on dying well. Most gladiators were slaves (often taken as prisoners of war), although some Romans voluntarily entered their ranks. There even were some female gladiators—they fought not only other women but also male dwarves.[21] Sometimes the women wore armor, but more often they fought bare-chested (to prove they were females).[22] Nero sometimes forced wives of senators to battle in the arena. In AD 200 the Emperor Severus banned combat by women.

Matches of gladiators were not always to the death; a loser who still lived and who had performed well could be spared to fight again. But probably most gladiators died in their first match, since well-known veteran gladiators often were pitted against novices. Gladiators did not always fight in pairs—sometimes many gladiators engaged in "battles." Julius Caesar once paid for a show involving 640 gladiators. He had wanted to employ more, but the Senate refused to allow it. In AD 108–109 the Emperor Trajan employed 10,000 gladiators and 11,000 wild animals in an entertainment lasting 123 days. Such entertainments continued until banned by Christian emperors in the fourth century.

Spectacles of death in the arena were so uniformly popular all across the empire that, in addition to the Colosseum at Rome (finished in 80 BC with a seating capacity of 50,000), the Romans built 251 amphitheaters spread all across the empire.[23] Many of these could seat 20,000 or more, and even the smallest could seat about 7,000.[24] Keep in mind that as of AD 100 only thirty-one cities in the empire had populations of more than 30,000.[25] Hence most arenas drew their spectators from villages, rural estates, and army camps.

To put the whole matter in perspective, it is credibly estimated that at least 200,000 people died in the Colosseum.[26] It seems quite conservative to estimate that an average of at least 10,000 would have died in each of the other 251 amphitheaters, or another 2.5 million. All of this for amusement! But, as Edith Hamilton pointed out, the "brutal, bloody Roman games had nothing to do with the spirit of play. They were fathered by the Orient, not by Greece."[27]

The Roman Army

In early days the Romans fought like Greeks, as did many of the other city-states in Italy. Like the Greeks, the Roman army consisted of citizen-soldiers who formed into phalanxes for battle, the front line consisting of the sons of the wealthiest families. Unfortunately, after having subdued the other Latin and Greek city-states in Italy, Rome's remaining enemies were mostly hill tribes, very mobile fighters who used the difficult terrain to their advantage; often the cumbersome phalanxes were unable to close with them to fight it out. Worse yet, in 387 BC the Gauls outmaneuvered the Roman phalanxes and sacked Rome. Subsequently, the Roman army was redesigned.[28]

Every Roman soldier still served a six-year tour of duty and was chosen by lot from an elite group of citizens who owned property and supplied their own equipment. But to increase maneuverability, the army reduced the amount of armor and made the shields smaller. The depth of the formation was reduced to three lines. The first line was the *hastati*, troopers in their first or second year of service, armed with a javelin and a sword. As they closed with the enemy, the *hastati* hurled the javelins and then fought with their swords. The second line, the *principes*, consisted of more experienced troops in their third through fifth years of service, more heavily armed and armored. If the *hastati* did not carry the day, they withdrew behind the ferocious, well-armored *principes*. The *triarii* were in their final year of service and were as heavily armored as the troops in the old phalanxes. They were armed with the long pikes of the phalanx troopers and formed a last line of defense behind which the *hastati* and *principes* could retreat if the battle went badly.

This is how things stood until Gaius Marius (157–86 BC) became consul. In response to a catastrophic defeat of Roman forces by Germanic tribes at Noreia on the Danube in 112 BC, Marius reorganized the Roman army. First, he dispensed with the three distinctive battle lines. Henceforth all soldiers carried the same arms and wore the same armor. Now "all available manpower could be brought into direct action," as Arther Ferrill observed in *The Fall of the Roman Empire*. "There was no wastage at the rear of a deep formation. . . . Roman soldiers were not expected to fight to the death before being replaced by men from the rear. There was a regular rotation of fighting waves."[29] The new basic Roman military unit was the legion, consisting of six thousand soldiers divided into ten cohorts, each of which consisted of six centuries.

But by far the most significant Marian "reform" was to change who could join and for how long. Gone were the elite citizen-soldiers serving for six years. Now anyone could join, even the poor and non-Romans. In addition, volunteers were encouraged to make long-term enlistments by being promised a comfortable retirement. The professional Roman army was born. Subsequently, the primary tactical advantage of the Romans involved training and "ferocious" discipline. Their arms were no different from those of their "barbarian" enemies—their shields had been copied from the Celts. But they were well trained to stand firm in their ranks and not to swing their swords but to make short, stabbing thrusts against opponents. As it had for the Greeks, this gave them a great advantage when fighting at close quarters. The legionnaires were also able to respond as whole units to appropriate bugle calls.[30]

Unlike the Greek Ten Thousand, however, the Roman army was not invincible—it suffered many horrific defeats. As mentioned, the most famous occurred at Cannae in 216 BC, when the Carthaginian forces under Hannibal outmaneuvered a much larger Roman force and then wiped out about fifty thousand Romans. The battle lost at Noreia on the Danube in 112 BC, which led to Marius's reforms of the army, cost the Romans as many as eighty thousand soldiers killed along with tens of thousands of camp followers. In AD 9 three legions were slaughtered by Germanic tribes at Teutoburg Forest. In AD 378 the Romans were routed by Goths in the Battle of Adrianople and lost about twenty-five thousand men. There were many other somewhat less costly defeats. The Romans were able to absorb such losses because the empire was huge, having a population of about sixty million. They maintained about three hundred thousand legionnaires in the first century and up to about six hundred thousand by the middle of the third century.[31]

This was the Roman army that sustained a great empire for five centuries. Its primary drawback was that, being a long-service professional force, the troops tended to give their loyalty to their generals rather than to Rome. This led to chronic political instability as the legions overthrew emperors and installed new ones on a regular basis. And as will be seen, later changes would erode the effectiveness of the legions.

The Rise of Christianity

In terms of the journey to modernity, the Christianization of the empire was the most beneficial aspect of the Roman era. I have told this story at great length in previous books.[32] Here a sketch will be sufficient.

In the aftermath of the crucifixion, probably fewer than two hundred people believed that Jesus was the Son of God (Acts 1:15). Even so, within a year or two (by about AD 35) there probably was a tiny congregation in the city of Rome. No doubt it was formed by the migration of a few believers from Palestine. Once established in the city, this new movement grew rapidly through conversions. By the time the Apostle Paul wrote to the Romans (about AD 57), there were "at least seven house churches in Rome."[33] Moreover, Christianity probably had already penetrated the Roman aristocracy.[34] Indeed, recent historians have refuted the traditional belief that early Christianity was based on poor people and slaves; they now accept that, as with most new religious movements, its primary appeal was to persons of privilege.[35] In addition, most early Christians were urbanites, as reflected in the fact that *pagan* is an unflattering term for a rural person—the equivalent of *rube* or *country hick*. The religious usage arose because eventually the cities were so Christianized that most believers in the old gods lived in rural areas.

From quite early times, Romans persecuted Christians. In the summer of 64 the Emperor Nero sometimes lit his garden at night by setting fire to a few fully conscious Christians who had been covered with wax and then impaled high on poles forced up their rectums. He also dispatched a few Christians to the Colosseum to be eaten by wild animals and had others crucified. But such attacks on Christians were scattered and episodic until 249, when the Emperor Decius initiated an empire-wide persecution against Christians for refusing to make a one-time sacrifice to the Roman gods—an act he demanded of everyone in the empire in hopes of getting the old gods to smile on Rome once again. As a result, many Christian bishops were searched out and executed, as were other prominent Christians. But the traditional Roman gods seem not to have been impressed: when Decius led his army to turn back an invasion by Goths, he was killed and his legions were annihilated.

Valerian succeeded Decius to the throne and continued the persecution of Christians. The hiding places of more bishops were discovered, and they, too, were tortured and killed. But no Christian victim came to a worse end than did Valerian himself, who led his forces east to meet a Persian threat, lost the battle, and was taken prisoner. The Persians humiliated him, tortured him at great length, and, after he died, stuffed his skin with straw and kept it in a temple as a trophy.

Valerian's son Gallienus became the next emperor. Like so many other emperors, Gallienus was murdered by the army, but not before he repealed all of his father's anti-Christian policies. (His wife was a Christian, as revealed by coins minted at the time.)[36] This done, everything was quiet until 303, when the last and most furious persecution commenced.

As had Decius, the Emperor Diocletian sought to enlist the old gods to set everything right. When, once again, the Christians refused to participate, his designated successor, Galerius, pushed him to crack down. So, despite the fact that Diocletian's wife and daughter were Christians,[37] he issued a decree, probably crafted by Galerius (who succeeded him as emperor two years later), that banned all Christian gatherings, ordered the seizure or destruction of all churches, required that all Christian scriptures be burned, barred Christians from public office, and prohibited anyone from freeing a Christian slave. Arrests, torture, and brutal executions began at once. All told, approximately three thousand Christian leaders and prominent members died, and thousands of others were sentenced to slavery.

But on his deathbed in 311, Galerius revoked all the anti-Christian decrees. He grumbled that the persecutions had been ineffective and then ordered Christians to pray for his recovery (and some probably did).

The persecutions were over. In part, they failed because Romans mistakenly thought that the way to destroy the Church was from the top down—that if deprived of their leaders, the rank and file would fall away. This probably would have destroyed pagan temples, but among Christians, behind every leader stood a line of members ready to step up into the role. In any case, the imperial persecutions came too late. Christianity had become too big to be stopped.

In 303, when the great persecution prompted by Galerius began, Christians already made up about two-thirds of the citizens of the city of Rome—and they were soon to make up the majority of everyone in the empire.[38] Then, after Constantine won the Battle of the Milvian Bridge and seized the throne in 312, he declared his conversion to Christianity. Subsequently every Roman emperor was a Christian, except for Julian (332–363), who served fewer than two years. The Christianization of Rome was complete.

But the "Romanization of Christianity" (to use Peter Heather's phrase) had begun.[39] Constantine meddled endlessly in church governance, and soon Christianity became a highly centralized bureaucracy modeled on the Roman state. Ironically, this new ecclesiastical structure was destined to long outlive the empire and to play a pivotal role in the rise of the West.

The Fall of Rome

In 410 the city of Rome was sacked by the Gothic[40] army of King Alaric. All across the empire the educated and privileged classes went into mourning—and have continued to do so through the centuries. Upon hearing the news, Saint Jerome (347–420) lamented that "the whole world perished in one city."[41] In 2006 the Oxford historian Bryan Ward-Perkins wrote that the fall of Rome had the tragic effect of "throwing the inhabitants of the West back to a standard of living typical of prehistoric times."[42]

Of course, Rome was not the capital even of the Western Empire at the time—the emperor had made Ravenna his new capital, easily defended because of its geography (on the Adriatic coast, more than two hundred miles north of Rome), but badly situated for any attempt to defend Italy. No matter, the city of Rome was of such immense symbolic significance that its dire fate was regarded as bringing an end to the empire. Technically, the Western Empire lingered for several more decades (the last emperor was deposed in 476), and the Eastern Empire lasted for another millennium. But when Gothic troops could prowl the streets of what had been the largest and most powerful city on earth, looting its palaces and public buildings, the Roman Interlude was over.

Assigning Blame

From the start, there have been vigorous and bitter efforts to explain this "calamity." The first seems to have been by the Byzantine pagan Zosimus, who published a *New History* written in Greek several decades after the last emperor in the Roman West was deposed. Early in his volume, Zosimus wrote that just as the historian Polybius (200–118 BC) had reported how "Romans acquired their sovereignty . . . I am going to tell how they lost it through their own blind folly."[43] He proceeded to anticipate Edward Gibbon (1737–1794) by blaming Christianity, but with a remarkable twist. Like Gibbon, Zosimus charged that "the precepts of Christian religion had the effect of debilitating the martial spirit." But as a pagan, Zosimus also agreed with those emperors who blamed Christians for offending the traditional gods of Rome, causing them to abandon the empire to its fate. Zosimus cited other Roman follies as well. He believed that everything had gone downhill since the republic had been abandoned for rule by an emperor. This transformation led to increasingly unsupportable taxation, moral depravity, corruption, weakening of the army, and needless appeasement of the barbarians. In his massive six-volume work, *The History of the Decline and Fall of the Roman Empire*, Gibbon put it all in elegant prose, but Zosimus had anticipated most of his conclusions—as Gibbon was fully aware.

Since Gibbon's time, explaining the fall of Rome has been a bustling cottage industry among professional historians. In 1984 a German professor published a collection of 210 theories of why Rome fell[44]—including a widely publicized claim that Romans became mentally incompetent because of lead poisoning caused by lead water pipes[45]—and more have been added since. Surely the strangest of the lot, even more bizarre than the lead-poisoning theory, is Kirkpatrick Sale's claim that Rome was so overfarmed that "millions of square miles of European soils were soon exhausted and the imperium collapsed of its own inability to feed itself."[46] This seems to have taken place without leaving any record of famine.

Nearly all the theories agree with Zosimus and Gibbon in placing the blame squarely on the Romans themselves—that Rome fell because of its internal failures and shortcomings. But as the historian A. H. M. Jones pointed out, "Most of the internal weaknesses which these historians stress were common to both halves of the empire"—and only the West fell.[47] For example, if Christianity weakened Roman resolve, why didn't the Eastern Empire fall too, since Christianity was even stronger in the East? Similarly, government bureaucracy and corruption afflicted the East every bit as much as they did the West.

Other scholars have argued that a severe economic decline precipitated the fall of Rome. The celebrated British historian Arnold J. Toynbee, for example, claimed that during its glory days Rome developed a plunder economy—that its standard of living was based on booty and loot from conquered territories—and that when the empire ceased expanding, revenues began to fall substantially and forced increasingly heavy taxation and then a recession.[48] Another twentieth-century historian, Michael Rostovtzeff, agreed that Rome fell mainly from economic decline and crisis:

Work was disorganized and productivity was declining; commerce was ruined by the insecurity of the sea and the roads; industry could not prosper, since the market for industrial products was steadily contracting and the purchasing power of the population was diminishing; agriculture passed through a terrible crisis. . . . Prices constantly rose, and the value of the currency depreciated at an unprecedented rate. . . . The relations between the state and the taxpayer were based on more or less organized robbery: forced work, forced deliveries, forced loans and gifts were the order of the day. The administration was corrupt and demoralized. . . . The most terrible chaos thus reigned throughout the ruined Empire.[49]

The trouble is that a very substantial body of archaeological evidence now indicates that during the latter days of the empire, the economy was booming.[50]

In any event, Alaric and his Goths did not overcome Rome by promising to stimulate the economy, reduce taxes, or stabilize the currency. Theirs was a military victory, and the fall of Rome occurred primarily on the battlefield. Why?

Military Shortcomings

In the nineteenth century the illustrious German historian Theodor Mommsen argued that the Emperor Constantine introduced a brilliant innovation to the Roman army by creating a central "strategic reserve." Generations of historians have elevated Mommsen's observation into the received wisdom—in 1976 the distinguished military analyst Eugene N. Luttwak hailed it as Rome's "Grand Strategy."[51]

When Constantine gained the throne in 312, Rome defended its frontiers—especially those along the Rhine and the Danube, facing the various Germanic "barbarians"—with a static, linear perimeter defense. The troops were stationed along the frontier in a series of fortresses, often linked by walls, from which they could move quickly to repel any intruders. When large groups of barbarians entered Roman territory, the nearest garrison troops attacked, knowing that reinforcements would be coming and confident that their superb battle readiness would allow them to stand fast even when greatly outnumbered.

Constantine decided that this system required too many troops and was vulnerable to a major breakthrough. He withdrew most of the troops from the frontier posts, leaving only enough scattered along the borders to deal with small matters such as bandit raids. Constantine then used the troops withdrawn from the borders to form a massive reserve army consisting of the best legions. These reserve forces were stationed in and around central cities, where it was easy to supply them—the cities being sufficiently close together so that the reserve force could fully assemble rapidly. In the event of a significant barbarian attack, the frontier guards would shut themselves up in their fortresses and send fast riders to summon the strategic reserve. Hence, any invader attacking at any point would always encounter Rome's biggest and best forces. Little wonder that so many modern, amateur strategists regard this as having been a brilliant move. But as Arther Ferrill noted so insightfully, this innovation contained the seeds of the decay and defeat of the legions.[52]

For one thing, it made it quite safe and usually profitable for Germanic tribes to raid the frontier areas. Incursions across the Rhine and the Danube became chronic; the fortress troops remained holed up and the raiders could be long gone before central-reserve forces arrived. This imposed such a severe burden on residents of border areas that they tended to leave, creating an inviting vacuum that subsequently led to negotiated "barbarian" resettlements on this land.

Second, the central-reserve troops were not out in remote areas spending their days training and chasing down raiders. They were exposed to all the delights that city folks can provide for soldiers. Zosimus recognized these deficiencies:

Constantine abolished this [frontier] security by removing the greater part of the soldiery from the frontiers to cities that needed no auxiliary forces. He thus deprived of help the people who were harassed by the barbarians and burdened tranquil cities with the pest of the military, so that several straightway were deserted. Moreover, he softened the soldiers, who treated themselves to shows and luxuries. Indeed (to speak plainly) he personally planted the first seeds of our present devastated state of affairs.[53]

Third, since the frontier troops were no longer expected to fight, they soon were unprepared to do so and no longer could contribute to victory. With the best troops reserved for the central force, the frontier defenders became, as Ferrill put it, "merely second-rate actors in defense policy."[54] Hence, even though on paper the Roman army was larger in the fourth century than in the second, effectively it was smaller.

Finally, as Ferrill remarked, "the worst feature of the new grand strategy was that it undermined the infantry."[55] The strategic reserve force depended on mobility. How fast could it get to where it was needed?

Cavalry could always get there long before the foot soldiers. So the cavalry became the favored force, even though throughout the entire era the major battles were decided by the infantry. It remained true then, as has been true throughout history, that cavalry were no match for well-disciplined infantry. This was especially true given that Roman cavalry, like all cavalry of that time, had no stirrups and rode on thin pads rather than saddles that supported their hips. Consequently, the cavalry could not charge behind a lowered lance without being vaulted off their horses. So cavalry in this era could only swing swords or axes, throw javelins, or shoot bows.

Nevertheless, the Roman the cavalry grew larger than the infantry. Worse yet, by late in the fourth century the infantry had lost their armor to the cavalry and now carried long swords unsuited for close fighting. The Roman military writer Flavius Vegetius Renatus reported in about 400 that the Roman soldiers had dispensed with "breastplates and mail and then the helmets. So our soldiers fought the Goths without any protection for chest and head and were often beaten by archers. Although there were many disasters, which led to the loss of great cities, no one tried to restore breastplates and helmets to the infantry. Thus it happens that troops in battle, exposed to wounds because they have no armour, think about running and not about fighting."[56]

Romanized "Barbarians"

As the Roman legions became less well armed and armored and less able to perform complex maneuvers, the "barbarian" armies were becoming better armed and armored and tactically far more sophisticated. This was demonstrated in 378 when a Goth force slaughtered the Romans in the Battle of Adrianople. Consider, too, that the Roman army was now filled with "barbarian" legionnaires and that there even were many Germanic generals leading the Roman forces. Although some historians see this as having undermined the loyalty and diligence of the Roman army, there is no evidence that while serving, the "barbarians" were other than loyal and dedicated.[57] But what is true is that the ranks of the "barbarian" armies were filling with veterans returning from Roman service and that many "barbarian" leaders had held Roman commands. Indeed, Alaric, who one day would lead the Gothic sack of Rome, served as a unit commander under Emperor Theodosius I and only returned to lead the Goths when the Romans denied him promotion to general (probably unfairly).[58] Or consider that Flavius Stilicho, the son of a "barbarian" Vandal leader, served as the consul of the Western Empire (which made him the effective supreme commander of the whole Roman army) for a number of years; in 402 he even defeated a Gothic army led by Alaric. In 408 Stilicho fell victim to a political conspiracy and was executed, whereupon, as Ferrill pointed out, "nearly thirty thousand allied barbarian troops marched north to join Alaric."[59]

Given all this intermingling, it is absurd to suppose that nothing rubbed off on the Goths, that they remained uncivilized "barbarians" through it all. Indicative of their eagerness to be "Romanized," soon after their initial contact with Rome, the Goths began to cut their long hair in the shorter Roman style.[60] More significantly, well before Alaric's day the Goths had become Christians—a Gothic bishop attended the Council of Nicaea in 325. In 341 the Goth Ulfilas was consecrated as a bishop by Eusebius, who was then the imperial bishop of Constantinople. Bishop Ulfilas completed a full translation of the Bible from Greek into Gothic in 383 (thus transforming Gothic into a written language).[61]

Nor was Gothic progress limited to copying the Romans. Consider that neither the Romans nor the Greeks had soap; it was invented by the northern "barbarians."[62] The Germanic farmers beyond the Rhine and the Danube possessed iron plows far superior to anything used by the Romans.[63] They also far surpassed the Romans in making trousers and laced boots, and they even had an early safety pin.[64] Perhaps more important, the Germanic "barbarians" were far better at metallurgy than were the Romans, and they produced swords and battle-axes of steel, with cutting edges that were "unequalled until the nineteenth century," according to historian Lucien Musset.[65] They also had ships and the navigational skills needed to successfully battle the Romans, not only in the North Sea but even in the Mediterranean. These matters will be expanded upon in chapter 4.

The point is that even though the Romans called all the Germanic groups "barbarians," Rome did not fall to a bunch of ignorant savages.

Sacked!

To a significant extent, the Persians caused the Gothic sack of Rome. By posing such a constant military threat from the East, they tied down large imperial forces that might well have been sent to the relief of the West. Instead, the Western Empire had to go it alone.

In October 408 Alaric led his powerful army of Goths (including the thousands of Roman veterans) over the Alps and into Italy. He was unopposed as the Emperor Honorius holed up in Ravenna. Lacking siege machines, Alaric probably had no intention of trying to take Rome. What he seems to have wanted was land and money, as well as Roman honors to make up for his having been passed up for promotion to general. To this end he marched his forces past the city of Rome and took possession of Ostia, Rome's port, through which passed the immense supplies of grain needed to feed the city. Fear of famine caused a panic in the city. At that point, in Ferrill's telling, the Senate offered "a ransom of five thousand pounds of gold, thirty thousand of silver, four thousand silk tunics, three thousand scarlet hides and three thousand pounds of pepper."[66] Alaric lifted the blockade but did not accept the ransom, demanding that in addition the Emperor Honorius agree to a treaty of alliance that gave permanent settlement to the Goths. Not being personally subject to the blockade, the emperor refused. Alaric resumed the blockade. Again there were negotiations. Finally, in August 410 Alaric surrounded the city. Then someone inside opened a gate and the Goths poured in.

There is debate about what happened next. Some historians claim it was the usual orgy of looting, rape, and massacre—"After three days of pillage, [Rome] was battered almost beyond recognition," in William Manchester's words.[67] Others claim it was an amazingly restrained performance. Peter Heather characterized it as "a highly civilized sack."[68] Everyone agrees that the churches were not looted and that the Senate was the only building that burned. In any event, it was the symbolic devastation of Rome that mattered most, and that lives on.

The End of the Interlude

But it was Rome that fell, not civilization. The Goths did not suddenly return to barbarism. Nor did the millions of residents of the former empire suddenly forget everything they knew. To the contrary, with the stultifying effects of Roman repression now ended, the glorious journey toward modernity resumed.

Part II

The Not-So-Dark Ages
(500–1200)

4

≈

The Blessings of Disunity

In response to the long-prevailing absurdities about how the fall of Rome plunged Europe into the "Dark Ages," some historians now propose that very little happened after the Western Empire collapsed—that the "world of Late Antiquity," as Peter Brown has identified the era from 150 to 750,[1] was one of slow transformation. Brown is, of course, correct that the history of these centuries can be told "without invoking an intervening catastrophe and without pausing, for a moment, to pay lip service to the widespread notion of decay."[2] But to deny decay does not require the denial of change.

The fall of Rome was, in fact, the most beneficial event in the rise of Western civilization, precisely because it unleashed so many substantial and progressive changes.

This chapter will examine the dramatic progress that began after Roman unity fell apart. Europe in this era was blessed with lasting disunity; periodic efforts to reestablish empires failed. Disunity enabled extensive, small-scale social experimentation and unleashed creative competition among hundreds of independent political units, which, in turn, resulted in rapid and profound progress. Thus, just as the Greek "miracle" arose from disunity, so too "European civilization . . . owes its origins and *raison d'être* to political anarchy," as Nobel Prize winner F. A. Hayek explained.[3]

Not surprisingly, most of the early innovations and inventions came in agriculture. Soon most medieval Europeans ate better than had any common people in history, and consequently they grew larger and stronger than people elsewhere.[4] They also harnessed water and wind power to a revolutionary extent. In addition, faced with constant warfare among themselves, medieval Europeans excelled at inventing and adopting new military technology and tactics, all of them consistent with the Western principles of warfare initiated by the ancient Greeks. In 732, when Muslim invaders drove into Gaul, they encountered an army of superbly armed and trained Franks and were destroyed. Subsequently, the Franks conquered most of Europe and installed a new emperor. Fortunately, the whole thing soon fell apart and Europe's creative disunity was reestablished.

The Myth of the Dark Ages

Belief in the Dark Ages remains so persistent that it seems appropriate to begin this chapter by quickly revealing that this is a myth made up by eighteenth-century intellectuals determined to slander Christianity and to celebrate their own sagacity.[5]

It has long been the "informed" opinion that after the fall of Rome came many centuries during which ascendant Christianity imposed an era of ignorance and superstition all across Europe. In her long-admired study of medieval philosophers, *The Age of Belief* (1954), Anne Fremantle wrote of "a dark, dismal patch, a sort of dull and dirty chunk of some ten centuries."[6] Fremantle's assertion merely echoed the anti-Christian fulminations of various eighteenth-century dissenters. Voltaire described the era following Rome as one when "barbarism, superstition, [and] ignorance covered the face of the world."[7] According to Rousseau, "Europe had relapsed into the barbarism of the earliest ages. The people of this part of the world . . . lived some centuries ago in a condition worse than ignorance."[8] Edward Gibbon called the fall of Rome the "triumph of barbarism and religion."[9]

More recently, Bertrand Russell, writing in the illustrated edition of his famous college textbook (1959), declared: "As the central authority of Rome decayed, the lands of the Western Empire began to sink into an era of barbarism during which Europe suffered a general cultural decline. The Dark Ages, as they are called."[10] In 1991 Charles Van Doren earned praise for his book *A History of Knowledge*, in which he noted that the fall of Rome had "plunged Europe into a Dark Age that lasted for five hundred years." It was an age of "rapine and death," since "there was little law except that of force." Worse yet, "life had become hard, with most people dependent on what they could scratch with their hands from the earth around their homes."[11] Van Doren blamed Christianity for prolonging this dismal era by disdaining consumption and the material world while celebrating poverty and urging contentment.[12] In 1993 the highly respected historian William Manchester summed up his views of the period "AD 400 and AD 1000" in his book title: *A World Lit Only by Fire*. He dismissed those who no longer believed in the Dark Ages on grounds that "most of what is known about the period is unlovely. . . . The portrait that emerges is a mélange of incessant warfare, corruption, lawlessness, obsession with strange myths, and an almost impenetrable mindlessness."[13]

Nevertheless, serious historians have known for decades that these claims are a *complete fraud*. Even the respectable encyclopedias and dictionaries now define the Dark Ages as a myth. *The Columbia Encyclopedia* rejects the term, noting that "medieval civilization is no longer thought to have been so dim." *Britannica* disdains the name Dark Ages as "pejorative." And *Wikipedia* defines the Dark Ages as "a supposed period of intellectual darkness after the fall of Rome." These views are easily verified.

There may have been some serious, but short-lived, dislocations associated with the collapse of Roman rule and the organization of new local political units. But the myth of the Dark Ages posits many centuries of ignorant misery based on four primary factors: (1) most cities were abandoned and fell into ruin; (2) trade collapsed, throwing local communities onto their own, very limited resources; (3) literacy all but disappeared; and (4) the standard of living of the average person fell to a bare subsistence level.

It is true that Roman cities and towns declined greatly in number and size after the fall of Rome. The population of the city of Rome dropped from about five hundred thousand in the year 400 to about fifty thousand in 600. Of 372 Roman cities in Italy listed by Pliny, a third disappeared soon after the fall.[14] Many towns and cities in Gaul and Britain "became like ghost towns, with small populations," according to Roger Osborne in *Civilization*.[15] All told, most of the empire's estimated 2,000 "cities" (mostly towns) suffered this fate.[16]

But these changes did not mean that the West had slid into backwardness. The truth is that most Roman cities no longer served any purpose. They had been funded by the state and existed only for governing: for collecting taxes, administering local rule, and quartering troops. As Osborne noted, "they were centres of consumption, not production, and had no autonomous reason for existence."[17] In contrast, the towns that arose or survived in post-Roman Europe were centers of trade and manufacturing—as were the many towns in the "barbarian" North, which continued to flourish. The towns and cities of this new era tended not to be large, because there were no state subsidies to pay for daily distributions of free food and entertainment for idle masses. Those people "now were not fed at all unless they made shift to feed themselves," as the historian A. R. Bridbury put it.[18]

Surely this was a major change. Just as surely, it was not decay.

With the demise of the fabulously rich Roman elite, the luxury trade bringing exotic food, jewels, and cloth from distant sources may have declined. But proponents of the Dark Ages myth propose that *all* forms of trade soon disappeared: in Van Doren's words, "the roads were empty of travelers and freight."[19] But it wasn't so—there was far more European trade *after* the fall. For one thing, although the Romans transported a lot of goods, it wasn't really trade but merely "a traffic in rent and tribute," in Robin Williams-McClanahan's apt phrase.[20] Coins and precious metals, food, slaves, and luxury goods flowed to Rome; little came back except tax collectors and soldiers. As Bridbury explained, Roman trade "did not generate income, it simply impoverished those from whom it was extorted."[21] Second, long before the fall of Rome the "barbarian" areas had established very active, dense, long-distance trade networks,[22] and these not only survived but soon were extended south and westward. Post-Roman Europe sustained busy trade networks dealing in practical things such as iron tools and weapons, pottery, glassware, and woolens. Most of these items were well within the means of ordinary people, and some of the goods traveled several thousand miles.[23]

"Everyone" knows that the fall of Rome soon resulted in an age of illiteracy. No doubt most people in the post-Roman world were unable to read or write. But this was nothing new: literacy was probably below 5 percent during the days of the empire as well.[24] It also is true that after the fall, fewer people wrote in Latin or Greek—since they did not speak them either. Meanwhile, many of the "barbarian" tongues already were, or soon became, written languages. For example, written Gothic dates from the fourth century and Old English from about the fifth.

As for the average person's standard of living, it is true that the state no longer subsidized food or made daily free distributions of bread, olive oil, and wine. But studies based on isotopic analysis of skeletons have found that people in the so-called Dark Ages ate very well, getting lots of meat, and as a result they grew larger than people had during the days of the empire.[25]

Finally, the Germanic North had already been "Romanized," even though it lay outside the empire. The historian Alfons Dopsch demonstrated that by the end of the first century the Germanic societies "had acquired most of the attributes of a fully articulated economic civilisation, including the use of coinage and the dependence on trade."[26] Moreover, when the Goths and Franks and other Germanic peoples took up residence in the empire, or later in what had been parts of the empire, they quickly assimilated. Thus it is that nowhere in modern Europe does anyone speak Frankish or Gothic. Instead, millions speak French, Spanish, and Italian—the Romance languages, which are, of course, merely "low" forms of Latin. This shift occurred very early.

What *did* decline during the so-called Dark Ages were literary pursuits. Manchester expressed the common theme: "Intellectual life had vanished from Europe."[27] In fact, little writing on any subject survives. As a result, echoing generations of scholars, the famous nineteenth-century artist Howard Pyle could complain, "Few records remain to us of that dreadful period in our world's history, and we only know of it through broken and disjointed fragments."[28] Although some writing from that era may have been lost, it appears that far less was written for several centuries after the fall of Rome than before or since.

Why? In large part because the wealthy leisure class inherent in the parasitical nature of the imperial system had fallen away. Under the empire, the immense wealth drained from the provinces had sustained the idle rich in Rome. When this flow of tribute disappeared, so did the leisure class. There ended up being far fewer persons who did not need to work for their livings and who had the leisure to devote themselves to writing and other "nonproductive" enterprises. It was a few centuries before the reappearance of persons free to produce artistic and literary works.

For generations of scholars, that alone was sufficient to call an era "dark," even if it was abundant in new technology—which these scholars probably would not have noticed in any event.

The Geography of Disunity

The map of medieval Europe's independent political units looks remarkably like a map of primitive cultures occupying this same area in 3000 BC.[29] That is because the geography proved inimical to unification. Europe was, in E. L. Jones's words, "a scatter of regions of high arable potential set in a continent of wastes and forests."[30] Unlike China or India, it was not one large plain but a multitude of fertile valleys surrounded by mountains and dense forests, each often serving as the core area of an independent state. Only a few sizable plains, such as those surrounding Paris and London, could easily sustain larger political units; the rest of the political units that developed were tiny—*statelets* is the appropriate term. We lack sufficient information to count the states and statelets of the early post-Roman period, but as late as the fourteenth century there were more than a thousand independent units spread across Europe.[31] Even today there are more than thirty.

Europe's geographic barriers created not only many political units but cultural and linguistic diversity too, which also impeded efforts at unification. It should be remembered that Rome was able to impose its rule on far less than half of Europe—only the area southwest of the Rhine and the Danube Rivers. Even in Britain, Hadrian's Wall separated the Roman area from that of the northern tribes. Within the empire, the Mediterranean substituted for a great plain facilitating central control from Rome. That is, Rome was essentially a waterfront empire encircling the great inland sea, and most Roman travel and trade was by boat. It is doubtful that the Romans could have controlled either Spain or the Levant had the legions been required to invade and supply themselves entirely by land. And once Rome fell, both areas splintered back into many small units.

Unlike Rome, however, most of Europe did not depend on the Mediterranean for waterborne tradeways. It had an immense advantage over Asia and Africa because of what Jones called "an abnormally high ratio of navigable routeways to surface area, which was a function of a long indented coastline and many navigable rivers."[32]

Migrations and Disunity

Our knowledge of the migrations of various groups into and across Europe is a confused mess. Most of the groups left no written accounts of their movements; the Roman reports are often wrong and almost always biased; modern archaeology has challenged a lot of what we thought we knew.

For example, every British schoolchild knows about the invasion of the Angles and Saxons, two related Germanic peoples who arrived in England during the fifth century and took over, as demonstrated by the fact that their language (Old English) soon dominated. In fact, the word *England* means "land of the Angles." The Anglo-Saxons' arrival in England and their rise to power is carefully attested by the Venerable Bede (672–735) in his esteemed *Ecclesiastical History of the English People.*

But archaeologists now challenge the claim that a substantial Anglo-Saxon migration took place.[33] As archaeology professor Peter S. Wells has documented, isotope studies of skeletons in what everyone has regarded as Anglo-Saxon cemeteries show "consistently that the individuals, whom earlier investigators would have interpreted as immigrants from the continent, were in fact local people." Anthropologists now believe that the famous migrations "rarely, if ever, involved the large numbers that many accounts indicate, especially in western and northern Europe." Instead, it now is believed that "small groups of elites, often with bands of their loyal warriors, sometimes moved from one region to another and quickly asserted their power over the peoples into whose land they moved."[34] That is, after the arrival of elite groups of Angles and Saxons, most people in England *became* Anglo-Saxons—or at least their descendants soon did.[35]

Obviously there were various "barbarian" groups on the borders of the Roman Empire. Obviously, too, many of these groups were large enough to pose a serious threat to Roman areas. And clearly some of them did enter the empire in large numbers as Roman rule faltered—the Ostrogoths and Visigoths, for example. But in the post-Roman period, it is difficult to know whether large groups, or only elites, were involved in migrations. During the fifth century, did great Frankish migrations occur into northern Gaul, or did Frankish warrior elites simply carve out many small kingdoms populated by locals? Whatever the case, cultural diversity increased dramatically, which increased disunity.

The proliferation of European political units had several important consequences. First, it tended to make for weak rulers. Second, it offered people some opportunity to depart for a setting more desirable in terms of liberty or opportunity.[36] Finally, it provided for creative competition.

Technological Progress

Perhaps the most remarkable aspect of the Dark Ages myth is that it was imposed on what was actually "one of the great innovative eras of mankind," in Jean Gimpel's words. During this period technology was developed and put into use "on a scale no civilization had previously known."[37] It was during the supposed Dark Ages that Europe took the great technological and intellectual leaps forward that put it ahead of the rest of the world.[38] The illustrious French historian Georges Duby pointed out that this was an era "of sustained growth" in the West, while in the surviving Eastern Empire it "was one of decay."[39]

The Agricultural Revolution

Long before the fall of Rome, the "barbarians" beyond the Rhine had invented a plow with an iron blade that was so much more effective than the one the Romans used that it resulted in a population explosion.[40] In several generations the Goths and others needed to expand their territories—with the results recounted in chapter 3. Soon after the fall of Rome, this plow was made even more effective as part of a revolution in farming methods.

Farmers in the Roman Empire depended on the scratch plow, which was nothing but a set of digging sticks arranged in rows. Scratch plows do not turn the soil but are simply dragged over the surface, leaving undisturbed soil between shallow furrows. This is not effective even for the dry, thin soils of southern Europe, and it is very unsatisfactory for the heavy, damp soils further north. The Germanic tribes rectified this problem by devising a plow with a heavy share (blade) that would dig a deep furrow. They added a second share at an angle to cut off the slice of turf being turned over by the first share. Then they created a moldboard to fully turn over the slice of turf. Finally, wheels were added to help move the plow from one field to another and to allow plowing at different depths. The fully developed heavy plow is known to have existed by the fifth century.[41]

With this new plow, land that the Romans could not farm at all became productive. Even on thinner soil, crop yields were nearly doubled by improved plowing alone. Shortly thereafter the harrow was invented, an implement consisting of a frame and teeth that is dragged over a plowed field to further break up the clods.[42]

The post-Roman era also brought greatly increased speed. Neither the Romans nor anyone else knew how to harness horses effectively for pulling. Horses were usually harnessed the same way as were oxen, which put the pressure on the horse's neck, with the result that a horse could pull only light loads without its strangling. Then, perhaps in the ninth century, a rigid, well-padded horse collar appeared in Scandinavia (possibly brought from China). It placed the weight of pulling on the horse's shoulders instead of neck, enabling a horse to pull even more weight than an ox could. Since horses could also pull such a load much faster than oxen, farmers using horses could plow more than twice as much land in a day. In addition, harnesses were modified so that two-horse teams could be placed in columns to increase pulling power. Farmers quickly made the switch to horses, whose productivity had already improved thanks to the earlier invention of iron horseshoes nailed to the hoof, probably made in Gaul during the fifth century. Horseshoes not only protected the hoof from wear and tear but also improved the horse's traction.

If this weren't enough, during the eighth century farmers stopped wearing out their land by constant planting. Instead, they adopted a system that divided their land into three plots—one planted in the fall (grain), one planted in the spring (of legumes such as peas and beans, or vegetables), and the third allowed to lie fallow (unplanted) and kept weed free, often by allowing livestock to graze on it, thus contributing fertilizer. The next year the plot that had been fallow was planted in the fall, the one that had been planted in the fall was planted in the spring, and the one that had been planted in the spring was allowed to be fallow. This, too, resulted in much greater production and more efficient use of labor, since plowing, sowing, and harvesting were spread more evenly around the calendar.

This agricultural revolution meant that most people in the medieval West ate far better than had all but the wealthy Romans. As a result, compared with the average Roman (or the average person elsewhere in the world), the average medieval European was healthier, more energetic, and probably more intelligent, since malnutrition stunts the brain as well as the body. In addition, the dramatic increase in the food supply sustained a long period of population growth.[43]

Wind and Water Power

Only after the fall of Rome did there arise economies that depended primarily on nonhuman power.[44] The Romans understood water power but, as noted, could see no reason to exploit it because they had slaves to perform needed tasks. By the ninth century, however, an inventory found that one-third of the estates along the River Seine in the area around Paris had water mills, most of these being on religious estates.[45] When William the Conqueror had the *Domesday Book* compiled in 1086, this forerunner of the modern census reported at least 6,500 water-powered mills operating in England, or one for about every fifty families.[46] Across the channel in Toulouse, early in the twelfth century a company known as the Société du Bazacle was founded to offer shares in a series of water-powered mills along the River Garonne. Because the shares were freely traded, Gimpel proposed that the Société "may well be the oldest capitalistic company in the world."[47] A century later, water mills had become so important that Paris had sixty-eight mills in one section of the Seine less than a mile long—an average of one mill every seventy *feet* of river.[48]

Europeans in the Dark Ages dramatically improved the productivity of these early water mills by building dams and developing so-called *overshot* mills. Most early water mills were of the *undershot* variety—that is, the water passed under the wheel, with the river's current providing all the force. Mills derived much greater power from overshot wheels, in which the water descended by a spillway to approximate a waterfall striking the top of the wheel; in this setup, both the speed and the *weight* of the water generated power. In most cases dams were needed to back up water so as to exploit its weight and pressure to generate power. Some very large dams were constructed at least as early as the twelfth century, including one at Toulouse more than 1,300 feet across.[49] There are many references to overshot wheels by the fourteenth century, but given the proliferation of large dams, they must have appeared much sooner.

Using various cranks and gear assemblies to increase the power of waterwheels and convert their motion from rotary to reciprocating action, Europeans were soon exploiting water power for all sorts of productive endeavors—sawing lumber and stones, turning lathes, grinding knives and swords, fulling (pounding) cloth, hammering metal and drawing wire, and pulping rags to make paper.[50] That last use offers a clear illustration of the point that invention per se is not the most critical factor to consider with technologies; more crucial is the extent to which the culture *values* inventions and puts them to use. As Gimpel pointed out, the Chinese had invented paper about a thousand years earlier, and the Arabs had been using it for centuries. Through all those years they continued to manufacture paper by hand (and foot). But almost as soon as paper reached Europe in the thirteenth century, a new production process emerged. "Paper had traveled around the world," Gimpel wrote, "but no culture or civilization on its route had tried to mechanize its manufacture" until medieval Europeans did so.[51]

Medieval Europeans quickly harnessed the wind as well. In Roman times large areas of what are now Belgium and the Netherlands had been under water. Medieval engineers developed windmills that allowed them to pump water away. Vast tracts of land were reclaimed for agriculture by thousands of windmills that pumped day and night throughout most of the Dark Ages.

Windmills proliferated even more rapidly than waterwheels because wind was everywhere. Engineers learned to take full advantage of the wind even when it shifted direction: the so-called post mill mounted the sails on a massive post that could turn with the wind. By the late twelfth century Europe was so crowded with windmills that owners began to file lawsuits against one another for blocking their wind.[52]

Transportation

The introduction of the horse collar not only revolutionized agriculture but increased trade as well. Beyond being limited to using oxen to pull heavy loads, the Romans had primitive carts and wagons that had no brakes and whose front axles could not pivot. Not surprisingly, anything of substantial weight seldom moved very far overland.[53]

After the fall of Rome, medieval innovators designed wagons with brakes and with front axles that could swivel, and they created harnesses that allowed large teams of horses to pull big wagons. The celebrated Cambridge economist Michael Postan noted the "Roman inefficiency in the use of draught animals. Where the Romans moved themselves and their goods on horseback, medieval men used carts."[54] As the horse became the primary draft animal, medieval Europeans also began to develop much larger, stronger breeds of horses.

Even with large, horse-drawn wagons, transporting goods overland remained expensive. In boat transportation, too, the Germanic peoples substantially improved on Roman technology. The improvements actually began well before the fall of the empire. Despite the long-standing image of the Germanic peoples as barbarians, as early as the first century they possessed sufficient nautical technology to attack Roman shipping in the Mediterranean. These were not Viking raids—those came much later. These attacks were conducted by Chauci, Franks, Saxons, Goths, and Vandals.[55] Moreover, whereas the Romans depended entirely on galleys, which were usually rowed, the Germanic boats already relied mainly on sails.[56]

The post-Roman era brought even greater innovation—most notably, the round ship, a sailing vessel with superior stability and increased cargo space. (It was called round because its hull was far wider relative to its length than had been the case with previous boats.) In many ways the round ship was an extension of the Viking transport ship the *knarr*.[57] The first fully developed round ships, called cogs, appeared in the tenth century.[58] The cog had no oars but was a true sailing ship, capable of long voyages with large cargoes. Like the Vikings, those possessed of cogs and their successors ventured out during the winter, something Roman galley captains had been loath to do.

Amazingly, for generations the notion of the Dark Ages had such a firm grip on historians that they clung to it despite their awareness that this was an era of remarkable inventiveness. S. C. Gilfillan decided that Marx must have been wrong to claim that invention is the mechanism by which civilizations rise, since during the Dark Ages civilization had declined while inventions "continued and even grew."[59] It did not occur to him that if this was an era rich in inventions, perhaps it wasn't "dark."

Manufacturing and Trade

For far too long historians were content to accept Roman claims about the Germanic people who came to dominate Europe. Most influential were the characterizations of Tacitus (AD 55–ca. 120), which shaped conventional thinking about the Germanics for nearly two millennia. Of the Germans, Tacitus wrote:

All have fierce blue eyes, red hair, huge frames. . . . Whenever they are not fighting, they pass much of their time in . . . idleness, giving themselves up to sleep. . . . They . . . lie buried in sloth. . . . It is well known that the nations of Germany have no cities, and that they do not even tolerate closely contiguous dwellings. They live scattered and apart. . . . They all wrap themselves in a cloak which is fastened with a clasp, or, if that is not forthcoming, with a thorn leaving the rest of the person bare. . . . They care but little to possess or use [gold and silver]. . . . Even iron is not plentiful with them as we infer from the character of their weapons.[60]

Nonsense. As the distinguished French historian Lucien Musset noted, the so-called barbarians were "admirable goldsmiths," and their "technological superiority extended also to a sphere of vital importance—metallurgy, and in particular the making of weapons. . . . They were able to produce a special steel for the cutting edge of their swords or battle-axes which was unequalled until the nineteenth century, and was infinitely superior to that which the imperial [Roman] arms factories were producing."[61] Much of this sophisticated metal work was done in the many Germanic cities scattered beyond the Rhine.[62] And not even the Germans were tough enough to go around wearing only a cape in the frozen North.

Nothing refutes these foolish notions about the Germans more fully than archaeological studies of a small Swedish island in Lake Mälaren, eighteen miles west of Stockholm.[63] Here an elaborate industrial community known as Helgö flourished from about 250 through 700, turning out what Peter S. Wells characterized as "large quantities of iron tools and weapons, bronze jewelry, gold ornaments, and others products . . . [including] locks and keys . . . [and] glass beads." Moreover, Helgö was closely linked to trading networks "throughout the continent," as demonstrated by coins found at the site, as well as "a bishop's crozier from Ireland" and even a "bronze Buddha figure made in India."[64] Nor was Helgö an anomaly: there were numerous industrial centers like it all over northern Europe.[65] Many of these trading centers were coastal; many others were situated on rivers, which served as Europe's main trade arteries until the advent of trains and trucks.[66]

Scholars such as the famous historian Henri Pirenne, who claimed that trade dwindled in Europe and did not begin to recover until the twelfth century,[67] were misled partly by the shift of the center of the

European economy from the old Roman southern area to the Germanic North. They focused on what may have been a decline in trade across the Mediterranean and failed to take account of the increased role of the major rivers linking northern and western Europe with the Black and Caspian Seas. In addition, they based their claims of a trade decline on the lack of imports of a few high-status commodities such as silks and spices without taking into account changes in taste.[68] For example, the importation of olive oil fell dramatically because the Germanic groups greatly preferred butter[69]—large amounts of which moved over the trade routes from what is now Denmark. As for a decline in the importation of silks, even the most affluent northern Europeans regarded fur as far more luxurious.

Finally, until very recently historians have relied almost entirely on literary evidence for their knowledge of the past. That is, if references to something declined in the written materials from some era, they have taken this as proof that this *something* declined. But that approach can be misleading, for a reason Wells identified: "Trade was an everyday affair and not of major concern to church officials, who were the principle sources of written information about this period."[70] In any event, there is by now abundant archaeological evidence to show that trade expanded rapidly during medieval times,[71] if for no other reason than that people could now put to personal use wealth that Rome had previously squeezed from them.[72]

High Culture

Even if Voltaire, Gibbon, and other proponents of the Dark Ages idea could be excused for being oblivious to engineering achievements and to innovations in agriculture, surely they must be judged severely for ignoring or dismissing medieval Europeans' remarkable achievements in music, art, and architecture.

The Romans and Greeks sang and played monophonic music: a single musical line sounded by all voices or instruments. It was medieval musicians who developed polyphony, the simultaneous sounding of two or more musical lines—hence, harmonies. Just when this occurred is unknown, but the practice was well established by the time the influential manual *Musica enchiriadis* was published around 900.[73]

Similarly, near the end of the eighth century an initial form of musical notation was developed (perhaps in Metz), and within two hundred years a fully adequate system was invented and popularized. These innovations allowed music to be accurately performed by musicians who had never heard it. That's why modern choirs can sing Gregorian chants.

The so-called Carolingian Renaissance that began late in the eighth century initiated innovations in art and architecture. Most of the surviving art consists of illuminated manuscripts and of metal work. The architecture was mainly devoted to churches and castles, and many of the buildings were very large and quite attractive.

The remarkable artistic era that emerged in eleventh-century Europe is known as "Romanesque," despite the fact that it was quite different from anything the Romans did. This name came from nineteenth-century professors who believed that Europe recovered from the Dark Ages only by *going back* to Roman culture. Hence, this could only have been an era of poor imitations of things Roman. In fact, Romanesque architecture, sculpture, and painting were original and powerful in ways that "even the late Roman artists would never have understood," as the art historian Helen Gardner wrote.[74]

The Romanesque period was followed, in the twelfth century, by the even more powerful Gothic era. It seems astonishing, but Voltaire and other eighteenth-century critics scorned Gothic architecture—extraordinary achievements including the Chartres Cathedral—and painting for not conforming to the standards of ancient Greece and Rome. These same critics mistakenly thought the style originated with the "barbarous" Goths—hence the name. As anyone who has seen any of Europe's great Gothic cathedrals knows, the artistic judgment of these critics was no better than their history. That is to say nothing of their disregard for the architectural inventions of the Gothic period, including the flying buttress, which made it possible to build very tall buildings with thin walls and large windows, thus prompting major achievements in stained glass.

Thirteenth-century artists in northern Europe were, moreover, the first to use oil paint and to put their work on stretched canvass rather than on wood or plaster.[75] Anyone who thinks that great painting began with the Italian "Renaissance" should examine the work of the Van Eycks.

So much, then, for notions that the centuries following the collapse of Rome were an artistic blank or worse.

Chronic Warfare, Constant Innovation

All historians, both early and late, agree that medieval Europe was a war zone. So much so that throughout the eleventh century the popes attempted to impose a cease-fire to get the nobility to stop making war on one another (often seemingly just for the sport of it). When Pope Urban II addressed an assembly of knights gathered outdoors at Claremont in 1095 to propose the First Crusade, he told them: "Christian warriors, who continually and vainly seek pretexts for war, rejoice, for you have today found a true pretext. . . . Soldiers of Hell, become soldiers of the living God."[76] Although many knights responded by joining the Crusade (as will be seen in the next chapter), they never did stop picking fights with one another.

But this chronic medieval warfare had a significant by-product: innovation. Within several centuries of the fall of Rome, Europeans had developed military technology that far surpassed not only the Romans' but that of every other society on earth.

Arms and Armor

Chain-mail armor probably was invented by the Celts—our first knowledge of it comes from a third-century-BC Celtic chieftain's burial in Romania. The Romans first encountered chain-mail armor when fighting against the Gauls, and subsequently the Germanics perfected it. Chain mail consisted of tiny rings of metal (preferably steel) closely linked—the standard was for each ring to be linked with four others. Some chain mail consisted of one layer, but more often it consisted of two or three layers.[77] With chain mail covering the arms and torso, sometimes the legs, and even the head and neck, Western knights during the Crusades often came away from an encounter with Muslim archers looking like porcupines, arrows sticking out in all directions, none of them having penetrated deeply enough to wound.[78]

Since a single chain-mail shirt might contain twenty-five thousand rings, it was very expensive, costing perhaps as much as "the annual income from quite a big village," according to the military historian Andrew Ayton.[79] A good sword cost about as much. The cost of arms tended to limit military participation to men of means—with a nasty exception.[80]

Although the English were famous for their longbows, and various

Germanic groups used excellent composite bows, the most popular and lethal weapon of medieval times was the crossbow, which was widely adopted during the tenth century.[81] The crossbow could penetrate even heavy plate armor from medium distance. Anyone could be trained to use a crossbow effectively in a week or two, since one just aimed and pulled the trigger. And that was the rub. Like the Colt revolver in the Old West, the crossbow was the great equalizer, allowing untrained peasants to stand up to aristocratic knights who had devoted their lives to learning military techniques. Under the direction of Pope Innocent II, in 1139 the Second Lateran Council declared the crossbow "a weapon hateful to God" and prohibited its use against Christians. That still permitted the crusaders to use crossbows against the Muslims; Richard the Lionheart had a large number of crossbowmen with him during the Third Crusade in 1191. In any case, the pope's prohibition had little influence: the Genoese several times deployed as many as 20,000 crossbowmen in a single battle,[82] and the French used 1,500 at Agincourt in 1415. What the pope's prohibition did accomplish was to cause crossbows to be little mentioned in contemporary accounts and subsequently by historians. Even some accounts of the death of Richard the Lionheart fail to mention that the wound that developed gangrene and killed him was from a crossbow.

The Cavalry Controversy

As pointed out in chapter 3, without stirrups a cavalryman could not charge behind a lowered lance without being vaulted from his horse. Thus it wasn't until the stirrup appeared sometime during the seventh century that there could exist the celebrated armored knight astride his great charger and armed with a long lance. Unfortunately, the development of this knightly heavy cavalry has led many historians badly astray. In his classic *Arms and Armour in Antiquity and the Middle Ages* (1871), Charles Boutell noted that "it was not possible that an infantry . . . should withstand the shock of mail-clad men-at-arms with their long lances, their strong swords, and their powerful horses. Hence, the serious fighting in those days took place between the mounted combatants."[83] R. Ewart Oakeshott agreed, writing in 1960, "The armoured cavalryman fighting with the lance and sword on a heavy horse became for the next 1,100 years the arbiter of war."[84] Similarly, Archibald R. Lewis claimed that the stirrup made "heavily armed cavalry carrying lances the decisive battle-troops of the period."[85] And the influential Lynne White believed that "the new military method of mounted shock combat" made cavalry the "backbone of [the medieval] army."[86]

If so, why did the knights, even though they rode to the battlefield, usually dismount when it came time to fight? For example, at the Battle of Agincourt (1415) both the French and the English had thousands of mounted knights, all of whom dismounted and marched into battle. Or if cavalry were the key to victory, why did the infantry overwhelmingly outnumber the cavalry in medieval European armies? As a typical example, for his Falkirk campaign in 1298, England's Edward I assembled a force of 3,000 heavy cavalry and 25,700 infantry.[87]

In fact, throughout the entire medieval era, battles were fought and won by infantry. Good commanders never committed their cavalry until the enemy infantry had broken ranks. The "glorious" knights on their chargers were reserved for riding down those poor souls who were already fleeing for their lives.

The Muslim Threat

Shortly before his death in 632, the Prophet Muhammad's forces, gathered in the Arabian Peninsula, began probing attacks into Byzantine Syria and Persia. These attacks were in keeping with what came to be known as Muhammad's farewell address, during which he said: "I was ordered to fight all men until they say 'There is no god but Allah.'"[88] That was entirely consistent with the Qur'an (9:5): "Slay the idolaters wherever ye find them, and take them [captive], and besiege them, and prepare for them each ambush." In this spirit, Muslim armies launched a century of successful conquests.

First to fall was Syria, in 636, after three years of fighting. Other Arab forces conquered the Persian area of Mesopotamia, known today as Iraq. Subsequently, the caliph al-Mansur built his capital city on the Tigris River. Its official name was Madina al-Salam (City of Peace), but everyone called it Baghdad (Gift of God). Eastern Persia, the area that is today Iran, soon fell to Muslim invaders as well.

Next, Muslim forces moved west. First up was the Holy Land, at that time the most western part of Byzantine Syria. Muslim forces entered it in 636, and in 638, after a long siege, Jerusalem surrendered to the caliph 'Umar. In 639 'Umar invaded Egypt, a major center of Christianity and also a Byzantine colony. Because the major Egyptian cities were strongly fortified, the Arabs massacred the villages and rural areas in hopes that Byzantine forces would be drawn into open battles. That occurred from time to time, but following each engagement, the Byzantines withdrew to their fortifications in good order. In 641 a new Byzantine governor of Egypt was appointed. For reasons that remain unknown, a month after his arrival by sea in Alexandria he arranged to meet the Muslim commander and surrendered the city and all of Egypt to him. A Muslim army of perhaps forty thousand then swept over the Byzantine cities along the coast of North Africa. In 711 Muslim forces from Morocco invaded Spain and soon pushed the defenders into a small area in the North, from which they never could be dislodged. A century later Sicily and southern Italy fell to Muslim forces.

Except for the one in Spain, all of the Muslim victories over Christians in the Middle East, North Africa, Sicily, and Italy had come against Byzantine forces—most of them low-quality fortress troops, all of them mercenaries. In Spain the Muslims had defeated a small Visigothic force—after several centuries of peace, the ruling Visigothic elite had felt no need to maintain a substantial army. Worse yet, a number of Visigothic leaders and their troops deserted to join the Muslims. After these easy victories, the Muslims were quite unprepared for what was to come.

The Battle of Tours/Poitiers

The Pyrenees Mountains contained the Muslim advance in northern Spain—for a few years. But in 721 Al-Samh ibn Malik al-Khawlani, the Muslim governor of Spain, led his troops north intent on annexing the Duchy of Aquitaine in southern Gaul (now France). His first step was to lay siege to the city of Toulouse. After three months, with the city on the brink of surrender, Duke Odo of Aquitaine arrived with an army of Franks. While Odo had been away gathering his forces, lack of opposition had encouraged Muslim arrogance. They had constructed no defenses around their camp, had sent out no scouts to warn of an approaching threat, and may not even have posted sentries. Taken completely by surprise when the Franks attacked, the Muslims fled, many without their weapons or armor, and most of them were slaughtered by Frankish heavy cavalry as they ran away. Al-Samh ibn Malik al-Khawlani was mortally wounded.

In 732, led by 'Abd-al-Rahmân, the Muslims tried again, this time with a far larger force. Muslim sources claim it was an army of hundreds of thousands; the Christian Chronicle of St. Denis swore that three hundred thousand Muslims *died* in the battle. More realistic is Paul K. Davis's estimate of an army of eighty thousand Muslims.[89] In any event, contrary to some historians who want to minimize the importance of the engagement, this was no mere raid or exploratory expedition. The Muslims came with a large army and drove deep into Gaul. The battle occurred only about 150 miles south of Paris, although it is uncertain precisely where it was fought. The best that can be done is to place it near where the rivers Clain and Vienne join, between Tours and Poitiers. Thus some historians refer to it as the Battle of Tours, while others call it the Battle of Poitiers.

As the Muslims moved north from Spain everything went well for them. They defeated a company of Franks attempting to defend Bordeaux and plundered the city. Then they slaughtered another small Christian army at the Battle of the River Garonne. At this point, according to Isidore of Beja's contemporary account, the Muslim commander "burned churches, and imagined he could pillage the basilica of St. Martin of Tours." But first he paused to regroup. Once again the Muslims were brimming with confidence. According to an anonymous Arab chronicler, "The hearts of 'Abd-al-Rahmân, his captains and his men were filled with wrath and pride."[90] Hence they sent out no scouts and failed to detect the approach of Charles Martel (688–741), de facto ruler of Gaul, who was leading an army of battle-hardened Franks.

Charles (Martel means "the hammer") was an unusually tall and powerfully built man, the bastard son of King Pépin II and famous for his military exploits. Even had he not confronted Muslim invaders, Martel would have been a major historical figure. By winning many battles against the Bavarians, the Alemanni, the Frisians, and the Saxons, he had founded the Carolingian Empire (named for him; Charles is Latinized as Carolus)—an empire later perfected by his grandson Charlemagne. Now, after gathering his troops, Martel marched south to meet the Muslim threat.

Taking the Muslims completely by surprise, Martel chose a battleground to his liking and positioned his dense lines of well-armored infantry on a crest, with trees to the flanks, thus forcing the Muslims to charge uphill or refuse to give battle. And charge they did. Again and again.

As noted, it is axiomatic in military science that cavalry cannot succeed against well-armed and well-disciplined infantry formations unless they greatly outnumber them.[91] In this instance, the Muslim force consisted entirely of light cavalry "carrying lances and swords, largely without shields, wearing very little armor," as military historians Edward Creasy and Joseph Mitchell recounted. Opposing them was an army "almost entirely composed of foot soldiers, wearing mail [armor] and carrying shields."[92] It was a very uneven match. As Isidore of Beja reported in his chronicle, the veteran Frankish infantry could not be moved by Arab cavalry: "Firmly they stood, one close to another, forming as it were a bulwark of ice."[93] The Muslim cavalry repeatedly rushed at the Frankish line, and each time they fell back after suffering severe casualties, with increasingly large numbers of bleeding and riderless horses adding to the confusion on the battlefield.

Late in the afternoon the Muslim formations began to break up, some of them withdrawing toward their camp, whereupon the Franks unleashed their own heavily armored cavalry for a thunderous charge.[94] The Muslim cavalry fled and thousands of them died that afternoon, including 'Abd-al-Rahmân, who was run through repeatedly by Frankish lancers.[95]

Many historians have regarded the victory at Tours as crucial to the survival of Western civilization. Edward Gibbon supposed that had the Muslims won at Tours, "Perhaps interpretation of the Koran would now be taught in the schools of Oxford, and her pulpits might demonstrate to a circumcised people the sanctity and truth of the revelation of Mahomet."[96] The nineteenth-century German military historian Hans Delbrück wrote that there was "no more important battle in world history."[97]

As would be expected, some more recent historians have been quick to claim that the Battle of Tours was of little or no significance. According to Philip Hitti, "Nothing was decided on the battlefield at Tours. The Muslim wave . . . had already spent itself and reached a natural limit."[98] And Franco Cardini wrote that the whole thing was nothing but "propaganda put about by the Franks and the papacy."[99] This is said to be consistent with evidence that the battle made no impression on the Muslims, at least not on those back in Damascus. Bernard Lewis claimed that few Arab historians made any mention of this battle at all, and those who did presented it "as a comparatively minor engagement."[100]

Given the remarkable intensity of Muslim provincialism, and the Islamic world's willful ignorance of other societies,[101] Damascus probably *did* regard the defeat at Tours as a minor matter. But that's not how the battle was seen from Spain. Spanish Muslims were fully aware of who Charles Martel was and what he had done to their aspirations. They had learned from their defeat that the Franks were not a sedentary people served by mercenary garrison troops, nor were they a barbarian horde. They too were empire builders, and the Frankish host was made up of well-trained citizen volunteers who possessed arms, armor, and tactics superior to those of the Muslims.[102] The Muslims tried to invade Gaul once more in 735, but Charles Martel and his Franks gave them another beating so severe that Muslim forces never ventured north again.

Martel defeated not only the Muslim invaders but nearly every other group in western Europe. At his death, the Frankish Realm included most of what had once been the Western Roman Empire except for Spain, Italy, and North Africa. Martel's conquests also extended to some of the Germanic areas that had never been part of Rome. His grandson expanded the realm to create a new "Roman Empire."

The Carolingian Interlude

Charlemagne (742–814) was the son of King Pépin III (Pépin the Short) and the grandson of Charles Martel (for whom he was named). In 768 he succeeded his father as king of the Franks, ruling along with his brother Carloman. A potential civil war between the two was averted when Carloman died in 771—but the tension between the two should have warned the Franks against divided rule.

Charlemagne was tall for his era (a study of his skeleton performed in 1861 estimated his height at slightly more than 6'2").[103] Although he had received little education, he was fluent in Latin and able to understand Greek. He married three times and had eleven legitimate children as well as a number of illegitimate children by his various concubines.

Soon after his brother's death, Charlemagne drove the Lombards out of northern Italy, adding it to his empire and placing Rome under his rule. In 795 Leo III became pope, despite opposition from the powerful Roman families who usually controlled the Church. Leo's opponents soon accused him of adultery and perjury and dispatched a gang to cut out his tongue and gouge out his eyes. Local soldiers saved Pope Leo, but he was formally deposed and shut up in a monastery. He escaped and fled to Charlemagne, who escorted him back to Rome and reestablished him in office. Two days later, on Christmas Day 800, Pope Leo crowned Charlemagne as Holy Roman Emperor.

During his reign, Charlemagne was almost constantly at war. Many of his campaigns were fought to extend the boundaries of his empire, and many others were to suppress rebellions against his rule. Most often he went campaigning in the East, usually against the Germanic Saxons, and here an additional motive played a central role—to stamp out paganism and impose Christianity. Thus, Charlemagne issued an edict making it a capital offense to resist Christianization and slaughtered thousands on those grounds. When he died in 814, his new empire included far more of Europe than the Romans had held.

Louis the Pious, Charlemagne's only surviving legitimate son, succeeded his father. But things began to fall apart when Louis chose to divide the empire among his three sons. Wars of succession broke out and the "empire" was rapidly divided into increasingly smaller pieces that soon numbered in the hundreds. Europe's precious disunity was restored!

Progress between Empires

The final blow to the myth of the Dark Ages is that Rome was not conquered by barbarians. In terms of some technologies such as metallurgy, the people of the North were well ahead of the Romans. They had cities. They had extensive trade networks. And when their turn came, they launched a postimperial era of progress. The Franks almost reimposed an empire that no doubt would have derailed that progress. Fortunately, the Carolingian Empire was short-lived.

5

Northern Lights over Christendom

W   estern civilization was born on the shores of the Mediterranean, but it came of age along the Atlantic Coast and beyond the great rivers that Rome's legions had been loath to cross. As we have seen, after the fall of Rome, Europe's social and cultural center of gravity shifted north. Even when the Carolingian Empire fragmented, the Vikings brought new energy and enthusiasm to continue the West's glorious journey. Remarkably, much of this story has been ignored and some has been falsified.

Despite the fact that historians have given many times more attention to the Carolingian Empire than to the Vikings, the latter played a far more significant and lasting role in the rise of the West than did the Carolingians. Charlemagne was never able to conquer Denmark (let alone Sweden or Norway), and even during his lifetime, seagoing Viking raiders had begun to terrorize Europeans living along the Atlantic coast and to plant colonies, eventually doing so in England, Scotland, Cornwall, Wales, Ireland, France, Iceland, Greenland, Newfoundland (briefly), and a multitude of coastal islands, including the Shetlands, Orkneys, and Faroes. Not content with these Atlantic possessions, in 860 Swedish Vikings sailed down the Dnieper River and captured Kiev. From there, a Viking fleet of two hundred longboats continued down the Dnieper into the Black Sea and attacked Constantinople. Although they were unable to breach the city's immense walls, the Vikings pillaged all the suburbs without interference from Byzantine forces, which must have greatly outnumbered the Viking raiders. Eight years later, in 868, the Vikings based in Kiev imposed a ruling dynasty on the whole of Russia that lasted for seven hundred years—the name Russia derives from *Rus*, a name applied to Swedish Vikings.

Finally, in the tenth century Vikings were ceded a large province on the west coast of France in return for protection against their raiding countrymen. This province became known as Normandy and its residents as Normans (Latin *northmanni* means "men of the North"). The subsequent triumphs of the Normans reveal that the prevailing view of the Vikings as backward barbarians who wore horned helmets and used skulls for drinking vessels is without any basis in fact. The Viking raiders may have been brutal (raiders usually are), but Scandinavia was as civilized as the more southern societies. In 1066 Duke William and his Normans sailed across the channel and easily conquered England. Far to the south, by 1071 Normans had driven out both Muslims and Byzantines and established the Norman Kingdom of Sicily, which included southern Italy. Then, in 1096, Normans played the leading role in the First Crusade—two of the four leaders were Normans.[1] And Richard the Lionheart, who led the Third Crusade, was a Norman (the great-great-grandson of William the Conqueror).

When the knights of the First Crusade arrived in the Holy Land, they so surpassed their Muslim adversaries in armor, weapons, and tactics that, although extremely outnumbered, they repeatedly routed Muslim forces.[2] Hence, although surrounded by an enormous Muslim world, and being very few in number, Christian knights were able to sustain crusader kingdoms in Palestine (so long as Europeans were willing to pay the substantial costs involved) and sent reinforcements when major crises arose. After two centuries European support dried up and the last knights came home. As the Crusades demonstrated, the real basis for unity among the Europeans was Christianity, which had evolved into a well-organized international bureaucracy. So for that era it would be more accurate to speak of Christendom rather than of Europe, since the latter had little social or cultural meaning at that time.[3]

Now for the details.

The Viking Age

From early days, historians have held the Vikings in contempt as brutal savages. Even the distinguished twentieth-century historian Norman Cantor wrote that the "Scandinavians had nothing to contribute to western European civilization. Their level of culture was no higher than that of the more primitive tribes among their German kinsmen. The unit of Scandinavian society was the same kind of war band that is depicted in *Beowulf*. . . . [They] had a penchant for drowning their rulers in wells."[4]

Such views of the Vikings as primitive barbarians are based entirely on reactions to Viking raiders without regard for, and perhaps with no knowledge of, the societies from which they ventured. But, as discussed in chapter 4, as early as the third century (and probably before) Scandinavia had many advanced manufacturing communities such as Helgö, and Viking merchants traveled a complex network of trade routes extending as far as Persia—tens of thousands of early Middle Eastern coins have been found in what is now Sweden.[5] Moreover, the Vikings had excellent arms, remarkable ships, and superb navigational skills.

Technology

Viking arms and armor were similar to those of the Carolingians, except that the Vikings made greater use of battle-axes. Otherwise, they had chain-mail armor (although they sometimes preferred to wear only heavy leather into battle to have freer movements), iron helmets (without horns), shields, spears, and long swords of fine steel. But if Viking arms and armor were standard, their boats were far superior to anything found elsewhere on earth at that time.

The magnificent Viking longships, such as the Gokstad ship reassembled and on display in Oslo, were used almost exclusively for warfare. For sailing the Atlantic and hauling cargo, the Vikings used a ship known as the *knarr*. Knarrs looked much like longships, but they were deeper and wider, and the decks were covered fore and aft, open only at midships. Knarrs often were more than fifty feet in length with a beam of about fifteen feet. The knarr enabled the Vikings to haul livestock and supplies to Iceland and Greenland for centuries. It also could sail in shallow water, making it a fine riverboat. It was primarily a sailing ship, using oars only when there was no wind. Under favorable wind and wave conditions the knarr probably could reach a speed of twenty knots.[6] None of the ships Columbus used on his first voyage could exceed about eight knots.

In contrast to the knarr, the longships (known as *skei*) relied mainly on oars, and they probably could (briefly) achieve a top speed of fifteen knots. Because of its shallow draft, the longship could sail in waters less than three feet deep and land on beaches, allowing Viking raiders to sail up rivers. Being double-ended, longships could reverse their direction without turning around. Although used for war, the longboats were not fighting ships but troop transports. The largest longship that archaeologists have discovered is 118 feet long. (Columbus's *Santa Maria* was only 75 feet long.) The longships were usually constructed of oak planks about an inch thick, which gave the boat considerable flexibility, and by overlapping the planks and riveting them together, the Vikings gave the longships great strength.

Together, the knarr and the skei gave the Vikings command of the water, whether salt or fresh. In addition, the shipbuilding industry must have been a major factor in the Scandinavian economy: "the foresters, carpenters, blacksmiths, sail-makers, rope-makers, and labourers involved must have been legion," Robert Ferguson observed in his Viking history.[7]

It took more than fine ships to sail from Norway and Sweden to Iceland, Greenland, and Labrador. The Greeks and Romans navigated by following the shore and by island hopping. The Vikings, by contrast, had several mechanical means for determining their latitude. They would sail along a particular degree of latitude and use well-established landmarks, the direction of currents, the appearance of seabirds, and remarkably accurate knowledge of astronomical cues to determine when to turn north or south.[8] Unfortunately, the Vikings who wrote the sagas were not interested in technology, so we know much less about Viking technology than might be expected. In fact, most of what we do know is the result of recent archaeology and scientific research. In 2011 French scientists reported that a particular kind of crystal, widely available in Scandinavia, can be used to accurately locate the sun even on very cloudy or foggy days.[9] This lends credence to traditions that the Vikings used a sort of sunstone.

Finally, the Vikings were experts at catching and drying codfish, and they relied on this form of "hardtack" to sustain them on long voyages.

Raids and Settlements

Viking voyagers discovered that none of the realms to the south could defend themselves against raiders from the sea and that there was enormous wealth to be taken, especially from the undefended monasteries. They took full advantage of the opportunity.

Viking raids began late in the eighth century; the first well-documented attack was in 793 on the monastery located on the island of Lindisfarne, off the east coast of England. As the twelfth-century chronicler Simeon of Durham reported, "They came into the church . . . laid everything waste with grievous plundering . . . dug up the altars and seized all the treasure from the holy church. They killed some of the brothers, took some away in fetters. . . . Some they drowned in the sea."[10] Other monks soon reestablished the monastery, but the Vikings came again; this process was repeated several more times until the monks finally abandoned Lindisfarne in 875. The same thing happened to the monastery at Iona on the west coast of Scotland, first raided in 794 and abandoned fifty years later. The Vikings also pillaged the monasteries off Ireland's west coast, beginning in 795. Throughout the ninth and tenth centuries the Vikings regularly raided the Frankish towns along the Atlantic coast and sailed up the Meuse, Seine, and Rhine Rivers and their tributaries, attacking and looting towns, churches, estates, convents, and monasteries.

It may have been that the Vikings were especially likely to raid church properties because they were undefended and wealthy. But it also has been suggested that they chose them, and were particularly brutal toward monks and nuns, because they were angry about vicious efforts to Christianize the North.[11] Especially provocative would have been the atrocities committed by Charlemagne, who, for example, had about 4,500 unarmed Saxon captives forcibly baptized and then executed. The Vikings seem to have known that Charlemagne had issued an edict imposing the death sentence on all who tried to resist Christianization.

As time passed, the Viking raids involved ever-larger fleets. In 832 an armada of about 130 ships—each ship transporting about fifty Vikings—attacked along Ireland's northern and eastern coasts. Twenty years later it was not unusual for a raiding party to have more than 300 ships. In 885 a fleet of 700 Viking ships sailed up the River Seine and laid siege to Paris (the raiders accepted a fortune in silver to leave).[12]

The Vikings also began to establish settlements—founding Dublin, Limerick, Wexford, and Waterford in Ireland and Skokholm and

Swansea in Wales, and claiming all of northern Scotland as well as the whole of Russia. During the 880s they established their most lasting and historically significant settlements, along the Frankish coast. From this secure coastal base the Vikings raided further inland. In 911 Charles the Simple, king of France, signed a treaty with the Viking leader Rollo, ceding to him a substantial coastal area around Rouen (an area the Vikings already held) to be known as the Duchy of Normandy. In return, Rollo agreed no longer to raid any Frankish areas, to defend the Seine so that no Vikings could threaten Paris, to convert to Christianity, and to marry Charles's daughter Gisela. Although both sides observed the provisions of the treaty, the boundaries of Normandy expanded substantially for about thirty more years.

Norman Triumphs

In principle, the dukes of Normandy were subjects of the kings of France, but they didn't act like it: they struck their own coins, levied their own taxes, raised their own armies, and named the officials of their own new archdiocese. The Normans also quickly won the support of the local Frankish population, both peasants and nobility—who, in effect, *became* Normans. In fact, most of the Viking settlers of Normandy married local women and welcomed some talented local men to their ranks. Soon most Normans in Normandy were at least partly of Frankish origins.

To England

In 1035, at the age of seven, William the Bastard (1028–1087) became duke of Normandy. He survived various threats to his rule, defeating rebel barons in 1047. As William consolidated his power, the king of France attempted to invade Normandy but was beaten badly in 1054 and again in 1057. William proved to be a popular leader and attached the county of Maine to Normandy in 1060. All the while he was eyeing the English throne, to which he had a tenuous claim. When Pope Alexander II recognized his claim, William assembled an invasion fleet—in part by promising English land and titles to his fellow Normans. Before William sailed he got word that Harald III, king of Norway, also a claimant to the English throne, had landed a Viking army near York. Knowing that Harald II, the Anglo-Saxon king of England, had marched his army north to meet the Norwegian Harald, William set sail across the channel.

The English overwhelmed the Norwegians and then rushed south to meet William and his Normans. The battle took place about six miles from Hastings on the road to London. This was the first appearance in England of crossbowmen, whose deadly volleys caused the English infantry to back up, whereupon William unleashed his heavy cavalry in a thundering charge. But the English infantry troops were sufficiently firm to turn back the cavalry. After another hour of fighting, one wing of William's infantry fell back. Seeing this, the English infantry broke ranks in pursuit—at which point the Norman cavalry rushed in and routed the English forces.

There followed some maneuvering and negotiations, but William's victory was not in doubt. He was crowned king of England at Westminster Abbey on Christmas Day 1066. William the Bastard was now to be known as William the Conqueror.

Soon after the battle most of the Normans returned to Normandy, with only about eight thousand remaining in England to form a ruling elite.[13] This is consistent with the many other instances considered in chapter 4 when "major" migrations involved only a small elite. In any event, this small number of Normans was sufficient to hold power. One might suppose that they soon were speaking English and assimilating. Not so—they remained a French-speaking elite for centuries.

William proved to be a very competent ruler, even though he spent most of his time back in Normandy. In 1085, to have full knowledge of the tax potential of England, he had an elaborate census taken to reveal the ownership and value of every parcel of land and of all livestock, the makeup of all villages (even noting each watermill), and all church properties. The English deeply resented this census as an intrusion; comparing it to the "final judgment," they called the completed assessment the *Domesday Book* (pronounced "Doomsday"). What the *Domesday Book* showed was that the Normanization of English property was nearly total; the English owned only about 5 percent of the land, and this was further reduced in subsequent decades.[14] As a consequence, the English (Anglo-Saxon) nobility fled—many to Scotland and Ireland, some even to Scandinavia.[15] And sometime in the 1070s a large group of Anglo-Saxons sailed from England to the Byzantine Empire.[16] There they served as effective mercenaries, helping Alexius I Comnenus seize the imperial throne.[17]

Finally, in part because Viking traditions limited the power of kings over the nobility, in 1215 the Norman barons imposed the Magna Carta on King John, thereby taking the first step toward democratic rule.

Kingdom of Sicily

Because of their fearsome reputations and unusual height, Normans soon discovered that they could earn premium wages as mercenaries, so many younger sons hired out all over the continent. The Byzantines engaged some to augment the forces they sent in 1038 to stop Muslim pirates operating from the ports of Sicily. It was a decision the Byzantines would always regret.[18]

The most famous living Byzantine general, George Maniakes, led an oddly assorted invasion force—Lombards forced into service, a few Byzantine regulars, and a substantial contingent of Norman mercenaries. Crossing over from southern Italy, Maniakes's army took Messina almost at once, won major battles at Rometta and Troina, and soon controlled more than a dozen fortresses in Sicily.[19] Then everything fell apart. Maniakes withheld the Normans' share of the booty, angering them and causing his most effective contingent to return to Italy,[20] Then, when the naval commander foolishly allowed the Muslim fleet to escape through the Byzantine blockade, Maniakes abused him physically and called him an effeminate pimp.[21] That naval commander was the emperor's brother-in-law Stephen. In revenge, Stephen sent a message to the emperor accusing Maniakes of treason. Maniakes was summoned to Constantinople and immediately thrown into prison. Stephen took command in Sicily—and made a complete mess of things before dying. His replacement, a court eunuch named Basil, was not much better.[22] The Byzantine army began a slow retreat, and then left Sicily altogether when it was called to quell a Lombard rebellion in Apulia, the southernmost province in the heel of Italy. Sicily was once again under uncontested Muslim rule.

The experience was eye-opening for the Norman mercenaries. They now knew that Sicily was rich, that the large Christian population would support an invasion, and that the Muslims were hopelessly divided. They also recognized that Constantinople was too far away and too corrupted by intrigues to sustain its rule in the West. So rather than help suppress the Lombard uprising, the Normans decided to lead it. In 1041 the Norman knights sneaked across the mountains and descended into Apulia.

The Normans were led by William of Hauteville, whose heroic

exploits in Sicily had earned him the nickname "Iron Arm." They quickly seized Melfi, a well-situated and fortified hill town, and accepted the submission of all the surrounding towns. The Byzantine governor assembled an army considerably larger than that of the Normans and rebels. He then sent a herald to the opposing camp offering either the Normans' safe return to Lombard territory or battle. In response, an enormous Norman knight smashed his mailed fist on the head of the Byzantine herald's horse; the horse fell dead on the spot. (Yes, this actually happened, historians agree.)[23] The battle began the next day.

The vastly outnumbered Normans routed the Byzantine forces, most of whom were killed in battle or drowned while trying to flee across the river. The Byzantine governor responded by importing many regular troops from Constantinople, but William Iron Arm and the Normans slaughtered this new Byzantine army, too. Even then the Byzantines did not accept defeat. They gathered another army and fought one more battle near Montepeloso. Again Iron Arm and his Normans prevailed, even taking the Byzantine governor prisoner and holding him for ransom. Never again were the Byzantines willing to fight an open battle with Normans in Italy; they contented themselves with defending strongly fortified towns and cities. Although they avoided further military catastrophes, they also failed to hold southern Italy, which slowly transformed into a Norman kingdom.

Soon the Normans turned their attention back to Muslim Sicily. In 1059 Robert Guiscard, the Norman duke of southern Italy, designated himself in a letter to Pope Nicholas II as "future [lord] of Sicily."[24] Two years later he and his brother Roger, with a select company of Normans, launched an invasion. They fortified Messina; formed an alliance with Ibn at-Tinnah, one of the feuding Sicilian emirs; and took most of Sicily before having to return to Italy. By 1071 Guiscard had driven the Byzantine forces out of southern Italy. The next year he returned to Sicily, captured Palermo, and soon took command of the entire island. Thus was created the Norman Kingdom of Sicily (which included southern Italy).[25] It only lasted for about a century, but Muslim rule never resumed.

Centuries after the Battle of Tours, West and East continued to clash on European turf. There was nothing preordained about the outcome of these conflicts. But here again we see the decisive impact of matters contemporary historians so often disregard—seemingly mundane matters such as military tactics and technology.

The Crusades

In 1095 Pope Urban II called on the knights of Europe to join in a crusade to free Jerusalem from Muslim rule and make it safe again for Christian pilgrims to visit their holy city. Although Muslims had controlled Jerusalem since 638, large numbers of Christians had continued making pilgrimages to Jerusalem through the centuries. Local Muslims welcomed the revenue they derived from the annual waves of penitent Christians. They permitted Christians to worship in their local churches—some of them having been built by Constantine early in the fourth century.[26] Then, at the end of the tenth century, the caliph of Egypt had prohibited Christian pilgrims, ordered the destruction of all Christian churches in the Holy Land, and demanded that the Church of the Holy Sepulchre and the cavern in the rock beneath the church that was believed to have been Christ's tomb be demolished. These desecrations caused a furious response across Europe, but calls for action subsided when the caliph was assassinated (by his own relatives) and his antipilgrim policies were reversed.

But the Muslims never completely returned to the policy of welcoming Christian pilgrims. They often enforced harsh rules against any overt expressions of Christian faith. For example, in 1026 Richard of Saint-Vanne was stoned to death after having been detected saying Mass. In addition, Muslim officials ignored frequent robberies and bloody attacks on pilgrim travelers, such as the incident in 1064 in which Muslims ambushed four German bishops and a party of several thousand pilgrims as they entered the Holy Land, slaughtering two-thirds of them.[27]

Making matters far worse, the Seljuk Turks—militant, recent converts to Islam—captured Jerusalem in 1071. In principle they allowed Christian pilgrims access to Jerusalem, but they often imposed huge ransoms and condoned local attacks. Soon only very large, well-armed, wealthy groups dared to attempt a pilgrimage, and even so, many died and many more turned back.[28] Pilgrims' dreadful tales of robbery, extortion, torture, rape, and murder once again aroused anger toward Muslims in the Holy Land. It was in this context that, in 1095, the Byzantine emperor Alexius I Comnenus appealed for Western forces to defend Constantinople from the threat of Turkish invaders. And it was in answer to this appeal that the pope organized the First Crusade.

Recruitment

There has been a great deal of antireligious nonsense written about the Crusades, including charges that the knights marched east not because of their religious convictions but in pursuit of land and loot. The truth is that the crusaders made enormous financial sacrifices to go—expenditures that they had no expectations of making back. For example, in order to finance a company of crusaders, Robert, Duke of Normandy (son of William the Conqueror), pawned the entire Duchy of Normandy to his brother King William of England for ten thousand marks, an amount that would have paid a year's wages to 2,500 ships' captains. To raise such a sum, the king had to impose a new tax on all of England (which caused many angry protests).[29] Similarly, Godfrey of Bouillon sold his entire county of Verdun to the king of France and mortgaged his county of Bouillon to the bishop of Liège.[30] Moreover, most of the crusaders knew they probably would never return, as expressed in many wills and letters they left behind.[31] In fact, very few of them did survive.

It is important to recognize that only a small percentage of Western knights heeded the pope's call to arms; nearly everyone stayed home. Those who did go were closely tied to one another by bonds of marriage and kinship. For example, Count William Tête-Hardi of Burgundy sent three sons and a grandson on the First Crusade; three men married to Tête-Hardi's daughters joined them, as did the husband of Tête-Hardi's granddaughter Florina, Sven of Denmark. Scandinavians such as Sven and Normans were extremely overrepresented among the crusaders, and many of the Franks who volunteered, like the Tête-Hardis, had Norman relatives.[32]

The First Crusade consisted of four main armies,[33] two of which were made up of Norman knights and led by Norman noblemen: Robert, Duke of Normandy, and Bohemond, Prince of Taranto (of the Norman Kingdom of Sicily). Aided by his nephew Tancred, Bohemond played the leading role in the success of the First Crusade.

Although Emperor Alexius had put out the call for help, he was apprehensive about having Prince Bohemond in Constantinople. And with good reason: Bohemond (ca. 1058–1111) was the son of Robert Guiscard, and along with his father he had repeatedly defeated Byzantine armies, some led by Alexius himself. Back in 1081, after taking control of Italy and Sicily, Guiscard and Bohemond had sailed their Norman troops across the Adriatic Sea, invading the primary Byzantine territory.

Alexius had marched north to expel the Normans, only to be badly defeated at the Battle of Dyrrhachium. While still in his early twenties, Bohemond defeated Alexius in two battles in northern Greece, thus putting the Normans in control of Macedonia and nearly all of Thessaly.

Bohemond was nearing forty when he arrived in Constantinople on April 9, 1097. He was still a commanding figure. Alexius's daughter Anna, who was fourteen at the time she met the Norman leader, wrote a remarkable sketch of Bohemond many years later: "The sight of him inspired admiration, the mention of his name terror. . . . His stature was such that he towered almost a full cubit [about twelve inches] over the tallest men." In fact, his real name was Mark; his father had nicknamed him Bohemond (after the mythical giant) because of his great size as an infant. Anna continued:

> He was slender of waist . . . perfectly proportioned. . . . His skin was . . . very white . . . His hair was lightish-brown and not so long as that of other barbarians. . . . There was a certain charm about him, but it was somewhat dimmed by the alarm his whole person inspired; there was a hard, savage quality in his whole aspect, due, I suppose to his great stature and his eyes; even his laugh sounded like a threat to others. . . . His arrogance was everywhere manifest; he was cunning, too.[34]

Bohemond's meetings with the Emperor Alexius were tense. But the two leaders appeared to come to an agreement, as Bohemond led his troops across the Bosporus to join forces with the crusader army commanded by Godfrey of Bouillon. A few days later a third crusader army, led by Raymond IV of Toulouse, arrived, followed in two weeks by the Duke of Normandy's forces. In all, probably about forty thousand crusaders were available for battle—or as many as fifty thousand fewer than had set out for the Holy Land. Some had turned back, but most had been lost to disease or in encounters fought with local forces along the route.

Alexius had never anticipated that thousands of high-ranking European nobles and knights would answer his call for help against the Turks. Few upper-class Byzantines engaged in military activities, and for centuries the armies of the empire had consisted of mercenaries and even slaves—often under the command of a eunuch.[35] Now Alexius was confronted with thousands of men who had come of their own free will and were dedicated to a cause; he and his court thought them to be dangerous barbarians.

In turn, the crusaders thought Alexius and his court were a bunch of decadent, devious plotters; the *Gesta Francorum*, the most influential eyewitness account of the First Crusade, often attaches a nasty adjective when referring to Alexius, such as "the wretched emperor."[36] They had supposed that Alexius would lead a joint force of Byzantine and Western warriors, but when the time came to attack the Turks, Alexius did not take command. Nor did he merge his army with the crusaders. Instead he sent a small contingent to accompany them only so far as needed to recover recently lost Byzantine territory. His position was that if the crusaders wanted to push on to the Holy Land, that was their own concern, but that "Jerusalem was strategically irrelevant to the empire."[37] The "barbarians" would have to go it alone. Thus began an antagonism between East and West that ultimately resulted in the sack of Constantinople in 1204 during the Fourth Crusade.

Victories

Although the crusaders held Alexius in contempt, they were not deterred by the lack of Byzantine troops. Rather, after defeating overconfident Muslim armies at Nicaea and Dorylaeum, they marched boldly on the city of Antioch, the main barrier to the Holy Land. Antioch, in what is today southern Turkey, was a strongly fortified city on the side of a mountain and with direct access to the sea. The crusaders lacked sufficient forces to surround Antioch, so the city continued to be resupplied. When winter came, the crusaders ran out of food and some starved to death. Of course, Emperor Alexius easily could have sent them supplies by sea, but he did not. He ordered the small contingent of Byzantine soldiers to withdraw.

Soon a large Muslim relief force arrived. Greatly outnumbered, the crusaders formed up as heavy infantry and gave the Muslims, all of whom were cavalry, a terrible defeat. As the Muslims began to retreat, Bohemond appeared with the remaining Christian cavalry, numbering perhaps three hundred. Their thundering charge turned the Muslim defeat into a massacre.

That still left Antioch unconquered. Making contact with Christians within the city, Bohemond found a Muslim in command of a tower who could be bribed to open a postern gate. That night Bohemond led a small group of Normans into the city, and they quietly took command of ten towers and a long stretch of wall, whereupon the remaining crusaders climbed into Antioch and wiped out the entire Muslim garrison.

Within a few days, however, a powerful new Muslim army arrived at the gates of Antioch, led by the Turkish sultan Kerbogha. In the face of this looming danger, Bohemond was acknowledged as the overall commander of the crusader army in recognition of his greater experience. Rather than accept a siege, he prepared the army to attack the Turks, realizing that this was the best military option, albeit "a dangerous gamble."[38] So on June 28 the remaining crusader forces marched through the Bridge Gate of Antioch to face Kerbogha's far larger host. The Turks attacked but recoiled after colliding with the well-armored, disciplined heavy-infantry formations. It was, in many ways, the Battle of Tours all over again. The Muslim cavalry attacked and died. The crusader ranks seemed impregnable. Soon the Turks began to withdraw and then to flee. The crusaders tromped along in their close formations, overran Kerbogha's camp, and killed everyone within reach. The only reason that some Turkish forces escaped was that the crusaders lacked the horses needed to catch them. To have triumphed so completely against such a powerful enemy seemed incomprehensible to many crusaders, even after the fact. The story spread that a contingent of mounted saints had descended from heaven and joined in the attack.[39]

So another major Muslim force had been destroyed and the road to Jerusalem lay open before the crusaders. But Bohemond did not plan to march down it. Instead, he accepted the offer to become the ruler of a new kingdom based in Antioch—he was extremely popular with the large Christian population remaining in the city. So while Bohemond remained at Antioch, his nephew Tancred led the Norman force from Sicily. Godfrey of Bouillon led the Normans and all the other remaining crusaders in their effort to take back Jerusalem.

By now there were fewer than fifteen thousand crusaders, only about a third the number of those who had reached Constantinople two years earlier. The Muslims had far greater numbers in their garrison in Jerusalem, which was "one of the great fortresses of the medieval world," in the words of the esteemed historian Sir Steven Runciman.[40] Worse yet for the crusaders, an overwhelming Muslim relief force was on its way from Egypt. At this point a priest had a vision that victory could be gained if the crusaders fasted for three days and marched barefoot around the walls of Jerusalem. So they did, mocked all the way by Muslims who crowded the city's walls to observe these foolish Christians. But two days later the crusaders gained a foothold on the walls, having built two movable wooden towers from which they fired lethal barrages from crossbows. From there they poured into Jerusalem and dispatched every one of the Muslim defenders.

There was no time to celebrate. The large Egyptian army was coming to retake Jerusalem. Even though by now there probably were fewer than ten thousand crusaders, they immediately marched south to meet the enemy, leaving only a token force in Jerusalem. At the town of Ascalon, fifty miles south of Jerusalem, they reached the Egyptian encampment and once again destroyed a far superior force. Very few Muslims escaped.

In celebration of this victory, most of the surviving crusaders boarded ships and sailed home. This left only about six hundred fighting men to defend the Holy Land.[41] Although the Muslims could have outnumbered the crusaders by several hundred to one, they had suffered such overwhelming defeats that it was a long time before they were willing to do battle again.

The Crusader Kingdoms

With Jerusalem in their possession, and having defeated the large Egyptian army sent to turn them out, the crusaders had to decide what to do to preserve their victory. Their solution was to create four kingdoms—independent states along the Mediterranean coast. These were the County of Edessa, named for its major city; the Princedom of Antioch, which surrounded the city of Antioch; the County of Tripoli, just south of the Princedom and named for the Lebanese coastal city of that name; and the Kingdom of Jerusalem, an enclave on the coast of Palestine roughly equivalent to modern Israel.[42]

Edessa was the first crusader state to be established. When the main body of crusaders marched south in 1098 to attack Antioch, Baldwin of Boulogne—brother of Godfrey of Bouillon—led a smaller force east to Edessa and managed to convince Thoros, the childless ruler of the city (who was a Greek Orthodox Christian), to adopt him as his son and heir. When Thoros was assassinated by angry subjects, Baldwin took over. Edessa also had the distinction of being the first crusader state to be retaken by Islam (in 1149).

After Bohemond captured the city of Antioch in 1098, he was named prince. His nephew Tancred became regent when Bohemond returned to

Italy in 1105 to raise a new army to fight the Byzantines. Bohemond died in 1111, making Tancred the permanent prince, although he too died the next year. The area remained an independent state until 1119, when it was joined to the Kingdom of Jerusalem (although Bohemond's descendants continued as princes). In 1268 Antioch fell to an army led by Baybars, sultan of Egypt, whose troops killed every Christian they could find.

The County of Tripoli was the last of the four crusader states to be established—in 1102. It came into being when Count Raymond IV of Toulouse laid siege to the port city of Tripoli. When Raymond died suddenly in 1105, he left his infant son as heir, so when the knights finally took the city, the county became a vassal state of the Kingdom of Jerusalem. It fell to Muslim forces in 1289.

By far the most important and powerful of the crusader states was the Kingdom of Jerusalem, which was also known at Outremer, the French word for "overseas" (outre-mer). Initially that term applied to all the crusader states, but it came to refer primarily to the Kingdom of Jerusalem. Godfrey of Bouillon, who led the capture of Jerusalem, was installed as the first ruler, with the title Defender of the Holy Sepulchre.

Despite its name, the Kingdom of Jerusalem included the city of Jerusalem for only about ninety years. As Muslim aggression built up, Western forces simply did not have enough troops to defend the long corridor linking Jerusalem with the coast. Consequently, it is absurd to claim, as many historians do, that the forces of Saladin prevented Richard the Lionheart from retaking Jerusalem during the Third Crusade. Richard knew that such a conquest was pointless and made no effort to take Jerusalem. Instead he overwhelmed Saladin's army at Arsuf, after which the Muslim leader signed a treaty restoring to Christian pilgrims the right of safe passage to and from Jerusalem.

Although few of the original crusaders remained to defend these kingdoms, two knightly religious orders eventually reinforced their ranks. These orders combined "monastic discipline and martial skill . . . for the first time in the Christian world," as the historian Thomas F. Madden pointed out.[43] The Knights Hospitallers were founded to care for sick Christian pilgrims to the Holy Land, but in about 1120 the order expanded its vows from chastity, poverty, and obedience to include the armed protection of Christians in Palestine. The Knights Templar originated as a military religious order in about 1119. Hospitallers wore black robes with a white cross on the left sleeve; the Templars wore white robes with a red cross on the mantel. The two orders hated each other, but together they provided the kingdoms with a reliable force of well-trained soldiers who built and garrisoned a chain of extremely well-sited castles along the frontiers.

Nevertheless, the existence of the kingdoms remained perilous, surrounded as they were by a vast and populous Muslim world. For many years, whenever the Muslim threat loomed especially large, new Crusades were mounted in Europe, bringing fresh troops east in support of the kingdoms. But eventually Europeans lost their fervor to defend—and, just as important, to *pay for* the defense of—the Holy Land, and Islamic forces ate away at the crusader areas.[44] Still, that the Kingdom of Jerusalem lasted until 1291, when its last fortress at Acre fell to a huge Muslim army, seems a remarkable achievement.

What the Crusades most revealed about the West was the superiority of its tactics and military hardware. Unwilling to shift from light cavalry, the Muslims were unable to dent crusader heavy-infantry formations. Beyond that, their arrows could not pierce the crusaders' mail armor unless shot from point-blank range, whereas the crusader crossbows were lethal at considerable range. Crossbows were widely used during the First Crusade, but during the Third Crusade, Richard the Lionheart fielded a large number of crossbow *teams*: a shooter supported by one or two loaders, facilitating a very high rate of fire. And of course Richard, like most crusader commanders, held in reserve a contingent of heavy cavalry that was irresistible when properly utilized. The few Muslim victories in the field were due to overwhelming numbers; their other victories involved sieges.

Crusader "War Crimes"

Of late, the alleged brutality of the crusaders is much lamented. In 1999, for example, the *New York Times* solemnly proposed that the Crusades were comparable to Hitler's atrocities.[45] The former priest James Carroll agreed, charging that the Crusades left a "trail of violence [that] scars the earth and human memory even to this day."[46] And the ex-nun and popular writer Karen Armstrong claimed that "crusading answered a deep need in the Christians of Europe," because Christianity has "an inherent leaning towards violence."[47] Carroll and Armstrong, along with many other modern authors, have gone so far as to claim that the Muslims who did battle with the crusaders were civilized and tolerant victims.

It is absurd to impose modern notions about proper military conduct on medieval armies; both Christians and Muslims observed quite different rules of warfare. One of these was that if a city surrendered before the attacking forces had to storm over the walls, the residents were supposed to be treated leniently. This was true no matter how long the siege had lasted. But when a city forced the attackers to storm the walls and thereby incur serious casualties, commanders (Muslims as well as Christians) believed they had an obligation to release their troops to murder, loot, and burn as an example to other cities that might be tempted to hold out in the future. This was the case in the fall of Jerusalem—the primary instance of a "massacre" that animates critics of the crusaders.

Many Western histories of the Crusades express such outrage against crusader "war crimes" but give little or no attention to the many massacres Muslims committed. As the British historian Robert Irwin noted, his country has "a long tradition of disparaging the crusaders as barbaric and bigoted warmongers and of praising the Saracens as paladins of chivalry." Irwin added, "Indeed, it is widely believed that chivalry originated in the Muslim East," with Saladin upheld as "the most perfect example of Muslim chivalry."[48] Another British historian, Christopher Tyerman, pointed out that such beliefs are neither recent inventions nor confined to Britain. Since the Enlightenment, Tyerman wrote, Saladin has "bizarrely" been portrayed "as a rational and civilized figure in juxtaposition to credulous barbaric crusaders."[49] In 1898 Germany's Kaiser Wilhelm visited Damascus and placed a bronze laurel wreath on Saladin's tomb. The wreath was inscribed: "From one great emperor to another."[50]

Much has been made of the fact that Saladin did not murder the Christians when he retook Jerusalem in 1187. Writing in 1869, the English historian Barbara Hutton claimed that although Saladin "hated Christians . . . when they were suppliants and at his mercy, he was never cruel or revengeful."[51] But as Muslim writers have acknowledged, Jerusalem was an exception to Saladin's usual butchery of his enemies. Indeed, Saladin had planned to massacre the knights holding Jerusalem, but he offered safe conduct in exchange for their surrender of Jerusalem without resistance. In most other instances Saladin was quite unchivalrous. For example, Saladin's secretary, Imad ad-Din, related the sultan's treatment of captured knights following the Battle of Hattin (1187): "He [Saladin] ordered that they should be beheaded, choosing to have them dead rather than in prison. With him was a whole band of scholars and sufis and a certain number of devout men and ascetics; each begged to be allowed to kill one of them, and drew his sword and rolled back his sleeve. Saladin, his face joyful, was sitting on his dais; the unbelievers showed black despair."[52] It thus seems fitting that during one of his amazing World War I adventures leading irregular Arab forces against the Turks, T. E. Lawrence "liberated" the kaiser's wreath from Saladin's tomb; it now resides in the Imperial War Museum in London.

Similarly, many Western historians have given little or no coverage to Baybars, sultan of Egypt, although he is much more celebrated than Saladin in Muslim histories of this period. When Baybars took the Knights Templar fortress of Safad in 1266, he had all the inhabitants massacred after promising to spare their lives during negotiations.[53] Later that same year his forces took the great city of Antioch. Even though the city surrendered after four days of siege, Baybars ordered all inhabitants, including all women and children, killed or enslaved. What followed was, as Thomas Madden observed, "the single greatest massacre of the entire crusading era."[54]

Since Bohemond VI, prince of Antioch, was away when this disaster befell his city, Baybars sent a letter telling him what he had missed:

> You would have seen your knights prostrate beneath the horses' hooves, your houses stormed by pillagers. . . . You would have seen your Muslim enemy trampling on the place where you celebrate Mass, cutting the throats of monks, priests and deacons upon the altars, bringing sudden death to the Patriarchs and slavery to the royal princes. You would have seen fire running through your palaces, your dead burned in this world before going down to the fires of the next.[55]

The massacre of Antioch is seldom reported in the many apologetic Western histories of the Crusades.

Of course, even though most of the crusaders went to war for God and at considerable personal cost, few of them adopted a religious lifestyle. They ate and drank as well as they were able, and most of them routinely violated commandments, especially those concerned with adultery and coveting wives. Moreover, they did not disdain the spoils of battle and looted as much as they were able—which wasn't much when balanced against the costs of crusading. And of course they were often cruel and bloodthirsty—after all, they had been trained from childhood to make war, face to face, sword to sword. No doubt it was "unenlightened" of the crusaders to have been typical medieval warriors, but it seems even more unenlightened to anachronistically impose the Geneva Conventions on the crusaders while pretending that their Islamic opponents were innocent victims.

Christendom

It was only though the auspices of the Church that a "European" effort such as the Crusades could be conceived and initiated. Indeed, the Church was the only entity that gave some semblance of political and cultural coherence to the West—despite the fact that, even by the time of the Crusades, much of the North had not yet been converted to Christianity

Two Churches

Ironically, the immense favoritism the Roman emperor Constantine showed toward Christianity did it substantial harm. Eamon Duffy, in his history of the papacy, pointed out that Constantine elevated the clergy to high levels of wealth, power, and status so that bishops "became grandees on a par with the wealthiest senators."[56] Not surprisingly, "there was a stampede into the priesthood," in the words of Richard Fletcher.[57] Soon Christian offices, and especially the higher positions, were dominated by sons of the aristocracy—some of them gaining bishoprics even before being baptized. Gaining a church position became a matter mainly of influence, commerce, and eventually heredity. Simony became the rule—an extensive and expensive traffic in religious offices, including even lowly parish placements. There quickly arose great clerical families whose sons followed their fathers, uncles, and grandfathers into holy offices. Even the papacy soon ran in families. Pope Innocent (reigned 401–417) was the son of his predecessor, Pope Anastasius (399–401). Pope Silverius (536–537) was the son of Pope Hormisdas (514–523). Many other popes were the sons, grandsons, nephews, and brothers of bishops and cardinals. Competition for high church offices became so corrupt that from 872 to 1012 a third of all popes died violent deaths, many of them murdered as a result of the constant intrigues among the Roman ecclesiastical families, and at least one killed by an irate husband.[58]

Of course, many who entered the religious life were neither careerists nor libertines. The "stampede" into the priesthood was accompanied by a rapid expansion of monasticism, which, perhaps surprisingly, also was dominated by the privileged: 75 percent of ascetic medieval saints were sons and daughters of the nobility, including the children of kings.[59] By the middle of the fourth century there were thousands of monks and nuns, nearly all of them living in organized communities; as time passed, the number of monks and nuns continued to soar.

In effect, two parallel churches arose. These can usefully be identified as the Church of Power and the Church of Piety.

The Church of Power was the main body of the Church as it evolved in response to the immense status and wealth bestowed on the clergy. It included the great majority of priests, bishops, cardinals, and popes until the Counter-Reformation began during the sixteenth century. Most clergy of the Church of Power were sensible and temperate men, but they tended to be worldly in both senses of that term—practical and morally somewhat permissive.

In contrast, the Church of Piety pressed for virtue over worldliness and constantly attempted to reform the Church of Power. Starting in 1046, the Church of Piety controlled the papacy for more than a century. Indeed, in 1073 a monk became pope (Gregory VII), and the next three popes also were monks, including Urban II, who launched the First Crusade. Even after the Church of Power recaptured the papacy, it was unable to silence the Church of Piety because the latter retained an unyielding base in monasticism, which had strong family ties to the ruling elites.

In practice, there was a division of labor between the two churches. The task of conversion, especially of pagan territories, was left to the Church of Piety, while the task of administering Christendom was undertaken by the Church of Power.

Christianizing the North

It was monks who converted the German "barbarians," and subsequently it was monks who undertook to convert the Vikings. Early on, many of the monks who missionized in Viking areas were martyred. But even when it became less dangerous, missionary monks had no choice but to try to convert the nobility and hope that their example would trickle down to the general population.[60] The realities of conversion dictated this strategy.[61]

For generations it was assumed that religious conversions were the result of doctrinal appeal—that people embraced a new faith because they found its teachings particularly appealing, especially if these teachings seemed to solve serious problems or dissatisfactions that afflicted them. If so, then to convert the Vikings might have been accomplished by preaching to mass audiences. But, surprisingly, when sociologists[62] took the trouble to go out and actually watch conversions take place, they discovered that doctrines are of secondary importance in the initial decision to convert. One must, of course, leave room for those rare conversions resulting from mystical experiences such as Paul's on the road to Damascus. But such instances aside, conversion is primarily about bringing one's religious behavior into alignment with that of one's friends and relatives, not about encountering attractive doctrines. Put more formally: *people tend to convert to a religious group when their social ties to members outweigh their ties to outsiders who might oppose the conversion, and this often occurs before a convert knows much about what the group believes.*[63]

Of course, one can easily imagine doctrines so bizarre as to keep most people from joining. It also is true that successful faiths sustain doctrines that have wide appeal. But while doctrines can facilitate or hinder conversion, in the normal course of events *conversion primarily is an act of conformity.* But then, so is nonconversion. In the end it is a matter of the relative strength of social ties pulling the individual toward or away from a group. This principle has, by now, been examined by dozens of close-up studies of conversion, all of which confirm that social networks are the basic mechanism through which conversion takes place.[64] To convert someone, you must be or become his or her close and trusted friend. When people convert to a new religion, they usually seek to convert their friends and relatives. Conversion, therefore, tends to proceed through social networks. This dynamic rules out mass conversions in response to sermons. In fact, social scientists have now discarded notions of "mass psychology" and "collective consciousness."[65]

A successful mission to a large population takes generations. The first missionaries must slowly form close ties with a few people who, in turn, may be able to attract some of their friends and relatives to the new faith. Of course, this supposes that the missionaries have free access to build such close interpersonal ties and are willing to be patient through many disappointing years. The Christian monks seeking to convert the Vikings had neither access nor time. To venture out among the Viking settlements was apt to be fatal, or at least unavailing, as the locals rejected contact. And the pressure was on the monks to achieve immediate results, since it was widely believed that if the Vikings could be brought to Christ they would cease their raids and invasions. Consequently, the monks focused on converting Viking rulers or on helping Vikings who had been raised as Christians outside Scandinavia to seize power.[66] As early as the eighth century, missionaries began to gather up Danish boys to be baptized and trained.[67]

The first Scandinavian king to be converted was the Dane Harold Klak, who was baptized in Germany in 826. His motives for becoming a Christian were not religious but political—by doing so he gained the support of the Carolingians. It is not certain that he ever returned to Denmark, but if he did, he was driven into exile the next year. Then, in about 965, Harold Bluetooth, the king of Denmark, was baptized. He, too, seems to have converted to gain Carolingian support. Subsequently Christians were intermittently persecuted in Denmark, and in 1086 King Canute IV was murdered in a church. His canonization as Saint Canute in 1188 is said to mark the triumph of Christianity in Denmark—although there still were few Christians aside from the nobility.

Next, consider Norway. Olaf Tryggvason grew up in England as a Christian. In 995 he seized Norway's throne, whereupon he attempted to convert the nobility by force, killing some who resisted and burning their estates. This aroused so much opposition that the nobility rebelled and, in the Battle of Svolder (about the year 1000), Olaf was killed. Fifteen years later, another Olaf (Haraldsson), who had been baptized in France, took the Norwegian throne. He, too, used the sword to compel Christianization, sparking rebellion. Driven into exile, he attempted to return after raising a new army in Kiev, but he was defeated and killed at the Battle of Stikklestad in 1030. Amazingly, once Norway was ruled by Christian nobles (converted in Denmark), history was rewritten to such an extent that the murderous Olaf Haraldsson became St. Olaf.

The conversion of the Swedish nobility also involved murder and forced conversions. Late in the eleventh century, Inge the Elder was king of Sweden and an ardent Christian (little is known of him, and nothing of the source of his Christianity). He was driven into exile when he tried to abolish pagan worship. After three years in exile, he returned with a band of armed followers and surrounded a hall in Old Uppsala, where his rival and his court were gathered. Inge and his men set fire to the building and killed all those who exited. Restored to the throne, Inge resumed his persecution of non-Christians.

Despite the success in baptizing Scandinavian kings and nobles, Christianity did not trickle down much among the people. The outward forms of paganism were muted, but the inward forms prevailed. As the great Danish historian Johannes Brøndsted pointed out, it was quite easy for Christianity to become the "public" faith in Scandinavia, "but far more difficult to overcome the complex [pagan] culture beneath." He quoted a twelfth-century Anglo-Danish monk: "As long as things go well and everything is fine, [the people] seem willing to acknowledge Christ and honor him, though as a pure formality; but when things go wrong," they turn against Christianity and revert to paganism.[68] Or, as the medieval Icelandic saga *Landnámabók* noted, Helgi the Lean "was very mixed in his faith; he believed in Christ, but invoked Thor in matters of seafaring and dire necessity."[69]

Brøndsted suggested that to the extent it can be said to have taken place at all, the conversion of Scandinavia occurred "only . . . when Christianity took over old [pagan] superstitions and usages and allowed them to live under a new guise."[70] Of course, since the baptizing of kings meant that Christianity became a state church, funded by tithes, it did not depend on popular support, and church officials had little motivation to work at convincing the masses. Thus, even today forms of paganism remain surprisingly popular in Scandinavia.[71]

Insofar as the Church of Power was concerned, it was enough that the Church of Piety had placed Christian state churches in power in Scandinavia. The tithes flowed in and all the formalities were properly observed.

An Organized Religion

Spanning hundreds of medieval states and statelets was a church structure based on geographic units—parishes and dioceses. A parish is the small, local area served by an ordained pastor (sometimes with assistant priests). A diocese is a set of parishes, presided over by a bishop. (An archdiocese is led by an archbishop.) After several centuries, all of Catholic Europe was divided into parishes and dioceses,[72] enabling the Church to act as the moral and administrative basis for continental unity.

To some extent, the Church could curb the worst excesses of the nobility—through excommunication, actual or threatened, or even by withholding the sacraments. Hence, Henry IV (1050–1106), the Holy Roman Emperor, was forced to humble himself and walk barefoot through the snow to gain the forgiveness of Pope Gregory VII. Henry's conflict with the pope involved the right to name bishops in Germany, but often the issues concerned moral lapses and abuses of power. The king of France was not permitted to go on the First Crusade because he was married to a woman who had not divorced her previous husband. The Church took a constant interest in marriage among the nobility, often blocking divorces or invalidating marriages between couples who were too closely related.

The Church also frequently, and surprisingly effectively, imposed sanctions on rulers who overstepped moral boundaries on mistreatment of their subjects. Consider the notorious case of Fulk III, Count of Anjou (972–1040). Fulk (called "the black count") was a "plunderer, murderer, robber, and swearer of false oaths, a truly frightening character of fiendish cruelty," in the words of Richard Erdoes.[73] The count had had his first wife burned to death in her wedding dress, allegedly for having sex with a goatherd. For that act, Fulk's confessor demanded that he make a pilgrimage to Jerusalem—and he went. Soon, however, he reverted to type, and whenever "he had the slightest difference with a neighbor he rushed upon his lands, ravaging, pillaging, raping, and killing."[74] Eventually, Fulk was required to make four pilgrimages to Jerusalem; he died on his way back from the last of them. Despite his relapses, Fulk's excesses would surely have known no bounds had it not been for the Church's interventions.

Although few medieval rulers were so extreme as Fulk, it was common for them to combine a tendency to violence and sin with deep religious devotion. By the tenth century Viking and Norman pilgrims were coming to Jerusalem who, it was said, "were very devoted to Christ if not to his commandments."[75] In some cases noblemen were told to make the whole trip to Jerusalem barefooted, and most obeyed.

The Church played other roles as well. With churchmen frequently acting as aides and advisers at royal court, the Church served as a universal diplomatic service, negotiating agreements and mediating disputes among rulers. As was the case during the Crusades, the Church also served as a major lending institution—until replaced by the rise of secular banks in the twelfth century (see chapter 6). Moreover, because of the constant movement of the religious, the Church became the primary conduit of news and gossip to the otherwise isolated courts.

Finally, the Church provided the intellectual life of the medieval West. All educated Europeans had been educated by the Church—all tutors were clergy or monks. Most music was church music, and all the pipe organs were in churches. Most of the great buildings were cathedrals. The graphic arts were mainly paid for by the Church. Most of the books were written by the religious, and all publications were the work of copyist monks. And, as will be seen in chapter 8, all the early scientists were monks or clergy—including many bishops and even an occasional cardinal.

This was Christendom.

Upside-Down History

For far too long, far too many historians have had a strong preference for empires. Not only have they continued to regret the fall of Rome, but they remember Charlemagne as the man who almost "saved" Europe and restored civilization, but whose heirs undercut his great achievements by subdividing his empire. That Charlemagne was a bloodthirsty tyrant is ignored or rationalized because, as R. H. C. Davis explained, "he was devoted to the cause of Christianity and Roman civilization."[76] Like a true Roman, Charlemagne was devoted to wars of conquest, leading his army somewhere to attack someone in almost every year of his forty-one-year reign. And he demonstrated his devotion to Christianity by pronouncing a death sentence on all who resisted becoming Christians.

In contrast, most historians have dismissed the Vikings as bloodthirsty enemies of civilization. As for the Normans, most historians have assumed that the sophistication shown by William the Conqueror and his nobles reflected their Viking forebears' rapid assimilation into Frankish culture. In fact, the Scandinavians were as civilized as the Franks, while William the Conqueror was certainly as able as Charlemagne, and considerably more tolerant.

6

Freedom and Capitalism

Compare Shakespeare's tragedies with those of the ancient Greeks.[1] Not that Oedipus was without faults, but he did nothing to deserve his sad end—he simply fell victim to his destiny. In contrast, Othello, Brutus, and the Macbeths were not the captives of blind fate. As Cassius pointed out to Brutus, "The fault, dear Brutus, is not in our stars, but in ourselves."[2] And in the end, each of these Shakespearian characters got what he or she deserved.

One of the most important ideas facilitating the rise of the West is the belief in *free will*. Whereas most (if not all) ancient societies believed in fate, Westerners came to believe that humans are relatively free to follow the dictates of their conscience and that, to a substantial degree, they make their own fate. This belief had remarkable behavioral consequences. Most important, perhaps, it created a tendency for people not to be resigned to things as they are but rather to attempt to make the situation better. Moreover, belief in free will led directly to valuing the *right* of the individual to freely choose, with the result that medieval Europe rejected slavery—the only culture ever to have done so without external compulsion. (Of course, eventually the West had to do it again in the New World.) The value placed on individual freedom, combined with the legacy of Greek efforts at democracy, led to new democratic experiments in the medieval Italian city-states. Meanwhile, the rise of large monastic estates having extensive commercial activities led to the invention of capitalism and to the reformulation of theological doctrines in ways favorable to commerce. Subsequently, capitalism gained a firm footing in the newly democratic Italian city-states, transforming them into major centers of banking, trade, and even manufacturing.

Free Will

Unlike the Greeks and Romans, whose gods lacked virtues and did not concern themselves with human misbehavior (other than failures to propitiate them in the appropriate manner), the Judeo-Christian God is a judge who rewards virtue and punishes sin.[3] This conception of God is incompatible with fatalism; the admonition to "Go and sin no more" is absurd if we are captives of our fate. Judaism and, later, Christianity were founded on the doctrine that humans have been given the capacity and hence the responsibility to determine their own actions. As Deuteronomy (30:19–20) puts it: "I call heaven and earth to witness against you today that I have set before you life and death, blessings and curses. Choose life so that you and your descendants may live, loving the Lord your God, obeying him, and holding fast to him."

Saint Augustine (354–430) wrote again and again that we "possess a will" and that "from this it follows that whoever desires to live righteously and honorably, can accomplish this."[4] The notion of free will, Augustine added, is entirely compatible with the doctrine that God knows ahead of time what choices we will make. Writing in refutation of Greek and Roman philosophers, he asserted "both that God knows all things before they come to pass, and that we do by our free will whatsoever we know and feel to be done by us only because we will it. But that all things come from fate we do not say; nay we affirm that nothing comes to pass by fate."[5] In other words, God knows what we will freely decide to do but does not interfere; it remains up to us to choose virtue or sin.

Augustine's views were echoed across generations of Christian thought. Thomas Aquinas (1225–1274), for example, taught that "a man can direct and govern his own actions" and that "the rational creature participates in the divine providence not only in being governed but also in governing."[6]

The idea of free will was not exclusive to the Judeo-Christian heritage. The Roman philosopher Cicero (106–43 BC) expressed views somewhat similar to Augustine's.[7] But for Jews and Christians, free will was not an obscure philosophical matter. Rather, it was the fundamental principle of their faith, without which the Ten Commandments were nonsense. Thus both Moses and Jesus taught that each individual must atone for moral lapses precisely because these are *wrong choices*.

Being central to Jewish and Christian thought, the doctrine of free will called into question the legitimacy of social structures and customs that limited the individual's ability to choose freely—especially slavery and tyranny.

The Abolition of European Slavery

If each of us has free will and is to be judged by our actions freely taken, what is the duty of Christians with regard to another's freedom to act? As the church fathers pondered the implications of free will, they grew increasingly uncomfortable with the institution of slavery and, especially after the fall of Rome, opposed it.

The historical record shows that slavery is far older than the pyramids and has been universal to all societies sufficiently affluent to afford it, including many aboriginal societies: the American Indians of the Northwest, for example, had extensive slavery long before the arrival of Columbus.[8] Moreover, according to the U.S. State Department's annual report, as many as twenty-seven million people around the world are exploited in modern slavery, most of them in Muslim nations and in central Africa.[9]

A slave is a human being who, in the eyes of the law and custom, is the possession, or chattel, of another human being or of a small group. Ownership of slaves entails absolute control, including the right to punish (and often to kill), to direct behavior, and to transfer ownership.

The existence of slavery is a function of human productivity. There will be a demand for slaves when the average person can produce sufficient surplus so that it becomes profitable to own them—when the costs of maintaining and controlling slaves are more than offset by their production. Slavery also can exist as a form of consumption, wherein sufficiently affluent people use slaves in nonproductive roles as personal servants, concubines, entertainers, and even bodyguards. Consumption slavery has been typical in Islamic societies.

All early empires made extensive use of slave labor. But as the classical scholar M. I. Finley explained, the Greeks and Romans achieved the first truly "slave societies," becoming highly dependent on "the large-scale employment of slave labor in both the countryside and the cities."[10] In fact, at the height of the empires, slaves may have outnumbered free citizens in both Athens and the city of Rome. There is no record that any voices were raised against slavery in either Greece or Rome.

Slavery began to decline in the latter days of the Roman Empire as a direct result of military weakness. No longer were victorious commanders dispatching throngs of prisoners to the slave markets. Since fertility was very low among Roman slaves, due both to privation and to a lack of women, their numbers declined.

But the successful military expeditions of the Germanic kingdoms produced a new source of slaves. Although no one really knows how many slaves were in Europe during, say, the sixth century, they seem to have been plentiful and their treatment was, if anything, harsher than in classical times. In the legal codes of the various Germanic groups that ruled in place of Roman governors, slaves were equated not with other humans but with animal livestock. Nevertheless, several centuries later slavery was on the way out.

Some historians insist that there was never an end to medieval slavery—that nothing happened other than a linguistic shift in which the word *slave* was replaced by the word *serf*.[11] These historians are the ones playing word games. Serfs were not chattel; they had rights and a substantial degree of discretion. They married whom they wished and their families were not subject to sale or dispersal. They paid rent and thus controlled their own time and the pace of their work.[12] If, as in some places, serfs owed their lords a number of days of labor each year, the obligation was limited and more similar to hired labor than slavery. Although serfs were bound to a lord by extensive obligations, so too was their lord bound by obligations to them.[13] No one would argue that medieval peasants were free in the modern sense, but they were not slaves.

The brutal institution had essentially disappeared from Europe by the end of the tenth century. Although most recent historians agree with that conclusion, it remains fashionable to deny that Christianity had anything to do with it. As Robert Fossier put it, "The progressive elimination of slavery was in no way the work of Christian peoples. The Church preached resignation, promised equality in the hereafter . . . [and] felt no compunction about keeping large herds of animals with human faces."[14] Georges Duby also dismissed any church role in ending slavery: "Christianity did not condemn slavery; it dealt it barely a glancing blow."[15] According to such historians, slavery disappeared because it became an unprofitable and outdated "mode of production."[16] Even the Yale scholar Robert S. Lopez accepted this view, claiming that slavery ended only when technological progress such as the waterwheel "made slaves useless or unproductive."[17] In this view, the end of slavery was not a moral decision but one of self-interest on the part of the elite. That same argument has been made concerning the abolition of slavery in the Western Hemisphere. Both claims are consistent with Marxist doctrine—but quite inconsistent with economic realities. Even as late as the start of the American Civil War, Southern slavery remained a profitable "mode of production."[18]

The fact is that slavery pays. But it is equally true that slaves are not nearly as productive as self-interested individuals performing the same tasks in pursuit of their own economic gain. That is, *owners* benefit from the possession of slaves, but *societies* gain far more from a free workforce. For example, Rome had a far stronger economy (and army) before the small independent farmers were pushed out by the slave-based estates (*latifundia*). Consequently, overcoming slavery gave Europe an immense economic advantage over the rest of the world.

But economics was not the decisive factor. Slavery ended in medieval Europe *only* because the Church extended its sacraments to all slaves and then banned the enslavement of Christians (and of Jews). Within the context of medieval Europe, that prohibition was effectively a rule of universal abolition.

In the beginning, the Church asserted the legitimacy of slavery, but it did so with a certain ambiguity. Consider the most-cited New Testament passage on slavery. Writing to the Ephesians (6:5–9), Paul admonished: "Slaves, be obedient to those who are your earthly masters, in fear and trembling, in singleness of heart, as to Christ . . . knowing that whatever good any one does, he will receive the same again from the Lord, whether he is slave or free." Those who eagerly quote this passage seldom go on to quote the next verse: "Masters, do the same to them, and forbear threatening, knowing that he who is both their Master and yours is in heaven, and that there is no partiality with him." That God treats all equally is fundamental to the Christian message: all may be saved. This encouraged the early Church to convert slaves and when possible to purchase their freedom—Pope Callistus (died 223) had himself been a slave.

So long as the Roman Empire stood, the Church continued to affirm the legitimacy of slavery. In 324 the Christian Council of Granges condemned anyone who encouraged discontent among slaves,[19] which suggests, of course, that such activities were taking place. But tension grew between support for slavery and the emphasis on the equality of all in the eyes of God. With the demise of the empire, the Church extended its embrace to those in slavery, denying them only ordination into the priesthood. The historian Pierre Bonnassie expressed the matter as well as anyone: "A slave . . . was baptised [and] had a soul. He was, then, unambiguously a man."[20] With slaves fully recognized as human and Christian, priests began to urge owners to free their slaves as an "infinitely commendable act" that helped ensure their own salvation.[21] Surviving wills show many manumissions.

The doctrine that slaves were humans and not chattle had another important consequence: intermarriage. Despite being against the law in most of Europe, mixed unions seem to have been prevalent by the seventh century, usually involving free men and female slaves. The most celebrated of these unions took place in 649 when Clovis II, king of the Franks, married his British slave Bathilda. When Clovis died in 657, Bathilda ruled as regent until her eldest son came of age. Bathilda used her position to mount a campaign to halt the slave trade and to redeem those in slavery. Upon her death, the Church acknowledged Bathilda as a saint.

At the end of the eighth century Charlemagne opposed slavery, as did the pope and many other powerful clerical voices. As the ninth century dawned, Bishop Agobard of Lyons thundered: "All men are brothers, all invoke one same Father, God: the slave and the master, the poor man and the rich man, the ignorant and the learned, the weak and the strong. . . . None has been raised above the other. . . . There is no . . . slave or free, but in all things and always there is only Christ."[22] At the same time, Abbot Smaragde of Saint-Mihiel wrote in a work dedicated to Charlemagne: "Most merciful king, forbid that there should be any slave in your kingdom."[23] Soon, no one "doubted that slavery in itself was against divine law," as the historian Marc Bloch put it.[24] During the eleventh century both Saint Wulfstan and Saint Anselm campaigned to remove the last vestiges of slavery in Christendom, and, according to Bloch, "no man, no real Christian at any rate, could thereafter legitimately be held as the property of another."[25]

But exceptions remained, all of them involving extensive interaction with Islam. In Spain, Christian and Muslim armies continued to enslave one another's captives taken in battle, and slave trading involving northern Italian export firms and Muslim buyers persisted into the fifteenth century, in defiance of the Church. The number of slaves involved in this trade was small. They were purchased from Slavic tribes in the Caucasus (the word *slave* is a corruption of *Slav*). A few were kept as a form of luxury goods by wealthy Italians such as the Medici, but most were exported to Islamic lands—white slaves being "more precious than gold in trading with Egypt," in Lopez's words.[26]

Although this residual slave trade withered away, slavery reappeared with a vengeance in the New World. The Church responded vigorously, with sixteenth-century popes issuing a series of angry bulls against New World slavery. But the popes had no serious temporal power in this era, and their vigorous opposition was to no avail.[27]

The theological conclusion that slavery is sinful has been unique to Christianity (although there are antislave passages in the Torah and several early Jewish sects rejected slavery).[28] In part this reflects the fact that it is possible for Christian theologians to propose new interpretations without engendering charges of heresy. So, for example, they could plausibly "correct" Saint Paul's understanding of God's will concerning slavery. By contrast, Buddhists, Confucianists, Hindus, and even Muslims reject the idea that sages or saints in times past may have had an imperfect understanding of religious truths. A second factor is that, of the major world faiths, only Judaism and Christianity have devoted serious and sustained attention to human rights, as opposed to human duties. Put another way, the other great faiths minimize individualism and stress collective obligations. They are, as the anthropologist Ruth Benedict so aptly put it, cultures of shame rather than cultures of guilt.[29] There is not even a word for freedom in the languages in which their scriptures are written.[30]

As for Islam, there is an insuperable barrier to theological condemnations of slavery: Muhammad bought, sold, captured, and owned slaves.[31] The Prophet did advise that slaves should be treated well: "Feed them what you eat yourself and clothe them with what you wear. . . . They are God's people like unto you and be kind unto them."[32] Muhammad also freed several of his slaves, adopted one as his son, and married another. In addition, the Qur'an teaches that it is wrong to "compel your slave girls to prostitution" (24:33) and that one can gain forgiveness for killing a fellow believer by freeing a slave (4:92). But the fundamental morality of the institution of slavery was not in doubt—and widespread slavery continues in many Islamic nations.

New Democracies

Christian theology also provided the moral basis for the establishment of responsive regimes. But political freedom did not emerge throughout Christendom. Rather, it appeared first in a number of Italian city-states. Why? Because as these city-states expanded foreign trade, they dispersed political power among a set of well-matched interest groups: not only the aristocracy, the military, and the clergy but also merchants, bankers, manufacturers, and the workers' guilds. Dozens of city-states in northern Italy separated power in this way. Let's look at two case studies: Venice and Genoa.[33]

Venice

Shielded by remarkable natural barriers and with unimpeded access to the sea, Venice fended off all Lombard efforts to subordinate it and instead became a province of the Byzantine Empire. This gave the growing city many commercial advantages, such as being free from Byzantine tolls or customs in its trade with the East. That commerce became increasingly important as Islam developed a trading network throughout the region, including Spain, Sicily, the toe of Italy, and North Africa. In fact, Venice probably was the first society to live by trade alone.[34]

It also was a pioneer in the return of democracy. Distance, and growing Venetian sea power, made Byzantium's sovereignty over Venice nominal at best. As far back as records go, Venice had been recognized as a dukedom and was administered by a duke, known as the *doge*. But Venice was unlike most other dukedoms in several ways. For one thing, the doge was not sustained by taxes or rents but owed his wealth to his active participation in commerce. The earliest known medieval reference to a monetary investment was in the will of Doge Giustiniano Partecipazio. When he died in 829, his estate included 1,200 pounds of "working *solidi*, if they come back safely from sea."[35] Second, the position of doge was not hereditary (although sons sometimes followed their fathers). According to Venetian tradition, even the very first doge was chosen by the "people," and Venetians enjoyed substantial political freedom from earliest days. If the "people" did not include all inhabitants of Venice, they did make up a substantial number—all those having wealth, military responsibilities, or business establishments, or who were members of the clergy. And as time passed, the "people" became an increasingly inclusive group. Meanwhile, the power of the doge was gradually reduced as elected councils took greater authority, leading to what came to be known as the *commune*—made up of the body of citizens with voting rights and the executives and legislators elected by them.

Venice was not the first Italian city-state to develop a commune; that honor may belong to Pisa.[36] But by the middle of the twelfth century, Venice's commune was in full operation, with five layers of government.[37] At the apex of this pyramid was the doge—a chief executive elected for life, but without regal pretensions, his powers being carefully limited by his oath of office. Below the doge was the Ducal Council, made up of six members, each representing a geographical area of Venice. Councilors were elected to serve a one-year term and could not be reelected until they had been out of office for two years. The councilors worked closely with the doge, who was required to gain their assent for major decisions. Beneath the council were the Forty and the Senate. The Forty were akin to a court of appeals, while the Senate consisted of sixty men who were particularly concerned with issues of commerce and foreign policy. The Forty and the Senate were selected from the Great Council (sometimes by election, sometimes by drawing lots), which also elected fleet commanders. Members of the Great Council, which often numbered more than a thousand, were selected from the General Assembly, which consisted of the thousands of voting Venetians. The General Assembly met irregularly, being summoned to ratify basic legislation and the choice of a new doge.

In early days, participation in Venetian politics was limited to various elites, but as time passed, and especially as Venice became a major manufacturing center as well as a trading port, the franchise was extended. The principal mechanism by which this was accomplished was by the organization of guilds—associations of persons engaged in a specific craft or trade. Guilds represented lawyers, physicians, glassblowers, apothecaries, jewelers, tailors, furriers, butchers, bakers, barbers, sailmakers, shopkeepers, and many others. Well organized and possessed of financial resources, the guilds became such a significant political force that they were assigned representation in the councils, thus giving the masses a significant voice in government. To this was added the influence of religious confraternities—lay fellowships that featured religious devotions but that also provided for mutual aid, rather like a modern fraternal lodge.

Venice and the other leading medieval Italian city-states were by modern standards medium-sized towns—in the year 1000, Venice had a population of about thirty thousand, and most of the other city-states were considerably smaller.[38] Everyone knew everyone else, current public opinion was transparent, and consensus often was easily achieved. This, combined with relatively open political institutions, allowed Venice to sustain a substantial degree of freedom and responsive governance.

Genoa

Situated on the western side of Italy at the head of the Ligurian Sea, Genoa occupied a strategically important coastal strip of land, where the best land route from Rome to France and on to Spain passed. This location helped make Genoa the dominant port in the western Mediterranean (a position solidified when the city-state defeated Pisa in a huge sea battle in 1284).

Unlike Venice, which was essentially independent from the start, Genoa had been dominated by the Lombards and then sacked by Muslim raiders in 934–35.[39] But by the end of the eleventh century it had established itself as an independent city-state.

Initially, Genoa was ruled by a council of nobles in the tradition of the Roman Senate. But, as happened in Rome, an autocratic coalition took over. This resulted in two civil wars, from 1164 to 1169 and again from 1189 to 1194. Neither war produced a winner, but the immense costs of these conflicts—which disrupted commerce and led to the loss of overseas colonies—made it evident that both sides would benefit by finding a lasting political solution.[40] Although the political system Genoa adopted seems bizarre, it was fully in accord with modern game theory—and it worked.

Called the *podesteria*, the setup involved a sort of city manager—a non-Genoese *podestá* hired each year to be military commander, chief judge, and political administrator.[41] Although an elected council of nobles selected the *podestá* and set policies and goals, during his one-year term the *podestà* had supreme authority and brought with him a company of soldiers and a set of judges. Neither the *podestà* nor his troops or judges were permitted to marry Genoans, to buy local property, or to engage in any commercial transactions, and at the end of the year he was required to leave and not return for several years. The system worked because the *podestà* had enough troops of his own so that combined with either Genoan faction he could defeat the other faction; at the same time, the *podestà* lacked sufficient troops to defeat either faction alone, preventing a dictatorship. This system worked so well that many other Italian communes adopted it.[42]

The Genoan system of government became more democratic in 1257 after a rebellion by guilds and confraternities. The council was expanded to thirty-two members, four elected from each of the city's wards, each set of four being divided equally between the nobility and the people. In place of an outside *podestà* serving for a year, the council elected a "captain" to administer the commune for a ten-year term. The fact that the first man elected captain, Guglielmo Boccanegra, was a rich commoner suggests that the real basis for the creation of a more democratic regime was Genoa's booming commercial economy. From a tiny town having perhaps ten thousand residents in 1100, by 1250 Genoa had a population of about fifty thousand, making it one of the largest cities in Europe.[43]

It needs to be emphasized that the Church vigorously advocated and defended democracy in northern Italy. Not only did the Church unequivocally assert moral equality, but it also ventured into the political arena, with bishops and cardinals playing a leading role on behalf of expanding the franchise.

Inventing Capitalism

Probably every leading textbook in introductory sociology gives substantial, positive coverage to Max Weber's famous thesis that Protestants invented capitalism, as he claimed in his *Protestant Ethic and the Spirit of Capitalism* (1904–5). But it isn't so! The rise of capitalism in Europe *preceded* the Reformation by centuries. In the 1970s the celebrated Fernand Braudel complained that Weber's "tenuous theory" had endured for decades even though "all historians have opposed" it and, more to the point, "it is clearly false." Braudel added, "The northern countries took over the place that earlier had so long and so brilliantly been occupied by the old capitalist centers of the Mediterranean. They invented nothing, either in technology or in business management."[44] Even these northern centers of capitalism were Catholic, not Protestant, during their critical period of economic development—the Reformation still lay well into the future.

Why my fellow sociologists persist in embracing Weber's thesis can only be attributed to historical ignorance. But historians' common objections to Weber's thesis also need correction. Capitalism was not invented in the Italian city-states, for all that they were fully developed capitalist centers by the end of the eleventh century. Weber was correct in asserting that capitalism had religious roots. It was not, however, originated by Protestants: capitalism first appeared in the great Catholic monastic estates back in the ninth century.

On Capitalism

What *is* capitalism? Several thousand books have been written on the subject, but very few authors explain what they mean by the term *capitalism*.[45] This is not because no definition is needed;[46] it is because capitalism is difficult to define, having originated not as an economic concept but as a pejorative term used by nineteenth-century leftists to condemn wealth and privilege. To adapt the term for serious analysis is a bit like trying to make a social-scientific concept out of a *reactionary pig*.[47] Although it might be good strategy to let readers supply their own meaning of capitalism, it seems irresponsible to base any analysis on an undefined term. Therefore: *Capitalism is an economic system wherein privately owned, relatively well-organized, and stable firms pursue complex commercial activities within a relatively free (unregulated) market, taking a systematic, long-term approach to investing and reinvesting wealth (directly or indirectly) in productive activities involving a hired workforce and guided by anticipated and actual returns.*[48]

The phrase *complex commercial activities* implies the use of credit, some degree of diversification, and little reliance on direct producer-to-consumer transactions. The term *systematic* implies adequate accounting practices. *Indirect* investment in productive activities extends the definition to include bankers and passive stockholders. The definition excludes profit-seeking ventures assembled for short-term activities, such as an elite-backed voyage by privateers or a one-shot trade caravan. It also excludes commerce conducted directly by the state or under extensive state control (or exclusive license), such as foreign trade in ancient China or tax farming in medieval Europe. Undertakings based on coerced labor such as Roman slave-based industries are excluded too. Most of all, this definition excludes simple commercial transactions—the buying and selling that has gone on among merchants, traders, and the producers of commodities through the centuries around the world.

Capitalism rests on free markets, secure property rights, and free (uncoerced) labor.[49] Free markets are needed for firms to enter areas of opportunity, which is precluded when markets are closed or highly regulated by the state. Only if property rights are secure will people invest in pursuit of greater gains, rather than hide, hoard, or consume their wealth. Uncoerced labor is needed so firms can attract motivated workers or dismiss them in response to market conditions. Coerced labor not only lacks motivation but also may be difficult to obtain and hard to get rid of. The capacity to motivate work and the systematic reinvestment of profits account for the immense productivity of capitalism.

Christianity and the Rise of Capitalism

Why have so many scholars overlooked Christianity's influence on the rise of capitalism? One reason may be that the Bible often condemns greed and wealth ("For the love of money is the root of all evil").[50] Similarly, many early church fathers—endorsing a view prevalent in the Greco-Roman world—believed commerce to be a degrading activity that involves great moral risk: it is difficult to avoid sin in the course of buying and selling.[51]

But note that the Bible does not directly condemn commerce or merchants. Moreover, soon after the conversion of Constantine (312 BC) the Church ceased to be dominated by ascetics, and attitudes toward commerce began to mellow. Augustine's writings reflected this change. He taught that wickedness was not inherent in commerce but that, as with any occupation, it was up to the individual to live righteously.[52] Augustine also gave legitimacy to free-trade practices when he ruled that price was a function not simply of the seller's costs but also of the buyer's desire for the item sold.

By the ninth century the Church was deeply involved in the earliest forms of capitalism.[53] Throughout the medieval era the Church was by far the largest landowner in Europe, and its liquid assets and annual income far surpassed not only those of the wealthiest king but probably those of all of Europe's nobility added together.[54] In addition to receiving many gifts of land, most monastic orders reinvested wealth in buying or reclaiming more land. Many monasteries established fifty or more outposts; by the eleventh century the huge monastic center at Cluny may have had a thousand priories.[55]

This period of great expansion was motivated in part by population growth and in even greater part by the immense increases in agricultural productivity.[56] Until this era the monastic estates were subsistence operations—they produced their own food, drink, and fuel; they made their own cloth and tanned their own leather; they maintained a smithy and often even a pottery. But as productivity increased, they began to specialize in particular crops or products. Some estates produced only wine, others grew grains, some raised cattle or sheep—the Cistercians at Fossanova specialized in raising fine horses.[57] The estates would engage in trade to secure their other needs. The rapid increase in agricultural surpluses also encouraged the founding and growth of towns and cities. Indeed, many of the monastic centers themselves became cities. Writing about the great monastery of St. Gall in Switzerland, Christopher Dawson noted that by 820 it was "no longer the simple religious community envisaged by the old monastic rules, but a vast complex of buildings, churches, workshops, store-houses, offices, schools and alms-houses, housing a whole population of dependents, workers and servants like the temple cities of antiquity."[58]

When estates grew into small cities and sustained many scattered outposts, and as they became specialized and dependent on trade, three important developments occurred. First, they evolved more sophisticated and far-seeing management. Unlike the nobility, the monasteries did not leave their affairs to the vagaries of inherited leadership. The essential meritocracy built into the orders ensured a succession of talented and dedicated administrators having the capacity to pursue plans of long duration. As Georges Duby put it, the new era forced monastic "administrators to turn their attention to the domestic economy, to reckon up, to handle figures, to calculate profits and losses, to think about ways and means of expanding production."[59]

Attendant to specialization was a second development, a shift from a barter to a cash economy. It simply was too complicated and unwieldy for a wine-making estate, say, to barter for its other needs, transporting goods hither and yon. It proved far more efficient to sell wine for cash and then buy whatever was needed from the most convenient and economical sources. Beginning late in the ninth century, the reliance on cash spread, with the monks in Lucca (near Florence) perhaps the first to adopt a cash economy. The system was well established across Europe when, in 1247, a Franciscan chronicler wrote of his order's estate in Burgundy that the monks "do not sow or reap, nor do they store anything in barns, but they send wine to Paris, because they have a river right at hand that goes to Paris, and they sell for a good price, from which they get all their food and all of the clothes they wear."[60]

The third development was credit. Barter does not lend itself to credit. The value of a future payment of, say, three hundred chickens can easily be disputed: are these to be old hens, roosters, or pullets? But the precise meaning of owing someone two ounces of gold is not in doubt. The great church estates began to extend one another monetary credit. Beyond that, as their incomes mounted, many monasteries and bishops became banks, lending to the nobility at interest. During the eleventh and twelfth centuries Cluny lent large sums at interest to various Burgundian nobles,[61] while in 1071 the Bishop of Liège lent the incredible sum of 100 pounds of gold and 175 marks of silver to the Countess of Flanders and subsequently lent 1,300 marks of silver and 3 marks of gold to the Duke of Lower Lorraine. In 1044 the Bishop of Worms lent 20 pounds of gold and a large (unspecified) amount of silver to Emperor Henry III.[62] By the thirteenth century, monastic lending often took the form of a *mort-gage* (literally, "dead pledge"), wherein the borrower pledged land as security and the lender collected all income from that land during the term of the loan and did not deduct this income from the amount owed.[63]

As University of Pennsylvania sociologist Randall Collins noted, the economic system that developed in this era was not merely a sort of proto-capitalism involving only the "institutional preconditions for capitalism, . . . but a version of the developed characteristics of capitalism itself." Collins referred to this as "religious capitalism," adding that the "dynamism of the medieval economy was primarily that of the Church."[64]

The Church's bursting treasuries had another effect. Monks began to leave their fields, hiring a labor force that proved more productive.[65] Thus, as "religious capitalism" unfolded, more monks worked as executives and foremen. In this way, the medieval monasteries came to resemble modern firms—well administered and quick to adopt the latest technological advances.[66]

The arrangement also allowed monks to retire into liturgical work, where they conducted endless paid Masses for souls in purgatory and for living benefactors who wished to improve their fates in the next world. Monks now enjoyed leisure.

The advent of leisure for clergy and other church officials had a profound impact on the rise of the West, for, as will be seen, in the centuries to come church figures played key roles in advancing science, economics, and learning.

The Virtue of Work

Just as important as these economic developments were changes in attitudes toward work that Christianity inspired. Notions of the dignity of labor were incomprehensible in ancient Rome or any other precapitalist society. Traditional societies celebrated consumption while holding work in contempt. In China, for example, the Mandarins grew their fingernails as long as they could (even wearing silver sheaths to protect them from breaking) to make it evident that they did no labor. Capitalism required and encouraged a remarkably different attitude, one that saw work as intrinsically virtuous. Max Weber identified this as the Protestant ethic, so-called because he believed it to be absent from Catholic culture. But Weber was wrong.

Belief in the virtues of work arose centuries before Martin Luther was born.[67] Despite the fact that many, perhaps even most, monks and nuns were from the nobility and wealthiest families,[68] they honored work not only in theological terms but also by actually doing it. In Randall Collins's words, they "had the Protestant ethic without Protestantism."[69]

In the sixth century Saint Benedict made evident the virtue of work, writing in his famous *Rule*: "Idleness is the enemy of the soul. Therefore the brothers should have specified periods for manual labor as well as prayerful reading. . . . When they live by the labor of their hands, as our fathers and the apostles did, then they are really monks."[70] In the fourteenth century Walter Hilton, the English Augustinian, wrote, "By the discipline of the physical life we are enabled for spiritual effort."[71] This commitment to manual labor distinguishes Christian asceticism from that found in the other great religious cultures, where piety is associated with rejection of the world and its activities. Eastern holy men, for example, specialized in meditation and lived by charity, whereas most medieval Christian monastics lived by their own labor, sustaining highly productive estates. Being of the world sustained a healthy concern with economic affairs. Although the Protestant-ethic thesis was wrong, capitalism was indeed linked to a Christian ethic.

Thus it was that, beginning about the ninth century, the growing monastic estates came to resemble "well-organized and stable firms" that pursued "complex commercial activities within a relatively free market," investing in "productive activities involving a hired workforce," "guided by anticipated and actual returns." If this was not capitalism in all its glory, it was certainly close enough.

A Theological Revolution

Just as Augustine's teachings had marked a shift in Christian attitudes toward commerce, Christian theologians who witnessed the growing economic activities of the great religious orders began to think anew about doctrines concerning profits and interest. In this way, the Church made its peace with early capitalism many centuries before there were any Protestants.

The Church had long opposed charging interest, a position inherited from the Jews. The basis for this doctrine was the Old Testament passage Deuteronomy 23:19–20, which admonishes: "You shall not charge interest on loans to another Israelite, interest on money, interest on provisions, interest on anything that is lent. On loans to a foreigner you may change interest, but on loans to another Israelite you may not change interest."[72]

Of course, the prohibition in Deuteronomy did not necessarily bar Christians from charging interest, since they were not Israelites. But the words of Jesus in Luke 6:34 were taken to prohibit interest: "If you lend to those from whom you hope to receive, what credit is that to you? Even sinners lend to sinners, to receive as much again. But love your enemies, do good, and lend, expecting nothing in return."

Interest on loans was thus defined as the sin of usury. As Benjamin Nelson wrote in his history of usury, as late as the Second Lateran Council in 1139 the Church "declared the unrepentant usurer condemned by the Old and New Testaments alike and, therefore, unworthy of ecclesiastical consolations and Christian burial."[73] But while widely condemned in principle, charging interest was pretty much ignored in practice. That is what allowed some of the great religious houses to venture into banking late in the ninth century. Likewise, bishops became second only to the nobility in their reliance on borrowed money. Many secured loans from private Italian banks that enjoyed the full approval of the Vatican. Documents from 1215 show that the Papal Court itself had usurers from whom prelates could obtain loans.[74]

Still, more traditional clergy continued to condemn usury and, more broadly, the pursuit of profit. Augustine may have approved of prices set on a free market, but were there no moral limits to profit margins?

During the thirteenth century Christian theologians declared that profits were morally legitimate. Echoing Augustine, Saint Albertus Magnus proposed that the "just price" is simply what "goods are worth according to the estimation of the market at the time of sale."[75] That is, a price is just if that is what uncoerced buyers are willing to pay. Adam Smith could not have found fault with this definition. Magnus's student Thomas Aquinas likewise recognized that worth is not really an objective value—"the just price of things is not absolutely definite"—but is a function of the buyer's desire for the thing purchased and the seller's willingness or reluctance to sell. Aquinas's respect for market forces is best revealed by his story about a merchant who brings grain to a country suffering a famine and who knows that other merchants soon will bring much more grain to this area. Is it sinful for him to sell at the prevailing, high market price, or should he inform the buyers that soon more grain will arrive, thus causing the price to decline? Aquinas concluded that this merchant can, in good conscience, keep quiet and sell at the current high price.

Aquinas was less clear about interest on loans. In some writings he condemned all interest as the sin of usury; in other passages he accepted that lenders deserved compensation, although he was fuzzy as to how much and why.[76] But many of Aquinas's contemporaries, especially the Canonists, were not so cautious. With the commercial economy rapidly expanding, they began detailing exceptions wherein interest charges were not usurious.[77] For example, if a productive property such as an estate was given as security for a loan, the lender could take all the production during the period of the loan and not deduct it from the amount owed.[78] Also, a lender could be compensated for the opportunity cost of not having the money available for other commercial opportunities.[79] In this same spirit it was deemed proper to charge interest for goods bought on credit.[80] Banks could not make straight loans at a fixed rate of interest because such deals would involve no "adventure of the principal." But it took little finesse for bankers to evade this prohibition by trading notes, bills of exchange, or currencies in ways that seemed adventuresome but that in fact had predictable returns.[81] In short, *usury* had become essentially an empty term.

Thus, by no later than the thirteenth century the leading Christian theologians had fully debated the primary aspects of emerging capitalism—profits, property rights, credit, lending, and the like. As the historian Lester K. Little summed up: "In each case they came up with generally favorable, approving views, in sharp contrast to the attitudes that had prevailed for six or seven centuries right up to the previous generation."[82] Capitalism was freed from all fetters of faith.[83]

It was a remarkable shift. After all, most of these theologians had taken vows of poverty, and most of their predecessors had held merchants and commercial activities in contempt. Other religions, too, condemned paying interest on loans, and they did not so dramatically revise their positions. In Islam, for example, the Qur'an (2:275) condemns all interest (*riba*) on borrowed money. Although medieval Muslims often ignored prohibitions on lending money at interest, this was almost exclusively to fund consumption, not for investment.[84] Religious opposition to interest, combined with the avarice of repressive regimes, prevented capitalism from arising in Islam—and still does.[85]

So what accounts for the theological revolution in Christianity? The shift occurred because the great monastic orders had begun actively participating in free markets. This direct experience caused monastic theologians to reconsider the morality of commerce. Of course, officials in the church hierarchy were far worldlier than those in religious orders. Few holding higher church positions had taken vows of poverty, and many displayed a taste for profligate living. As we saw in chapter 5, many church officials purchased their positions—sometimes before being ordained or even baptized![86] The worldly aspects of the medieval Church were an endless source of scandal and conflict, culminating in the Reformation. But they paid serious dividends in the development of capitalism. The Church didn't stand in the way; in fact, it justified and even played an active role in the commercial revolution of the twelfth and thirteenth centuries.[87] Had this not occurred, the West may have ended up like the nations of Islam.

Capitalist City-States

Although capitalism developed in the great monastic estates, it soon found a receptive setting in the newly democratic Italian city-states. In the tenth century these city-states emerged as the banking and trading centers of Europe. Subsequently they industrialized and began producing a large volume of manufactured goods for export across the Mediterranean and to northern Europe and the British Isles. For example, eyeglasses (for nearsightedness as well as farsightedness) were mass-produced by plants in both Florence and Venice, and tens of thousands of pairs were exported annually.

Perhaps the most striking aspect of Italian capitalism was the rapid perfection of banking. The Italian bankers quickly developed and adopted double-entry bookkeeping. To facilitate trade, they invented bills of exchange, making it possible to transfer funds on paper rather than transporting coins or precious metal over long distances, which was both difficult and dangerous. Italian bankers also initiated insurance to guard against loss of long-distance shipments by land or sea. Perhaps the most important of all the Italian banking innovations was the perfection of modern arithmetic, based on the adoption of Hindu-Arabic numerals and the concept of zero. Even addition and subtraction were daunting chores for Romans, given their cumbersome numeral system. The new system was revolutionary in terms of its ease and accuracy. Arithmetic schools sprang up in all the leading northern Italian city-states, eventually enrolling students from as far away as northern Europe.[88]

Banks proliferated. By the thirteenth century there were 38 independent banks in Florence, 34 in Pisa, 27 in Genoa, 18 in Venice—a combined total of 173 in the leading Italian city-states.[89] Most of these Italian banks had foreign branches, too. In 1231 there were 69 Italian banking branches operating in England and nearly as many in Ireland. In fact, until well into the fifteenth century every bank in western Europe was either in Italy or was a branch of an Italian bank.[90]

The proximate cause of the rise of Italian capitalism was freedom from the rapacious rulers who repressed and consumed economic progress in most of the world, including most of Europe. Although their political life often was turbulent, these city-states were true republics able to sustain the freedom capitalism requires. Second, centuries of technological progress had laid the necessary foundations for the rise of capitalism, especially the agricultural surpluses needed to sustain cities and to permit specialization. In addition, Christian theology encouraged the idea of progress, which justified long-term investment strategies, and provided moral justifications for the business practices fundamental to capitalism.

The Freedom Factor

If there is a single factor responsible for the rise of the West, it is freedom. Freedom to hope. Freedom to act. Freedom to invest. Freedom to enjoy the fruits of one's dreams as well as one's labor.

So much of that freedom emerged during the so-called Dark Ages. The ramifications would be felt for centuries to come.

Part III

Medieval Transformations (1200–1500)

7

❧

Climate, Plague, and Social Change

I f historians have been rather inattentive to matters of geography, they have been even less attuned to the implications of climate and disease. Of course, the obvious effects of climate—that Eskimos use sleds and Bedouins do not—have always been noted. What has been given little attention are significant climatic *changes*. In part this is because until Hubert Lamb wrote about them in 1965,[1] it was not widely recognized that there had been any substantial climatic changes since the end of the Ice Age, twenty thousand years ago, despite the fact that the history of medieval Europe hinges on two major shifts in climate. By the same token, although the conquest of many chronic diseases is regarded as an essential feature of the rise of modernity, historians have largely ignored epidemics, which have had far more dramatic effects on the course of history. Incredibly, generations of historians dismissed the death of nearly half the world's population from the Black Death (1346–1351) as of little significance compared with, say, the Hundred Years' War (1337–1453). Serious historical studies of the Black Death did not begin until well into the twentieth century,[2] and even now these studies are pursued as an isolated subject matter.

For example, in his well-received *Civilization: A New History of the Western World* (2006), Roger Osborne devoted one sentence to the Black Death and none to plagues; he gave two sentences to the Ice Age and made no mention of more recent climate changes. In his huge and celebrated *Europe: A History* (1996), Norman Davies gave nearly three pages (out of 1,365) to the Black Death, but like so many other historians, he treated it as a self-contained event, writing only two paragraphs on any social effects. Davies also gave one page to climate, but mostly to discredit it as being of historical significance.

Breaking with tradition, this chapter is focused on two extraordinary developments in the middle of the fourteenth century: the Black Death and the so-called Little Ice Age, when the weather turned bitterly cold. Ironically, these twin catastrophes seem to have made several important positive contributions to the rise of modernity.

Medieval Climates

Amid the bitter contemporary conflicts over whether the climate is getting warmer, and if so why, the most basic fact about earth's climate has been nearly forgotten: that warming and cooling trends are quite common. Because substantial changes in the climate occur very slowly, people tend to regard their current climatic conditions as normal. Not so. For example, beginning sometime in the eighth century, the earth began to heat up, producing what now is known as the Medieval Warm Period, which lasted from about 800 to about 1250. As temperatures rose, the growing period lengthened all across northern Europe; the Arctic ice pack receded, making it much safer to sail in the North Atlantic; and it became possible to farm successfully as far north as Greenland. Then temperatures began to drop until early in the fourteenth century, when the Little Ice Age dawned; this era of very cold winters and short summers lasted until about 1850. During the coldest decades of the Little Ice Age, in the seventeenth century, the Baltic Sea froze over, making possible sleigh rides from Poland to Sweden; the Thames River froze in London, as did all the Atlantic harbors in Europe.[3]

To make matters more confusing, both eras saw considerable variation from year to year—unusually cold years during the Medieval Warm Period and unusually warm years during the Little Ice Age. In fact, such abnormal conditions could sometimes last for a decade. But the important point is that both eras had substantial influence on the course of history.

The question arises, how do we know that these climatic periods took place? Until recent times our only sources were literary—as when a medieval diarist noted that "this was a year without summer" or an English pastor wrote to a friend about ice skating on the Thames. Then came archaeological evidence, such as analysis of skeletons showing how the Viking colony on Greenland slowly died out from malnutrition. But we now have a far more general, accurate, and sensitive database on the climate obtained from tree rings and from ice cores drilled in glaciers in many parts of the earth. Ice cores have annual layers similar to tree rings. Chemical and isotopic analyses of ice cores reveal many aspects of climate, including temperature ranges, ocean volume, precipitation, chemistry of the lower atmosphere, volcanic eruptions, solar variability, and even the prevalence of forest fires. Because of the great depth of some glaciers, it has been possible to reconstruct the climate for a period stretching back several hundred thousand years.[4] Of course, a recent scandal concerned the falsification of these data on behalf of the man-made global warming thesis, a fraud that involved minimizing the warmth of the Medieval Warm Period and maximizing the temperatures of the Little Ice Age to create the so-called hockey stick graph of temperatures for the past millennium. Now that this fraud has been detected, there can be no doubt that such warm and cold periods occurred and that they greatly influenced human events.

The Medieval Warm Period

No one benefited more from the warm conditions that prevailed from about 800 to about 1250 than did the Vikings. The lengthening growing season in Scandinavia greatly increased crop yields, and this, in turn, fed a larger population. The newly benign climate also enabled the Vikings to undertake voyages of discovery and settlement that had been impossible in colder times.[5] The receding ice pack, the reduced prevalence of icebergs, and the reduction in the number and severity of storms at sea favored Viking voyaging across the North Atlantic.

First came the discovery and settlement of Iceland. The Vikings initially reached Iceland by accident, after getting lost while sailing from Norway to the Faroe Islands. Next, a boatload of Swedes accidentally reached the island and stayed for the winter. The first Viking to intentionally sail there, in the 860s, was Flóki Vilgerðarson, who stayed only one winter and named the island Iceland after seeing drift ice in the fjords. The first settler of Iceland was Ingólfr Arnarson, a Norwegian chieftain who arrived with his family in 874. Within the next sixty years all the land on Iceland had been claimed by settlers and a government had been established. The first Christian bishop of Iceland was consecrated in 1056.

Although several Vikings had sailed to Greenland soon after the initial settlement in Iceland, it was not until 982 that someone settled in Greenland. The first settler was a Norwegian under a three-year exile from Iceland for killing several men. When his period of exile had passed, Eric the Red recruited settlers from Iceland to colonize the southern coast of Greenland, an area then quite suitable for farming. Trade with Scandinavia flourished—in 1075 a Greenlander shipped a live polar bear as a gift to King Ulfsson of Denmark. (The coat of arms of the Danish royal family still includes a depiction of a polar bear.) Even at its peak, however, the Viking population of Greenland was probably no more than three or four thousand.[6]

Finally came Vinland. Although this settlement is recorded in several Norse sagas, as well as in Adam of Breman's eleventh-century *Description of the Northern Island*, for centuries historians dismissed the claim that Leif Eriksson had sailed his knarr from Greenland to the north coast of America as pure mythology. Then, in 1914, William A. Munn, after close study of the sources, proposed that the Vikings had landed and made their base at L'Anse aux Meadows in northern Newfoundland. No respectable scholar took him seriously. But in 1960 Helge and Anne Stine Ingstad found extensive remains of a tenth-century Viking village at precisely the spot Munn had proposed.[7] It is now accepted that this was the main Viking settlement in North America and that the Vikings had camped in many other coastal sites. None of this could have happened except for the Medieval Warm Period.

Meanwhile, it was golden days in Europe as well. Wine grapes grew so plentifully in England that local officials in various parts of the continent attempted to limit the import of English vintages. So much new land was cleared or reclaimed by pumping out marshes, especially along the coast, that it would be five hundred years before Europe matched the extent of land under cultivation.[8] As food became abundant, the population of Europe soared from about 25 million in 950 to about 75 million in 1250.[9] Given that the medieval economy rested primarily on agriculture, this was an era of considerable prosperity. Studies of coinage offer one window into this prosperity.[10] Another comes from the nearly two centuries during which wealthy Europeans funded the Crusades and subsidized the crusader kingdoms. But the most obvious manifestations of abundance are the great Gothic cathedrals constructed during this period: Notre Dame (1163), Canterbury (1175), Strasbourg (1190), Chartres (1194), Reims (1212), Amiens (1225), and dozens more. As the archaeologist Brian Fagan concluded, "Like the Norse conquests, cathedrals too were a consequence of a global climatic phenomenon, an enduring legacy of the Medieval Warm Period."[11]

And then it ended—brutally.

The Little Ice Age

During the winter of 1310–11 Londoners danced around fires on the frozen Thames River—something that had never happened before. Then, starting in the early spring of 1315, rain poured down for weeks and weeks, making it impossible to farm. All across western Europe dikes were destroyed by floods, and new lakes and marshes appeared. In August the weather turned bitterly cold. Hunger began to spread. The next spring, heavy rains again prevented planting, and so again there was no harvest, nor was there fodder for the flocks. Famine became widespread. Meanwhile, intense gales battered the coastal areas. By 1317 all of northern Europe was starving—even the nobility.

Although the weather returned to normal that summer, the misery continued, because people had been so weakened, so much of the seed stock had been eaten, and even the horses and oxen used for plowing had been consumed. By the time the famine ended in 1325, perhaps 10 percent of the population had died of starvation and starvation-related diseases.[12] Even then, although the famine was over, agricultural production continued to decline because of bad weather. Grain yields can be measured in terms of the ratio of seeds of grain harvested to seeds planted. In about 1200 the ratio for wheat was 5 to 1; by 1330 it had fallen to about 1.5 to 1. Barley fell from 10 to 1 to about 3 to 1 during the same period. Rye fell from about 4 to 1 to less than 2 to 1.[13] It barely paid to farm until new, more productive varieties, better suited to shorter growing seasons, were developed. (By the sixteenth century the ratio for these three grains had risen to 7 to 1.)[14]

With colder weather came more severe storms. The worst were enormous gales that drove tidal waves onto the western Atlantic shores, drowning tens of thousands. In 1282 storm-driven waves broke through the barrier coastal dunes of Holland, creating an inland sea extending about sixty miles from the coast and about thirty miles wide. Known as the Zuiderzee, it continued to expand during new storms. In 1287 a new immersion drowned an estimated fifty to eighty thousand Dutch; a flood in 1421 destroyed seventy-two villages and drowned another ten thousand.

Meanwhile, far fewer boats were reaching Iceland from Norway and Denmark, and no boats were going to or from Greenland—the last Viking boat visited Greenland in 1406, and then only because it had been blown off course. Since Greenland had no forests, the Greenland Vikings could not build boats or even repair them. Unable to leave, and unable to grow grain in the deteriorating climate, the Greenland Viking population was wiped out by the end of the fifteenth century.

Still another catastrophe arrived in October 1347, when a galley from Cairo docked in the Sicilian port of Messina. On board were a number of rats, all of them with fleas. The Black Death had come to Europe.[15]

The Black Death

The Black Death was the bubonic plague (*Yersinia pestis*). (Although this identification was long disputed, recent analysis of human skeletons settled the debate.)[16] Bubonic plague is carried by fleas that are borne by rats; humans become infected when they are bitten by a flea with the disease. There has been a long controversy over whether the plague can be directly transmitted from one human to another or whether the disease always requires a flea bite. The consensus is that direct contact with bodily fluids of an infected person possibly can transmit the disease to another person, but almost always a flea bite is involved. Symptoms appear within several days of becoming infected, and most victims die after two or three days of intense pain and vomiting.

Of course, humanity had suffered many devastating plagues before. From 165 to 180 a plague had raged across the Roman Empire, with the famous emperor Marcus Aurelius among the victims. In 541–42 the plague of Justinian began somewhere near Constantinople and spread worldwide.

But the Black Death was far more deadly than these. It seems to have originated in China, perhaps in 1346. From there it traveled west, reaching the Middle East and North Africa in 1347.[17] Europeans could do nothing to prevent the Black Death from reaching them. Merchant ships brought cargoes of infected rats and dying crews not only to Messina but to most, if not all, of the other Mediterranean ports. And Europe had an enormous rat population ready to become hosts for infected fleas.

The plague raged across Europe for four years, 1348–51, beginning in the south and moving north. Although the mortality rate may have varied from one region to another, everywhere huge numbers died. In 1351 Pope Clement VI asked his staff to calculate the number killed by the plague in Europe. They arrived at a figure of 23,840,000, or about 30 percent of the total population.[18] Apparently, this total was based on actual reports and was not influenced by the fact that Revelation 9:18 predicts that "a third of mankind" will be killed by plague. Many modern scholars accept the 30 percent estimate, although some have supported estimates as high as 60 percent.[19] The latter is quite credible if one adds in the next outbursts of plague that took place in 1361 and 1369. The same range of rates is proposed for the world as a whole, yielding estimates that at least 100 million and perhaps as many as 200 million perished. Since even the lowest estimates are staggeringly high, there seems little point in quibbling as to which figure is best.

The horror of what took place is difficult to imagine. The great Italian philosopher and literary intellectual Francesco Petrarch (1304–1374) wrote to a friend of "empty houses, derelict cities, ruined estates, fields strewn with cadavers, a horrible and vast solitude encompassing the whole world."[20] Parish registers from the Burgundian village of Givry show a population of about 1,200 in 1340, with deaths averaging about 30 a year; then, in a fourteen-week period in 1348, 615 deaths were recorded.[21] There wasn't room in the graveyard for such a number, and soon bodies were being pushed into trenches, layer upon layer.

Contemporary accounts from across Europe report the dedication of nuns and monks in caring for the afflicted and seeing to their burial, but there was no keeping up. Everywhere there were piles of putrefying corpses and many houses and cottages in which everyone lay dead. An agonized Italian father wrote about conditions in the city of Siena:

> And none could be found to bury the dead for money or friendship. Members of a household brought their dead to a ditch as best they could. . . . And in many places in Siena great pits were dug and piled deep with the multitude of dead. . . . And I . . . buried

my five children with my own hands. And there were also those who were so sparsely covered with earth that the dogs dragged them forth and devoured many bodies throughout the city.[22]

Nowhere was there any safety, not even in remote villages. Not even in Iceland, where the fatality rate may have been as high as 60 percent.[23]

Reactions

It has become routine for historians to claim that the Black Death caused people to lose confidence in Christianity, and especially in the Church. Perhaps some people did, but quoting passages from the *Decameron* does not establish the state of popular opinion.[24] Nor does it inspire confidence when historians claim that a lack of church attendance reveals a falling away in response to the Black Death. What this does reveal is that most historians are ignorant of the fact that church attendance was *always* low in medieval times, even in Italy.[25] In fact, scattered data suggest that as the plague progressed, people became increasingly likely to bequeath legacies to the Church.[26] The only reliable evidence of a widespread religious reaction to the Black Death concerns an intense, if somewhat grotesque, deepening of faith.

The Flagellants

The Flagellant movement began well before the outbreak of the Black Death, being first reported to have appeared in Italy in 1259 in response to a famine. But it burst into a mass movement in the earliest days of the Black Death as the belief spread that God had sent the plague to punish humanity. As King Magnus II of Sweden put it, "God for the sins of man has struck the world with this great punishment of sudden death. By it, most of our countrymen are dead."[27]

Beginning in Hungary and spreading rapidly through Germany, tens of thousands of Christian men[28] organized themselves into companies and began to travel from town to town, whipping themselves and one another in atonement for their sins. To join, a man had to agree to remain active for at least thirty-three and a half days (symbolizing Christ's years on earth), make prior restitution of all his debts, gain permission from his wife (if married), and agree to obey the leaders absolutely. Flagellants entered towns together, never stayed in one place more than one night, swore never to speak to a woman, and vowed not to sit on cushions or to shave or bathe.[29]

At first the Church supported the Flagellants—Pope Clement VI even invited a company of them to Avignon (where the papacy was in exile from Rome). The Flagellants often had pronounced moral effects on communities they visited, as guilt-stricken adulterers made public confessions and thieves returned stolen goods.[30] Soon, however, leading Flagellants became blatantly heretical. Philip Ziegler recounted in his history of the Black Death: "Certain of the Brethren began to claim a measure of supernatural power. It was commonly alleged that the Flagellants could drive out devils, heal the sick and even raise the dead. Some members announced that they had eaten and drunk with Christ or talked with the Virgin. One claimed that he himself had risen from the dead."[31] Unordained leaders of the movement began hearing confessions, granting absolution, and imposing penances. Pope Clement responded in 1349 by condemning the Flagellants as a heretical sect, whereupon some leaders were seized and executed. Meanwhile the Black Death continued.

Blaming the Jews

Inevitably, the persistent question was, why had the plague struck? In response, the story began to spread that the Jews were poisoning the wells with plague. (Out of their concern for keeping kosher, Jews often maintained their own wells rather than drink from those maintained for the public.) This rumor seems to have originated in Spain, where the initial attacks on Jews took place—twenty Jews were killed in Barcelona, eighteen in Cervera, then a few in Catalonia and Aragon.[32] But attacks on Spanish Jews were quickly suppressed by local bishops, armed with a bull issued by Pope Clement:

Mandate to Protect the Jews
October 1, 1348

We . . . are mindful of our duty to shelter the Jews, by reason of the fact that our savior, when he assumed mortal flesh for the salvation of the human race, deemed it worthy to be born of Jewish stock. . . . Recently, however, it has come to our attention . . . that some Christians out of rashness have impiously slain

several Jews . . . after falsely blaming the pestilence on poison-
ings by Jews, said to be in league with the devil, when in fact
it is the result of an angry God striking at Christian people for
their sins. . . . It does not seem credible that the Jews . . . are
responsible . . . because this nearly universal pestilence . . . has
afflicted and continues to afflict the Jews themselves.

We order all of you [bishops] by apostolic writing . . . to warn
your subjects, both the clergy and the people, during the service
of mass in your churches, and to expressly enjoin them on pain of
excommunication, which you may then inflict in those who trans-
gress, that they not presume to seize, strike, wound, or kill Jews.[33]

The papal order was obeyed nearly everywhere. Contrary to historians who allege many Jewish massacres that never happened,[34] there were
no more attacks on Jews in Europe except in a series of cities along, or
near, the Rhine River. Perhaps as many as twenty thousand Jews were
murdered in Erfurt, Mainz, Speyer, Strasburg, Augsburg, Cologne,
Munich, Nuremberg, Frankfurt, and Stuttgart.[35] This was an area with a
long history of bloody anti-Semitic outbursts, beginning in 1096.[36] Here
some families proudly claimed to be descendants of *"Judenbreter"* (Jew
roasters),[37] harking back to previous pogroms. Why here? Because the
Rhine basin was, as the historian Shulamit Magnus put it, a "politically
fractured area,"[38] wherein neither church nor state had effective control.
Consequently, there was little or no restraint on popular outbursts. For
this same reason, heretical Christian movements were highly successful
here too, as was Luther's Reformation (see chapter 14). Unfortunately, the
vicious anti-Semitic culture of these cities did not die out with the wan-
ing of medieval times, but lived on to support Hitler's "Final Solution."

Stagnant Demography

In the aftermath of the huge loss of life from the Black Death, Europe's
population became stagnant: pre–Black Death levels of population were
not regained until well into the sixteenth century. This has puzzled many
demographers whose theories suppose that such population catastrophes
are followed by a rapid recovery due to an accelerated birthrate.[39] This
is the sort of controversy that only academics could sustain, and it has

prompted a deluge of interpretations of the dubious theories of Thomas Malthus (1766–1834).[40] Nonetheless, the primary reason Europe's population did not grow is obvious: the plague did not vanish after 1352! Instead, there were new outbursts, again and again. Nor were these minor outbreaks. In 1361 a new epidemic killed millions—anywhere from 10 to 20 percent of Europe's population succumbed. A third outburst in 1369 probably killed another 10 percent all across Europe.[41] "The best estimate," according to Ziegler, "is that from 1349 to 1450 [the] European population declined between 60% and 75%."[42]

It would have taken an impossibly high fertility rate to have made up these losses. In fact, during this era the fertility rate was unusually low. Here demographers have offered plausible explanations. Given that the fatality rate for the plague was higher for men than for women, far more women than usual never married and never had children. In addition, because the plague hit young adults especially hard, the surviving population was disproportionately elderly.[43]

But having a far smaller population was not entirely a misfortune for most of those who survived.

The End of Serfdom

Before the Black Death struck, serfs did most of the farming in Europe. A serf was a peasant to whom a landowner provided a parcel, as well as housing, in return for labor in the landowner's fields. Serfs had a hereditary right to their land; in return they were bound to their land and their landlord—that is, they couldn't be dispossessed, but they couldn't leave. In addition to providing serfs with land, the seigneurs (as landowners were called in England as well as on the Continent) provided them with protection.[44]

Not all medieval peasants were serfs. Many freely rented their land without any additional obligations to a landlord. The *Domesday Book* showed that at the end of the eleventh century, 12 percent of the population of England consisted of free peasants, while 35 percent were serfs.[45] The proportion of free peasants to serfs began to increase by the start of the fourteenth century, and the immense loss of life caused by the Black Death so accelerated this trend that serfdom soon disappeared in western Europe.[46]

A direct result of the Black Death was an immense amount of agricultural land having no surviving owners or heirs. Consequently, surviving landowners greatly expanded their holdings. As their fields doubled and tripled in size, they faced an immediate crisis: a serious shortage of labor. So landowners began to compete for labor, with the result that both wages and conditions of employment improved. In England, for example, a plowman's average wage rose from 2 shillings a week in 1347 to 7 shillings in 1349 and to 10 shillings, 6 pence, in 1350.[47] Similar increases occurred everywhere. Perhaps even more important, conditions of tenancy changed dramatically too. Unless freed from the rules binding them to the land, serfs simply deserted and signed on as free tenants elsewhere—to which their new landlords turned blind eyes. To keep their tenants, landlords had to emancipate them from serfdom. Moreover, new lease agreements increasingly favored the peasant farmer: landlords agreed to furnish seed, oxen or horse teams, and better housing, all for lower rents. Lack of tenants also prompted many landowners to abandon farming in favor of the far-less-labor-intensive grazing of livestock—especially sheep and cattle. This development, combined with the greater affluence of the laboring classes, increased the consumption of meat; the increase in protein intake was quickly reflected in growth and strength.

Rapidly growing opportunities in expanding industries and other forms of urban employment also improved the situation of the peasantry.[48] In fact, the real wages of urban construction workers were as high in the mid-fifteenth century as at the end of the nineteenth century.[49] In England in the late fourteenth century, the rapidly growing industry of woolen manufacturing offered wages that attracted many workers away from rural employment, thereby putting increased upward pressure on wages.[50] It should be noted that the demand for woolen garments grew partly in response to the increasingly colder climate.

As a result of the financial and legal gains made by medieval workers, the financial circumstances of the elite declined substantially. With many fewer mouths to feed, prices for agricultural products declined, which reduced landowners' incomes. As the distinguished A. R. Bridbury put it, "Members of the landed classes . . . were outstandingly the casualties of the movements of these momentous times."[51] Consequently, all across western Europe the aristocratic landowners attempted to prohibit higher wages by law. In France a 1349 statute limited wages to pre-1348 levels.

It was ignored. So in 1350 a new statute limited wage increases to 33 percent above the 1348 level. In England, an Ordinance of Labour in 1349 froze wages. Then in 1350 Parliament enacted a statute that attempted the same thing. But the market overruled them. "All of these efforts were for naught," the historian Robert S. Gottfried wrote, "and landlords discovered that the only way to keep laborers was to pay the going rate."[52]

Nevertheless, tensions between the peasants, who demanded greater freedom, and the aristocracy, who wanted a return to unchallenged serfdom, led to several peasant revolts—the Jacquerie in France in 1358, the Revolt of the Ciompi in Italy in 1378, and the English Peasants' Revolt (or Wat Tyler's Rebellion) in 1381. All these revolts were ruthlessly suppressed. But their goals were largely achieved by economic forces. As the historian Jim Bolton aptly put it: "Change came, almost inexorably, and it did so because the economic events of the last quarter of the fourteenth century, and especially those resulting from the sudden decline in population, gave peasant tenants an irresistible bargaining position. By the late 1380s, [aristocratic efforts to restore serfdom] had largely failed, in the face of tenant resistance and economic realism."[53]

Innovations?

In a charming, posthumously published book,[54] the twentieth-century historian David Herlihy proposed the plausible thesis that the labor shortages caused by the Black Death stimulated the invention and development of labor-saving technology. This hypothesis is especially attractive given that, as seen in previous chapters, societies often ignored innovations when labor was sufficiently cheap, as when Romans ignored watermills in favor of having slaves grind grain by hand. Indeed, Herlihy proposed that water and wind power were widely adopted subsequent to the Black Death to replace hand labor.

Printing was another innovation said to have received vital stimulus from the fourteenth-century labor shortage. According to Herlihy, "Numerous scribes were employed to copy manuscripts. . . . As long as wages were low, this method of reproduction based on intensive human labor was satisfactory enough. . . . But the late medieval population plunge raised labor costs. . . . The advent of printing is thus a salient example of the policy of factor substitution which was transforming the late medieval economy."[55] In passing, Herlihy also suggested that labor shortages caused the development of larger ships with fewer crew members and the rapid adoption of firearms by western European armies.

It is an elegant thesis, and I must confess my disappointment that Herlihy's hypotheses are not supported by the evidence. Water power was widespread across western Europe several centuries before the Black Death (as seen in chapter 4), and water-powered fulling mills were the basis for the explosive growth of the English woolen industry in the thirteenth century. The critical factor was that hand labor could not compete even if paid only a bare subsistence wage; the fulling machines were just too efficient.[56] English woolens were so cheap that they quickly dominated the entire European market. The same is obviously true of printing presses versus scribes. The press did come into existence after the Black Death reduced the number of scribes, but so long as books were hand-copied they would have remained too expensive for any but the deepest pockets. Even an overabundant supply of scribes could not have kept the much-less-expensive printers from taking over the market. As for ships, they did not suddenly become much larger and crews smaller in the wake of Black Death labor shortages; the long-established trend in that direction merely continued. Finally, European armies adopted firearms to compensate not for a shortage of troops but for a shortage of troops who were bulletproof.

Thus far, no one has discovered any credible examples of labor-saving technologies prompted by the labor shortages resulting from the Black Death.

In contrast, a number of innovations can plausibly be attributed to the Little Ice Age: glass windowpanes, storm doors, skis, ice skates, sunglasses (first used for preventing snow blindness), distilled liquor, trousers, knitted clothing, buttons, and chimneys.[57]

To consider the widespread social impact such inventions had, consider the last example. The chimney did much more than keep rooms well heated and smoke free, important as those developments were. It fundamentally changed the way people organized their homes and lived their lives.

Evidence of human use of fire goes back at least 400,000 years, and some scholars date the first use of fire to much earlier. When humans took shelter in huts, they took their campfires with them, relying on openings in the roof to let out the smoke—an inefficient method that resulted in smoky rooms and let in cold drafts and rain. Fireplaces improved safety by containing the fire in an inflammable hearth but did nothing to solve the smoke and draft problems. These were somewhat minimized by limiting structures to one great hall heated by a central hearth.

The chimney first appeared sometime in about the twelfth century and initially was adopted only by the very rich. Unfortunately, too many medieval historians[58] assume that lower-class housing continued to lack chimneys until nearly modern times. They should have consulted art historians—many paintings from the early fifteenth century show chimneys on most buildings in rural areas as well on even very modest homes in cities.[59]

Because chimneys work best in relatively small rooms, soon the great rooms were abandoned or used only in summer. Medieval buildings became subdivided into small rooms, each with its own fireplace and chimney. With many small rooms came a degree of privacy previously unknown and with it a new sense of modesty. "The bedroom, in particular, became one of the most cherished rooms in the later Middle Ages," concluded LeRoy Dresbeck in his study of the medieval winter climate, "and the chimney helped to alter sexual customs of this period."[60] That is, sex became a private rather than a semipublic activity.[61]

Misreading History

Generations of historians and social scientists embraced Thomas Malthus's claim that the famine of 1315–18, the devastation by the Black Death, and other such catastrophes were "positive checks" on population, triggered (seemingly automatically) to keep the populace proportionate to the food supply. That is, famines and plagues are the normal results of their being too many people. During the 1960s and early 1970s the Malthusian theory of population reigned supreme in academia, as every sociology textbook (including early editions of mine) warned that we could expect tragedy to strike at any moment. Stanford University's Paul Ehrlich pontificated in his bestseller *The Population Bomb* (1968): "The battle to feed all of humanity is over. In the 1970s the world will undergo famines—hundreds of millions are going to starve to death." Also in the late 1960s, the celebrated scientist C. P. Snow told the *New York Times*, "Perhaps in ten years millions of people in the poor countries are going to starve to death before our very eyes. . . . We shall see them doing so upon our television sets."[62]

Nothing of the sort happened, of course. And it has slowly dawned on historians and social scientists that Malthusian theory tells us nothing about the disasters of the fourteenth century either. The famine of 1315–18 was caused by weather, not overpopulation. Prior to the sudden, nearly total destruction of crops, the food supply was quite sufficient. As for the Black Death, it was caused by bubonic plague, and it struck as hard or harder in sparsely settled places such as Iceland as it did in crowded London and Paris.

In any event, for good and for ill, both the climatic changes and the Black Death had significant influences on the course of Western civilization.

8

The Pursuit of Knowledge

T he most fundamental key to the rise of Western civilization has been the dedication of so many of its most brilliant minds to the pursuit of knowledge. Not to illumination. Not to enlightenment. Not to wisdom. But to *knowledge*. And the basis for this commitment to knowledge was the Christian commitment to *theology*.[1]

Theology is in disrepute among most Western intellectuals. The word is taken to mean a passé form of religious thinking that embraces irrationality and dogmatism. So, too, *Scholasticism*. According to most dictionaries, the word *scholastic* often means "pedantic and dogmatic," denoting the sterility of medieval church scholarship. John Locke, the eighteenth-century British philosopher, dismissed the Scholastics as "the great mintmasters" of useless terms meant "to cover their ignorance."[2] In the twentieth century, Sir William Dampier spoke for most conventional academics when he complained that scientific thought was "quite foreign to the prevailing mental outlook" of the Scholastics, who were enmeshed in a "tangle of astrology, alchemy, magic and theosophy" and were absolutely hostile to experimentalism.[3]

Not so! The Scholastics were fine scholars who founded Europe's great universities, formulated and taught the experimental method, and launched Western science.

As for theology, it has little in common with most religious thinking, being a sophisticated, highly *rational* discipline that has its roots in Judaism and in Greek philosophy but is fully developed only in Christianity.

159

The pursuit of knowledge was inherent in theology, as efforts to more fully understand God were extended to include God's creation—thus inaugurating an academic enterprise known as *natural philosophy*, defined as the study of nature and of natural phenomena. During medieval times, a long line of brilliant Scholastic natural philosophers advanced Western knowledge in ways leading directly to the Copernican "Revolution" and the extraordinary scientific achievements of the sixteenth and seventeenth centuries.

Theology and Natural Philosophy

Sometimes described as "the science of faith,"[4] theology consists of formal reasoning about God. The emphasis is on *discovering* God's nature, intentions, and demands, and on understanding how these define the relationship between human beings and God. Theology necessitates an image of God (one God, not many gods) as a conscious, rational, supernatural being of unlimited power and scope.

That is why there are no theologians in the East: those who might otherwise take up such an intellectual pursuit reject this first premise of theology. Consider Taoism. The Tao is conceived of as a supernatural essence, an underlying mystical force or principle governing life, but one that is impersonal, remote, lacking consciousness, and definitely not a being. It is the eternal way, the cosmic force that produces harmony and balance. According to the ancient Chinese philosopher Lao-tzu, the Tao is "always nonexistent" yet "always existent," "unnamable" and the "name that can be named," both "soundless and formless" and "always without desires."[5] One might meditate forever on such an essence, but it offers little to *reason* about. The same applies to Buddhism and Confucianism. Although the popular versions of these faiths are polytheistic and involve an immense array of small gods (as is true of popular Taoism), the "pure" forms of these faiths, as pursued by the intellectual elite, are godless and postulate only a vague divine essence. Buddha specifically denied the existence of a conscious God, and, in the words of the scholar Bradley Clough, "Buddhists have even gone so far as to say that belief in such a God often leads to ethical degradation."[6]

But even the first premise of a conscious, all-powerful God is not enough to sustain theology; it is also necessary to think it is legitimate to apply human reason to questions about God. That is why there are no Muslim theologians. Just as Muslim clerics have rejected science as heretical because they believe that natural laws imply limits on Allah's freedom to act, so too do they deny the legitimacy of relying on reason to expand their understanding of Allah. All that needs to be understood about Allah is written in the Qur'an. The proper role for Muslim thinkers is to interpret scripture—that is, to ensure that the people follow Allah's commands.

In contrast, Christian theologians have devoted centuries to reasoning—about God's nature and about the very meaning of God's teachings. Over time some theological interpretations have evolved dramatically. For example, although the Bible does not condemn astrology—and the story of the Wise Men following the star might even seem to suggest that it is valid—in the fifth century Saint Augustine *reasoned* that astrology is sinful because to believe that one's fate is predestined in the stars stands in opposition to God's gift of free will.[7] This was not a mere amplification of scripture; it was an example of careful deductive reasoning leading to a *new doctrine*: the Church prohibited astrology. Similarly, as outlined in chapter 6, medieval Christian theologians deduced that previous doctrines that accommodated slavery were wrong—that slavery was in fact against divine law. As these examples demonstrate, great minds could, and often did, alter or even reverse church doctrines—on the basis of nothing more than persuasive reasoning.

Leading Christian theologians such as Saint Augustine and Thomas Aquinas were not what today might be called strict constructionists. They celebrated reason as the means to gain greater insight into divine intentions. Recall from chapter 6 how they reworked doctrines concerning commerce. Recall, too, Tertullian's instruction from the second century: "Reason is a thing of God, inasmuch as there is nothing which God the Maker of all has not provided, disposed, ordained by reason nothing which He has not willed should be handled and understood by reason."[8] Or consider again the passage from *The Recognitions*: "Do not think that we say that these things [Christian doctrines] are only to be received by faith, but also that they are to be asserted by reason. For indeed it is not safe to commit these things to bare faith without reason, since assuredly truth cannot be without reason." In fact, the statement stands as perhaps the most compelling and influential linkage of faith and reason. It goes on:

And therefore he who has received these things fortified by reason, can never lose them; whereas he who receives them without proofs, by an assent to a simple statement of them, can neither keep them safely, nor is certain if they are true; because he who easily believes, also easily yields. But he who has sought reason for those things which he has believed and received, as though bound by the chains of reason itself, can never be torn away or separated from those things he hath believed. And therefore, according as any one is more anxious in demanding a reason, by so much will he be the firmer in preserving his faith.[9]

Such views prompted the noted British historian R. W. Southern to reflect that Scholastic theologians tended "to make man appear more rational, human nature more noble, the divine ordering of the universe more open to human inspection, and the whole complex of man, nature and God more fully intelligible, than we now can believe to be plausible." But, Southern concluded, "regarded simply as an effort to comprehend the structure of the universe and . . . to demonstrate the dignity of the human mind by showing that it can know all things—this body of thought is one of the most ambitious displays of scientific humanism ever attempted."[10]

Given this commitment to the pursuit of knowledge, Christian theology and natural philosophy were closely linked during medieval times. As the distinguished historian Edward Grant noted, "Within Western Christianity in the late Middle Ages . . . almost all professional theologians were also natural philosophers. The structure of medieval university education also made it likely that most theologians had early in their careers actually taught natural philosophy."[11] In contrast, natural philosophy was highly controversial within Islam, something to be "taught privately and quietly" at some risk, and it was never taught by prominent Muslim religious thinkers. But in the West, Grant explained, "natural philosophy could attract talented individuals who believed that they were free to present their opinions publicly on a host of problems that formed the basis of the discipline."[12]

It would be difficult to exaggerate the importance of the bond between theology and natural philosophy for the rise of Western civilization. As a result of this bond, the pursuit of knowledge about the natural world became central to the medieval university curriculum and led, ultimately, to the rise of Western science.[13]

Inventing Universities

Perhaps in deference to the political correctness of our times, or perhaps because of ignorance, there have been many recent efforts to place the first universities in China, India, or Persia. Of course, many of the ancient empires had schools devoted to teaching religious culture as well as institutions that sheltered those devoted to contemplation and meditation. But just as there are no theologians in the East, none of these ancient institutions was devoted to the pursuit of knowledge. Rather, as the prolific Harvard scholar Charles Homer Haskins put it, "Universities, like cathedrals and parliaments, are a product of the Middle Ages."[14] More specifically, they were the product of the medieval Church.

The word *university* is a shortened version of the Latin *universitas magistrorum et scholarium*, which can be translated as "community of teachers and scholars." Most of what became medieval universities had been schools imparting religious culture, maintained by cathedrals and monasteries, many dating from the sixth century. The first universities were created specifically to go beyond such instruction. They were devoted to "higher learning," to the active pursuit of knowledge.

The first university was founded in Bologna, in northern Italy, in about 1088—just after the Norman invasion of England and just before the First Crusade. Next came the University of Paris in about 1150, Oxford ca. 1167, Palencia ca. 1208, and Cambridge ca. 1209. Twenty-four others followed before the end of the fourteenth century, and at least twenty-eight more opened during the following century, including one as far north as Uppsala in Sweden (in 1477).

These new institutions distinguished themselves by not limiting their scholarly work to reciting the received wisdom. Instead, the Scholastics who founded universities esteemed innovation. Marcia L. Colish's description is enlightening:

They [the Scholastic faculty] reviewed past authorities and current opinions, giving [their] analysis of them and [their] reasons for rejecting some and accepting others. Altogether, the methodology already in place by the early twelfth century shows the scholastics' willingness, and readiness, to criticize the foundation documents in their respective fields. More than simply receiving and expanding on the classical and Christian traditions, they set aside ideas of those traditions deemed to have outlived their usefulness. They also freely realigned the authorities they retained to defend positions that those authorities might well have thought strange and novel. [Commentaries] were now rarely mere summaries and explications of their author's views. Scholastic commentators were much more likely to take issue with their chosen author or to bring to bear on his work ideas from emerging schools of thought or the scholastics own opinions.[15]

Of crucial importance, the great medieval universities were dominated by empiricism from the start.[16] If it was possible to put an intellectual claim to observational tests, then that was what should be done. Nowhere was the Scholastic commitment to empiricism more fully displayed than in the study of human physiology. It was the Scholastics, not the Greeks, Romans, Muslims, or Chinese, who based their studies on human dissection.[17] During classical times the dignity of the human body had forbidden dissection,[18] which is why Greco-Roman works on anatomy are so faulty. Aristotle's studies were limited to animal dissections, as were those of Celsius and Galen. Human dissection was also prohibited in Islam. But with the founding of Christian universities came a new outlook on dissection. This new outlook was predicated on the assumption that what was unique to humans was a soul, not a body, meaning that dissections had no theological implications. Further, adequate medical knowledge required direct observation of human anatomy. In any case, too many murderers had escaped detection because the bodies of their victims had not been subjected to careful postmortems.

In the thirteenth century, local officials (especially in Italian university towns) began to authorize postmortems in instances when the cause of death was uncertain. Late in the century, Mondino de' Luzzi (1270–1326) wrote a textbook on dissection, based on his study of two female cadavers.[19] Then, in about 1315, he performed a human dissection in front of an audience of students and faculty at the University of Bologna. From there, human dissection spread rapidly through the Italian universities—given added impetus by the calamity of the Black Death. Public dissections began in Spain in 1391, and the first one in Vienna was conducted in 1404.[20] Dissection became a customary part of anatomy classes. As Edward Grant observed, the "introduction [of human dissection] in the Latin west, made without serious objection from the Church, was a momentous occurrence."[21]

The rise of human dissections reflected the autonomy of medieval universities. As Nathan Schachner explained:

> The university was the darling, the spoiled child of the Papacy and Empire, of king and municipality alike. Privileges were showered on the proud Universities in a continuous golden stream; privileges that had no counterpart, then, before, or since. Not even the sacred hierarchies of the Church had quite the exemptions of the poorest begging scholar who could claim protection of a University. Municipalities competed violently for the honour of housing one within their walls; kings wrote siren letters to entice discontented groups of scholars from the domains of their rivals; Popes intervened with menacing language to compel royalty to respect the inviolability of this favoured institution.[22]

The faculty benefited from this privileged status. Despite slow transportation and limited means of communication, scholars moved from one university to another amazingly often. They could do so because language barriers were not a problem: all instruction, everywhere, was in Latin. Then, as today, one gained fame and invitations to join other faculties by *innovation*. It was not who knew Aristotle word for word, but who had found errors in Aristotle. As William of Auvergne (1180–1249), a professor of theology at the University of Paris, put it: "Let it not enter your mind that I want to use the words of Aristotle as authoritative for the proof of things I am about to say, for I know that a proof from an authority is only dialectical and can only produce belief, though it is my aim, both in this treatise and whenever I can, to produce demonstrative certitude."[23] Even better was to have discovered something unknown to the classical world.

So much, then, for the claims that Scholastics merely recited dogma or debated theological minutiae.

Cradle of Learning: The University of Paris

For all the dozens of universities that flourished in the Middle Ages, by far the most important, both as a model for the others and for the achievements of its faculty, was the University of Paris.

This university quickly became the largest and most prestigious institution of higher learning in Europe, at least partly because of the attractions of the city itself. Even then, Paris had a reputation as a sophisticated and beautiful city, very large for that era, having a population of about a hundred thousand in 1200.[24] As the capital of France, it also featured a dazzling court and the excitement inherent in constant intrigues and affairs of both heart and state.[25]

The roster of University of Paris graduates and faculty stands as a glittering array of the most famous medieval intellectuals. While the university was still the cathedral school of Notre-Dame de Paris, the almost legendary Peter Abelard (1079–1142) was a student and later held the chair in natural philosophy. Thomas Aquinas (1225–1274), the most admired of medieval scholars, served as regent master of theology at the university. Later graduates included Ignatius Loyola (1491–1556) and John Calvin (1509–1564). And, as will be seen, most of the great natural philosophers who took part in the Copernican "Revolution" were associated with the University of Paris.

Students

Many readers will suppose that medieval universities were quite small, consisting of a few masters and, perhaps, a hundred students. In fact, by the year 1200, only fifty years after its founding, the University of Paris is estimated to have had from 2,500 to 5,000 students and several hundred faculty.[26] Many of these students came from far away, even from Scandinavia. In 1167—the year Oxford was founded—King Henry II prohibited English students from attending the University of Paris. Shortly thereafter the ban was lifted, and thus began several centuries of close connections between Oxford and Paris.

Students were very young, most entering at age fourteen or fifteen. Keep in mind that back then, the world was run mostly by young men, life expectancy being rather short. Most students, observed the historian Hastings Rashdall, "were of a social position intermediate between the highest and the very lowest—sons of knights and yeomen, merchants, tradesmen or thrifty artisans."[27] Still, a surprising number of students were impoverished; some even received permission from the chancellor to beg door-to-door. To give alms to a student beggar "was recognized as a work of charity in the medieval world," Rashdall noted.[28]

The area surrounding the University of Paris came to be known as the Latin Quarter—a name that persists today. This was because students were encouraged to speak only in Latin, in and out of class. Nevertheless, few students had real fluency in Latin. (Neither did most clergy, from parish priests to cardinals.)[29] Such deficiencies in Latin were not usually a serious problem, because, as Grant pointed out, "most of the students at medieval universities departed after two years or less without acquiring a bachelor's degree."[30] For most students, it was enough simply to have been at university.

It wasn't only in Latin that most undergraduate students failed to live up to the faculty's high standards. Recalling his days as a student in Paris from about 1205 to 1210, Cardinal Jacques de Vitry wrote: "Simple fornication was held to be no sin. Everywhere, publicly, close to their brothels, prostitutes attracted the students who were walking by on the streets and squares of the city with immodest and aggressive invitations."[31] It was, of course, against regulations for students to accept such invitations. But many students flouted those and other rules, not only bedding prostitutes but also being rowdy and drinking too much.[32]

This dissolute, sometimes even criminal behavior had an amazing result: it gave the university complete independence from local authorities. Here is how it happened.

Gaining "Academic Freedom"

In March 1229, at the start of the pre-Lenten Carnival—which was much like a modern Mardi Gras, complete with masks and uninhibited behavior—a group of University of Paris students became embroiled in a conflict with a tavern owner over their bill. A fight broke out, other patrons supported the owner, and the students were beaten and thrown into the street. The next day the students returned with reinforcements and clubs, broke into the tavern, beat the owner and patrons, smashed everything, and then rioted in the streets.

City officials demanded punishment. University officials took shelter in the exemption of the Church from local courts, since the university was a religious institution. But Blanche of Castile, the mother of

Louis IX who was then serving as regent of France, demanded retribution. The university then allowed the city to take action against the students. Unfortunately, the city guardsmen picked out a group of students who had not taken part in the riot and even killed several of them.

The university went on strike. Faculty refused to teach and all classes were canceled. Many students went home; some went to other universities, including Oxford and Cambridge.[33] The strike caused a severe economic pinch in Paris.

After two years, Pope Gregory IX, himself a graduate of the university, issued a bull that guaranteed the institution total freedom from local authorities—including ecclesiastical leaders—by placing it directly under papal patronage and control. The university thus had the right to establish its own rules and statutes, as well as the exclusive right to punish violations. Even criminal cases brought against faculty and students could be heard only in an ecclesiastical, not a civil, court. The pope's bull became the university's charter, which, in turn, served as the model for other new universities.

In addition to granting the ecclesiastical exemption from civil authorities, the charter placed all power in the hands of the faculty. They decided whom to admit to their ranks and whom to dismiss. Summed up in two words, the university enjoyed virtually unlimited "academic freedom."

Curriculum

The curriculum was similar throughout medieval universities. At the undergraduate level, it consisted of the seven liberal arts: grammar, rhetoric, and logic formed the trivium; arithmetic, geometry, astronomy, and music made up the quadrivium. Under the appropriate art, students studied the Latin classics, the astronomy of Ptolemy, the complete works of Euclid, and Aristotelian logic—the last of which, according to the historian Charles Homer Haskins, formed "the backbone of the arts course." The prominence of logic made perfect sense, for it "was not only a major subject of study itself, it pervaded every other subject as a method and gave tone and character to the medieval mind."[34]

The graduate level of studies was organized into four divisions: theology, law, medicine, and natural philosophy. There were, Haskins noted, "relatively few students of theology."[35] Several reasons explained the dearth of theology students: theological training was not required for the priesthood; many monastic orders offered their own instruction; it took a long time to complete the work for an advanced degree; the books—still copied by hand—were expensive; and the anticipated income was low compared with what one could earn from medicine or law.[36]

Faculty

As is true today, most university students were not very serious about learning, let alone playing any role in the pursuit of knowledge. That was the domain of some advanced graduate students but primarily of the faculty. "Publish or perish," however, had not yet come into vogue. Consequently, only dedicated scholars with something to say devoted time to the pursuit of new knowledge (and the world was spared the flood of trivia churned out by careerist faculty in modern times).

Teaching was the primary faculty obligation. The great Scholastic scholars held classes every day during the school year. They usually lectured to large groups of students, often dictating from books because texts were so scarce and expensive in the days before the printing press.

The faculty also ran the university. They elected a rector or chancellor to administer the institution—though, in a reflection of the faculty's power, the Paris rector's term was limited to just three months.[37] As Haskins pointed out, "As there were no endowments of importance there were no trustees, nor was there any system of state control. . . . Administration in the modern sense was strikingly absent. . . . In a quite remarkable degree the university was self-governing."[38]

How, then, were universities funded? How were faculty paid? Entirely by student fees—often paid directly to a professor by those registering for his class. Nonpayment was a problem. One professor ended his lecture course by saying: "Next year I expect to give ordinary lectures well and lawfully as I always have, but no extraordinary lectures, for students are not good payers, wishing to learn but not to pay, as the saying is: All desire to know but none to pay the price. I have nothing more to say to you beyond dismissing you with God's blessing and begging you to attend mass."[39]

Scholastics and the Copernican "Revolution"

Just as there were no "Dark Ages," there was no "Scientific Revolution." Rather, the notion of a Scientific Revolution was invented to discredit the medieval Church by claiming that science burst forth in full bloom (thus owing no debts to prior Scholastic scholars) only when a weakened Christianity no longer could suppress it. But, as will be seen in chapter 13, the great scientific achievements of the sixteenth and seventeenth centuries were produced by a group of scholars notable for their piety, who were based in Christian universities, and whose brilliant achievements built on an invaluable legacy of centuries of Scholastic scholarship.[40]

The start of the so-called Scientific Revolution is usually attributed to Nicolaus Copernicus (1473–1543). According to the fashionable account, Copernicus was an obscure Catholic canon in far-off Poland, an isolated genius who somehow discovered that, contrary to what everyone believed, the earth revolves around the sun. Moreover, the story goes, the Church made unrelenting efforts to suppress this view.

There is far more fiction than fact in this account. Rather than being some obscure Pole, Copernicus received a superb education at the best Italian universities of the time: Bologna, Padua, and Ferrara. The idea that the earth circles the sun did not come to him out of the blue; he learned the fundamentals leading to the heliocentric model of the solar system from his Scholastic professors. What Copernicus added was not a leap but the implicit next step in a long line of discovery stretching back centuries.

Robert Grosseteste (ca. 1175–1253)

A Norman raised in England, Robert Grosseteste attended Oxford, studied and taught at the University of Paris from 1208 to 1213, returned to become chancellor of Oxford, and then became Bishop of Lincoln, the largest diocese in England, which included Oxford. Grosseteste was a remarkable polymath who made important contributions to optics, physics, and tides. He refuted Aristotle's theory of the rainbow—Grosseteste being the first to realize that rainbows involve refracted light.[41] He also pursued astronomy, being careful to distinguish it from astrology, as many of his contemporaries did not.

But perhaps his most important contributions involved what has come to be called the scientific method. One of these contributions was what he called the principle of "resolution and composition"—which involved reasoning from the particular case to the general and then back again. For example, by looking at a particular case, one can formulate a universal law about nature and then apply this law to make predictions about all the other relevant cases—such as by formulating a law about eclipses of the moon and then testing that law by applying it to eclipses of the sun.

Note the emphasis on observation as the basis of all science. Grosseteste's commitment to empiricism was such that he introduced the notion of the controlled scientific experiment to Western thought. The fundamental principle is that, as one historian of science summarized, "when one controls his observations by eliminating any other possible cause of the effect, he may arrive at an experimental universal of provisional truth."[42]

John of Sacrobosco (1195–1256)

His real name may have been John of Holywood; he probably was either English or Irish, he may have attended Oxford; but he most certainly served on the faculty of the University of Paris, beginning in 1221. Although little is known about Sacrobosco, he wrote two influential books, both of which survive. The first was *Algorismus*, which introduced Hindu-Arabic numerals and new methods of numerical calculation for the first time to the European universities. His second, *Tractatus de Sphaera* (usually referred to as *Sphere*), was a readable astronomy textbook based on Ptolemy's cosmology. The title reflects the claim that the earth and all the heavenly bodies are spherical. *Sphere* was required reading for European university students for the next several centuries, often praised for its clarity.[43]

Albertus Magnus (ca. 1200–1280)

The son of the Count of Bollstädt in Bavaria, Albertus was educated in Italy at the University of Padua, and then he taught at a number of German universities before taking the position of master of theology at the University of Paris (where Thomas Aquinas was his dedicated student). In 1248 Albertus returned to Germany and in 1260 he was appointed Bishop of Regensburg. He resigned after three years to return to his scholarship. Author of thirty-eight books, he was so celebrated during his lifetime that his colleagues, including Roger Bacon, added the title "Magnus" (the great) to his name. He was regarded as one of the theological giants of medieval times, but he also put to empirical testing claims that Aristotle and other classical Greek philosophers had made about nature. In doing so he became "perhaps the best field botanist of the entire Middle Ages," according to historian of science David Lindberg.[44]

Committed to observation and experimentation, Albertus made significant contributions in many other fields, including geography, astronomy, and chemistry—hence his colleagues gave him the title *Doctor Universalis*. Perhaps most important, he inspired his colleagues and students not merely to accept classical scholarship but to challenge the received wisdom and seek reliable observations.[45]

Roger Bacon (ca. 1214-1294)

This brilliant Englishman is often identified as "the first scientist" in that he fully embraced Grosseteste's commitment to the experimental method and expanded on it at length. Born in Somerset, he entered Oxford at thirteen and eventually became a master there, lecturing on Aristotle. Moving on to the University of Paris in about 1240, he spent a few years on the faculty but then joined the Franciscan Order and ceased teaching, devoting his time to writing.

Initially, Bacon's Franciscan superiors prevented him from publishing, but Pope Clement IV ordered Bacon to write for him. Bacon responded by sending the pope his *Opus Majus*. It is an amazing work. Written in only a year of frantic effort, the available modern edition runs to 1,996 pages. In it, Bacon displayed knowledge of many different fields: mathematics; the size and position of heavenly bodies; the physiology of eyesight; optics, including refraction, mirrors and lenses, the magnifying glass, and spectacles; an accurate recipe for gunpowder; calendar reform; and on and on—"a veritable library covering all aspects of natural science," in the words of biographer Brian Clegg.[46]

Bacon also stressed empiricism as opposed to authority. He declared: "Authority has no savor, unless reason for it is given, and it does not give understanding, but belief. For we believe on the strength of authority, but we do not understand through it. Nor can we distinguish between sophism and demonstration, unless we know to test the conclusion by works."[47] As illustration, Bacon noted that some had argued (wrongly) that Aristotle claimed hot water freezes faster than does cold water. This was not a matter to be accepted on Aristotle's authority or by consulting other learned persons, Bacon said. Instead, one must take a container of hot water and one of cold, put them outside in cold weather, and see which freezes first.

Bacon's general discussion of the experiment rested on the work of his predecessor Robert Grosseteste. Putting theories to further tests and making appropriate observations—this is what both Grosseteste and Bacon, and probably most Scholastic scientists, meant by the experimental method. That approach represented an extraordinary departure from the Greeks as well as from early Christian thinkers, who believed in the superiority of ideas and abstract forms to empirical reality. To the Scholastics' predecessors, reason, not observation, was the true test of any philosophical claim. This was a powerful tradition that proponents of experimentalism had to overcome. Only because Bacon, Grosseteste, and other Scholastics fought and won the battle for empiricism was it possible for the rise of science to occur.

Finally, *Opus Majus* was filled with remarkable predictions about future inventions, including microscopes, telescopes, and flying machines. The Oxford historian John Henry Bridges noted that Bacon's "scientific imagination" made these forecasts possible. But "what may [best] be said," Bridges added, "is that he set the world on the right track towards their discovery"—namely, by outlining a method that called for "experiment and observation combined with mathematics, when mathematics were available, and when they were not available, then experiment and observation pursued alone."[48]

Campanus of Novara (1220–1296)

Born in Lombardy, Giovanni Compano (Campanus is the Latinized version of his name) served as chaplain to four successive popes. Meanwhile he earned a reputation as a mathematician—Roger Bacon considered him one of the world's greatest mathematicians. But Campanus's greatest contributions came as a sophisticated translator and commentator on two extraordinary works of knowledge. First was his translation of Euclid's *Elements*, wherein the great ancient Greek mathematician presented his complete work of geometry. Campanus's translation became the standard textbook in European medieval universities. And, of course, geometry was the essential tool for study of the cosmos. To this, Campanus added a second invaluable translation: Ptolemy's second-century treatise on planetary theory, the *Almagest*. Although Ptolemy had the earth at the center of the solar system with everything else in orbit around it, the geometry of his system was so well constructed that calculations based on it yielded accurate predictions of future states and allowed accurate calculations of the dates for Easter and of eclipses. It was very important that Campanus gave Scholastic scholars access to Ptolemy's complete work because it revealed how complicated it was to have everything in orbit around the earth.[49]

Theodoric of Freiberg (1250-1310)

A German who studied at the University of Paris and later returned as a member of the faculty, Theodoric formulated the first geometrical analysis of the rainbow and backed it up with solid experimental findings, leading to what has been called "the most dramatic development of 14th and 15th century optics."[50] Theodoric was the first to realize that rainbows are caused not by either refraction or reflection but by *both within a single raindrop*. Using spherical flasks and glass globes filled with water, he was able to create rainbow effects in his laboratory.[51] Theodoric's use of a specially constructed experimental apparatus was widely admired and copied by Scholastic natural philosophers.

Thomas Bradwardine (1290-1349)

Thomas Bradwardine was an Englishman educated at Oxford who then stayed on as a professor in Merton College and eventually became chancellor of the university. He left Oxford to serve as confessor to Edward III at the Battle of Crécy (August 26, 1346), and in 1349 he was elected Archbishop of Canterbury. Forty days later Bradwardine died of the Black Death.

Bradwardine was the leading member of the group known as the Oxford Calculators, pioneers in formulating and quantifying theorems in kinetics and dynamics—they were the first to formulate the mean speed theorem. As the prominent American mathematician Clifford Truesdell explained:

> The now published sources prove to us, beyond contention, that the main kinematical properties of uniformly accelerated motions, still attributed to Galileo by the physics texts, were discovered and proved by scholars at Merton college. . . . In principle, the qualities of Greek physics were replaced, at least for motions, by the numerical quantities that have ruled Western science ever since. The work was quickly diffused into France, Italy, and other parts of Europe. Almost immediately, Giovanni di Casale and Nicole Oresme found how to represent the results on geometrical graphs, introducing the connection between geometry and

the physical world that became a second characteristic habit of Western thought.[52]

William of Ockham (ca. 1285-1349)

Another Englishman who studied at Oxford, William of Ockham joined the Franciscans and then spent his academic career on the Continent. He was constantly in trouble with the pope while enjoying the protection of the Holy Roman Emperor, Louis IV of Bavaria. Like Bradwardine, Ockham died during the outbreak of the Black Death, but it is unknown whether that was the cause of his death.

Today, Ockham is remembered primarily for his principle known as *Ockham's razor*, which stresses parsimony in the formulation of explanations. As he expressed it, explanations should "not be multiplied beyond necessity." Too often this is misrepresented as saying one should prefer the simplest explanation, but the simplest might well be an inferior explanation. What Ockham meant was that theories should include no more terms and principles than are needed to explain the matters in question. Hence, if two theories are equally efficient, prefer the one that is simpler.

But Ockham's razor was not Ockham's important contribution to understanding the cosmos. Because the Greeks thought vacuums could not exist, they assumed that the universe was a sphere filled with transparent matter. That meant heavenly bodies would need to constantly overcome friction to keep moving. This notion prompted many Greek philosophers to transform the sun, moon, stars, and other bodies into living creatures having the capacity to move on their own, while others imagined various sorts of pushers in the form of gods and spirits. Early Christian scholars assumed that angels pushed the heavenly bodies along their courses. It was Ockham who did away with the need for pushers by recognizing that space is a frictionless vacuum. He then anticipated Newton's First Law of Motion by proposing that once God had set the heavenly bodies in motion, they would, facing no friction, remain in motion ever after.[53]

Jean Buridan (1300-1358)

Born in France, Jean Buridan was a student at the University of Paris and then joined the faculty. Buridan differed from most of his academic colleagues by remaining a secular priest rather than joining a religious order.

Many stories persist about his alleged amorous affairs, but whether or not they are true, he was regarded as a glamorous figure around Paris.

Buridan made a pivotal contribution when he introduced the concept we now know as *inertia*, which explained Ockham's insight that things in motion will tend to remain in motion. Aristotle and his followers, including most Scholastics of Buridan's era, believed that a body remained in motion only when an external force was continuously applied. So, for example, Aristotelians held that a projectile would fall immediately to the ground were in not for eddies or vibrations in the air around it applying motive force. Buridan shifted the focus from imposed forces to a property of the moving body itself: he called this property *impetus*. As he described it: "After leaving the arm of the thrower, the projectile would be moved by impetus given to it by the thrower and would continue to be moved as long as the impetus remained stronger than the resistance, and would be of indefinite duration were it not diminished and corrupted by a contrary force resisting it or by something inclining it to a contrary motion."[54]

Oddly enough, although Buridan extended Ockham's physics, they became bitter opponents on several theological issues.[55]

Nicole Oresme (ca. 1320–1382)

The next vital step toward the heliocentric model was taken by the most brilliant (and sadly neglected) of the Scholastic scientists, Nicole Oresme. Born in Normandy, Oresme attended the University of Paris and then joined the faculty. In 1364 he was appointed dean of the Cathedral of Rouen, and in 1377 he was appointed Bishop of Lisieux.

Among his many major achievements, Oresme firmly established that the earth turned on its axis, which gave the illusion that the other heavenly bodies circled the earth. He began by noting that the movements we observed of the heavenly bodies would appear exactly the same whether the earth turned or these bodies were circling the earth. So there were no observational data to settle the matter. Oresme reasoned, however, that the earth's spinning offered a far more economical explanation than did the notion that an immense number of heavenly bodies all circled the earth.

The idea that the earth rotates had occurred to many people through the centuries, but two objections had always made it seem implausible. First, if the earth turned, why wasn't there a constant wind from the east caused by the rotation? Second, why did an arrow shot up into the air not fall well behind (or in front of) the shooter? Oresme addressed both objections by proposing that the motion of the earth was imparted to all objects on the earth or close by, including the atmosphere.[56]

Albert of Saxony (ca. 1316-1390)

A farmer's son born in Germany, Albert was recognized for his brilliance in childhood, which led to his being sent first to the University of Prague and then to the University of Paris. After earning his master's degree at Paris, he joined the faculty. Subsequently he convinced the Duke of Austria to found the University of Vienna, and in 1365 he became its first rector. The next year he became Bishop of Halberstadt (the diocese in which he was born) and served until his death.

Albert was a student of Jean Buridan, and he extended the theory of impetus and made it more precise, noting that although air resistance slows the motion of an object, gravity alone pulls it to earth after the impetus is spent. But Albert's most important contribution was the textbook *Physics*, which carefully summarized the work of all his predecessors and constructed many original proofs of major propositions. This text was read throughout Europe for several centuries.[57]

Pierre d'Ailly (1350-1420)

Born in France and educated at the University of Paris, Pierre d'Ailly joined the university's faculty in 1368, serving as chancellor from 1389 through 1395. He then was consecutively Bishop of Le Puy, of Noyon, and of Cambrai before becoming a cardinal in 1411.

In 1410 he published *Image of the World* (*Ymago mundi*), a widely read work of cosmology that included his calculation that the circumference of the earth was 31,500 miles—higher than the actual distance of 24,901 miles, but a considerable improvement over Plato's estimate of about 40,000 miles.[58] The book also suggested that only a small sea separated East and West, which greatly misled Columbus. More important, d'Ailly's book spurred interest in questions about the relationship between earth and the stars.[59]

Nicholas of Cusa (1401-1464)

A German who became Bishop of Brixen and then was elevated to cardinal in 1448, Nicholas of Cusa was educated at the great Italian University of Padua, where he learned that the earth turns in response to "an impetus conferred upon it at the beginning of time." Based on eclipses, he noted that the earth was smaller than the sun but larger than the moon. But what of the earth's position—was it fixed? Nicholas observed that "whether a man is on the earth, or the sun, or some other star, it will always seem to him that the position he occupies is the motionless center, and that all other things are in motion."[60] It followed that humans could not trust their perceptions that the earth was stationary in space. Indeed, according to Nicholas, the earth moved through space.[61]

Nicolaus Copernicus (1473-1543)

All this prior theorizing was well known to Copernicus—Albert of Saxony's *Physics*, for example, was published at Padua in 1492, just prior to Copernicus's becoming a student there.

So what did Copernicus contribute? He put the sun in the middle of the solar system and had the earth circling it as one of the planets. What gave such special luster to his work was that he expressed it all in mathematics.[62] He worked out the geometry of his system so as to permit the calculation of future positions of the bodies involved, which was essential for setting the dates of Easter, the solstices, and the like. But these calculations were no more accurate than those based on the Ptolemaic system dating from the second century. That is because Copernicus failed to realize that orbits in the solar system are elliptical, not circular. To make his system work, Copernicus had to postulate loops in the orbits of heavenly bodies that accounted for the seeming delays in the completion of those orbits. There was no observational support for this contention.

Consequently, everything in Copernicus's famous book, *On the Revolutions of the Heavenly Spheres*, is wrong, other than the placement of the sun in the center. It was nearly a century later that Johannes Kepler (1571–1630), a German Protestant, got things right by substituting ellipses for Copernicus's circles. Now each heavenly body was always where it was supposed to be, on time, with no loops needed.

Of course, even with Kepler's additions, there still was no *explanation* of why the solar system functioned as it did—of why, for example, bodies remained in their orbits rather than flying off into space. The achievement of such an explanation awaited Isaac Newton (1642–1727). But over several previous centuries, many essential pieces of such a theory had been assembled: that the universe was a vacuum; that no pushers were needed because once in motion, the heavenly bodies would continue in motion; that the earth turned; that the sun was the center of the solar system; that the orbits were elliptical.

This record of systematic progress explains why the distinguished historian of science I. Bernard Cohen noted that "the idea that a Copernican revolution in science occurred goes counter to the evidence . . . and is the invention of later historians."[63] Most of Cohen's sophisticated colleagues agree.[64] Copernicus added a small step forward in a long process of normal science, albeit one having immense polemical and philosophical implications.

It should be noted, too, that the scholars involved in this long process were not rebel secularists. Not only were they devout Christians; they all were priests or monks—even bishops and cardinals.

And one more thing: they all were embedded in the great Scholastic universities. In fact, nine of the thirteen who preceded Copernicus were faculty at the University of Paris.[65]

Faith and Reason

The pursuit of knowledge did not suddenly appear in the seventeenth century. From early days, Christian theologians were devoted to natural philosophy. That provided the fundamental basis for the creation of universities, thus giving an institutional home to science. The Christian thinkers who studied and taught at these universities were responsible for remarkable advances in an era supposedly short on progress.

Similar (and similarly unappreciated) advances were occurring in industry and technology.

9

Industry, Trade, and Technology

There is a growing illusion, fostered by an assortment of revisionist scholars, that Europe's industrial and technological lead over the rest of the world developed only recently, having come out of nowhere at the end of the eighteenth or even as late as the nineteenth century.[1] Some even claim that the West stole it all from Asia, which supposes that Asia was already industrialized before a sudden decline into backwardness.[2]

It may well be true, as these revisionists claim, that the total value of what was being traded in China during, say, the sixteenth century was greater than that of European trade.[3] But that difference reflects only a greater volume based on a larger population. It tells us nothing about how the trade goods were created or about the technological merits of what was being bought and sold. Eyeglasses, for example, were being sold only in Europe at this time, and in large quantities there, but a hundred pounds of rice outweighed and may well have cost more than a pair of eyeglasses.

In any event, despite the fact that these matters are being solemnly debated in academia, no serious reader needs me to refute such nonsense; I also ignored "respectable" claims that the Black Death came from outer space.[4]

The reality is that medieval Europe saw the rise of banking, elaborate manufacturing networks, rapid innovations in technology and finance, and a busy network of trading cities. Also evident in this period were the first stirrings of what eventually became the Industrial "Revolution." Europe had long been ahead of the rest of the world in technology, but by the end of the sixteenth century that gap had become a chasm.

Consider military capabilities. Europe's sixteenth-century navies consisted of large, heavily armed, sophisticated sailing ships that could go anywhere and sink anything.[5] Only in European armies did the rank and file bear firearms and were they backed up by maneuverable field artillery.[6] In addition to this huge technological superiority were the tactical and training advantages that had favored the West since the days of ancient Greece. Those advantages would continue to favor the West for centuries, in fact. As late as 1900, after the Chinese army was fully equipped with modern firearms and artillery imported from the West, 409 Western soldiers—armed only with rifles, pistols, three machine guns (with very little ammunition), and a homemade cannon—withstood the Imperial army's fifty-five-day attack on the embassy compound in Peking. Holding off thousands of Imperial forces, the Western troops suffered casualties of nearly 50 percent but still stood firm.[7]

And military technology was just the beginning.

Capitalism Moves North

For several centuries, buyers for the Italian city-state exporting companies crisscrossed northern Europe seeking goods for resale around the Mediterranean. At first they did their buying at the great trade fairs held periodically in the Champagne region and other northern locations, but eventually they bought directly from local producers. This was especially true of woolen cloth from Flanders. To facilitate these transactions, many Italian banks opened branches in Flanders. These banks were sophisticated capitalist firms, run by well-trained executives hired and promoted on the basis of ability, not family ties.

In Flanders, the Italians not only organized a backward, inefficient woolen industry but also dealt with a repressive, counterproductive set of merchant weavers' guilds. With the full backing of the local ruler in return for regular permission fees, the merchant weavers' guilds in the various towns and cities of Flanders operated as cartels, restricting the industry and punishing nonconformists. For example, anyone found to have varied the formula for a popular scarlet dye faced a huge fine—and if he didn't pay, he would lose his right hand.[8] Guild rules limited the number of looms firms could own, usually to fewer than five. They controlled prices and forbade bargaining, thereby limiting any benefits of increased efficiency. The weavers' guild also set the length of the working day and required all firms to comply.[9]

The guild set wages as well. The wage levels applied not only to hired weavers but also to wool washers, carders, spinners, dyers, fullers, shearers, and everyone else in the industry. Because only weavers with their own shops could belong to the guild, management alone dictated wages. No variations in wages were allowed from one firm to another, and any and all forms of collective bargaining for higher wages were prohibited not only by guild rules but usually by local law as well. The result was an unproductive and uncreative wool industry.

As Italian bankers surveyed this scene, they realized the immense economic gains to be made if they overcame the guild system. They approached the problem with both a carrot and a stick. The stick involved inviting large numbers of cloth makers to emigrate to Italy, where they were given special privileges in exchange for launching a woolen industry. For example, as the economic historian Eleanora Carus-Wilson pointed out, a statute enacted in Padua in 1265 exempted "foreigners who came into the city to make cloth . . . from all tolls and customs duties and later also from personal taxes."[10] The carrot was the promise of far greater incomes for everyone if the guilds surrendered. The bankers eventually won everyone over and delivered as promised, supplanting the merchant weavers' guilds with well-managed firms that integrated the entire woolen industry: importing the fleeces, coordinating all the steps and hiring all the subcontractors necessary to turn wool into cloth, and then exporting the cloth based on market conditions. In addition to its more expensive luxury woolens, Flanders soon began to produce less expensive varieties, which led to an immense increase in sales.

The woolen industry prospered in Flanders for several centuries, despite a great deal of social turmoil and war. Then, late in the thirteenth century, France annexed southern Flanders. Although northern Flanders held off the French, the destruction of the wool industry in the South had serious consequences: some companies moved north to escape French taxes and repression, many others went to Italy, and still others went to England. Eventually the whole of Flanders was taken over by the Spanish, who wrecked its commercial and industrial institutions. At the end of the fifteenth century the continental woolen industry and aggressive capitalist firms were driven north to Amsterdam. All this gave England a huge opportunity.

English Capitalism

As in Flanders, capitalism came to England in the form of Italian semi-colonialism. Italian banks proliferated in England (and Ireland) during the thirteenth century,[11] a fact acknowledged in the Magna Carta, signed in 1215, which guaranteed the rights of foreign merchants to enter the country and conduct their business without hindrance. By the start of the thirteenth century London had foreign merchant enclaves quite similar to those Western colonialists formed in Asia centuries later. But this was *semi*colonialism because foreign merchants operated in England only at the pleasure of the Crown and were not backed by military pressure.

Secure behind the Channel, the English had become one of the major Western powers, blessed with exceptionally productive agriculture, vast mineral resources, and abundant water power. So it was only a matter of time before they went into business for themselves, imposing unfavorable taxes and duties on foreign firms and products. Even so, it was the remarkable rise of political freedom that gave greater impetus to English capitalism. As made explicit in the Magna Carta, the English merchant enjoyed secure property rights and free markets, unlike early capitalists in southern Italy and those in the Walloon area of Flanders, who were destroyed by despots. Freedom and the security of property spurred innovation, with the result that English industries developed or exploited technologies far superior to those used by their European competitors. When the Industrial "Revolution" began in the eighteenth century, it was not a revolution at all but part of an *evolution* of invention and innovation that had begun in England perhaps as early as the eleventh century.

As was the case in Flanders, capitalism first came to England in response to the woolen trade, and the early development of English capitalism took place almost entirely within this single industry. Therefore, close examination of how capitalism transformed the English woolen industry offers the most revealing perspective on the rise of English industrial capitalism.

From Wool to Woolens

The basic contours of this story are clear in table 9–1 (all figures have been rounded). In the thirteenth century England was, in effect, a vast sheep ranch serving the continental woolen industry. English exports of cloth were so insignificant that no tax records exist, but exports of wool climbed rapidly, from an annual average of 17,700 sacks in 1278–80 to 34,500 sacks in the first decade of the fourteenth century, or almost 9 million fleeces (the standard sack of wool contained about 260 fleeces).[12] But the dynamic soon changed. The first statistics on cloth exports become available in the middle of the fourteenth century, and the annual figure jumps from 4,400 bolts exported in 1347–48 to 31,700 bolts at the beginning of the fifteenth century. Meanwhile, fleece exports dropped, from about 33,700 sacks of wool a year to only 13,900. From the turn of the century on, cloth exports rose rapidly and fleece exports declined: by 1543–44 annual English cloth exports amounted to 137,300 bolts, and fleece exports were down to an insignificant 1,200 sacks.

Table 9–1: English Wool Exports: 1278–1544

Years	Average Annual Export of Cloths (in Bolts)	Average Annual Export of Fleeces (in Sacks)
1278–1280	-	17,700
1281–1290	-	23,600
1301–1310	-	34,500
1347–1348	4,400	-
1351–1360	6,400	33,700
1401–1410	31,700	13,900
1441–1450	49,400	9,400
1501–1510	81,600	7,500
1531–1540	106,100	3,500
1543–1544	137,300	1,200[13]

The table reflects the rise of the English woolen industry, propelled by the development of English cloth-making firms and the imposition of taxes and export duties specifically designed to keep the superb English wool out of the hands of foreign weavers. Not surprisingly, as the domestic woolen industry took off, the English no longer needed to import most of their cloth. During 1333–36, imports averaged about 10,000 bolts of cloth a year; just two decades later, by 1355–57, the number of imported cloths had dropped to about 6,000 bolts per year.[14] The English eventually dominated the world woolen market, maintaining their preeminence for centuries.

One factor in this rise to prominence was the superiority of English local wool. Even in the early thirteenth century, when English woolen manufacturing operated on a small scale, wealthy Europeans would buy only English cloth,[15] the best of which was often dyed scarlet and esteemed by European royalty. The Venetians were concerned enough about their English rivals to impose a special import tariff on English woolens in 1265. The lesson was not lost on the English Crown, and ten years later the king imposed an export duty on English fleeces. This meant, of course, that English cloth makers could buy the superior English fleeces much cheaper than could cloth makers in Flanders and Italy and could sell the finished cloths abroad for less.

But there was more to English control of the wool market than just having the best fleeces and favorable government tax policies. Like the Italian woolen industry before it, the English industry benefited from substantial immigration of skilled artisans from Flanders. In 1271 King Henry III decreed that "all workers of woollen cloths, male and female, as well as of Flanders as of other lands, may safely come into our realm, there to make cloths," and he made them tax-exempt for five years.[16] In 1337 Edward III extended these benefits to Flemish cloth makers and even sent recruiters among them. Some entrepreneurs brought their entire firm, workers and all, to England. These people were not simply inclined to flee the civil disturbances that beset Flanders; they were drawn to England because of greater freedom, political stability, lower costs, finer raw materials, and superior technology—and, most of all, higher wages and profits.

Perhaps the most remarkable feature of the English wool industry was dispersion—the fact that English woolen firms were scattered throughout the rural countryside. This dispersion, which became a defining characteristic of many other English industries, occurred owing to both technological and political reasons.

The Thirteenth-Century Industrial Revolution

In 1941 Eleanora Carus-Wilson pointed out that from very early days the English woolen industry had migrated from urban locations to villages and rural areas. Why? Several factors were involved, but water-powered fulling mills played such an important role that Carus-Wilson entitled her famous paper "An Industrial Revolution of the Thirteenth Century."[17]

Fulling is a major step in producing good cloth. When cloth comes from the loom it is quite loose. The process of fulling involves submerging a cloth in water (usually containing a natural clay detergent called fuller's earth) and beating it vigorously. Proper fulling will shrink the cloth, making the fabric tighter and stronger, and make the surface smoother and softer.[18] Three traditional methods of fulling were used: a submerged cloth was beaten with the feet, with the hands, or with clubs. A wall painting in Pompeii shows a nearly naked fuller standing in a trough, stomping on a cloth. These traditional methods were still used in Flanders, Italy, and, for a time, England. But then, in the eleventh or twelfth century (historians disagree on the precise date), a new method was introduced: two wooden hammers were attached to a drum and turned by a crank to raise and drop on the cloth. The real breakthrough came when this device was hooked to a water mill (one probably constructed to grind grain). As a result, a single operator overseeing a series of hammers could perform the work that had previously required a crew of fullers—and he could do it much more quickly, too.[19]

This is why Carus-Wilson observed that the invention of the fulling mill "was as decisive an event [for the woolen industry] as were the mechanization of spinning and weaving in the eighteenth century."[20] Whether fulling mills developed in the eleventh or twelfth century, they were so common in the thirteenth century that they revolutionized the English industry, leaving the Continent far behind. Fulling gave English cloth a significant advantage on the international market. With many fewer fulling mills, cloth makers on the Continent could full only *some* of their cloths, which entailed a large sacrifice in quality.[21]

The ascendance of the fulling mill helps explain the English woolen industry's marked preference for villages and rural areas on good streams.[22] Such locations had several additional advantages. Moving water was useful for dyers, who needed to rinse excess dye from their cloths. Moreover, locating in rural areas permitted firms to escape repressive guild regulations, to pay lower taxes than those imposed by towns and cities, and to pay lower wages (the cost of living was lower in rural areas than in cities).[23]

Why didn't the woolen industry on the Continent similarly disperse to small towns and villages? Because in Europe only the cities provided enough freedom and property rights to sustain industry. In the European countryside rule by the nobility prevailed, and everyone had to fear the local lord's avarice. But in England, freedom and security prevailed throughout the realm, and medieval English industrialists did not need to huddle in crowded, expensive, disorderly, filthy cities—many devoid of water power—as their counterparts in Flanders, in Holland, along the Rhine, and in Italy were forced to do. As a result, the English woolen industry was remarkably decentralized.

Exploiting the advantages of the fulling mill was but the first step in England's mechanization of the textile industry. Soon after the fulling mill came the gig mill, for raising the pile on fabrics. Then came the knitting machine (1589), the flying shuttle (1733), the spinning jenny (1770), the spinning mule (1779), and the power loom (1785). When James Watt built the first practical steam engine in 1776, there all these inventions were, waiting to be hooked up. Technological innovation was the hallmark of English capitalism.

Finally, dispersion and relatively unfettered capitalism may have contributed to the international dominance of English woolens by producing more fashionable and attractive products. As A. R. Bridbury put it, to explain the success of English woolens, it is not enough to invoke better fleeces or lower prices; what should be stressed is "art and skill . . . the exotic dyeing of these cloths and . . . the subtle blending of design and colour in their creation . . . the search for making cloth which would be more fashionable internationally."[24] In European textile centers the guilds often exerted the dead hand of tradition on colors and designs, and originality nearly always suffers when creative people are crowded together and fully aware of one another's work. Greater variations in styles and quality turned up in England's dispersed woolen industry, where designers couldn't look over one another's shoulders. Moreover, capitalist managers were free to respond to market feedback by shifting production toward popular goods. In modern terminology, the English woolen industry was *market driven*.

Coal Power

The growth of the woolen industry marked the beginning of England's rise to international commercial prominence. The English became the world's first truly industrial nation by applying the lessons learned from woolens to other opportunities. The crucial next step came when England shifted to coal-powered industries, a development that illustrates the dynamic link between capitalism and technological innovation.

As had most civilizations since ancient times, England had long depended on wood power. Wood was an inferior fuel to coal, but unlike coal, it was relatively abundant, close at hand, and easy to transport. Wood and charcoal (created from wood) thus were used not only to heat buildings and to cook and bake but also for metallurgy and making bricks, glass, soap, salt, pottery, and much more. The low temperatures produced by wood fires imposed severe limits on the quality of these products. For example, most weapons and armor were made of bronze and brass because these were alloys of soft metals that melted at a relatively low temperature. It was well known that iron was superior for these purposes, but it required far higher temperatures.

As London's population swelled in the twelfth and thirteenth centuries, the price of firewood rose correspondingly. At Hampstead, about five miles from London, the price of firewood nearly doubled between the 1270s and the 1290s; in Surrey, about twenty miles from London, the price jumped about 50 percent between the 1280s and the 1330s.[25] As the price gap between coal and wood narrowed, more firms needing industrial heat switched to coal, importing it by water from Newcastle to London. The competitive price of coal in England partly reflected technical improvements in mining and transportation, but to a far greater extent the growing market for coal *prompted* the invention and adoption of such technology. In addition, just as water power caused the woolen industry to cluster near streams, the switch from wood to coal caused many industries to cluster near coal mines.[26]

Even in England, where high-quality coal was abundant, it soon proved necessary to follow seams well below ground. Boring rods were invented to locate seams. Underground mining necessitated removal of the water that often flooded mine shafts. The Romans had dealt with seepage by hand-bailing via bucket brigades. The English met the problem with a variety of pumps driven by water power or by horses turning a wheel. They powered ventilating fans the same way to force fresh air down mine shafts.[27] These techniques were used on the Continent too, and some probably originated there, but the English exploited them more extensively because their mines were managed on a far larger scale.

An additional problem facing mining industries involved how to transport heavy loads of coal or mineral ores. Toward the end of the reign of Elizabeth I, unknown inventers in southern Nottinghamshire found the solution by installing metal rails to support horse-drawn wagons— later known as trams or trolleys. Two techniques were used. One was like the modern railroad in that the wagon wheels were flanged so that they stayed on the track. The second was known as a "plateway" and involved a flange attached to the rails to guide the wagon wheels. The latter approach was the preferred method at first, because the wagon could proceed normally when it reached the end of the rail line, having no flange on its wheels. But the other method became popular because it cost much less to attach a flange to wagon wheels than to put one all along a track.

The great virtue of rails was to reduce friction so that much less power was needed to move a load. A wagon set in motion on a rail will roll about five times as far after the power is removed as will one set in motion on a paved highway.[28] Consequently, a horse could pull a far heavier load along rails than down a road. So, long before steam engines, England had an extensive system of rails in industrial areas. Little wonder that the locomotive was invented in England and that England led the world in the development of railroads. In truth, the extensive horse-drawn rail system virtually demanded perfection of the locomotive once Watt's stationary engine proved practical and reliable.

The transition to coal accelerated England's technological advances. Now able to work iron properly, both to smelt the ore and to produce molten iron, by the early sixteenth century the English were manufacturing the finest cannons in Europe. Cast from iron, these weapons had much greater range and dependability—and were far cheaper to produce—than the brass and bronze weapons cast on the Continent. Come the battle with the Spanish Armada, the English ships were outnumbered, but the Spanish were outgunned.

Capitalism was essential to England's industrialization. Mining coal—and keeping the mines well ventilated, dry, and served by rail systems—required substantial investments, sophisticated management, and a large, dependable labor force. So English firms got larger and more complex, a trend that was surprisingly little affected by plagues, wars, and political turmoil. Of course, English capitalism could develop as it did only because the English enjoyed unparalleled levels of freedom.

The Hanseatic League

As the English prospered and innovated, so did a group of German city-states ranged along the coast of the North Atlantic and the Baltic Sea. Surprisingly, it was the English who gave the merchants of these cities a clear sense of their common commercial interests, even giving them their name. *Hansa* was a term the English used to designate the right of merchants to form associations, and eventually it referred only to foreign merchants in London.[29] When the merchants from these German cities organized a formal manufacturing and trading bloc, they adopted their English designation and came to be known as the Hanseatic League.

The league was dominated by a few larger cities, primarily Lübeck, Hamburg, Rostock, Danzig, Bremen, Cologne, Antwerp, and Bruges, but most member towns had fewer than a thousand inhabitants.[30] Not that the larger cities were very large. Bruges was the largest of them, with about 60,000 residents in 1400. More typical were Danzig, with 8,500, and Hamburg, with 22,000. Or course, there were only about 50,000 Londoners at that time.[31]

Using the coastal waterway as well as the major rivers, the Hanseatic League prospered by trade along two axes: east-west and north-south. Furs and beeswax came from Russia and Finland; copper and iron from Sweden; dried codfish from Norway; cattle, butter, and huge amounts of salted herring from Denmark; grain, timber, and amber from Prussia and Poland; woolens, linens, candles, and salt from Flanders and western Germany. To give some sense of the volume of the Hanseatic trade, "One convoy of three ships sailed from Riga to Bruges with 450,000 pelts," according to historians Ronald Findlay and Kevin O'Rourke.[32] Most of the bow staves English archers used were imported from eastern Europe by Hansa merchants in London.[33] In addition, all the masts used by the large sailing ships—many of them at least a hundred feet tall—were imported from Sweden. The Hanseatic city-states also did a great deal of business with the Italian city-states—the latter exporting spices, silks, brocades, armor, and eyeglasses while importing fur, metal, and hardwood. This trade, too, was conducted by sea, the Italians continuing to use galleys long after the northerners had shifted to sailing ships.

As early as the thirteenth century, then, economic specialization had already developed in Europe, and the Hanseatic League was the primary mechanism making it possible. Flanders, for example, could devote nearly its entire economy to woolen and linen cloth, relying on its trading partners for food and drink.

Eventually the Hanseatic League was broken up by the rise of more powerful nation-states and wars among them. But the elaborate network of commercial trade continued to flourish.

Asian Enterprises

Despite the economic success of Flanders, England, and the Hansa merchants, the Italian city-states remained the dominant trade center of Europe. With Genoa, Florence, and Venice leading the way, they did a booming business with England and northern Europe and all around the Mediterranean, and by the late thirteenth century they had established regular trade relations all the way to China. The historian J. R. S. Phillips noted that in about 1340 "the Florentine merchant and banker Francesco Balducci di Pegolotti could write that the route from Tana on the Sea of Azov to Peking, via Turkestan and Mongolia, was safe by day and night, and could give detailed instructions on how to reach China, together with information on local currencies and customs duties."[34]

Perhaps because of centuries of humbug over the authenticity of Marco Polo's account of his travels, it has too often been overlooked that even if the Polo family were fictional, Italian merchants maintained a lucrative trade network all across Asia, and especially with China. In fact, the Polos did exist and they did travel to China, notwithstanding sensational recent claims that Marco got no farther east than Persia.[35] Sensible historians[36] are not misled by the many errors and omissions in *The Travels of Marco Polo* (1298) because, as was always known, Marco did not write the book—if published today the authorship would read, *by Marco Polo as told to Rustichello of Pisa*. Rustichello included a lot of nonsense because he set out to write a bestseller, and he succeeded despite the fact that all books had to be hand-copied. *The Travels* circulated all over Europe, in many translations. More than eighty copies made in the fourteenth and fifteenth centuries have survived, and there are extreme variations among them, some containing a substantial amount of fiction, and some very little.[37] Ironically, the earliest doubters of Polo's story questioned his account because he failed to report then-common fables about the East, such as people without heads, their faces on their chests.

In any event, the Italians carried on a lucrative trade with China. This was possible despite the fact that Chinese goods had to be transported most of the way by overland caravans and therefore had to be small and light. It is estimated that the annual import from Asia to Venice amounted to only one thousand to two thousand tons.[38] But these were extremely valuable tons, consisting of luxury goods such as silk and spices. For centuries, of course, the overland routes from China to the West had been known as the Silk Roads. Even though the Italians had developed their own silk industry early in the thirteenth century, silk was so much cheaper in China that it paid the Italian merchants to transport it all the way west. Even then, Chinese wages were far below those paid in the West, which reflected a lower standard of living. In return for silks and spices, China was an eager importer of Flemish linens.[39] In 1340 a Genoese merchant took several Frankish warhorses to China, where they were highly prized as "heavenly steeds," being so much larger and stronger than Chinese horses.[40]

Italian trade with China became far more perilous when Muslims conquered Armenia in 1337. A decade later the Black Death disrupted trading activities all across Europe and Asia. Finally, Italian trade with China became impossible in 1368 with the fall of the Mongol dynasty in China and the rise of the Ming dynasty, which held all foreigners in contempt.

Europe's Superior Technology

It should be noted that Marco Polo's reports of the glories of China were concerned with such things as the splendor and wealth of Kublai Khan's palaces, grand public works, and the fertility of Chinese fields and orchards. It was not an account of technological marvels.

And with good reason: the most remarkable technological progress in that era was occurring in Europe. From 1200 through 1500 European technology was rapidly improving in such critical areas as metallurgy, ships, and armaments. These improvements allowed the West to greatly increase its lead over the rest of the world.

The Blast Furnace

Perhaps the single most important technological breakthrough of medieval times was the blast furnace, which made it possible to cheaply produce large amounts of superior iron and, therefore, better cannons, better firearms, better plowshares, and better tools of all sorts. Blast furnaces are so-called because they introduce blasts of air into the furnace box to increase the heat of the coals, which results in superior iron. Like so many other inventions, blast furnaces are said to have been first developed in China, but once again, being first had little lasting importance. Recall from chapter 1 how the Chinese court destroyed the iron industry that had briefly flourished during the eleventh century. In any event, the first blast furnaces in Europe seem to have appeared in Sweden in about 1150,[41] and there is no evidence to suggest that the Vikings learned the technique from the Chinese. The technology of blast furnaces spread rapidly from Sweden all across Europe, eventuating in a major industrial complex in England.[42]

Carracks and Galleons

The Belgian historian Henri Pirenne famously proposed that during the tenth and eleventh centuries Europe regained the capacity to sail the Mediterranean after having been driven to land by Islam. He wrote that the "Mediterranean had been a Roman lake" until late in the seventh century, when it became "a Moslem lake."[43] Pirenne based his conclusion on trade statistics showing a decline in the import of papyrus, silks, and spices, which he interpreted as a withering of trans-Mediterranean trade. But Pirenne should have consulted the historical record of naval engagements, which shows that during the time in question, the Mediterranean was a Byzantine lake. Many times Muslim leaders assembled navies, only to have them utterly destroyed in encounters with the Byzantines.[44] And, as discussed in chapter 4, the decline in trade that concerned Pirenne reflected not naval capacities but rather a northward shift in trade routes and, as A. R. Bridbury observed, "the virtual extinction of European demand for" the items Pirenne focused on.[45]

Pirenne was correct, however, that by the tenth century the navies of various Italian city-states such as Venice and Genoa were routinely sinking any Muslim naval forces that challenged them.[46] Indeed, during the Crusades, not only could the Italians sail wherever they wished, but also ships from France, Normandy, England, and Denmark routinely hauled knights and supplies to the Holy Land.[47] The few times that Muslims attempted to challenge crusader fleets, they were quickly sunk.[48] Of course, the "ships" on both sides were mostly galleys and could not venture far beyond the Strait of Gibraltar without hugging the coast. Meanwhile, Europeans living along the Atlantic developed a far superior vessel.

Chapter 4 discussed the invention of the cog sometime in the tenth century, the first round ship propelled entirely by sails. The cog was a huge step beyond the galleys that had dominated European seagoing vessels since ancient times, being far larger and much more seaworthy. But early in the fifteenth century came an even more dramatic naval breakthrough—the three- or four-masted carrack. A typical three-masted carrack flew six sails and was sufficiently large to weather severe storms at sea—often displacing more than a thousand tons and having multiple decks. The carrack, like the Viking ships, was clinker-built: the planks forming the hull were overlapped and fastened to one another, and then internal braces were added to increase strength. Clinker-built ships were very strong and their hulls were somewhat flexible.

Carracks could be very large. Possibly the largest was the *Grace Dieu*, built for King Henry V of England in 1416 at Southampton (archaeologists found its wreck in 1933).[49] The *Grace Dieu* was 184 feet long, with a 50-foot beam and a forecastle that soared more than 50 feet above the water; her main mast was about 200 feet tall. With a deck load of large cannons, the carrack was a deadly warship, and its great holds made it ideal as a merchant cargo ship. Both Vasco da Gama and Columbus sailed in carracks, although two of the ships Columbus used on his first voyage were much smaller, being advanced versions of the cog known as caravels.

A century later came the galleon, a far more deadly fighting ship, the definitive model being built in the 1550s.[50] The great drawback of the carrack as a fighting ship was that its guns were limited to the main deck, because to cut more than two or three gunports in the clinker-built hull weakened the ship. To make lower gun decks possible, the galleon was caravel-built: frames were attached to the keel to create a basic skeleton of the ship, and then the hull planks were attached to this frame butted edge to edge, not overlapped, and caulked to be watertight. The galleon was also streamlined, with a lower superstructure to make the ship more stable in the water and much faster. The galleon's gun decks could pack a huge punch: forty-eight cannons were typical, in addition to the guns on the main deck.[51] The major fighting ships in the Spanish Armada (1588) were galleons, as were the leading English ships that stood them off. Although the carrack continued to be preferred as a cargo ship, galleons were used to form the annual Spanish treasure fleets as protection against pirates and English privateers.

Artillery and Firearms

There is a learned debate over whether gunpowder was brought to the West from China or invented independently in Europe.[52] The great Scholastic scholar Roger Bacon published a formula for gunpowder in a cryptogram in 1242 and then openly in his *Opus Tertium* (1267), and Albertus Magnus, Bacon's colleague at the University of Paris, included an effective recipe for gunpowder in a manuscript dated 1270. Whatever the origins of the West's knowledge of gunpowder, the Chinese had gunpowder at about the same time or slightly before it appeared in Europe. But they made very little use of it; they built some cannons but soon seemed content to use gunpowder for fireworks, which were used primarily to scare away evil spirits.

In contrast, a few years after gunpowder became known in the West, church-bell makers all across Europe were busy casting cannons. Soon armies were using the technology on the battlefield. King Ferdinand IV of Castile used cannons against the Moors at Gibraltar in about 1306. In 1314 artillery was reportedly used in Flanders, and cannons were certainly used in the Siege of Metz in 1324 and by the English against the Scots in 1327. Edward III used five or six cannons against the French in the Battle of Crécy in 1346, and they are said to have "struck terror in the French army . . . it being the first time they had seen such thundering machines."[53] By 1350 the great Italian scholar Petrarch described cannons as being "as common and familiar as other kinds of arms."[54]

The use of cannons only increased, especially as they became maneuverable. Early cannons were massive and lacked wheels; they were carted to the battlefield and unloaded where they were expected to be of the most use. But before the end of the fourteenth century smaller cannons mounted on wheeled carriages were widely in use in Europe: in 1377 the

Duke of Burgundy's forces included 140 cannons, all of which were on wheels.

As Europeans learned to cast smaller, stronger cannons, the range and accuracy of the weapons improved. Whereas the earliest cannons fired stone projectiles, iron cannonballs were soon adopted. Being of uniform size and shape, iron cannonballs were much more accurate. At the end of the first century of the cannon's existence, an anonymous chronicler wrote: "Hardly a man and bravery in matters of war are of use any longer. . . . The gruesome artillery pieces have taken over so much that fencing, fighting, hitting and armour, weapons, physical strength or courage are not of much use any more. Because it happens so often and frequently that a virile brave hero is killed by some forsaken knave with a gun."[55]

The "gun" referred to here was a cannon—individual firearms took a bit longer to develop. The first individual firearms appeared early in the fifteenth century but were so heavy that they had to be supported by a metal rod (or stand) resting on the ground. By the start of the sixteenth century, however, individual firearms had been greatly streamlined. Called arquebuses, they were first used by the Spanish in 1503 to route a much larger French army. Their use quickly spread even though the weapon was difficult and dangerous to use. The arquebus was fired by detonating its powder charge through a touchhole using a burning slow match; carrying a burning match while also carrying a large amount of gunpowder was too often a fatal combination. Arquebuses also had a massive recoil and took a long time to reload.

When muskets appeared in the late fifteenth and early sixteenth centuries, they were a significant improvement. They could be reloaded more quickly, and a slow match was no longer required: the musket was fired by a flintlock—when the trigger was pulled, a spring-loaded hammer was released that struck sparks from a piece of flint, thus igniting the powder change. Musketeers soon became the pride of European armies, often receiving double pay.[56] For a few years, pike men were placed within the lines of musketeers to protect them from cavalry charges. Then the bayonet was invented, allowing musketeers to withstand cavalry on their own.

Forces lacking either artillery or musketeers had no chance against the new gunpowder armies of Europe. Moreover, as European cannons improved, they made Europe's warships invincible. In 1509 eighteen Portuguese ships met a Muslim fleet of more than a hundred ships at the port of Diu on the coast of India. The Muslim fleet seemed in an impregnable position, being supported by land-based artillery. But the great Portuguese cannons outranged even the land-based artillery, and soon no Muslim ship was afloat.[57] As will be recounted in detail in chapter 13, this outcome was reenacted six decades later, at Lepanto in 1571, when a Spanish and Italian fleet destroyed the huge Ottoman fleet aiming to seize control of the Mediterranean.

The World Beckons

By this time Europeans were fully aware of the commercial opportunities available to enterprising travelers to the East. Indeed, as early as 1291, two Genoese brothers, Ugolino and Vadino Vivaldi, secured financial backing for a voyage to the Indies. They loaded two large galleys with supplies and sailed out the Strait of Gibraltar. Whether they planned to sail west across the Atlantic or south around Africa is unknown—they were never heard from again.[58] But the idea of such voyages was becoming increasingly popular, while the carrack made them seem far more feasible.

10

Discovering the World

One of the most significant steps toward modernism came with the dawning of the Age of Discovery. Europeans had long wanted a secure sea route to Asia, but now they had the ships and the navigational technology equal to the task.

The era of European voyages of exploration began early in the fifteenth century when the Portuguese ventured into the Atlantic. By 1433 they had discovered the Azores, colonized Madeira, and begun exploring the West African coast, slowly progressing southward until rounding the tip, whereupon Vasco da Gama sailed all the way to India in 1497. This was an extremely long voyage, but it produced immense wealth for the Portuguese, who gained complete control over the Indian Ocean and established colonial trading enclaves on the subcontinent.

Meanwhile, Columbus anticipated a short passage to the Indies by sailing west. To his dying day Columbus refused to admit that he had discovered a New World and that the Indies were many thousands of miles further on. Still unaware that Columbus had not reached the Indies, the Italian Giovanni Caboto—remembered as John Cabot—convinced merchants in England to fund a voyage, which in 1497 reached the shores of North America, probably Newfoundland or Labrador. Then, in 1500, Pedro Alvares Cabral claimed Brazil for Portugal. Soon thereafter, voyages to the New World became commonplace.

Europe's Knowledge of Geography

The Greeks knew the earth was round, as did the Scholastics. The existence of climate zones also was well known. But over the centuries there was considerable disagreement as to the earth's circumference and hence the distance from Europe's Atlantic coast to the Indies. The actual circumference of the earth is 24,902 miles. Plato guessed that the distance was about 40,000 miles and Archimedes estimated it to be about 34,000 miles. Marinus of Tyre, another Greek, set the distance at about 18,000 miles. His estimate became extremely influential because in the second century the great Greek astronomer and cartographer Ptolemy based his maps on that figure. Roger Bacon repeated Ptolemy's circumference figure, which misled Columbus into believing that his voyage to the Indies would need to cover only three or four thousand miles, instead of about fourteen thousand. It was not until the sixteenth century that the Flemish cartographer Gerardus Mercator published a map giving the proper distance around the equator.

Asian Vistas

If there were doubts about the route westward to the Indies, Europeans were fully aware of the existence of Africa and the basic geography of the Eurasian landmass. European merchants had traveled east over the Silk Roads to China since the days of the ancient Greeks, and Alexander the Great had marched victoriously as far as the Indus River in modern Pakistan. The fabulously rich Roman elite offered a nearly insatiable market for luxury goods from the East—"spices, pearls, perfumes, gums, ivory and precious stones," as one author put it.[1] Roman traders used both the Silk Roads and a sea route to reach India. The latter involved following the coast from the Egyptian shores of the Red Sea to northern India. Apparently, Roman merchants did not go beyond India, even though Chinese silk was one of their most valued imports: Pliny the Elder (23–79), who objected to the drain on Roman wealth, complained in his famous *Natural History* that "toil [had] to be multiplied; so have the ends of the earth to be traversed; and all that a Roman dame may exhibit her charms in transparent gauze."[2]

After the fall of Rome, the demand for Eastern luxury goods plummeted, as did trade with Asia. But by the time of the Carolingians a brisk commerce in silk and other Eastern products had resumed, mostly by land despite the impediment of Muslim settlements. Then, beginning in the thirteenth century, a series of Christian missionaries made the journey all the way to Mongolia and China and returned to write about their travels.

One of the first to go was Giovanni da Pian del Carpine, also known as Joannes de Plano (1182–1252), an original Franciscan and personal friend of St. Francis of Assisi.[3] At the age of sixty-five, Giovanni was chosen by Pope Innocent IV to lead a mission to the Great Khan in Mongolia. The group left Lyon on Easter Day 1245 and rode to the Mongol camp on the Volga River. From there it was directed to proceed to the court of the Khan in Mongolia, about three thousand miles farther east. Upon arrival, Giovanni obtained an audience with the Khan and presented him with a letter from the pope—which, among other things, invited the Khan to become a Christian. In response, the Khan gave Giovanni a letter for the pope demanding that Innocent and all the kings of Europe come and swear allegiance to him. After Giovanni's slow and dangerous journey home, the pope appointed his emissary archbishop of Antivari, a city on the Balkan Peninsula across the Adriatic from Bari, Italy. Giovanni's careful account of his trip, known as the *Tartar Relation*—at that time Europeans mistakenly identified the Mongols as Tartars—offers an excellent description of the Mongols' manners and customs and provides a fine assessment of Mongol military capacity and tactics, with suggestions of how to defeat them.

Next was William of Rubrouck (ca. 1215–ca. 1295).[4] In 1248 William, also a Franciscan, accompanied the French king Louis IX (later to become Saint Louis) on the Seventh Crusade. Then, in 1253, as directed by the king, Rubrouck set out with several companions to convert the Mongols. Their journey covered thousands of miles before they arrived at the Khan's court in Karakorum, Mongolia. The Khan received Rubrouck courteously but did not convert. During his stay, Rubrouck also encountered some Europeans, many of them Nestorian Christians. In July 1254 he began his journey back, taking a year to get home. Rubrouck was an acute observer and accurate reporter whose account of his journey was especially valuable as to geographical matters—for instance, that the Caspian was an inland sea rather than being an extension of the Arctic Ocean, as many in Europe had believed. An English translation of *The Journey of William of Rubruck to the Eastern Parts* was published in 1900.

John of Montecorvino (1247–1328), also a Franciscan missionary, was in China at about the same time as Marco Polo.[5] Unlike Polo or his Franciscan predecessors, Montecorvino went by boat from India and reached Peking in 1294. Upon his arrival he discovered that the great Kublai Khan had just died. But that did not deter Montecorvino: he was not a messenger to the Khan but was committed to a serious effort of conversion. He built a number of churches, bought many young Chinese boys from their parents and raised them as Christians, is credited with making about six thousand converts, and served as the first Bishop of Peking. He also translated the New Testament into Uyghur (a Mongol language). When Montecorvino died in Peking in 1328, the Christian mission seemed bound for considerable success—centers had been established in three additional Chinese cities. But then, in 1368, the Chinese drove the Mongols out of China and the obsessively isolationist Ming Dynasty expelled or killed Christians.

But it was too late to close the door. Europeans had a good working knowledge of the geography as well as the riches of Asia.

The Western Hemisphere?

Controversy continues as to what fifteenth-century Europeans might have known about the existence of the Western Hemisphere. The English merchants who funded John Cabot's voyage may have been aware that their local fishing fleet had been sailing to and from the Great Banks fishery off the coast of Newfoundland for many years. Of course, there is nothing to suggest that they thought this was anything more than a large island, like Iceland and Greenland. As for the latter two, the Danes surely knew of them, as did the Vatican—the pope had been appointing Bishops of Iceland since 1056, and in 1126 Greenland had become an official diocese. Even so, knowledge of these two islands offered no hint that beyond them lay two continents stretching nearly from pole to pole.

As for the Viking knowledge of Vinland, there is a fascinating dispute over the authenticity of the so-called Vinland map. Found in 1957 bound in a fifteenth-century copy of Giovanni's *Tartar Relation*, it is a map of the world that shows Iceland and Greenland and beyond them another substantial island identified as *Vinlanda Insula*. When Yale University published the map in 1965, along with an extensive set of studies affirming the map's authenticity, a swarm of angry academics pounced, denouncing it as a modern forgery. In early days the critics seemed to carry the day with various pieces of evidence including chemical analysis.

Since then, the supporters of the map's authenticity have rallied,[6] and there is no current consensus as to whether the map is genuine.

If the Vinland map is authentic, it is a charming historical artifact. But it is irrelevant to the larger historical picture in that it played no role in prompting voyages west. Even had Columbus seen it, he would not have taken Vinland for the Indies, let alone for a new continent—on the map it appears to be just another northern island.

Navigational Technology

Aside from the Vikings, until late in the fifteenth century sailors around the world had pretty much navigated by following coastlines or island hopping. This approach was sufficient for sailing the Mediterranean, which is densely packed with islands and has narrow north-south dimensions, putting most locations in sight of land.[7] But technological developments from the twelfth century onward made sailing across empty oceans possible.

The first major achievement was the magnetic compass.[8] Like so many other medieval inventions, the magnetic compass is generally attributed to the Chinese. The Chinese may have been the first to discover that a magnetized needle floating in liquid points north. But the Chinese found this phenomenon to be of interest primarily for performing magical rites; they may not have used this device aboard ships until long after Europeans were doing so. Moreover, there is no reason to believe that the knowledge that a floating magnetized needle points north reached Europe from China. The magnetic properties of naturally occurring lodestones were widely known in the ancient world—they were noted by the Greek philosopher Thales in the sixth century BC. In any event, a floating arrow pointing north is a far cry from a useful navigational instrument. The invention of the magnetic compass actually occurred when medieval Europeans added the compass card. That is, Europeans were the first to place a circular card directly beneath the magnetized compass needle, marked off into a thirty-two-point scale with north at zero. This not only allowed mariners to know which way was north but also enabled them to set an accurate course in *any* direction—expressed in points from north: "Helmsman, hold steady at 24 points." Such a course could be followed even in the dark and without any need for landmarks. The first recorded use of a compass in the West was in 1187, but it probably had been used for some time before then.

Next came the astrolabe, a device for determining one's latitude from the position of major heavenly bodies.[9] The basic theory on which the astrolabe was based was well known to the ancient Greeks, who used crude devices for locating one's latitude, though not at sea. The real breakthrough came in 1478, when a Spanish rabbi, Abraham Zacuto (1452–ca. 1514), combined a precise metal astrolabe with a set of astronomical tables showing the positions of the sun, the moon, and five planets at different dates. This combination allowed navigators to easily calculate their latitude with great accuracy. In addition to serving local Jewish congregations, Zacuto taught astronomy at the universities of Zaragoza and Cartagena.[10] When the Jews were expelled from Spain in 1492, Zacuto went to Portugal, where he was appointed Royal Astronomer.[11] Zacuto's astrolabe and tables were quickly adopted—Vasco da Gama used them on his first trip to India.[12]

Even with a compass and an astrolabe, to follow a course it was necessary to know one's speed. By the fifteenth century a ship's speed was calculated by throwing overboard a slab of wood attached to a bridle of three lines connected to a single line. The single line was knotted at regular intervals. With tension on the line, the slab of wood remained (roughly) in place in the water, so the length of line—the number of knots—let out over a timed period (usually measured by an hourglass) could be translated into the distance traveled in the time period, and hence the boat's speed. Eventually speed came to be expressed in terms of the number of knots per hour, which remains the nautical standard.[13]

Finally, given the ability to determine where a ship was and where it had been, navigators began to keep records to make a voyage easy to retrace. These records, which the French called "routiers" (the English corrupted the word to *rutters*), were simply a set of written directions for sailing from one particular place to another. For example, "Leaving this harbor, sail a course of [so many] points until reaching the [whatever] degree of latitude and then turn west and sail along this degree of latitude for three hundred nautical miles." Sailing instructions were eventually replaced with charts that depicted a particular area, accurately oriented as to compass headings and having an accurate distance scale.

It was now feasible to go exploring.

The Rise of Portugal

Portugal is said to have been founded in 1128, when Dom Afonso Henriques proclaimed himself Prince of Portugal after defeating forces led by his mother in the Battle of São Mamede. Subsequent Portuguese princes slowly drove the Moors from the southern areas, completing the reconquest by 1250 (Moors remained in southern Spain until 1492). Nevertheless, a fully independent Portugal was not achieved until 1385, when John of Avis defeated the Castilians and became King John I.

The new Kingdom of Portugal became a major maritime power and the leader in oceanic explorations. The first step was the conquest of Ceuta, a major Muslim port city in North Africa directly across from Gibraltar. In 1415 a Portuguese force led by King John I and his sons, including Prince Henry (soon to be known as Henry the Navigator), attacked Ceuta from the sea and by nightfall had routed the Muslim defenders. Despite several attempts to retake the city over the years, Muslims did not regain control of Ceuta until Morocco was granted independence from Spain in 1956. With Ceuta in hand, the Portuguese turned their attention westward to the Atlantic.

Henry the Navigator

A thrilling romantic tale once surrounded Prince Henry the Navigator (1394–1460). For centuries historians credited him as "a precocious genius and innovator" who established and directed an advanced school of navigation, nautical astronomy, and mapmaking somewhere along the barren cliffs of Sagres, near Cape St. Vincent.[14] There, it was said, a group of experts worked in secrecy to gather knowledge and direct expeditions of discovery. It was believed that these experts assembled a vast amount of information and developed a set of navigational techniques far ahead of anyone else but that it all was lost because of excessive secrecy at the time and later generations' negligent destruction of the records. It is true that various European authorities and investors often kept navigational knowledge and voyages secret. But, alas, the rest of the story about Prince Henry's school seems to have been made up by early biographers, each of whom kept adding to the legend.[15]

What Prince Henry did accomplish was to finance many voyages of exploration—his abundant funds coming from his being administrator of Ceuta and from his appointment by the pope as Governor of the Order of Christ, a rich Portuguese religious order that was an offshoot of the Knights Templar. In keeping with this position, although he did not take holy orders, Prince Henry is thought to have been a lifelong celibate and to have occasionally worn a hair shirt, as did many ascetics of that era.[16]

Exploring the "Atlantic Mediterranean"

The initial voyages Henry sent forth were short ones into the Atlantic. Portugal was ideally situated to explore the area that has been called the "Atlantic Mediterranean," which stretches from the coasts of Portugal and West Africa to the Azores and the Canaries.[17] As the historian Felipe Fernández-Armesto observed, the name derives from the fact that "the area was a 'middle sea' surrounded by mainlands and archipelagoes which constituted, for a while, the practical limits of navigation."[18]

Europeans had long had some awareness of Atlantic islands in this area. In the year 75 the Greek historian Plutarch claimed to have met a sailor just back from two Atlantic islands that probably were what are today known as Madeira and nearby Porto Santo.[19] The Canary Islands also were known in ancient times; the Romans visited them, and Ptolemy included them quite accurately on one of his second-century maps. More recent knowledge of these islands probably stemmed from a mapping expedition Portugal's King Afonso IV sent out in 1341. Reasonably placed representations of the Azores, Madeiras, and the Canaries appeared in the famous *Medici Atlas* published in 1351, probably in Genoa.[20] Whether or not he had knowledge of this atlas, Prince Henry surely knew of the results of the expedition his ancestor Afonso had sent out. Thus it is no surprise that he was determined to claim these nearby islands.

First up were the Madeiras. A voyage sent by Prince Henry reached them in 1419, and settlers landed there in 1420. The settlers included members of the minor nobility as well as some convicts to serve as field workers. From the start, Madeira was a profitable venture, exporting a substantial amount of wheat to Portugal. Then came a bonanza based on raising sugarcane. By 1480 the Dutch had devoted more than seventy ships to transporting raw sugar from Madeira to Antwerp, where it was refined and distributed. Within ten years Madeira had become the major producer of Europe's sugar.[21]

In 1427 the Portuguese captain Diogo de Silves reached the Azores. It is not known whether he was sent there or encountered them by accident. But in 1431 or 1432 Prince Henry had cattle and sheep placed on the Azores to resupply ships voyaging in the area, and in 1439 Portuguese settlers were landed. These were mainly convicts and other undesirables, since volunteers could not be found.[22] Eventually the Azores proved especially valuable as a rest stop for ships returning from the Americas.

Finally, in the 1450s Portuguese explorers discovered the Cape Verde Islands, an archipelago lying nearly six hundred miles off the coast of Africa and much farther south than the Azores and Madeiras. Despite the name, the islands were not very green, nor were they very fertile. But this location proved of considerable use for the newly resurrected slave trade (see chapter 11).

Although they tried several times, the Portuguese were never able to annex the Canary Islands, which remained in the control of their natives until the Spanish finally overcame their resistance in 1495. Whereas the Azores, Madeiras, and Cape Verdes were uninhabited, the Canaries were inhabited by a Neolithic culture of white, blue-eyed people, many of them having blond hair, who may have shared a common origin with the Berbers of North Africa. These natives grew wheat and raised goats, sheep, and pigs. No one knows when they arrived. The Spanish attempted to enslave them, but the pope prohibited those efforts.[23] Eventually these indigenous peoples were assimilated. The Canaries became a major stopover for Spanish fleets crossing the Atlantic.

The long-term value of the islands of the "Atlantic Mediterranean" was substantial, but in the short term the passage around Africa was far more lucrative.

Down the Coast of Africa

The most surprising feature of the *Medici Atlas* was its depiction of Africa. A century before the Portuguese began their slow and careful probes down the African West Coast, the Medici map showed the sharp eastward bend of the Gulf of Guinea. It also showed that the Atlantic and Indian Oceans joined below the tip of the continent and therefore that it would be possible to sail around Africa and on to India. Historians now regard all this as a lucky guess, but one can't help but wonder about unknown voyages. Whatever the case, Prince Henry seems to have been certain that Africa could be sailed around, based on his belief in legends concerning Prester John and on the Bible's implication that all the great oceans are connected. But Henry did not send out ships to trace this supposed route; he only sent his captains on a series of small incremental voyages along the coast.

Initially, neither Portuguese nor Castilian voyagers sailed south of Morocco's Cape Juby because of treacherous currents that could smash a ship against the shore. Moreover, the coastline from the Strait of Gibraltar down to the Senegal River was forbidding, being largely a rocky desert inhabited only by small bands of nomads. As the historian Ronald Fritze noted, before 1433 Prince Henry sent fifteen different ventures to round Cape Juby, but each time his captains lost their nerve and turned back.[24] Finally, in 1434 Gil Eannes, a member of the prince's household, made it around Cape Juby safely by staying farther out to sea, and he returned to tell about it.[25] Asked by Prince Henry to repeat his feat, Eannes did so. Exploration down the African coast was now on. But it went very slowly, more attention being given to initiating a slave trade than to explorations, although Diogo Gomes did explore the Gambia River in 1457. Explorations were further delayed by the disastrous Portuguese attempt to conquer Morocco in 1458–59.

The last voyage Prince Henry commissioned left early in 1460 and sailed at least five hundred miles south of the Gambia River, charting the coast. Henry died before it returned, but the prince's dream of sailing around Africa to India did not die with him. A major next step was taken in 1488, when Bartolomeu Dias sailed around the Cape of Good Hope and several hundred miles up the East Coast of Africa.

To India

The same year Prince Henry died,[26] Vasco da Gama was born in a small seaport on the southwest coast of Portugal.

Little is known of da Gama's early life or education, although he was well versed in astronomy and might have been a student of the rabbi-astronomer Abraham Zacuto.[27] In 1492 King John of Portugal placed da Gama in command of a force that seized all the merchandise aboard French ships in Portuguese harbors in retaliation for the French seizure of a Portuguese ship loaded with gold. Da Gama did this so well that the king of France quickly returned the Portuguese ship and all its gold cargo. Da Gama may have been entrusted with other missions by the king, possibly some of them secret. What is known is that in 1497 da Gama was selected to lead a long-planned expedition around Africa to India.

On July 8, 1497, da Gama sailed with a fleet of four ships and a total crew of 170 men. Two of the ships were large carracks (see chapter 9), the *São Gabriel* and the *São Rafael*, each being 89 feet long and displacing about 170 tons. A third was a slightly smaller caravel, *Berrio*, and the fourth was a supply boat, name unknown, and lost at sea. Both carracks had large deck cannons—perhaps ten on each ship, making them very powerful fighting ships for their time. This made it possible for da Gama to loot Arab merchant ships encountered along the East Coast of Africa, this being a Muslim-controlled area. Da Gama regarded all Muslims as the enemy because the Portuguese were still at war with Muslims in North Africa and on the Mediterranean.[28]

After nearly a year at sea, on May 20, 1498, da Gama landed near Calicut, India. He was not well received by the king. Although a Hindu, the king was influenced by Muslim merchants, who may have regarded da Gama as a rival (little did they know!). Still, Da Gama had gained valuable cargo by plundering Muslim ships along the way: when he sailed for home on August 29, his cargo was worth sixty times the cost of the expedition, including the construction of his ships.

Da Gama's return voyage was far more difficult than the trip out. Because of prevailing westerly winds, his trip from Malindi on the African coast to India had taken only 23 days. It took 132 days in the other direction. In the end, only 60 of da Gama's original crew of 170 lived to return to Portugal.

Upon his homecoming in September 1499, da Gama received both wealth and honors—the king gave him the title Admiral of the Indian Seas. He made a second voyage in 1502 with a fleet of eighteen ships and more than eight hundred men. This allowed him to overawe the Indian king and establish a fort and trade center at Cochin, south of Calicut.

After da Gama's second voyage, new Portuguese fleets were sent to India. They quickly took command of the Indian Ocean, and hence of trade with India, by sinking several Muslim fleets and defeating attempts to drive them from Cochin.[29] In 1510 Portuguese forces seized the kingdom of Goa, well to the north of Calicut, and they held it as a trade center and colony until ousted by the Indian army in 1961.

In 1524 Vasco da Gama was named Viceroy of India and made his third voyage, landing in Goa and then sailing to Cochin. There, on Christmas Eve 1524, he died of malaria and was buried in St. Francis Church. In 1539 his body was returned to Portugal and reburied in a coffin decorated with gold and jewels.

Columbus Sails

While the Portuguese explored Africa and India, amazing things were happening on the Atlantic.

In 1485 Cristóbal Colón (as Christopher Columbus was known and as he signed his name) asked King John II of Portugal to finance his plan to sail west to the Indies. Supported by his advisers, the king turned him down. The Portuguese did so not because they thought the world was flat (as all the textbooks used to claim)[30] but because they correctly believed that Columbus was badly underestimating the circumference of the globe. They believed the voyage would be impossible without stops to resupply.

Despite misjudging the distance, Columbus had done a great deal of research in preparation for a voyage west. Having taught himself Latin, he read many great works on astronomy and geography, including Ptolemy's *Almagest* and Cardinal Pierre d'Ailly's *Image of the World*. We know this because, as the historian Samuel Eliot Morison wrote, "fortunately we have his own copies of these works, amply underlined, and their margins filled with his [commentaries]."[31] Columbus had also gained invaluable knowledge by voyaging down the West Coast of Africa with Portuguese traders. In 1476 he sailed with a Genoese convoy that visited Bristol, England; Galway, Ireland; and possibly Iceland. Somewhere along the line he seems to have learned about the trade winds—the somewhat circular prevailing wind system over the Atlantic. On his first voyage to America he sailed along southern latitudes, where winds blowing from the east propelled him in five weeks from the Canaries to the Bahamas. For his return voyage, instead of clawing his way back against these easterlies, he sailed up to northern latitudes and was propelled home by prevailing winds from the west, which, as they approach Europe, bend south toward Portugal and Spain.

Having been rejected by the Portuguese, Columbus unsuccessfully approached both Genoa and Venice. Then, in May 1486, he presented his plan for sailing to "the land of spices" to Queen Isabella of Castile. She referred it to a group of experts, who, like those in Portugal, recommended against funding on grounds that Columbus was badly underestimating the distance involved. Eventually, Columbus had his brother Bartolomé present his plan to Henry VII of England. After long hesitation, Henry expressed his willingness, but by then Columbus had received a commitment from the new kingdom of Spain, created by the marriage of

Isabella of Castile and Ferdinand of Aragon, who had together driven the last Moors from the peninsula.

It had taken two years of negotiations and the commitment of some private Italian investors to foot half the costs to gain the approval of the Spanish monarchs. The terms under which Columbus launched his voyage were very generous—according to his son, that was because the king and queen didn't really expect him to return.

So, finally, on August 3, 1492, Columbus sailed west in three ships. The largest was the carrack *Santa María*, which was about 85 feet long. Second largest was the caravel *Pinta*, about 69 feet, and the third was the caravel *Niña*, about 55 feet.[32] Columbus's crew amounted to ninety men and boys. He sailed first to the Canaries, where he stocked up on provisions and made some minor repairs. Then, on September 6, he headed west. Five weeks later, a lookout on the *Pinta* spotted land. Columbus had reached the Bahamas. It is unknown on which of these islands he first landed. Because he was convinced that he had reached the Indies, he identified the inhabitants—"they go naked as when their mothers bore them," Columbus recorded[33]—as "Indians." As do most historians, I shall use that term to identify members of the indigenous population of the New World.

Next, Columbus explored the coast of Cuba and then the north coast of Hispaniola ("New Spain," now Haiti and the Dominican Republic). Here, too, the inhabitants went naked. Columbus also was surprised that the Indians he encountered lacked metal weapons, and anything else made of metal except for golden trinkets. He wrote in his journal: "A thousand would not stand before three of our men. . . . I believe that with the force I have with me I could subjugate the whole island, which I believe to be larger than Portugal, and the population double."[34]

The *Santa María* ran aground off the coast of Hispaniola and had to be abandoned. With an unneeded crew, Columbus reached an agreement with the local chief and left behind thirty-nine men to form a settlement he named La Navidad (Christmas—the day the ship ran aground). After kidnapping about a dozen natives, Columbus headed back for Spain. Seven or eight of the captured Indians survived the voyage and became a local sensation—they were baptized and then accompanied Columbus back on his second voyage.

On October 12, 1493, Columbus sailed again, this time with seventeen ships and 1,200 men, including crew members, some soldiers (including a cavalry troop of twenty lancers), and a large company of colonists. His fleet soon arrived in what we now know as the Lesser Antilles. After touching shore at Dominica, Columbus turned northwest to Guadeloupe, where he made a shocking discovery. As Samuel Eliot Morison described it, "In the course of their wanderings, the searching Spaniards learned a good deal about the manners and customs of the Caribs, the tribe from which the word 'cannibal' is derived [as is the word *Caribbean*]. In huts deserted by the natives they found human limbs and cuts of human flesh partly consumed, as well as emasculated boys who were being fattened to provide the main dish for a feast."[35]

In these politically correct times, many deny that the Caribs (or any other native people) were cannibals, claiming that Columbus and his companions made it all up.[36] I will refute this nonsense in detail at the end of the chapter 11. Here it is sufficient to note that the Caribs themselves were colonialists, having invaded the islands from the Orinoco River area of South America in the thirteenth century; they dined not on one another but on the less ferocious tribes over whom they ruled.

Columbus and his men sailed to St. Croix, where they had a brief skirmish with Caribs, and then on to Hispaniola. There Columbus discovered the fate of his colony, La Navidad. After he had left, the Spaniards at La Navidad became a marauding gang roaming the island in search of gold and women. The local natives (not Caribs) soon had had enough and ambushed Columbus's men, killing them all—these Spanish colonists were sailors, not soldiers. Since what little building had been done at La Navidad lay in ruins, Columbus founded a new settlement a few miles away, naming it Isabela (with only one *l* even though the queen's name had two). Soon after that, he returned to Spain.

Columbus made two more voyages to the New World, steadfastly denying, of course, that it was other than the Indies. The last voyage was a disaster. Columbus and his men were shipwrecked and marooned on Jamaica for nearly a year—the new Spanish governor of Hispaniola hated Columbus and refused to come to his aid. Help eventually arrived and Columbus was able to return to Spain. There he died on May 20, 1506. By then Spanish fleets were making regular voyages to the Caribbean. Little more than a decade later, Hernán Cortés invaded Mexico. Colonization of the New World was well under way.

It is worth noting that the Columbus story illustrates the importance of political disunity for European progress. Had all of Europe been ruled by an emperor, one rejection would have meant that Columbus would never have sailed west[37]—just as the Emperor of China beached Zheng He's fleet and halted all further voyaging only fifty years before Columbus set sail (as seen in chapter 2). Instead, Columbus was able to make his case to several courts, and competition among them seems to have influenced Queen Isabella to change her mind. Clearly, too, competition continued to play a major role in sustaining Europe's Atlantic explorations.

Cabot's "Rediscovery"

Giovanni Caboto (1450–1499) was an Italian with a checkered past, whose voyages were of little significance until they were used as the basis for English claims to North America. A native of Venice, he probably engaged in maritime trade with the Muslims and also seems to have been involved in construction. He fled Venice in 1488 as a debtor and settled in Valencia, where he appears to have bid on a project to improve the harbor. From there he went to Seville and began a construction project involving a stone bridge, but it was canceled. It was then that Caboto began seeking support for an Atlantic voyage. Refused funding, he went to England in 1495.

It is uncertain whether John Cabot, as he now was known, based his plans on Columbus's voyages or had arrived at them independently before Columbus sailed. In any event, he found King Henry VII, who had too late offered to back Columbus, willing to listen to his scheme to sail a more northern (and therefore shorter) route to the Indies. But the king gave him only a letter of patent. Financial support came from merchants in Bristol. In 1496 Cabot set sail in one small ship but, it is believed, soon turned back. The next year he sailed again with one ship and a crew of about eighteen. Almost nothing is known of the voyage except that Cabot seems to have reached the New World somewhere around Newfoundland—in effect rediscovering the Viking Vinland. Cabot went ashore once, going inland only about two hundred yards. He seems to have followed the coast south for a few hundred miles before turning back to England. Going to see the king, Cabot was awarded £10 and a lifetime pension of £20 per year.[38]

In 1498 Cabot finally had enough backing for a substantial effort and set forth with five ships. The fate of this fleet is in doubt. Many believe it simply disappeared, probably sunk in a storm. We do know that in that year, payment of Cabot's pension ceased, suggesting official acknowledgment of his having been lost at sea.[39] But a few historians have accepted claims made by the late Alwyn Ruddock of the University of London, who said she had found several obscure documents suggesting that Cabot returned to England in 1500 after two years of explorations down the North American coast that went as far south as the Caribbean. For many years Ruddock was believed to be working on a book based on her discovery, but she died in 2005 with it still unpublished, leaving instructions that all her files be destroyed.[40] Even if Ruddock's claims were valid, Cabot's voyages mattered little except as evidence that once launched, voyages to the New World rapidly escalated.

America

As the sixteenth century began, Europeans continued to believe that the voyages to the West had reached the Indies, even if they had not yet found a mainland resembling China. Then came voyages by the superb navigator and cartographer Amerigo Vespucci. During two (or possibly four) voyages from about 1499 through, perhaps, 1504, Vespucci sailed so far down the coast of South America that he realized this was no group of islands off the coast of China but a huge new continent. After his last voyage, King Ferdinand appointed Vespucci as chief navigator of Spain, responsible for authorizing and planning voyages to the New World. Vespucci also publicized his conclusions about a new continent and sketches of the coast he had sailed along, which led the great mapmaker Martin Waldseemüller to name this new continent America on the world map he published in 1507. Had Columbus hit either of the continents rather than arriving in the Caribbean, and had he been willing to draw the proper conclusion, the New World might have been named Columbia.

Hinge Point

The three decades from 1490 through 1520 changed the world. In 1490 no one knew there were two huge continents located only about 3,500 miles west of Europe. By the end of 1520, Ferdinand Magellan's expedition, financed by Charles V of Spain, had reached the Pacific on its voyage around the globe.

The Age of Discovery ushered in conquest and colonization—and the dawn of modernity.

Part IV

The Dawn of Modernity
(1500–1750)

11

New World Conquests and Colonies

The Age of Discovery involved much more for Europeans than reaching India and finding the New World. Of equally great importance was their discovery of the extraordinary military superiority they held over the rest of the world. A few Portuguese ships repeatedly sank huge Muslim fleets in the Indian Ocean, and the Portuguese needed only small forces to overawe Eastern rulers. And in the New World, tiny bands of Spanish conquistadors prevailed against incredible odds. It was surely to be expected that Europeans would use their advantages over other societies to exploit them, especially given the enormous riches involved.

Initially the Spanish were the major colonial presence in the New World (with the Portuguese controlling Brazil), but other Europeans soon took up New World colonizing as well—the French, English, and Dutch.

Nearly at once, New World colonialism resulted in the resumption of slavery by Europeans. Before it ended, millions of enslaved Africans were transported across the Atlantic, huge numbers of them dying during the voyage. This did not, however, introduce slavery into the Western Hemisphere: in pre-Columbian times indigenous societies widely practiced slavery, from the Incas in the south to the Indians of the Pacific Northwest.

Of course, Western colonialism had other dreadful consequences: scores of native cultures were smashed and millions of people perished, mostly from diseases to which they lacked immunity. This story is sad enough without the immense amount of misrepresentation, exaggeration, and plain foolishness that has been added during the past century.

The Spanish Conquests

The first successful European colony in the New World was Columbus's La Isabela on Hispaniola, which was quickly inhabited by 1,300 men. Soon the Spanish settlers at La Isabela were joined by African slaves—in 1574 a census of Hispaniola's nonindigenous population revealed 1,000 Spaniards and 12,000 African slaves.[1] This was typical of the extractive Spanish model of colonization—small numbers of Spaniards (mostly soldiers and administrators) ruling large numbers of indigenous people and slaves, with the primary aim of sending valuable exports (including as much gold and silver as possible) to Spain. This model of Spanish colonialism is discussed at length in chapter 12.

Of course, only a small amount of the wealth Spain extracted from the New World came from the Caribbean. Most of it came from Spain's continental conquests—especially Mexico and Peru.

Cortés and the Conquest of Mexico

In 1519 Hernán Cortés invaded Mexico with six hundred men, fifteen of them mounted. Opposing him were tens of thousands of well-disciplined and organized Aztec warriors. Against these odds, how did the Spanish prevail? Two factors were involved.

The first was vastly superior military technology and training. Man for man the Spanish conquistadors were the class of Europe in this era. While all European armies had adopted cannons, the Spanish had eagerly adopted firearms sooner than anyone else. As early as 1503 Spanish infantry armed with arquebuses overwhelmed a French army that outnumbered them by four to one but was without individual firearms. The same result was obtained against the Swiss in 1522.[2] Little wonder that, as the scholar Keith Windschuttle observed, the conquistadors "found Aztec weapons [made of wood and stone] so inconsequential that they abandoned their own heavy metal armour in favor of quilted cotton."[3] And, just as the French and Swiss troops had been in Europe, the Aztecs were mowed down by the hundreds by volleys the Spanish arquebusiers fired from upward of a hundred yards.[4] In addition, the conquistadors had brought fifteen cannons with them to Mexico, and these "shredded wave after wave" of Aztecs, according to Victor Davis Hanson.[5]

But were it not for a second factor, the Aztecs enjoyed such a numerical advantage that they might have, quite literally, stomped the Spanish to death. Cortés responded by enlisting several thousand warriors from local tribes.[6] He was able to recruit local allies because the Aztecs were brutal tyrants who every year sacrificed tens of thousands of men, women, and children seized from subordinated tribes. When the Spaniards arrived in Mexico they were astounded by the immense ritual slaughters taking place. Bernal Díaz del Castillo, who accompanied Cortés, wrote that "in the plaza [of Mexico City] where their oratories stood, there were piles of skulls so regularly arranged that one could count them, and I estimated them at more than one hundred thousand. I repeat again that there were more than one hundred thousand of them. . . . We had occasions to see many such things later on . . . for the same custom was observed in all the towns."[7] These monumental piles of skulls represented the huge numbers put to death each year atop the Aztec temples.

For most of the twentieth century it was claimed, especially in textbooks, that tales like that of Díaz were falsehoods, told to justify Spanish imperialism. But these Spanish reports are verified by Aztec frescoes, by their sacred texts, and, most of all, by archaeology. Indeed, Harvard's David Carrasco was moved to write a remarkable book on human sacrifice among the Aztecs after viewing a ritual receptacle where the "skeletal remains of forty-two children lay as a messy remnant of a fifteenth-century, precious offering to the rain gods."[8] The victims were all around five years old and had been sacrificed, probably by having their throats cut. Carrasco noted that human sacrifices were conducted in more than eighty different places in the Aztec capital and in hundreds of other ceremonial centers. Every year there were eighteen major ceremonies that required extensive human sacrifices.

Although most victims were men, Carrasco reported that "women and children were also sacrificed in over a third of" the ceremonies, which were "ritually choreographed" and performed before large crowds.[9] An adult male victim usually was held down on a sacrificial stone atop a pyramid, his chest was slashed open, and the priest snatched his still-beating heart and held it aloft to the sun. The head of the victim was usually severed and placed on a rack—soon to be a skull added to the ceremonial collection. Then "the body, now called 'eagle man,' was rolled, flailing down the temple steps to the bottom where it was skinned and dismembered."[10] The choice cuts were distributed to the onlookers, who took them home and ate them. When females were sacrificed they sometimes had their living hearts ripped out, too, but more often their necks were stretched back over the edge of the stone and then they were slowly beheaded, after which their hearts were extracted. At that point the priest often skinned the victim and wore her skin as the slaughter continued.[11]

How many victims were consumed by these ceremonies? In 1487, well before any contact with Europeans, the Aztecs inaugurated their great new Templo Mayor. The day began with four lines of victims, each line stretching for two miles. The historian and anthropologist Inga Clendinnen has estimated the total number sacrificed on that occasion as twenty thousand, although others have placed the number as high as eighty thousand.[12] This was, of course, a onetime occasion. During regular festivals, the numbers killed at a particular temple probably ran around two thousand a day,[13] and there were hundreds of these sacrificial sites. Hence, piles of skulls numbering into tens of thousands were widespread, just as Díaz reported.

Little wonder, then, that Cortés could enlist warriors from tribes eager to overthrow the Aztec Empire. Granted, the Spanish Empire that replaced the Aztecs had many unpleasant aspects. But at least the days of human sacrifice and cannibalism were over.

Pizarro Seizes Peru

Cortés's victory over the Aztecs pales in comparison with that of his second cousin Francisco Pizarro's defeat of the Incas.[14] With 167 conquistadors, only about 8 of them having arquebuses, and four very small cannons, Pizarro marched on the huge Incan Empire, which stretched for 2,500 miles along the West Coast of South America. There, faced with about 80,000 battle-hardened Incan warriors, Pizarro triumphed without losing a single man.

Prior to his victory, Pizarro had led two expeditions to Peru. The first started from Panama in 1524, consisting of 80 men and 40 horses. It sailed as far as present-day Colombia and then turned back after a skirmish with hostile natives. The second expedition set out in 1526 with two ships, 160 men, and a few horses. Pizarro's forces reached Peru and went ashore at Tumbez, a small Incan coastal city, where they were amazed at the fine buildings, the friendliness of the people, and the amount of gold and silver on display. Then, taking aboard several llamas, some fine cotton and alpaca fabrics, and two boys (whom Pizarro taught Spanish and then used as interpreters), he sailed back to Panama.

The new governor of Panama refused to allow Pizarro to mount another expedition, whereupon Pizarro returned to Spain and appealed to the king. The king authorized a third attempt on the condition that Pizarro raise a force of at least 250 men. Unable to obtain this total, Pizarro sailed clandestinely with only 180 men—106 foot soldiers and 62 cavalry. Back in Panama, he assembled his invasion forces and in 1532 headed to the coast of Peru.

Landing again at Tumbez, the Spanish were shocked to find the city in ruins. A civil war had erupted in which two royal heirs contested for the throne. Shortly before Pizarro's arrival, Atahualpa had defeated his brother Huáscar and now was the emperor. He possessed a huge, battle-tested army.

Informed of Pizarro's arrival on his coast, Atahualpa lured the Spanish deep into his mountain empire until they had entered Cajamarca. The city was largely deserted, but beyond Cajamarca, along a line of hills, Atahualpa had assembled his host—outnumbering the Spanish about four hundred to one. Pizarro held his nerve and sent an envoy to invite Atahualpa to meet him in Cajamarca the next day. The emperor accepted.

The Spanish were betting their lives on being able to take Atahualpa prisoner. Atahualpa had plans of his own, according to Kim MacQuarrie in *The Last Days of the Incas*: "to capture and kill the Spaniards, to make eunuchs out of the survivors, and to breed powerful and majestic animals" from the Spaniard's warhorses. Although these were the only horses the Incas had ever seen, they immediately grasped their value.[15]

The meeting with the Incas was to take place in the town's plaza, which was a square of about six hundred feet per side and surrounded on three sides by low stone buildings. In preparation, the Spanish concealed their four small cannons inside several buildings, where they would have unobstructed fields of fire across the plaza. They also found good firing positions for the arquebusiers. Pizarro hid his cavalry and infantry inside the buildings as well. It would be left to the Dominican friar Vincente de Valverde to meet Atahualpa.

At the appointed hour Atahualpa entered the plaza, borne on a huge litter carried by eighty of his senior chiefs and accompanied by thousands of warriors, who packed the plaza.[16] He was surprised that no Spaniards were in sight but relaxed a bit when Valverde came forward to meet him. Suddenly, at Pizarro's signal, the cannons and the arquebusiers fired; the doors were flung open and both the cavalry and the infantry charged, slaughtering Incas with their razor-sharp cutlasses. Far exceeding their own expectations, the Spanish quickly reached Atahualpa's litter and slaughtered the bearers; Pizarro himself dragged the Incan emperor into one of the buildings. The carnage continued in the plaza until the last living Incan warrior had managed to flee the city, leaving behind as many as seven thousand dead (many had been trampled to death by their comrades).[17] No Spaniard was even wounded.[18] And with the emperor now held hostage, the huge Incan army up on the hills was powerless to act.

Pizarro set Atahualpa's ransom at a room full of gold. It was soon paid. But fearing to let him go, the Spanish—against Pizarro's wishes—executed Atahualpa and installed his brother Túpac Huallpa as a puppet ruler. When Túpac died suddenly, another brother, Manco Inca, took the throne and allied himself with the Spanish. Meanwhile, the Spanish under Pizarro and Hernando de Soto (who later explored what is now the American Southwest) managed to conquer the Incan capital of Cuzco with the support of some tribes seeking to overthrow Incan rule. At this point many tribes joined the Spaniards, helping defeat a number of Incan rebellions.

Thus, forty years after Columbus's first voyage, Spain had conquered the two mighty New World empires, precipitating what seemed to be an inexhaustible flow of gold and silver.

The Latecomers

The Spanish and Portuguese not only established New World colonies well before any other European nation; the Spanish also claimed by far the richest areas. The latecomers could settle a few Caribbean islands, but mostly they had to be content with the "leftover" Northern Hemisphere.

The French

Amazingly, Italy played no role in the exploration of the New World despite the fact that Italians dominated the ranks of the initial voyagers. The first of the "Spanish" explorers was the Genoan Cristóbal Colón. The first "English" explorer was the Venetian Giovanni Caboto. And the first "French" explorer was the Florentine Giovanni da Verrazzano.

Although neglected by Western historians until the 1950s, Verrazzano sailed west with the backing of King Francis I of France in 1524 and explored the Atlantic Coast from Newfoundland to the Carolinas, entering both New York Harbor and Narragansett Bay. On a second voyage, in 1527, Verrazzano went south and explored the coast of Brazil, returning with a cargo of brazilwood, a fine hardwood. In 1528 he made a third voyage, exploring Florida and the Bahamas before going ashore on Guadeloupe. There he was set upon and eaten on the beach by Caribs while his horrified companions looked on from their ship, too far from shore to intervene.[19]

Six years after Verrazzano's death, Jacques Cartier sailed the northern route across the Atlantic and claimed an area in Canada for France, although he was under the misapprehension that he had reached Asia.[20] In 1535 Cartier sailed west again, with three ships and 110 men. This time he sailed down the St. Lawrence River. He stopped at the site of what is now Montreal, prevented from going on because of a waterfall in the river. Cartier was convinced that beyond the waterfall lay the "northern passage" that would lead to the Orient. On a third voyage, in 1541, he founded a colony on the present site of Quebec and sent a ship loaded with what he thought were diamonds and gold back to France. The diamonds turned out to be quartz crystals, the gold to be iron pyrite (or fool's gold, as it came to be known), and the colony failed. What did survive was Cartier's designation of the area as Canada, based on the Indian word *kanata* (meaning "village").

Next up was Samuel de Champlain.[21] In 1608 he sailed with a group of settlers to reestablish the colony at Quebec. By this time, "Canada" was being referred to as "New France." The settlement was a success, the fur trade boomed, and chronic wars began with the Iroquois Indians, the Huron Indians siding with the French. Champlain died and was buried in Quebec, which remains a French-speaking city even though the English seized Canada in 1759.

Robert de La Salle greatly expanded French territorial claims in the New World by canoeing down the Mississippi River to New Orleans in 1682 and naming the huge area drained by the Mississippi and north to Canada as Louisiana, in honor of Louis XIV of France. In 1763 Louisiana was ceded to Spain as part of the treaty ending the Seven

Years' War. In 1765 several thousand French refugees from Nova Scotia (driven out by the English) settled in southern Louisiana—today they are known as Cajuns. In 1800 Napoleon Bonaparte reacquired Louisiana for France following a victory over Spain. In 1803 Napoleon sold the whole region—totaling 828,000 square miles—to the United States for $15 million.

The English

In 1576, eighty years after Cabot had sailed west from England, Martin Frobisher reached Baffin Island, just west of Greenland. It was a very brief visit during which several of his crew were taken captive by the Inuit and never seen again. Nevertheless, upon his return to England, Frobisher secured funds for a larger expedition from Queen Elizabeth and a merchant group chartered as the Company of Cathay. Embarking with three ships and 150 men, he did little exploring but brought about two hundred tons of ore back to England. Assays of this ore were contradictory (eventually the ore turned out to be fool's gold), but local enthusiasm remained high. Hence, a large voyage of sixteen ships set out in June 1578 with plans to set up a colony. Frobisher's third expedition landed in southern Greenland, but conflict among the participants prevented colonizing (which probably would not have survived an arctic winter). Back in England, Frobisher became involved with the flourishing privateers who preyed upon Spanish shipping and went out with a fleet headed by Sir Walter Raleigh, taking a rich Spanish prize. He died in 1594 after suffering a gunshot wound while taking part in the siege of the Spanish Fort Crozon in Brittany.

In 1587 Raleigh established the first major English colony in North America on Roanoke Island, just off the coast of present-day North Carolina.[22] Three years elapsed before Raleigh returned to Roanoke, having delayed in part to help defeat the Spanish Armada in 1588. When Raleigh did reach Roanoke in 1590, no one was there. What happened to these colonists has been pursued ever since as one of history's great mysteries. For a variety of other reasons, Raleigh was beheaded by order of King James on October 29, 1618, eleven years after the founding of the first successful English New World colony: Jamestown, Virginia.

Sir Francis Drake sailed around the world in 1577–1580, robbing Spanish treasure ships as he went and extensively exploring the western coasts of South and North America on his way.[23] He then made a brilliant attack on the Spanish fleet gathered in the Cádiz harbor and two years later played a leading role in the defeat of the Armada. But he established no New World colonies.

Initially the most lucrative English colonies were in the Caribbean: Saint Kitts (1624), Barbados (1627), and Nevis (1628). In 1655 the English took Jamaica from Spain, and in 1666 they colonized the Bahamas. All of these island colonies specialized in producing sugar and rum.

Of course, eventually the English colonized the entire East Coast of North America, having defeated the French in Canada and seizing New Amsterdam from the Dutch, renaming it New York.

The Dutch

The Dutch were remarkably successful in colonizing Asia, keeping many of these colonies until after World War II. They also founded successful colonies in the New World. The most famous of these was the New Netherlands, located on the Hudson River in what is now New York State. Fort Nassau was founded in 1614 on the site of modern Albany, and New Amsterdam was founded in 1625 on what now is known as Manhattan Island. In 1655 the Dutch annexed the Swedish settlement of Fort Christina (in modern Delaware), ending Sweden's involvement in the New World. But within twenty years the Dutch lost these North American settlements, ceding them to the English in 1674, following their third war with England.

Unfortunately, one of the most immediate and longest-lasting effects of European colonialism in the New World was slavery.

Slavery

As will be seen, the arrival of Europeans in the New World brought with it diseases such as smallpox and measles to which the Indians had no natural immunity, dying by the millions. Much less notice has been taken of the fact that, especially in the Caribbean, there were tropical diseases such as yellow fever (which originated in Africa) to which Europeans had no immunity, and they, too, died in large numbers. It was against this background that European colonialists confronted the need for laborers.[24]

Recall that the Portuguese had exiled convicts to labor in their Atlantic island possessions when it proved impossible to recruit volunteers.

Faced with a similar problem, the Spanish tried to impose slavery on the indigenous population of the Canaries but were deterred from doing so not only by the pope but also by the rebelliousness of the natives. This labor problem became acute in the New World, particularly on the Caribbean islands best suited to plantation agriculture, which required a huge labor force. Here, too, efforts to enslave the native population failed for several reasons. First, those natives exposed to Europeans suffered a high death rate. Second, the Indians were rebellious, and it took so much force to coerce them to work that it wasn't profitable. Third, the Church condemned enslavement of the Indians, with the missionary Bartolomé de las Casas's book *A Brief Account of the Destruction of the Indies* (1542) playing a major role. Nor was it possible to recruit workers from Europe, given the death rates. Only the immense gains to be made in running plantations were enough to justify the risks, and even those Europeans who came to the Caribbean stayed only long enough to become rich.

But it wasn't long before European colonizers recognized that a suitable labor force, having substantial immunity to tropical diseases, could be purchased, cheaply, on the west coast of Africa.

The Slave Trade

Despite being politically correct, it is absurd to claim that Europeans forced slave trading on Africans.[25] The enslavement and sale of black Africans by other black Africans goes back at least to ancient Egypt—the pharaohs bought large numbers of black slaves. Moreover, as the historian John Thornton pointed out, slavery was intrinsic to "many if not all pre-colonial African societies."[26] By the time the New World was discovered, the exportation of black slaves had been going on for several thousand years—in recent centuries, mostly to Islamic societies—and African dealers were well organized and prepared to offer a seemingly endless supply of prime laborers.

From the first shipment in about 1510 until the very end when Cuba abolished the slave trade in 1868, about 9.5 million slaves *reached* the New World slave markets, meaning that at least 15 million (and probably more) began the journey from the African interior. The distinguished historian Philip Curtin calculated that of the roughly 9.5 million who survived the trip, about 400,000 went to North America, 3.6 million to Brazil, 1.6 million to Spanish colonies, and the remaining 3.8 million to British, French, Dutch, and Danish colonies in the Caribbean.[27]

The slave trade was extremely profitable. In Africa some slaves were obtained by raiding another tribe and selling the captives, but most were sold by their own tribal leaders, who remained in power partly because of the wealth they could shower on their supporters from the sale of slaves. Between 1638 and 1702 prices in the West African ports averaged £3.8 (English pounds) per slave. During this same period, the average price per slave upon arrival in an English colony was £21.3. Of course, there were many costs to be subtracted, including the not infrequent loss of an entire ship and its cargo, but most slave merchants expected to turn a profit of 200 to 300 percent in a period of three to four months.[28]

Powerless Popes

Even some Catholic writers parrot the claim that it was not until modern times that the Roman Catholic Church repudiated slavery.[29] Nonsense! As seen in chapter 6, the Church took the lead in outlawing slavery in Europe, and Thomas Aquinas formulated the definitive antislavery position in the thirteenth century. A series of popes upheld Aquinas's position. First, in 1435, Pope Eugene IV threatened excommunication for those who were attempting to enslave the indigenous population of the Canary Islands. Then, in 1537, Pope Paul III issued three major pronouncements against slavery, aimed at preventing enslavement of Indians and Africans in the New World.[30]

Historians have almost uniformly ignored these papal efforts against slavery, in part perhaps because so many Catholics involved in New World slavery ignored them. In fact, many Catholic slave owners and dealers probably knew nothing of them. In this era the popes had very little power among the Spanish and Portuguese. The Spanish ruled most of Italy and in 1527 had even sacked Rome. Under the resulting treaty, it was illegal even to publish papal decrees in Spain or in Spanish colonial possessions without royal consent, and the king of Spain appointed all Spanish bishops.[31] When Jesuits read a papal bull against slavery in public in Rio de Janeiro, a mob attacked the local Jesuit college and injured a number of priests. When a similar effort to publicize the pope's attack on slavery was made in Santos, the Jesuits were expelled from Brazil. Eventually all Jesuits were violently expelled from Latin America, and then from Spain.

Even if bulls against slavery were ignored in the New World, the Catholic Church's efforts resulted in less brutal treatment of slaves in Catholic than in Protestant societies.

Catholic Slave Codes

When I began to read works on slavery, I was stunned to discover that it was widely considered unacceptable to mention variations in the treatment of slaves across different settings. In his Pulitzer Prize–winning *Problem of Slavery in Western Culture* (1966), for example, David Brion Davis condemned as apologies for slavery all claims that variations in treatment had existed. According to Davis, "Negro bondage was a single phenomenon, or *Gestalt*, whose variations were less significant than underlying patterns of unity."[32] He was especially disdainful of claims that because of slave codes originating with the Catholic Church, slavery was less destructive in Catholic areas—a disdain expressed by most other historians as well, none louder than Marxists such as Marvin Harris.[33]

To be sure, slavery is an abomination in any circumstances. But these historians distort the record when they deny that slaves were treated more brutally in some areas than others.

The *Code Noir* (Black Code) was formulated in 1685 by Louis XIV's minister of finance in collaboration with leading French churchmen to regulate the treatment of slaves in French colonies (slavery was, of course, illegal in France).[34] To the extent that it hasn't simply been ignored by most recent historians, the *Code Noir* has been fraudulently characterized. Peter Gay wrote that the code was "extraordinarily severe—toward the slave, of course."[35] Davis complained that, despite the fact that Article 39 ordered officers of justice "to proceed against the masters and overseers who will have killed their slaves or mutilated them," "there is apparently no record of a French master being executed for killing a slave."[36] But Davis failed to quote the context of this statement given in his source, which reported that "there are records of cases having been brought against [masters and overseers], although no master appears to have suffered the death penalty."[37]

Most of the misrepresentations have been the result of omissions. Many historians have noted that the *Code Noir* prohibited slaves from carrying guns or from gathering in crowds. But these same writers have not reported that owners were required to have their slaves baptized, provide them with religious instruction, and permit them the sacrament of holy matrimony, which served as the basis for prohibiting the selling of family members separately. Slaves were exempted from work on Sundays and holy days (from midnight to midnight), with masters being subject to fines or even to the confiscation of their slaves for violating that provision. Other articles specified minimum amounts of food and clothing that masters must provide and ordered that the disabled and elderly must be properly cared for.

The Spanish *Código Negro Español* included most of the provisions of the *Code Noir* and also guaranteed slaves the right to own property and to purchase their freedom. Specifically, slaves were enabled to petition the courts "to have themselves appraised and to purchase themselves from even unwilling masters or mistresses at their judicially appraised market value."[38] They could do so because the *Código* gave slaves the right to work for themselves on their days off, including the eighty-seven days made up of Sundays and holy days. In rural areas, slaves typically were permitted to sell the produce raised in their own gardens and keep the proceeds.[39]

These were not empty promises. As Columbia University historian Herbert S. Klein pointed out, "the lower clergy, especially at the parish level, effectively carried this law into practice."[40] They did so by maintaining close contacts with their black parishioners and also by baptizing newborn slaves in formal church services that emphasized their humanity, holding church weddings for slave couples, and holding a church ceremony when a slave was freed.[41]

In contrast, the British and Dutch colonies had no regulations governing the treatment of slaves. They did not baptize slaves. As the historian Robert William Fogel reported, masters had the acknowledged right to "apply unlimited force to compel labor," even if this resulted in death.[42] Slaves were not allowed to marry, and for a long time it was illegal to set a slave free. In 1661 the English colony of Barbados adopted a slave code holding that should an owner decide to sentence a slave to death for an infraction, two neighbors should be brought in on the hearing and sentencing, although this was not mandatory.[43] In Barbados the legal prohibition on freeing a slave was lifted, but it was replaced by a tax so heavy as to prevent such an action from occurring.

Far too many recent historians say that legal codes didn't matter. David Brion Davis argued that no claim for better treatment of slaves in French and Spanish colonies could be assumed because of a "lack of detailed statistical information."[44] He was wrong. Reliable statistics establish that the death rate for slaves was substantially higher in English than in French and Spanish colonies.[45] In addition, there were some long-available statistics that somehow no historian had noticed—until I did so.[46] Compare the situation in heavily Catholic Louisiana with that in the rest of the

South, which was largely Protestant. Louisiana came under the French *Code Noir* in 1724. Then, when Louisiana shifted to Spanish control in 1769, slaves there were subject to the *Código*, which included the right to buy their freedom. France regained Louisiana in 1800, and even after the area was sold to the United States in 1803, Catholic norms concerning slavery were deeply rooted there. Those norms had a real impact: the U.S. Census of 1830 found that a far higher percentage of blacks in Louisiana were free (13.2 percent)[47] than in any other American slave state— all of them overwhelmingly Protestant. The contrast is especially sharp in comparison with other neighboring states having similar plantation economies: Alabama (1.3 percent), Mississippi (0.8 percent), and Georgia (1.1 percent). In New Orleans in 1830, an astonishing 41.7 percent of the city's blacks were free, compared with 1.2 percent in nearby Natchez, 1.0 percent in Montgomery, and 3.9 percent in Nashville. Historians like Davis could have easily consulted such census data to recognize the truth: slave codes mattered.

Of course, even the best of slave codes did not abolish the moral outrage that is slavery. But we would do well to remember that had it not been for the rise of Western modernity, slavery would still be everywhere. Even today, it exists in too many places.

Assessing the Consequences of Colonialism

It is time for a final assessment: was the European settlement of the Americas truly a brutal act of genocide, the destruction of a more peaceful world populated by noble savages?

Myths of the "Noble Savage"

As European colonialism spread, nearly at once Europe's intellectuals responded on the side of the colonized, depicting the Indians as "noble savages," as people unsullied by civilization and therefore innocent, honest, gentle, moral, peaceful, kind, and generous.

Among the influential proponents of the doctrine of the noble savage was the French *philosophe* Jean-Jacques Rousseau (1712–1778), who glorified humans in the "state of nature." To which his friend Voltaire responded, "Never has so much intelligence been employed to render us stupid."[48] Unfortunately, this stupidity reached new heights late in the twentieth century as common sense and evidence were overwhelmed by political correctness.

Representative is the historian David E. Stannard's claim that "social practices of certain native Americans in the pre-Columbian era—from methods of child rearing and codes of friendship and loyalty, to worshipping and caring for the natural environment—appear far more enlightened than do many dominant ideas that we ourselves live with today."[49] A huge chorus has extolled Native Americans for their "reverence for the earth, kinship with all forms of life, and harmony with nature," as J. Donald Hughes put it.[50] Wilcomb Washburn of the Smithsonian Institution proposed that "the Indians were the first ecologists."[51] According to the title of Kirkpatrick Sale's book, the arrival of Europeans in the New World resulted in "The Conquest of Paradise."[52]

To make these claims required the denial of many obvious historical facts. One of the first to be denied was the existence of New World cannibalism—indeed, it has been widely proposed that cannibalism never existed *anywhere* as "a prevalent cultural feature."[53] That is, cannibalism has no doubt occurred from time to time, but always as the isolated work of deranged or desperate persons—as when starving persons on a life raft eat the first to die. According to the anthropologist William Arens, there never has existed a society in which cannibalism took place as a legitimate activity, and all claims to the contrary are fantasies and lies. Thus, Arens said, Columbus never actually saw any cannibalism by the Caribs but was taken in by the tales of other Indians "who were eager to fill him with gossip about their enemies."[54]

Arens's claim was seized on eagerly by writers determined to mark the five hundredth anniversary of Columbus's first voyage in 1992 with vitriolic attacks on Columbus and the European settlement of the Americas in general. For example, Kirkpatrick Sale flatly denounced the claim that the Caribs were even hostile, let alone cannibals, as "a bogey, born of Colón's own paranoia or stubborn ferocity and spread to his comrades, to the chroniclers of Europe, and to history."[55] Similarly, numerous scholars denied that the Aztecs ate their sacrificial victims; a few even argued that the Aztecs didn't engage in human sacrifice.[56]

In fact, many societies, including many in the Western Hemisphere, have practiced cannibalism. Even if we were to agree with Arens, Sale, and others that all the many eyewitness accounts are mere bigotry or errors of interpretation, there is overwhelming *physical evidence* to sustain the claims of cultures of cannibalism. In many different places, involving many different tribes, archaeologists have found solid evidence of human bones that have been cooked and scraped clean precisely like the bones of animals that have been cooked and eaten.[57]

In any case, the eyewitness accounts are so numerous and detailed that they cannot all be dismissed. Writing in 1519, Bernal Díaz del Castillo reported on the Aztecs' practices: "Every day we saw sacrificed before us three, four or five Indians whose hearts were offered to the idols and their blood plastered on the walls, and the feet, arms and legs of the victims were cut off and eaten, just as in our country we eat beef brought from butchers."[58] Later, Díaz recounted seeing the sacrifice of some of his fellow conquistadors, in which the Aztecs "kicked their bodies down the steps, and the Indian butchers who were waiting below cut off the arms and feet."[59] Finally, the Caribs ate Verrazzano while his companions watched from on board their ship.

It is certainly true that Europeans did dreadful things to Indians. But not even the wildest critics of Columbus and of the Western colonization of the New World claim that the Europeans engaged in cannibalism.

It has been proclaimed far and wide that Europeans taught the Indians to scalp.[60] Vine Deloria explained, "Scalping . . . was introduced prior to the French and Indian War by the English."[61] That claim was even confided to millions of viewers of a TV Western shown on NBC in 1972.[62] But here, too, archaeological evidence prevails, having unearthed the pre-Columbian remains of North American Indians who were scalped.[63] "Probably the most dramatic skeletal example of prehistoric violence in North America comes from the Crow Creek site in central South Dakota," the historians Michael Haines and Richard Steckel wrote. "Archaeological excavations revealed about 486 skeletons within a fortification ditch on the periphery of the habitation area. The site . . . dates to about 1325 A.D. . . . Analysis revealed that 90% of the individuals had cut marks characteristic of scalping."[64]

Many of the same writers who deny cannibalism have been equally adamant that before the arrival of Columbus, North American Indians were very peaceful—that they learned war from the white man. D'Arcy McNickle proposed that at least 70 percent of North American tribes were pacifists.[65] Kirkpatrick Sale affirmed this claim, saying that at least that many tribes had no battle legends or war myths. Of those war myths that have been passed down, he added, "virtually every one of them involves horses," meaning that they date from after Europeans brought horses to the New World.[66]

But the pre-Columbian Indians unearthed in South Dakota did not scalp themselves. Nor had they dug a fortification ditch for exercise. Warfare was chronic everywhere in the New World.[67] Even the Viking sagas report attacks by natives in Vinland, and Champlain found himself involved in a long-standing war between the Iroquois and the Hurons. Extensive pre-Columbian fortifications exist in the southeastern United States, and battlefields complete with skeletons have been found. Even in the American Southwest, among the allegedly peaceful Hopi and Zunis, warfare was constant and bloody.[68] And, of course, the Aztecs and the Incas were warrior nations who imposed a brutal colonial rule on other tribes in their regions and also engaged in frequent civil wars.

It also has become a virtual article of faith that, unlike the white man, Native Americans lived in close harmony with nature and had a reverence for the earth that prevented them from doing damage to the ecology. Some writers even have claimed that this is why they "chose" not to develop technology as the Europeans had done.[69] In truth, the inhabitants of the New World had no notions about ecology, and to the extent that any were easy on the environment, it was the unintended consequence of their lacking the capacity to do more. Moreover, there is ample evidence of Indian activities inconsistent with reverence for the earth—including deforestation and worn-out fields. As the distinguished environmental archaeologist Karl Butzer put it: "The empirical evidence . . . contradicts the romantic notion that the Native Americans had some auspicious recipe to use the land without leaving a manifest and sometimes ugly imprint upon it."[70] This is nowhere more fully demonstrated than in the remains of the Mayan Empire.

The Mayan Empire was to the south of the Aztecs', located on the Yucatan Peninsula, and it flourished from about the third through the tenth centuries. Judging from their massive ruined cities, the Mayans probably were more advanced than either the Incas or the Aztecs. Although they had no metal tools, they grasped the concept of zero and had a fully developed written language that scholars did not decipher until the 1960s and '70s. For many years one of the great historical mysteries was what caused the precipitous fall of the Mayan civilization. For in the tenth century, suddenly the Mayans abandoned their great cities, and those who survived lived at a far lower level of intellectual and material sophistication. Today, after a great deal of excavation and study, it is believed that the Mayan Empire succumbed to a combination of ecological disaster and endemic warfare. The Mayans appear to have cleared too much of the rain forest for cropland, slowly wearing out the soil to such an extent that they were helpless when faced with a minor decline in rainfall.[71] As the ecology went sour, Mayan cities were raided by unknown outsiders who committed a number of massacres, as archaeological evidence including skeletons and evidence of vandalism has indicated.[72] The point being that the Mayans were neither ecologists nor pacifists.

Most of those who celebrate the superior virtues of pre-Columbian American Indian societies remain silent about their practice of slavery, despite the fact that the enslavement of Indians by Indians was widespread. Of the few writers who have acknowledged this fact, most have brushed it off as not being *real* slavery. Thus Morton Fried argued that those said to be slaves ought to be called "captives," since so-called slavery among the Northwest Indians "bears little resemblance" to real slavery.[73] Ronald and Evelyn Rohner agreed. In their monograph on the Kwakiutl Indians of the Northwest, they admitted that the Kwakiutl "had slaves who were usually war captives from other tribes. Slaves contributed little to the traditional social system except to give prestige to their owners; we give them no further attention." Perhaps it was on these grounds that for decades no mention of slavery was included in undergraduate textbooks on North American Indians or in the "definitive" *Smithsonian Book of North American Indians* published in 1986.

The truth is that slavery was widespread in pre-Columbian North America—at least thirty-nine societies had slavery, according to the Standard Cross-Cultural Files. And slavery among the Northwest Indians was as brutal as anywhere else.[74] Bondage was not only lifelong but also hereditary: as the anthropologist Leland Donald showed, masters held "complete physical control over their slaves, and could even kill them if they chose." And they often did choose to kill the old, sick, or rebellious.[75] Hence, by 1990 even the Smithsonian was willing to acknowledge that the Northwest Indians had real slavery and to condemn "the standard view . . . that slaves were mere prestige goods" and "lived as well as their masters."[76]

It should also be noted that in the nineteenth century American Indians began to acquire black slaves. In 1838, when the Cherokee

Indians were forced to leave Georgia for resettlement in the Oklahoma Territory—the famous "Trail of Tears"—they took along a number of their black slaves.[77]

Finally there is the charge of genocide. Everyone agrees that, lacking any immunity to communicable European diseases such as smallpox, measles, and typhus, the indigenous populations of the Americas suffered a catastrophic death rate—millions died within a few years after contact. In recent decades, however, many have characterized this calamity as genocide and identified Columbus as the chief villain. Native American activist Russell Means charged: "Columbus makes Hitler look like a juvenile delinquent."[78] The title of David E. Stannard's 1997 book said it all—*American Holocaust: The Conquest of the New World*.

Consider the unknown captain of the galley that rowed into the port of Messina in October 1347, aboard which were rats infested with fleas carrying the Black Plague. Should we identify him as the perpetrator of genocide and worse than Hitler? Why not? The galley captain *unintentionally* and *unknowingly* transmitted an epidemic disease to a population lacking immunity. So did Columbus. What happened in the New World was an unpreventable catastrophe; grumblings about the intentional spread of disease are unwarranted.[79] As the historian Stafford Poole put it, "The term [genocide] applies to a calculated, deliberate extermination of an identifiable people for racial or other reasons. . . . There are other terms to describe what happened in the Western Hemisphere, but genocide is not one of them."[80]

Why Were the Americas Behind?

These days, whenever anyone asks why the inhabitants of the Western Hemisphere were so far behind Europe, at least in terms of science and technology, the usual response is insulting: Indians were far too wise to pursue such a foolish and wicked path. Kirkpatrick Sale assured his readers that Indians "certainly could have developed [advanced technologies] if they felt any need to do so. . . . If they did not anywhere use the plow, for instance, that may have been because their methods of breaking the soil with a planting stick worked just as well with a tenth the effort, or because they had learned that opening up and turning over whole fields would only decrease nutrients and increase erosion, or because their thought-world would not have allowed such disregardful violence." In the same paragraph Sale touted the bow and arrow as "far easier, faster, and safer than the musket."[81] Sale's knowledge of farming equals his knowledge of weaponry. The Indians did not plow because it is impossible to do so with wooden implements.

The question persists: why did none of the many pre-Columbian societies of the Western Hemisphere ever learn to work metal other than gold and silver, which are too soft to use for tools or weapons? This is especially hard to explain since both North and South America are abundant in iron ore, copper, and tin (for making bronze), and since a number of pre-Columbian cultures knew how to mine. Nevertheless, when the conquistadors arrived, it was wooden clubs against steel cutlasses.

What seems even more remarkable is that this has become a semi-taboo topic. It is taken up only in books by generalists having secure circumstances (as in the present instance); there is no ongoing discussion in scholarly journals, an outlet sustained by academics, many of them lacking tenure and most of them vulnerable to politically correct criticism.

In any event, among those who have addressed the topic, there is widespread agreement that a major factor in the lack of progress in the Western Hemisphere was the absence of large, domesticated mammals, chiefly cattle, sheep, horses, donkeys, camels, and water buffalo. In the more advanced parts of the globe these animals supplied a great deal of animal protein as well as the power to pull plows, carts, and chariots. They also provided mounts for cavalry as well as messengers. Jared Diamond insightfully noted that although the Spanish had been established in Panama for more than twenty years before Pizarro marched against the Incas, and although he had made two previous sorties into Incan territory, the Incan leaders remained ignorant of the existence of Spaniards until Pizarro marched inland in 1532. Diamond attributed this ignorance to the lack of communication within the Incan empire resulting from its having no written language and no mounted messengers.[82] As Thomas Sowell pointed out, horses and camels had connected Europe and China, thousands of miles apart over the Silk Road, but given the animals' absence in the Western Hemisphere, it was not possible "to connect the Iroquois on the Atlantic seaboard of North America with the Aztecs of Central America . . . or even be aware of their existence."[83]

In addition, before the invention of wind and water power, oxen, horses, water buffalo, and sometimes even camels were a major source of mechanical power. "In contrast," Diamond wrote, "the Americas had only one species of big domestic mammal, the llama/alpaca, confined to a small area of the Andes and the adjacent Peruvian coast. . . . [But] the llama never bore a rider, never pulled a cart or plow, and never served as a power source or vehicle of warfare."[84] Finally, microbes originating in mammal species have frequently crossed over to humans; they were the origin of the infectious diseases to which Europeans and Asians had developed substantial immunity and which, upon contact, ran rampant among the indigenous Americans.[85]

The lack of large mammals was no doubt a major factor in the gap between Europeans and Indians, as the radical transformation of the Plains Indians once they had horses would attest. But much more must have been involved. Granted that the Indians lacked horses or oxen to pull wagons, but surely they would have been better off pulling wagons by hand rather than toting everything on their backs. They knew about the wheel (but used it only on toys), and the Aztecs, Incas, and Mayans even had roads—but they continued to use humans as their beasts of burden. Perhaps this resulted partly because they lacked the idea of progress. But many societies had no such notion and still advanced far beyond the Aztecs, Incas, and Mayans, let alone other Indian societies. Consider that the Iron Age began more than three thousand years ago, and Bronze Age societies flourished in Sumer and Babylon more than six thousand years ago. But five hundred years ago even the Incas and the Aztecs were essentially still in the Stone Age, using flint arrowheads and tipping their wooden clubs with rocks.

Other scholars have suggested that Europeans benefited greatly from the fact that the Eurasian landmass, lying essentially from east to west, occupies a limited range of latitudes and therefore has only modest variations in climate. This climate facilitated the spread of plants and animals (and of technologies involving both), and the same basic crops, such as wheat, grow nearly everywhere. In contrast, the north-south layout of the Western Hemisphere maximizes climatic variations and impedes the spread of plants and animals. As Sowell put it: "Bananas could not spread from Central America to Canada."[86] Indeed, the temperate zones of North and South America are so distant, and separated by such a wide tropical belt, as to make transmission of knowledge or of crops unlikely. Consequently, there were no potatoes or tomatoes in what is now Idaho, nor were there pumpkins or corn (maize) in what is now Argentina.

The more advanced a society is, the less its technology has originated locally: it learns of, and builds on, innovations from far and wide. In that sense, debates about whether stirrups and gunpowder were independently invented in Europe or imported from China are pointless. What matters is that Europeans had both and made great use of them—and of innumerable other inventions and new techniques that spread among them, often with amazing speed, as in the case of cannons. In contrast, the Western Hemisphere saw minimal diffusion of innovations.

This brief sketch suggests several promising lines toward a general explanation of the relative lack of technological progress in the pre-Columbian Americas. It would seem to be a worthwhile intellectual challenge for someone to pursue.

The Universality of Colonialism

Perhaps the primary conclusion to be drawn from these historical episodes involves the fundamental similarity of human nature. Just as there is nothing surprising about the fact that the Mayans, Aztecs, and Incas imposed great empires on those unable to resist them, so too it was to be expected that Europeans would impose empires on the people of the New World, especially since those indigenous peoples lacked metal weapons but were not short of precious metals. It surely is an instance of moral progress that colonialism has become unacceptable—at least in most Western societies. But it is pointlessly anachronistic to suppose that sixteenth-century Europeans, Aztecs, or Incas should have known better.

12

The Golden Empire

"Spain" did not fully exist until nine months before Columbus sailed on his first voyage. Isabella I of Castile had married Ferdinand II of Aragon in 1469, enabling the merger of the two kingdoms, but the reconquest of Granada from Muslim rule was not achieved until January 2, 1492. Even then, having a population of fewer than eight million people, Spain was only a minor power in Europe. That quickly changed in 1516, when Charles V became king of Spain. Charles was a Habsburg and heir to several other crowns, making him ruler of huge areas of Europe. The Spanish Empire was born.

Charles came by these territories through legitimate succession. He defended and expanded them with a powerful army and navy financed by the incredible flow of gold and silver from his colonies in the New World. Charles was succeeded in 1555 by his son Philip II, under whom the empire reached its zenith. In addition to all his father's crowns, Philip was king of Portugal and briefly held the title of king of England and Ireland, by his marriage in 1554 to Queen Mary I (known to history as "Bloody Mary"). When Mary died in 1558, Philip lost his claim to the throne, which went to Elizabeth I, who was soon to become his nemesis. Eventually, Philip's efforts to impose Spanish rule on England failed when his "Invincible Armada" was thwarted by Elizabeth's "Sea Dogs." Then Philip's campaigns to stamp out the Reformation ended in the defeat of his army in the Netherlands, leaving Spain buried in mountains of debt, having nothing left of the incredible riches brought from the New World.

It soon became obvious that, even at its imperial height, Spain had remained a backward nation.[1] Even so, Spain had accelerated the rise of the West by opening the New World, pushing England into a global role, and spurring the rise of Dutch capitalism.

Building an Empire

The conquest of Granada from the Moors was a long and expensive undertaking. The need for new sources of income to offset these costs is thought to have been an important consideration in Queen Isabella's change of heart about funding Columbus. Of course, she had in mind profits from voyages to the real Indies to obtain cargoes of spices and silks. As things turned out, Columbus's mistake yielded far greater wealth, all of which was spent on a century of imperial undertakings.

Torrents of Gold and Silver

Spanish gold fever began when Columbus noticed that many Indians wore golden trinkets. Forty years later, when Pizarro demanded a room filled with gold as ransom for the ill-fated Atahualpa, the Incas brought more than fifteen thousand pounds of the precious metal. The next year, when the Spanish took the Incan capital of Cuzco, they captured an even larger amount of gold. Soon the Spanish also began to export silver, which was far more abundant than gold, albeit less valuable. Between 1521 and 1590 an astonishing two hundred tons of gold and more than eighteen thousand tons of silver were exported to Spain. And these are only the official figures. It is estimated that as much as an additional 50 percent was smuggled into Spain to avoid giving the crown its legal share.[2] To grasp the magnitude of this flow of precious metals, consider that, even counting only the official figures, these imports tripled Europe's supply of silver and increased the gold supply by about 20 percent.[3]

Initially the gold and silver came from stocks in the possession of Indians. But by midcentury the overwhelming amount came from mines, some already in use by Indians but many newly discovered—in Mexico, Peru, Colombia, and elsewhere. In 1546 the Spanish found the incredibly productive silver mines at Petosí in what is now Bolivia. Despite its extreme altitude, being 13,420 feet above sea level, for a few years Petosí became a boomtown with perhaps one hundred thousand residents.

At first the mining at Petosí and elsewhere was done by a mixed labor force—some Indian slaves (despite efforts against it) but mostly hired workers, many of them Indians and some Spaniards. But in 1608 black slaves began to work the mines, and soon they did most of the mining.

Because precious metals are heavy, elaborate arrangements were needed to transport them to Spain. First, llamas or mules were used to carry the refined metals to the western coast. Then ships carried the gold and silver to Panama. Mule trains hauled the treasure across the isthmus to the Atlantic shore, where it was stored under guard and periodically loaded on ships forming the Spanish treasure fleet, consisting of big, well-armed carracks, and later galleons, that convoyed the treasure back to Spain. Such security was necessary because pirates and privateers lurked everywhere, as will be seen.

Empire via Inheritance

Against all odds, Charles V was heir to three of Europe's most powerful royal dynasties. First was the House of Habsburg, rulers of much of modern Germany and Austria. Second was the House of Valois-Burgundy, rulers of the Burgundian Netherlands and kingdoms stretching from the North Sea to the Alps, among them Brabant, Limburg, Luxembourg, Holland, Zeeland, Namur, Franche-Comte, Flanders, and Artois. Finally, Charles was heir to the House of Trastámara of Castile and Aragon (which now formed Spain), as well as Sicily, Sardinia, and Naples—the last three covering all of Italy south of the Papal States. This immense patrimony made Charles the most powerful ruler in Europe. In 1519, after paying stupendous bribes, he gained the title of Holy Roman Emperor. Given the Spanish possessions in the New World as well as Asia, his was the first empire on which it was said "the sun never sets."[4]

But Charles was not content. In 1527 his superbly armed troops (most of them mercenaries) overwhelmed a force assembled by France, Venice, Milan, and the pope, and took Rome. Unfortunately, Charles already was afflicted by what became a chronic problem for the new empire. Despite the immense influx of gold and silver, his debts had mounted rapidly, and hence his troops had gone unpaid for some months. The result was that when they entered Rome, the imperial soldiers broke ranks and went on a spree, looting and setting fire to the city.[5] Although Charles expressed his most sincere regrets for the "Sack of Rome," as it became known all across Europe, this outrage worked to his advantage—never again did either he or his son Philip face papal opposition. To the contrary, the Vatican became a willing and substantial source of imperial loans. In addition, a year later Genoa allied itself with Charles. In 1530 he took control of Florence, and five years later Milan became part of the Spanish Empire. All seemed well.

But trouble was brewing in Germany, where conflicts concerning the Protestant Reformation had broken out. It was Charles V, acting as Holy Roman Emperor, who had initially ordered Luther to appear at the Diet of Worms in 1521, promising him a safe conduct. When that episode left matters even worse than before, Charles outlawed Luther and his followers. Soon the Lutheran princes in Germany formed the Schmalkaldic League to defend the Reformation. Eventually Charles outlawed the league, and in 1547 he defeated Lutheran forces at the Battle of Mühlberg. But in 1552 the Protestant princes found a new ally in the Catholic monarch Henry II of France, and together they forced Charles's armies to retreat to the Netherlands.

Three years later Charles, now in ill health, abdicated in favor of his son Philip. In addition to the immense Spanish Empire, Philip inherited a mountain of debts and an impending revolt in the Netherlands. Perhaps worst of all were the continuing threats to the treasure ships on which his precarious finances depended.

Pirates of the Caribbean

For all their fame, the actual pirates of the Caribbean played a minor, if colorful, role in looting Spain's treasures. The pirates were groups of seamen, many of them deserters, who managed to secure a ship or two to attack and capture small merchant ships—usually only those sailing alone. Far more devastating were the *privateers*, who often sailed in fleets of large warships and who claimed legal standing under authority granted by the government of England, France, or Holland. This authority took the form of a letter of marque, which defined whose shipping could be attacked and specified how the spoils would be divided—a substantial share always going to the monarch who issued the letter. The incredible wealth being transported from the New World to Spain proved irresistible to both pirates and privateers, but usually only the latter could muster sufficient forces to confront the powerful Spanish treasure fleet.

The earliest known attack by privateers on Spanish treasure occurred in 1521, when Cortéz sent a precious cargo taken from the Aztecs back to Spain aboard three ships. Included were half a ton of gold, much silver, many boxes of pearls, and three live jaguars. But only part of it reached Spain. Two of the ships were intercepted by French privateers under the command of Jean Fleury. The French ambushed the Spanish ships just off the coast of Portugal and took the treasure to Paris, where they presented it to the king (receiving a generous slice for themselves).[6] Although legally these were French warships acting on orders from the king, they were privately owned. The Spanish denied the distinction between pirates and privateers, and they hanged Fleury as a pirate when they caught him in 1527.

But if the French were the first, from the Spanish perspective the English were the worst. Once Elizabeth was securely on the throne, English privateers posed the major threat to Spanish shipping, not only on the high seas but also in Caribbean waters. English privateers even launched ground attacks on Spanish ports and storehouses in the New World. In response, the Spanish took to calling Elizabeth the "Pirate Queen." And so she was.[7] Nothing makes this clearer than the early career of Francis Drake.

Francis Drake was a hero from quite a young age, and time has not diminished his fame. At age thirteen he was apprenticed to the owner-captain of a small ship plying the coastal trade with France and the Netherlands. The elderly captain grew so impressed with Drake that upon his death he bequeathed the ship to the young man.

Drake made his first voyage to the New World at age twenty-two, in command of the *Judith*, a fifty-ton, three-masted ship, as part of a fleet assembled and commanded by John Hawkins, with Queen Elizabeth as one of the major investors. Hawkins was Drake's second cousin and eventually became the chief designer and commander of England's stunning victory over the Spanish Armada, with Drake as his second in command. Hawkins had gained his reputation as a privateer by capturing a number of Portuguese slave ships off the coast of Africa and then selling their human cargoes in the Caribbean slave markets. But his raids on the Spanish had rather mixed results—on Drake's second voyage with Hawkins, in 1568, most of the English fleet was destroyed and only Drake and Hawkins managed to sail back to England. Following this ordeal, Drake decided to go it alone.

In 1569 Drake sailed to the Caribbean with two small ships. Nothing more is known of the venture, which he later called a "reconnaissance."[8] In 1572 Drake led a tiny force of seventy men on two ships to intercept the annual Spanish treasure shipment while it was stored in the town of Nombre de Dios on the Isthmus of Panama. The attack was a success—the town was taken and the treasure was captured. Drake was badly wounded, however, and his men were so committed to their captain that they abandoned the treasure to carry him back to his ship.

But Drake was not ready to quit. He continued raiding Spanish ships, and in 1573 he found an ally in Guillaume Le Testu, a French pirate. Even together they lacked sufficient naval forces to attack the Spanish treasure fleet. Then Drake and Le Testu hit upon the idea of ambushing the mule train that brought the treasure overland from the Pacific to the Atlantic shore. On April 1, 1573, Drake, Le Testu, and thirty-five English and French sailors lay in wait for the treasure mule train. As dawn broke, it arrived—"190 mules tended by slaves and guarded by forty-five soldiers," in the words of maritime historian Samuel Bawlf.[9] The trap was sprung, the soldiers and slaves fled, and the treasure was taken. In addition to substantial amounts of gold and gems, it included fifteen tons of silver. Drake's men hid the silver they could not carry in the surrounding forest and then staggered off with their loads, heading for the beach. Le Testu had been wounded in the fight to seize the mule train and could not keep up. He insisted that the others go on, though two French sailors volunteered to accompany him. Soon the Spanish captured Le Testu and one of his sailors, torturing them to reveal Drake's plan. Then Le Testu was beheaded and the sailor was drawn and quartered. So when Drake and his men reached the shore, they saw seven boatloads of Spanish soldiers patrolling. Drake's own ships were nowhere to be found. They had been delayed by unfavorable winds, but the Spanish soon concluded that they had arrived too late to keep Drake from sailing and abandoned their vigil. The next day Drake's ships arrived and everyone boarded and sailed away.

When Drake arrived in England with a huge treasure—valued at more than £40,000, or, as Bawlf noted, "roughly one-fifth of Queen Elizabeth's annual revenues"[10]—it was an inauspicious moment. Elizabeth had just signed a new peace treaty with Spain in which she had agreed to keep her seamen from attacking Spanish shipping. With the queen's connivance, Drake simply lay low for a time, carefully preserving the large royal share of his booty.

Strange to tell, however, Drake's most fabulous capture of Spanish treasure took place during his circumnavigation of the globe. Late in 1578, unbeknownst to the Spanish, Drake had sailed his flagship the *Golden Hind* around the southern tip of South America and into the Pacific. Drake's ship, originally named the *Pelican*, had been built to his specifications. She was a bit more than one hundred feet long and about twenty-one across. Her hull was double-planked, yet she drew only thirteen feet, which meant Drake could sail in shallow waters. Her main mast was about ninety feet tall and she could fly an extra amount of sail to increase her speed. The ship was heavily armed for her size, with seven gun ports on each side for extremely long-range cannons, with four more of these cannons on her main deck as well as many smaller guns.[11] The queen had paid for construction of the *Golden Hind* and had also provided the new, smaller eleven-gun *Elizabeth* for Drake's voyage.

Spanish ships in the Pacific sailed without fear of attack, since pirates and privateers were confined to the Atlantic. Consequently, Drake was able to take unsuspecting prizes. Among them was the *Nuestra Señora de la Concepción*, a cargo ship much larger than Drake's *Golden Hind*, and better known as the *Cagafuego* (Spanish for "shitfire"). Drake was able to sail right up to the *Cagafuego* because her captain believed that his was a Spanish vessel. The treasure taken on that day was huge: twenty-six tons of silver, eighty pounds of gold, many jewels, and thirteen chests full of coins. To make room for it all, Drake discarded his ship's ballast and replaced it with silver bars. Then he continued on his voyage up the Pacific coast, taking several other prizes along the way, before heading west to complete his circle of the earth. Finally, in 1580, Drake returned to England with enormous treasures. He stated that his backers received £47 for each £1 they had invested—Queen Elizabeth's share probably amounted to £264,000, or considerably more than her year's income from all other sources.[12] She would soon need every penny of it to prepare the fleet to face the Armada.

Spain's Low-Country Wars

When Philip II succeeded his father, he gained a huge empire that sprawled from Asia to Austria, sustained by the largest standing army in Europe since the fall of Rome. This elite force enrolled more than two hundred thousand men, recruited from all over Europe—large numbers of them from Ireland, Flanders, Italy, and Germany, with perhaps 20 percent of them from Spain.[13] They were superbly armed, well-trained, fierce in battle, and extremely expensive—so costly as to consume "ten times more revenue than all other functions of the [empire's] government combined," according to the historian William S. Maltby.[14] This was not a frivolous expense. Given the many challenges to Philip's rule, he had either to bear these costs or surrender substantial portions of his patrimony.

Indeed, there was nothing frivolous about Philip. He was known as "Philip the Prudent," and he devoted nearly every day of his long reign to sitting at his desk in the Escorial, the royal residence near Madrid, corresponding with officials throughout his vast realm, trying to control events and keep his empire solvent.

Aside from being diligent, Philip was said to have been a pleasant and gracious man. But as a Habsburg he had inherited a severely deformed lower jaw that interfered with both his eating and his speaking—the same deformity had afflicted his father. The "Habsburg Jaw" was the consequence of many generations of inbreeding: nearly all Habsburg males married first cousins, or their aunts, or their nieces.[15] In addition to these physical difficulties, Philip spent many of his years in mourning. He was married four times—three of his wives were immediate relatives, and each of these three died in childbirth. The fourth, Mary of England, died during the fourth year of their marriage (possibly of uterine cancer). In addition, most of his children died very young—between 1517 and 1700, half of all Habsburg children died before their first birthdays. As it happened, Philip's foreign affairs were equally unfortunate.

Radical Dutch Protestants

Philip was an unflinchingly dedicated Roman Catholic. He always regretted that his father had granted Luther a safe conduct pass instead of having him seized and executed. But when he took the throne he was confronted with a substantial Protestant minority in the Netherlands that his father had tolerated. Initially he did nothing. Then he adopted what he took to be a sensible and humane plan. He would convert the Protestants by greatly improving and strengthening the Catholic Church.

At the time only four bishops served the entire Netherlands, leaving even many of the larger cities without one. The lack of bishops reflected a church that was without an effective presence in most places. So Philip secured the pope's permission to appoint sixteen new bishops. But there was little funding available to finance this huge new apparatus: a diocese was expected to be self-funding, but these new ones lacked the strong parish structures needed to bring in sufficient money. Worse yet, the prospect of a stronger, more active Catholic Church frightened Protestants, including the nobility, since it implied a more vigorous persecution of "heretics." Philip's move also infuriated Catholic nobles, who had traditional rights to appoint church officers.[16] These divisions were exacerbated in 1566 when Calvinist radicals struck.

The *Beeldenstorm*, or Iconoclastic Fury, involved roving bands of radical Calvinists who, opposing all religious images and decorations in churches, stormed into Catholic churches in the Netherlands and destroyed all artwork and finery. Many scholars have tried to explain this frenzy of image breaking as caused by the dislocation of many textile workers and a sudden rise in the price of food. If so, how is one to account for the fact that only churches were attacked? Why no attacks on government officials or town halls? Why no looting of shops and foodstores?[17]

The *Beeldenstorm* reached Antwerp on August 21. As the iconoclasts proceeded they drew large, cheering crowds and no opposition. "All forty-two churches in the city were ransacked," wrote the historian Jonathan Israel, "the images, paintings, and other objects hauled into the streets, smashed, and the plate pilfered, the work continuing at night under torches."[18]

But there was no cheering in the Escorial. Philip II decided that the time had come to impose serious governance on the Netherlands, in the form of Don Fernando Álvarez de Toledo, third Duke of Alba. At the head of ten thousand troops (and hundreds of attractive mounted "courtesans"),[19] Alba marched from Milan (then a Spanish province), through the Alpine passes, and into the Rhine valley, along what then was known as the Spanish Road. He arrived in Brussels on August 22, 1567, almost exactly a year after the *Beeldenstorm* had hit Antwerp.

Then the bloodbath began. It is not clear how many iconoclasts Alba rounded up, if any, for his wrath was directed against treason far more than heresy. He defined treason as ever having favored any degree of local sovereignty. Hence no one was safe, not even solidly Catholic nobility—a number of whom were beheaded.[20] The main effect of Alba's brutality was to drive the upper classes into opposition, including William of Orange, who went on to lead the Dutch fight for independence.

Fighting Dutchmen

The rebellious Dutch launched a fearsome opposition from the sea. The "Sea Beggars" (also known as *Gueux*) were formed in 1568 by Hendrik, Count of Brederode, and a number of Protestant nobles intent on an independent Netherlands. They were ridiculed as beggars when they had petitioned the governor-general of the Netherlands for religious toleration; when their petition was denied, they took up the name as a badge of honor. They soon assembled a fleet of very fast, small, shallow-draft fighting ships able to ply the complex waters off the Dutch and Flemish coasts, almost with impunity. Their raids caused Alba to station large garrisons at major ports, including Antwerp, where he also had built a very large fortress. But the Spanish troops, though providing some protection for dockyard areas, were useless against attacks on shipping. The Sea Beggars soon had imposed an effective blockade of Antwerp and other southern Netherlands ports. An exodus of import and export firms began.

In 1572 Alba imposed a new and onerous tax, which prompted the Sea Beggars not only to raid ports but also to take and hold them. Brill was the first, but within weeks other ports were taken. This was, of course, war. Alba proceeded via a series of sieges, taking Haarlem in 1573. Later in the year Alba was replaced by Don Luis de Requeséns, who went north with instructions from Philip II to attempt a negotiated settlement. The talks dragged on and on. Often enough the participants found a basis for agreement, but each time Philip II rejected their efforts on the grounds that there could be no toleration of Protestants.

Meanwhile, like his father before him, Philip neglected to pay his troops. In November the imperial army mutinied, and, after sacking several minor towns, a horde of troops arrived at Antwerp, at that time still a loyal outpost of the empire. What followed became known as the Spanish Fury. Thousands died, seldom without great suffering. Jervis Wegg recounted: "The Spaniards hanged men up by their legs and arms and women by their hair; they flogged people and burnt the soles of their feet to extort the hiding place of their wealth."[21] Young women were dragged screaming to the newly built fortress. No one was safe—not the poor, who often were killed because they had no money to give, and not even the clergy, who were forced (even tortured) to reveal where their valuables, including altar chalices and plates, were hidden.[22] The factor of the Fugger Company, then the largest German financial firm, estimated that the Antwerp merchant community lost at least two million crowns in gold and silver coins.

Once the troops departed, Antwerp switched sides, joining the Protestant Union of Utrecht, thus becoming the major center of resistance in the southern Netherlands. Now rather than being blockaded by the Sea Beggars, Antwerp's shipping enjoyed their protection. Still, the city's commercial life had been severely curtailed.

In 1578 Don Alessandro Farnese, Duke of Parma, replaced Requeséns as governor-general of the Netherlands. Parma, a distinguished general, resumed the campaign to crush the Dutch Revolt. He launched several unsuccessful attacks on Antwerp before laying siege to the city in 1584. A year later it fell, and Antwerp was back in Spanish hands to stay. But it no longer was much of a prize. Once again it was cut off from the sea by blockade. And its population was greatly reduced by the flight of Protestants, who took their commerce with them. Antwerp never recovered its financial glory.

Most of those who fled Antwerp took their capitalist enterprises north to Amsterdam. Economic historians date the boom in Amsterdam as beginning in 1585, the very year Antwerp fell to the Duke of Parma. In Amsterdam there was freedom and toleration, taxes required citizen approval, and access to the Rhine and the Meuse allowed the Dutch to dominate the rich and very active Baltic trade. Foreign merchants and traders who once clustered in Antwerp now clustered in Amsterdam—especially the English.

If the Netherlands had once been reclaimed from the Atlantic, now the ocean rescued the Dutch by providing superb defensive water barriers. Fighting at home and for their homes, using arms of their own manufacture, funded by a booming commercial economy, having unimpeded access to the sea and a stalwart English ally, the Dutch could afford to fight on and on and then some more. To oppose them, the Spanish Empire depended on expensive mercenary troops, using arms of foreign manufacture, mainly supplied from abroad. Lacking control of the sea, the Spanish had to bring everything overland, following the Spanish Road just as had Alba's battalions. The costs of all this were staggering.

The Queen and Her Pirates Prevail

As the 1580s began, things were not going well for Philip II. The Dutch had not been dislodged despite repeated onslaughts. Then, in 1585,

Queen Elizabeth sent her small but effective army, made up of 6,350 infantry and 1,000 cavalry commanded by the Earl of Leicester, to the Netherlands in support of the Dutch cause. (She had long permitted the Sea Beggars to use English ports.)[23] Elizabeth also bought shares in stock companies organized to finance raids on Spanish shipping—especially on the treasure ships from the Orient and the Americas. To make things worse, the French continued to connive against Spain, always ready to attack from the rear.

Something had to be done. Putting first things first, Philip II and his advisers decided to remove England from the equation. They would transport their invincible battalions from the Netherlands across the English Channel, overrun the irregular forces Elizabeth could muster against them, replace her with a Catholic monarch, and that would be that.

It was a wonderful design. It might well have succeeded had England also been ruled by a despot—but the plan was doomed against a free nation "of shopkeepers," where technology blossomed, enterprise was cultivated, and the queen was a devoted capitalist and pirate.

In 1587 the Spanish began to assemble the great fleet needed for the invasion of England. The plan was to sail north into the English Channel and inflict such damage to the English ships that the Armada could then protect a vast flotilla of barges and small ships conveying the Duke of Parma's veterans from the Netherlands to the English coast. Special arrangements were well in hand for barges capable of carrying cavalry units with their horses, ready to ride through the surf and attack all comers. The main assembly ports for the Armada were to be Cádiz (just west of the Strait of Gibraltar) and Lisbon.

Drake's Raid

Fully aware of Spanish intentions, the English decided to make a disruptive raid, a plan that bore "all the signs of Elizabeth's personal intervention," observed Garrett Mattingly in his history of the Armada.[24] The English force was commanded by Sir Francis Drake, who had been knighted by Elizabeth in 1581. Although he was one of Elizabeth's favorites, Drake was not an officer in the Royal Navy. In keeping with the English affinity for free enterprise, private citizens could command the queen's ships, and English battle fleets often were a mixture of both royal and privately owned ships.

Drake planned to strike against both Cádiz and Lisbon, hoping to find their harbors jammed with ships not yet ready to fight. The makeup of his fleet reveals much about a truly "capitalist" approach to warfare and about the unique nature of the English merchant fleet. Drake began with four powerful ships of his own. Then Elizabeth put four of her best royal galleons under Drake's command and authorized him to complete his fleet by recruiting as many merchant ships as London merchants would agree to furnish.

Of what use could merchant ships be to a battle fleet? None, if they were the wide, deep, lightly gunned, cumbersome ships that continental merchants used. But English merchants built fighting ships and overcame the commercial deficiencies of these vessels by scorning bulky cargoes in favor of light, valuable goods. Built to take their place in the line of battle, these ships had narrow bottoms for speed, and their hulls spread to their greatest width above the water in order to provide for gun decks. As the historian Violet Barbour pointed out, the way to distinguish a royal man-of-war from a large English merchant ship was not on the basis of shape, number of gun ports, or rigging but only "by the decoration lavished upon her," for the queen's ships had a great deal of scrollwork and carving and impressive figureheads.[25]

Recognizing the military value of merchant ships, Drake convinced the Levant Company to provide him with nine, plus a number of frigates and pinnaces for scouting, communication, and inshore service. The merchants' motives were not purely patriotic. Drake's fleet was in fact commissioned as a stock company, and participants (including the queen) were to receive shares in all prizes and loot the expedition acquired. As Mattingly noted, the voyage had "some of the aspects of a private commercial venture."[26]

Upon arriving at Cádiz on April 29, 1587, Drake saw everything go as he had hoped. The harbor was crowded. The Spanish ships were mostly without crews, and many lacked guns and sails. Drake sailed in, sank some thirty ships, and sailed out again with a large number of prize vessels, which he dispatched for England. Drake then sailed for Portugal's Cape Saint Vincent, where he positioned his fleet to harass the coastal trade and intercept squadrons trying to reach Lisbon (which he had judged as too strong to attack once surprise was lost). Again he wreaked havoc on the Spanish, taking many prizes and supplies.[27] These blows were sufficient to cause the Spanish to postpone the sailing date for their immense Armada until the next year. Drake kept it all in perspective, writing to Elizabeth's spymaster Francis Walsingham, "Prepare in England strongly and most by sea!"[28]

The Armada Sinks

When the Armada did sail the following year, several extreme flaws in the Spanish plan were revealed. The English fleet could not in fact be defeated because it refused to fight in the traditional manner. Rather than closing for deck-to-deck infantry battles, the nimble English vessels stood off and relied on powerful broadsides from cannons, which outranged the Spanish guns. The Spanish ships were stuffed with troops eager to put the English sailors to the sword, but their cannons lacked range, weight, and number and also began to run short of powder and shot. Fighting so close to home that crowds on the shore could see some of the battle, the English were constantly resupplied with powder and shot carried out on lighters.

Even so, the Armada did well enough as it battled its way up the English Channel that it remained mostly intact and was still a potent naval force as it passed the coast of Flanders, where the Duke of Parma awaited. Now a second major tactical flaw was revealed. The Armada was capable of sheltering the barge flotilla, and indeed, bringing the flotilla out from shore might have forced the English to close in for deck-to-deck fighting. So why didn't Parma's veterans come out? Because the Dutch Sea Beggars were blockading Flanders, and their ships could sail in the shallow coastal waters, out of reach of the Armada. Had the barges pushed out, then, the sea soon would have been full of drowning Spanish soldiers and riderless cavalry horses.

So the Spanish troops sat on the beach and the Armada continued north, pounded all the way by the longer-range English guns. Eventually, having passed to the north of Scotland, the Armada decided to swing west to circle around Ireland and hence back to Lisbon. Now came terrible storms, and dozens of Spanish ships were wrecked along the Irish coast; for many weeks bodies kept washing up on Irish beaches.

That it was storms that had done the worst damage to the Armada revealed much about the two navies. English naval construction was so superb and their seamen so adept that, as the historian G. J. Marcus pointed out, during Elizabeth's entire forty-five-year reign "not a single English warship was lost through shipwreck; while over the same term of years, entire squadrons of Spaniards were overwhelmed by the sea."[29]

Spanish Realities

When Philip II died in 1598 it was already obvious that the Spanish Empire was in decline. It would be another century before the empire no longer played a significant role in European affairs, but Spain's neighbors were already exploiting its fading power. The British and the Dutch ruled the seas and were not only colonizing North America (as were the French) but also intruding into Spanish's colonies in the Caribbean. The English even welcomed and taxed pirates (real ones) in their new Caribbean ports. Worse yet, attacks on Spanish treasure ships continued, with English battle fleets now involved. Thus, in 1592, a six-ship English squadron, lying in wait just off the Azores, intercepted the enormous carrack *Madre de Deus* (Mother of God) and seized the largest treasure ever. She was the biggest ship the English had ever seen: as Harvard scholar David S. Landes recorded, the *Madre de Deus* was "165 feet long, 47 feet of beam, 1,600 tons, three times the size of the biggest ship in England; seven decks, thirty-two guns plus other arms."[30] As for treasure, "chests bulging with jewels and pearls, gold and silver coins . . . 425 tons of pepper, 45 tons of cloves, 35 tons of cinnamon," and much else. The total value was estimated at £500,000, and "a large share of this catch was owed to the queen."[31] The loss of this treasure was a terrible blow to the Spanish economy.

How had such a level of Spanish vulnerability come to pass?

Financial Ruin

Despite the torrent of gold and silver from the New World, the wealth of the Spanish Empire was largely illusory given its staggering debts. The problems began with Ferdinand and Isabella, who never managed to balance their budgets. Charles V assumed their substantial debts at his coronation and expanded them on a properly imperial scale, starting by borrowing more than a half million gold guilders from the banker Jakob Fugger to gain the Holy Roman Emperorship. This, too, was but a drop in the bucket. During his reign Charles secured more than five hundred loans from European bankers, amounting to about 29 million ducats.[32] Much of this amount still had not been repaid when his son Philip II ascended to the throne in 1556, and a year later Philip declared bankruptcy. Nevertheless, only five years later debt was again so high that the empire paid out 1.4 million ducats—more than 25 percent of the total annual budget—as interest on current loans.[33] By 1565 the imperial debt in the Low Countries alone stood at 5 million ducats, and interest payments plus fixed costs of governing produced an additional deficit of 250,000 ducats a year.[34]

The same pattern held for the empire as a whole—debt dominated everything. During the first half of the 1570s, Philip II's revenues averaged about 5.5 million ducats a year, while his total expenditures often nearly doubled that amount, with interest on his debts alone exceeding 2 million a year.[35] No one was too surprised when again in 1575 Philip disavowed all his debts, amounting to about 36 million ducats. By doing so, however, he left his regime in the Netherlands penniless. As his governor-general complained, "Even if the king found himself with ten millions in gold and wanted to send it here, he has no way of doing so with this Bankruptcy."[36] To send it by sea was far too risky. Only a few years before, in 1568, the Spanish had tried to sneak four small coasters with 155 chests of ducats to Antwerp to pay the Duke of Alva's soldiers. But the English intercepted the boats, and most of the cash ended up in Queen Elizabeth's treasury.[37] To send money by a letter or bill of exchange also was impossible, because Spanish bankers in the Netherlands could no longer pay such an amount, and other bankers would not honor Spanish credit. Eventually the northern Netherlands was lost in large part for lack of money to pay the troops on time. The empire struggled through many subsequent bankruptcies.

Backward Spain

Since the start of the seventeenth century, Western historians have devoted immense effort to explaining the "decline of Spain." The English traveler Francis Willughby wrote in 1673 that Spain had fallen on bad times because of: "1. A bad religion. 2. The tyrannical Inquisition. 3. The multitude of Whores. 4. The barrenness of the Soil. 5. The wretched laziness of the people very like the Welsh and Irish . . . 6. The expulsion of the Jews and Moors. 7. Wars and plantations."[38] Forty years later the Florentine ambassador to Spain noted that "poverty is great here, and I believe it is due not so much to the quality of the country as to the nature of the Spaniards, who do not exert themselves; they rather send to other nations the raw materials which grow in their kingdom only to buy them back manufactured by others."[39] Such views persisted. As the distinguished historian J. H. Elliot summed up in 1961, "It seems improbable that any account of the decline of Spain can substantially alter the commonly accepted version of seventeenth-century Spanish history, for there are always the same cards, however we shuffle them."[40] But then Henry Kamen produced a whole new deck: *Spain never declined because it never rose!*[41]

Kamen's brilliant revision of the conventional wisdom turns on a crucial distinction between Spain and the Spanish Empire. The empire was a *dynastic* creation, not one built by Spanish expansion or conquest, aside from its foothold in the New World. Spain's subsequent contributions to the empire consisted mainly of military recruits and gold and silver brought from the New World. These massive amounts of specie brought no significant benefits to Spain itself; rather, they caused inflation throughout western Europe and financed the empire's large, well-equipped armies to fight the French, Protestant German princes, various Italians, the Dutch, and the English. In fact, the costs of empire bled wealth from Spain, which remained an underdeveloped, feudal nation. Once Spain's backwardness was no longer obscured by the grandeur of the empire, it was incorrectly seen as a decline from better times.

Impoverished Spain depended on imports not only for manufactured products but even for sufficient food. Spanish agriculture was hampered by poor soil and by the strange institution known as the *Mesta*. Spanish sheep grew high-quality fleeces—not as good as those of English sheep but better than could be found elsewhere—and Spain had, in fact, replaced England as the source of wool for the Flemish and Italian cloth industries. The *Mesta* was an organization of sheep owners who had royal privileges to sustain migratory flocks of millions of sheep. The flocks moved all across Spain—north in the summer, south in the winter—grazing as they went, making it impossible to farm along their routes.[42] When conflicts arose with landowners, the crown always sided with the *Mesta* on grounds that nothing was more important to the economy than the wool exports. The government's protection of the *Mesta* discouraged investments in agriculture, so Spain needed to import large shipments of grain and other foodstuffs.[43]

Geography also made it difficult to unite a Spanish nation or even to carry on domestic commerce. Rough mountain ranges created easily defended enclaves (as Wellington was to demonstrate during the Napoleonic Wars), but these same natural barriers greatly handicapped commercial transport and, as Elliot put it, "added terrifyingly to prices."[44] For example, it cost more to transport spices from Lisbon to Toledo than it did to buy the spices in Lisbon.

As for manufacturing, Spain had little, and most of what did exist soon perished when the flood of gold and silver from the Americas allowed far greater reliance on imports. Nor did Spain develop much in the way of an indigenous merchant class, its commercial life remaining in the hands of foreigners, most of them from Italy. This was a source of pride among leading Spanish citizens—known as the hidalgos. Manufacturing and commerce were for inferior people and nations, so let others toil for Spain, was how they put it.[45]

So while the empire dominated northern Europe, Spain itself remained frozen in feudalism and produced mainly young men, many of them from the nobility, with no opportunities except as professional soldiers. These well-trained, long-service, well-equipped Spanish soldiers were the most feared and formidable fighting force in Europe. But they fought for the empire, not Spain. Their victories were far from home—in the Low Countries, in Italy, and along the Rhine. And the means to pay them came thousands of miles across the Atlantic.

Spain could not even arm these fine soldiers. It had no weapons factories; it made no gunpowder; it cast no cannons or even any cannonballs. When an urgent shortage of balls arose in 1572, Philip II wrote to Italy asking that two Italian experts in casting cannonballs be sent at once to Madrid, because "there is no one here who knows how to make them."[46] This led nowhere. When the huge Armada sailed against England in 1588, all its guns and cannonballs were imported, as was most everything else aboard, including the supply of ship's biscuit. Of course, the ships weren't built in Spain either.

Colonial Drift

Although the defeat of the Armada had been a terrible blow, Spanish imperialism suffered more important defeats elsewhere. In 1594 the Dutch began to intrude in the Caribbean. The English soon did likewise, and in 1605 they laid claim to Barbados in the West Indies. The New World no longer was uncontestedly Spanish. Nor was it any longer an unlimited source of silver. Costs of mining had risen substantially as it became necessary to work deeper veins. In addition, the demand for Spanish imports began to fall sharply in the Americas. The problem was that Spanish colonists had essentially re-created the Spanish economy. They now produced their own grain, wine, oil, and coarse cloth equal to that they had long imported from home. Spanish merchants, who had long prospered from trading with the Americas, soon found themselves overstocked. As Elliot put it: "The goods which Spain produced were not wanted in America; the goods that America wanted were not produced in Spain." Beginning in the 1590s, Spain became less important to the economies of its American colonies, and Dutch and English interlopers became more active.[47]

The Spanish were especially vulnerable to these incursions because their colonies were so thinly settled. Perhaps the most remarkable aspect of Spanish settlement of the New World, especially from early in the sixteenth century until well into the nineteenth, is how few came over. Spanish emigrants to the New World were required to register at the House of Trade in Seville, and during the course of the entire sixteenth century only about 56,000 did so. At one time historians assumed that this total was exceeded many times over by illegal immigrants, but it now is accepted that the number of unregistered emigrants was small.[48] Likewise, the estimate that somewhat more than 300,000 Spaniards went to the New World from 1500 to 1640 is now thought to be much too high.[49] But even this figure would have left most of Latin America unsettled by Europeans.

There were many reasons why the Spanish did not voyage west in large numbers. For one thing, unlike England, Spain was not abundant in "shopkeepers" or people having the outlook required to become successful smallholders. Spain was a land of huge estates and of agricultural laborers only slightly above serfdom. Nor were there glittering prospects of becoming a successful shopkeeper or smallholder in a New World that was also dominated by feudal landowners—although the prospects were more promising there than in Spain.

Second, the voyage was extremely dangerous. Many died aboard ship from various diseases or from running out of water. Also, the Atlantic was wide and stormy, and Spain's inferior ships, poor maintenance, and relatively unskilled sailors meant that large numbers of ships were lost. Between 1516 and 1555 about 2,500 ships left Spain for the Indies. Of them, about 750—or 30 percent—were lost.[50]

In addition, most of those who did emigrate did not plan to stay; they intended merely to sojourn in pursuit of sudden wealth. Many, perhaps most, of those who hit it rich returned to Spain, where they expressed immense relief to be back. Correspondence from this era shows that those who traveled to the colonies often expressed regrets over having come.

Finally, the authorities in both Spain and the colonies restricted immigration. Because the Spanish colonial economies were fueled mainly by the mining and exporting of gold and silver, the authorities regarded additional population as doing nothing but adding to the costs of subsidizing life in the colonies. To limit newcomers, whenever possible the authorities refused entry unless one had relatives already established in a colony.

Emigrants from Britain came to the British colonies in North America in far greater numbers than came to Latin America from Spain—an estimated 600,000 between 1640 and 1760.[51] Many others came from the Netherlands, France, Germany, and other parts of Europe. They did not come in search of feudal estates or to mine gold and silver. Most of them came because of the high wages prevailing in the colonies and the extraordinary opportunities to obtain fertile farmland or to set up a workshop or store. They had no interest in going back. Moreover, because they came in British ships, and began coming a century later, their voyages were safer, less debilitating, and shorter. Although most became smallholders, the droves of immigrants to the northern colonies did not generally become subsistence farmers.[52] Their family farms were huge by comparison with European peasant plots, and they shared in the profits from exporting their crops and hides to Britain as well as feeding the nonagricultural colonists. In contrast, the Spanish colonies imported not only manufactured goods but also large amounts of food, paid for mainly with precious metals from mines, many of which the Spanish crown owned outright.

Of course, the Spanish Empire didn't just drop dead, or even stop fighting. In 1590 and again the next year imperial troops in the Netherlands turned south and fought unsuccessful campaigns against the French. And soon these same northern armies were embroiled in the Thirty Years' War. But the news, both economic and military, continued to be mostly bad. In 1596 the empire once again declared bankruptcy, then again in 1607, 1627, 1647, and 1653. In 1638 the French captured the fortress at Breisach on the Rhine, thus closing the Spanish Road from Italy to the Netherlands. Thereafter, Spanish troops and supplies could reach the Netherlands only by sea, subject to attack by both the English and the Dutch navies.

By this time the tide had so irrevocably turned that people now began to publish treatises to explain the "decline of Spain." But it was the empire that had declined; Spain had never risen. As Douglas C. North explained in a book that helped win him the Nobel Prize in economics, Spain's "economy remained medieval throughout its bid for political dominance. Where it retained political sway, as in the Spanish Netherlands, the economy of the area withered."[53]

Europe's Military Revolution

The final blow to Spanish power came as a result of a dramatic shift in military might. Just as Spain's immense and powerful army melted away for lack of funds, a revolution in military organization and technology transformed other European armies, thus reducing Spain to a second-rate power.[54]

The fundamental cause of this military revolution was the proliferation of individual firearms. When all the infantry had muskets, a substantial change in tactics allowed armies to maximize firepower: after a front line fired a volley, it shifted to the rear to begin reloading while another line moved to the front. These maneuvers needed to be highly coordinated, with each line moving in perfect unison and each trooper reloading with precision. To achieve all this required a standing, professional army that drilled constantly. Professional troops also were needed because inexperienced soldiers were unreliable in the face of coordinated fire, including that of mobile artillery. In addition, the new style of warfare created the need for a highly trained officer corps—hence the founding of military academies. All these developments made warfare prodigiously expensive.

Nevertheless, the Dutch, French, Swedes, Austrians, and various German principalities all took part in the military revolution (the British were content to spend most of their money on a superior navy). Despite the fact that the Spanish army in the sixteenth century had anticipated many of these innovations, by the seventeenth century it was small, unprofessional, and out of date.

Legacy of a Flawed Empire

Despite everything, it must not be overlooked that it was the Spanish who created the global society. No doubt the Chinese *could* have sent

Zheng He's fleet east to the Americas, but they did not. And many European rulers *could* have funded Columbus, but it was Isabella and Ferdinand who did. As for the tragic epidemics that resulted from contact, they would have occurred whenever *any* outsiders, including the Chinese, reached the New World—as was bound to happen, if not in 1492 then surely within the next several decades. The fact remains that it was the Spanish who funded the first voyage and the Spanish who rapidly followed up: by the time of Columbus's third voyage they had already set up an administrative apparatus in the Caribbean and a busy maritime network.

As for the fall of the Spanish Empire, ironically, perhaps no monarchs in history were more conscientious, honest, or hardworking than Charles V and his son Philip II. Between them they carefully built the Spanish Empire and ruled it for more than eighty years. Nearly every day they rose early and worked diligently at administering this sprawling entity. Had they been wastrels or playboys, they might have done much less damage to the economies in their charge. In contrast, the "Pirate Queen" ran a relaxed regime, treating her Sea Dogs more like business partners than subjects, and they responded with brilliant initiative. In the end, it was this English free-enterprise approach that was the final undoing of the Spanish Empire.

13

The Lutheran Reformation:
Myths and Realities

Ayear after Charles V became king of Spain, Martin Luther nailed his Ninety-Five Theses to the Wittenberg church door, initiating the Reformation. The careers of the two would be closely intertwined in the brutal religious conflict that soon followed.

A remarkable number of myths have gathered around the Reformation. Many of these reflect the anti-Catholic bias of the historians who long dominated what was written in English and much that was written in German. The conventional myths proclaim that the emergence of Protestantism was caused by enlightened factors such as the spread of literacy and that it had many equally marvelous consequences, including a remarkable revival of popular piety and the spread of religious liberty. Unfortunately, many of the admirable claims about the Reformation aren't true. The rise of Protestantism was anything but the triumph of tolerance: it was a criminal offense to say Mass in Lutheran Germany; John Calvin tolerated no dissenters; and Henry VIII *burned* dissenters. That hardly anyone went to church in either the Protestant or the Catholic areas of Europe quashes all claims of a popular revival.

Of course, *the* Reformation is itself a misnomer: there were several independent and quite different Reformations, the primary instances being Lutheranism, Calvinism, and Anglicanism. But the first, most analyzed, and most important of these three Reformations—and therefore the one that will be our main focus—was the one Martin Luther led.

Luther and Lutheranism

Martin Luther (1483–1546) was the son of a well-to-do German family.[1] His father may have been of peasant origins but soon owned copper mines and smelters, and he served for many years on the council of the city of Mansfeld in Saxony. After four years in prep schools, in 1501 the young Luther enrolled in the University of Erfurt, one of the oldest and best universities in Germany. His father hoped he would become a lawyer, but after a few months in law, he transferred to theology. Luther received his bachelor's degree in 1502 and his master's in 1505. He then entered an Augustinian monastery and in 1507 was ordained a priest. After being appointed to the faculty at the University of Wittenberg in 1505, he received his doctorate in 1512. Except for several short breaks caused by his conflict with the Church, Luther remained at Wittenberg for the rest of his life.[2]

In 1510 a pivotal event in Luther's life took place when he was selected as one of two German Augustinians to go to Rome to present an appeal concerning their order. Only ten years later, Ignatius Loyola (1491–1556), founder of the Jesuits, would be advised not to go to Rome, for there his faith might be shaken by the city's "stupendous depravity."[3] Luther received no such helpful warning, and, although impressed by the history and grandeur of Rome, he was shocked by the open blasphemy and impiety of the clergy, including priests who thought it amusing to recite parodies of the liturgy while celebrating Mass. This was not some anti-Catholic tale Luther later told to justify his break with Rome. Many other devout visitors to Rome reported similar abuses. For example, the celebrated Erasmus (1466–1536) noted from his own visit to Rome only five years prior to Luther's that "with my own ears I heard the most loathsome blasphemies against Christ and His Apostles. Many acquaintances of mine have heard priests of the curia uttering disgusting words so loudly, even during mass, that all around them could hear."[4] And like Erasmus before him, Luther remained within the Church even after seeing such dreadful excesses. Instead he committed himself to reform. Even so, it was not until about seven years later that Luther did anything other than continue teaching.

It was the local sale of indulgences that finally prodded Luther to act. The basis for indulgences was the doctrine that the temporal penalty for all sins must be remitted by good works or penance before a soul can enter heaven. Since at death most people have sins whose temporal penalties have not been fully remitted, their souls must linger in purgatory—a kind of semi-hell—until they have endured sufficient punishment, or cleansing, to purge their sins (hence "purgatory"). This doctrine stimulated many good works, and the Church assigned each such work a value as to time remitted from one's sentence to purgatory. For example, service in a Crusade brought complete remission of time in purgatory. Soon it became accepted that gifts to the Church allowed individuals to gain credits for time off their stay in purgatory. The Church formalized this practice by selling signed and sealed certificates known as *indulgences*, some of them specifying a period of remission, others providing dispensations to commit, or for having committed, various sins. Then, in 1476, Pope Sixtus IV authorized the sale of indulgences to the living to shorten the suffering of their dead loved ones in purgatory. As a popular sales slogan put it, "As soon as a coin in the coffer rings, the soul from purgatory springs."[5] The Church's yield from indulgences was enormous, especially because it sent out trained officials to lead local sales efforts.

In 1517 Johannes Tetzel, a prominent Dominican indulgence salesman, organized a campaign in areas near Wittenberg, the proceeds to go to rebuilding Saint Peter's basilica in Rome and to repay the archbishop of Metz the huge price he had paid to buy his office. Drafts of some of Tetzel's sermons survive. The following excerpt is typical: "Do you not hear the voices of your dead parents and other people, screaming and saying 'Have pity on me, have pity on me. . . . We are suffering severe punishments and pain, from which you could rescue me with a few alms, if you would."[6]

Luther was disgusted by the sale of indulgences. In fact, his Ninety-Five Theses focused specifically on critiquing this practice rather than offering a general attack on church practices. The document he nailed to the door of the Wittenberg Castle church, which became known as the *Ninety-Five Theses on the Power and Efficacy of Indulgences*, was a proposal to debate the issue. Contrary to myth, the act of nailing his theses to the church door was not an act of defiance: the Wittenberg faculty routinely used the castle church door as a bulletin board.[7] Still, Luther's proposal prompted a swift reaction.

He posted his theses (written in Latin) on October 31, 1517. By December at least three different printers in three different cities had produced German translations. During the next several months translations were published in France, England, Italy, and beyond.[8] Probably because Luther's critique became so widely known outside the Latin-reading elite, the Church responded angrily. Pope Leo X ordered Luther to Rome. Had Luther gone, he probably would have become just another obscure martyr to reform. But the German Elector Frederick objected to his summons (he, too, opposed the sale of Roman indulgences in Germany), and the Church agreed to have Luther instead appear before Cardinal Cajetan in Augsburg.

Arriving in Augsburg on October 7, 1518, with a safe conduct from Frederick, Luther discovered that the cardinal had no interest in anything but a retraction of his theses. When Luther refused, he was ordered into seclusion until he was ready to conform. Soon rumors reached Luther that the cardinal was planning to violate his safe conduct and send him to Rome in chains. Friends helped Luther to escape back to Wittenberg, where the faculty rallied to his cause and petitioned Frederick to protect him. This amounted to an irreconcilable break with the church hierarchy. Luther responded in 1520 by publishing three famous and defiant tracts, now known as the "Reformation Treatises."

Written in German, Luther's tracts denounced the Roman Church for bleeding Germany: "Every year more than three hundred thousand gulden [gold coins] find their way from Germany to Rome, quite uselessly and fruitlessly; we get nothing but scorn and contempt. And yet we wonder that princes, nobles, cities, endowments, land and people are impoverished."[9] He wrote of Rome and the pope in colorful, violent language: "Hearest thou this, O pope, not most holy, but most sinful? O that God from heaven would soon destroy thy throne and sink it in the abyss of hell! . . . O Christ, my Lord, look down, let the day of thy judgment break, and destroy the devil's nest at Rome."[10]

Luther also proposed radical changes in both practice and doctrine. He called for an end to the sale of indulgences, to saying Masses for the dead, and to all "holy days" except for Sundays. He declared that the whole congregation, not just the priest, should sip the communion wine. Moreover, he proposed that priests be allowed to marry and that no one be permitted to take binding monastic vows before the age of thirty. (Later he advised the dissolution of all religious orders and that there be no more vows of celibacy.) As for doctrine, Luther asserted the absolute authority of Holy Scripture and that each human must discover the meaning of scripture and establish his or her own, personal relationship with God. Most radical of all, Luther proposed that salvation is God's gift, freely given, and is gained entirely by faith in Jesus as the redeemer. That is, salvation cannot be earned or purchased by good works. Consequently, there is no purgatory, since no atonement for sins, other than that wrought by Christ, is necessary or possible. One either has faith and is saved or lacks faith and is damned. Good works are the result, or fruits, of faith.

On June 15, 1520, the Church officially condemned Luther's writings, and copies were burned in Rome. In response, the students at Wittenberg burned official pronouncements against Luther. Despite Luther's widespread popularity in Germany, the pope officially excommunicated him in January 1521. Next, Luther was ordered to appear before the Imperial Diet meeting in Worms—his safe conduct provided by Charles V, king of Spain and Holy Roman Emperor. Luther's friends urged him not to go, fearing for his life. But Luther refused to be deterred. It was the most important decision of his life and changed the course of Western history. Luther's journey to Worms was not that of an unimportant, excommunicated monk. Crowds of supporters thronged along the roads, and "he was attended by a cavalcade of German knights," in the words of the Luther scholar Ernest Gordon Rupp.[11] During his hearing before the Diet, Luther refused to budge, closing with his immortal "Here I stand."

A rump session of the Diet organized by members loyal to Rome declared Luther an outlaw, but it was an empty gesture. A large number of German princes formed ranks in defense of Luther and in rebellion against the Church (thus retaining the huge sums that Rome had extracted from their realms). Luther exulted: "I declare, I have made a reformation which will make the pope's ears ring and heart burst."[12]

Causes of the Reformation

Explanations of the Lutheran Reformation must distinguish between the appeal of the phenomenon itself—the stimulus—and factors that may have influenced responses to Lutheranism. The latter can be distinguished into *background* factors, such as Catholic shortcomings; *operative* factors, including characteristics of individuals and groups that governed their choices; and *situational* factors, such as freedom to choose.

Unfortunately, discussions of the causes of the Lutheran Reformation have been tightly focused on the virtues of the stimulus—on the appeal of the set of doctrines Luther offered. Much of this discussion is irrelevant because it centers on theological intricacies that very few of those who embraced Lutheranism understood or cared about. To be sure, Luther's basic message—that each individual controls his or her own salvation, since it is gained by faith alone, and that the intercession of the Church is unnecessary—was bound to have appealed widely in this time and place. Even so, Lutheran doctrine is of limited help in explaining the rise of Lutheranism because the doctrine was a constant, while the success or failure of Lutheranism was a variable. That is, everyone in Germany who could possibly have cared was aware of Luther's message, but only some people in some places turned Lutheran. Why them?

Many background factors have this same shortcoming—they are effectively constants, not variables. Defects of the Catholic Church were the same everywhere; what varied were responses to them. The same is true of the catalogue of "real causes" that a host of social scientists have assembled: the demise of feudalism (supposing it had ever existed), the growth of a money economy, the rise of credit, the expansion of trade, industrialization, urbanization, the expansion of the bourgeoisie, increased taxes, and population growth, among others.[13] Even if we accept that all these changes were taking place, they explain nothing about the success of the Lutheran Reformation because they were as prevalent in areas that remained Catholic as they were in those that embraced Lutheranism.

The same shortcoming also applies to two silly explanations historians have offered for the Lutheran Reformation. Some scholars have cited the Black Death as a cause, presumably because it resulted in a widespread loss of confidence in the Church.[14] But as noted in chapter 7, what evidence there is strongly contests the claim that people turned away from religion in response to the Black Death. In any case, there was a lag of nearly two centuries between the outbreak of plague and Luther's challenge to the Catholic Church. Some historians have suggested another silly cause: celibacy. That is, they argue that Luther, along with many priests and nuns, seized the opportunity to escape their vows.[15] As is so often the case with efforts to trace complex social affairs to simple matters of sexuality, these claims trivialize human events. In addition, the Black Death was of memory everywhere, and sexual urges are universal, whereas acceptance of Lutheranism was variable.

Let us turn, then, to operative and situational variables that might account for why some areas in Germany, but not others, became Lutheran.

Pamphlets and Printers

Luther's Reformation was the first social movement for which printed materials played an important role—the printing press was only just coming of age. Luther produced many pamphlets (often only four to six pages long) outlining his various disagreements with Rome, each written in vernacular German, and printers across Germany and in other parts of Europe pumped out copies. Between 1517 and 1520 Luther turned out thirty pamphlets and short essays. These were published by more than twenty printing firms, and it is estimated that they sold more than three hundred thousand copies altogether.[16] In 1522 Luther's translation of the New Testament into German appeared, and it became his bestselling work.[17]

Keep in mind that copyrights didn't exist in this era and printers produced their own editions of anything they thought would sell. Luther protested when other printers rushed out his New Testament before the printer in Wittenberg had sold out his copies. But it was the existence of aggressive local printers that spread Lutheran materials so widely and quickly. In most of the rest of Europe printers operated only in the largest cities, but in Germany printers existed even in many of the smaller towns. Hence, books and pamphlets did not need to be transported long distances; most of Luther's writings were available locally as soon as the enterprising printer had obtained a copy elsewhere. In one famous incident, a copy of one of Luther's tracts was stolen from the printer's shop in Wittenberg and appeared in print in Nuremberg before the Wittenberg edition came out.[18]

Connections between printers, printing, and the Reformation have been well tested in a remarkable new study by Hyojoung Kim and Steven Pfaff.[19] These young sociologists assembled data for each German town having a population of two thousand or more in 1520. Their goal was to test explanations of the success of the Reformation by seeing what factors determined which of these 461 towns turned Lutheran and which remained Catholic. They used as their measure whether and when each town officially outlawed saying the Catholic Mass, which is well documented.

Among the many factors Kim and Pfaff studied about each town were whether it had a local printer and whether this printer had produced an edition of Luther's Bible. Consistent with an immense historical literature, the sociologists hypothesized that towns with printers who had published Luther's Bible were more likely to turn Lutheran. And the results? Not so! During the early days of the Reformation there was no correlation between printers of Lutheran Bibles and turning Lutheran; in later days the correlation was negative—towns where Luther's Bible was printed were significantly *less* likely to have turned Lutheran. This suggests—contrary to what many scholars have suggested[20]—that printers churned out Lutheran literature because it was so profitable, not necessarily because they agreed with it. In fact, that is precisely what Luther and many of his fellow reformers believed. They often complained that the printers were merely profiteering from their work—Luther denounced printers as "sordid mercenaries."[21]

The emphasis historians have placed on pamphleteering and printing is understandable, since nothing of the sort had been seen before. But it seems excessive to claim, as Lawrence Stone did, that without "the printing press . . . it is probable that there would have been no Reformation at all."[22] Indeed, assessments of the impact of printed materials on the success of the Lutheran Reformation too often overlook a critical factor: no more than 5 percent of Germans in this era could read.[23] This helps explain why the Reformation was a middle- and upper-class phenomenon that left the masses virtually untouched. Most people in Germany were counted as Protestants or Catholics because their community had accepted or rejected the Reformation, although they remained impervious to the whole matter, being, at best, semi-Christians.

Professors and Students

The Reformation began at the University of Wittenberg. As the distinguished scholar Paul Grendler put it, "The activities of the first four or five years of the Lutheran Reformation resembled a young faculty uprising."[24] As word of Luther's activities spread, enrollment at Wittenberg nearly doubled by 1520, and soon it was the largest university in Germany. Many students attended Luther's theological lectures, and nearly all of them heard Philipp Melanchthon (1497–1560), Luther's confidant and ally.[25] After completing their studies at Wittenberg, most students went home and devoted themselves to spreading the Reformation. Lutheranism attracted strong support in many other universities as well, especially at the University of Basel. In addition to taking the Reformation home with them, many students soon became professors of theology and began to train more activists. A study of prominent Reformation leaders found that nearly all of them were, or had been, university professors.[26]

It turns out, however, that this is a one-sided and misleading view of the connection between academia and the Reformation. Many other universities were hotbeds of anti-Lutheran, orthodox Catholicism. The University of Cologne, for example, came to be called the "German Rome," and the University of Louvain was equally anti-Lutheran. Students from these universities went home and served as staunch defenders of the Church.

Apparently universities, at least in Germany, keep their records forever. Records remain for each student who enrolled in the sixteenth century, with the student's hometown detailed. Even the enrollment lists for specific classes, including those Luther taught, can be reconstructed. For their set of 461 towns and cities, Kim and Pfaff identified the number of residents who were enrolled in Wittenberg and in Basel from 1517 through 1522. They also identified the number who attended Cologne and Louvain. Finally, they created a measure of the total number of students from a town or city who enrolled in any university.

The results are compelling. The rate at which a town's young people went off to a university had no impact whatsoever on whether the town turned Lutheran or stayed Catholic. But if the larger proportion of students had gone off to Wittenberg or Basel, the city or town had a high probability of becoming Lutheran. Conversely, where enrollments in Cologne and Louvain predominated, the probability was that the town or city remained Catholic. Finally, university towns were more likely to remain Catholic than were towns and cities lacking a university. Despite the prominence of students and faculty in the Lutheran movement, universities tended to be conservative in the sense of upholding traditions. This also helps explain the negative correlation between printers and Lutheranism—university cities all had active presses.

Responsive City Governance

The backbone of the Lutheran Reformation was provided by the urban bourgeoisie: the merchants, bankers, lawyers, physicians, manufacturers, schoolmasters, shopkeepers, and bureaucrats, as well as members of the highly skilled guilds, such as printers and glassblowers, and many local priests. This does not mean, of course, that all or nearly all members of these groups favored Luther. It merely means that most of Luther's support came from these groups.

It is well known that these urban groups formed the base of Lutheran recruitment.[27] But why? Did it have something to do with city governance?

These urban supporters were effective because many German towns and cities had sufficient autonomy to make Lutheranism the only lawful faith without suffering outside interference—at least not until the Wars of Religion began. The importance of local political autonomy can be seen through an examination of so-called Free Imperial Cities.[28] These cities owed no allegiance to local princes; paying their taxes directly to the Holy Roman Emperor (which is why they were called Imperial Cities), they remained in complete control of their own tax systems as well as their internal affairs.

There were about sixty-five Free Imperial Cities, but some can be ignored because they were tiny, having no more than a thousand residents.[29] A few had less political freedom than the others because they were situated in a powerful duchy or principality, which made the city fathers act cautiously lest they provoke outside interference. But most of the Free Imperial Cities were located in the area along the Rhine known as the "Borderlands," where there were no large governmental units and thus little threat of external interference. Fortunately for purposes of research, this Borderland area had a number of similarly sized cities that were not Free Imperial Cities. Some of these cities were ruled by a prince bishop, others by a nearby prince, but in either case the local laity had little authority.

To test the hypothesis that where the local bourgeoisie were in control, Lutheranism was far more likely to have been adopted, I collected information on all forty-three significant Free Imperial Cities and the twelve other cities located in the Borderlands. Of the Free Imperial Cities, nearly two-thirds (61 percent) became Protestant, while three-fourths (75 percent) of the non–Imperial Cities remained Catholic.[30] Using a slightly different set of cities, Kim and Pfaff found very similar results.

Hence, local political autonomy played an important role in the success of Luther's Reformation. But so did autocracy. Aside from the cities, many larger political units ruled by strong princes or kings turned Protestant too.

Royal Self-Interest

We come now to an apparent contradiction about the spread of Luther's Reformation. In most of Europe, the decision to embrace Lutheranism or to remain steadfastly within the Catholic Church was made by an autocratic ruler—a king or a prince. Nearly without exception the autocrats opted for Lutheranism in places where the Catholic Church had the *greatest* local power and chose to remain Catholic in places where the Church was extremely weak. To see why things turned out this way, it will be useful to contrast France and Spain, on one hand, with Denmark and Sweden.

Beginning in 1296, when King Philip of France successfully imposed a tax on church income, papal authority steadily eroded in France. In 1516 the subordination of the Church to the French monarchy was formalized in the Concordat of Bologna, signed by Pope Leo X and King Francis I. The concordat acknowledged the king's right to appoint all higher church posts in France: ten archbishops, eighty-two bishops, and every prior, abbot, and abbess of all the many hundreds of monasteries, abbeys, and convents. This gave the king full control of all church property and income. As the esteemed historian Owen Chadwick noted, "When he [King Francis] wanted ecclesiastical money, his methods need not even be devious."[31] His appointees simply delivered.

If anything, the Spanish crown had even greater power over the Church. It had long held the right to nominate archbishops and bishops, to fine the clergy, and to receive a substantial share of the tithes. Then, in 1486, King Ferdinand and Queen Isabella gained the right to make all major ecclesiastical appointments, to prohibit appeals from Spanish courts to Rome, to impose taxes on the clergy, and to make it illegal to publish papal bulls and decrees in Spain or its possessions without prior royal consent.[32] Of course, as Spain became the center of the Holy Roman Empire, these policies were extended to many portions of Italy and to Portugal, the Netherlands, Austria, and southeastern Germany.

In contrast, in Denmark in 1500 the Church owned from a third to half of all tillable land and required all laypeople (including the nobility) to pay tithes. None of this income was shared with the crown, and much of it went directly to Rome. The pope also had sole authority to make ecclesiastical appointments in Denmark. Thus, when Christian III became king of Denmark in 1534, he seized an immense opportunity by declaring for Lutheranism and confiscating all church properties and income in his realm.[33]

Meanwhile, Sweden had successfully rebelled against Danish rule and crowned King Gustavus I in 1528. The new king was desperate for funds, and here, too, the Church possessed unchallenged authority and immense wealth. So Gustavus opted for Protestantism and confiscated all church possessions and income.[34] To gain support among the nobles, Gustavus sold them appropriated church property at bargain prices. Even so, the church possessions he kept increased the crown's lands fourfold.[35]

The same principle of self-interest accounts for the decisions of other rulers. German princes with much to gain from becoming Lutheran did so; others, such as prince bishops who already possessed control of church offices and income, remained Catholic. And did any king gain more from stripping the Church of its wealth and power than did England's Henry VIII? Consider that from the shrine dedicated to Saint Thomas à Becket alone, Henry's agents confiscated 4,994 ounces of gold, 4,425 ounces of silver gilt, 5,286 ounces of silver, and twenty-six cartloads of other treasure—and this was regarded as a trivial portion of the wealth confiscated from the Church.[36]

In many instances, too, it was very much in the self-interest of the urban bourgeoisie for local church property to be confiscated and church authority curtailed. The Church's extensive holdings in the Free Imperial Cities—about a third of all property in most cities—went *untaxed*. Adding to the burden were the clergy and members of religious orders, who made up as much as 10 percent of a city's population; these members of the Church were exempt from all taxes (including tithes to the Church) and all duties of citizenship (such as taking their turn as sentries on the walls, as all able-bodied nonclerical males were required to do). So the cities, too, had much to gain by expelling the Church. As the twentieth-century British Catholic writer Hilaire Belloc summed up, the Reformation benefited immensely from "the chance presented to territorial lords, large and small, from kings down to squires, of looting Church property."[37]

It is all well and good to note the widespread appeal of the doctrine that we are saved by faith alone, but it also must be recognized that Protestantism prevailed only where the local rulers or councils had not already imposed their rule over the Church. Pocketbook issues prevailed.

Consequences of the Reformation

An amazing number of consequences have been traced to the Lutheran Reformation—some of them immediate, some of them occurring far later; some of them plausible, some of them as nutty as the claim that Hitler was Luther's direct heir.[38] (Granted that Luther was a bitter anti-Semite, but so were many others in that era, including leading Catholics,[39] and Hitler was a quite militant atheist.)

The Revival of Mass Piety?

The most widely accepted belief about the Lutheran Reformation is that it touched the hearts and souls of the German masses to such an extent that it resulted in a huge revival of popular piety. As Lawrence Stone put it, the combination of Luther and the printing press "made the Bible available to the unsophisticated. . . . The result was the most massive missionary drive in history, a combined assault on indifference, cynicism, paganism, and ignorance . . . [making] the sixteenth century the era of the rise of Christian Europe." Stone then explained that the Reformation "achieved such immediate success" because it was able "to harness the powerful feelings of separatism and nationalism."[40]

But it wasn't so. Eventually even Martin Luther admitted that neither the tidal wave of publications nor all the Lutheran preachers in Germany had made the slightest dent in the ignorance, irreverence, and alienation of the masses. Luther complained in 1529, "Dear God, help us! . . . The common man, especially in the villages, knows absolutely nothing about Christian doctrine; and indeed many pastors are in effect unfit and incompetent to teach. Yet they all are called Christians, are baptized, and enjoy the holy sacraments—even though they cannot recite either the Lord's Prayer, the Creed or the Commandments. They live just like animals."[41]

Luther's despair was not merely due to his having unrealistic expectations. Rather, Luther and his colleagues were properly distressed on the basis of carefully collected evidence. Beginning in 1525 and continuing until after Luther's death in 1546, official visitors made systematic observations of local churches, interviewing Christians and writing up their evaluations in formal reports. The distinguished American historian Gerald Strauss extracted these reports, noting, "I have selected only such instances as could be multiplied a hundredfold."[42] Here is a sampling of the reports Strauss published.

In Saxony: "You'll find more of them out fishing than at service. . . . Those who do come walk out as soon as the pastor begins his sermon." In Seegrehna: "A pastor testified that he often quits his church without preaching . . . because not a soul has turned up to hear him." In Barum: "It is the greatest and most widespread complaint of all pastors here-abouts that people do not go to church on Sundays. . . . Nothing helps; they will not come . . . so that pastors face near-empty churches." In Braunschweig-Grubenhagen: "Many churches are empty on Sundays." In Weilburg: "Absenteeism from church on Sundays was so widespread that the synod debated whether the city gates should be barred on Sunday mornings to lock everyone inside. Evidence from elsewhere suggests that this expedient would not have helped."

Nevertheless, it is not clear that having a large turnout at Sunday services would have been desirable. In Nassau: "Those who come to service are usually drunk . . . and sleep through the whole sermon, except sometimes they fall off the benches, making a great clatter, or women drop their babies on the floor." In Wiesbaden: "[During church] there is such snoring that I could not believe my ears when I heard it. The moment these people sit down, they put their heads on their arms and straight away they go to sleep." In Hamburg: "[People make] indecent gestures at members of the congregation who wish to join in singing the hymns, even bringing dogs to church so that due to the loud barking the service is disturbed." In Leipzig: "They play cards while the pastor preaches, and often mock or mimic him cruelly to his face; . . . cursing and blaspheming, hooliganism, and fighting are common. . . . They enter church when the service is half over, go at once to sleep, and run out again before the blessing is given. . . . Nobody joins in singing the hymn; it made my heart ache to hear the pastor and the sexton singing all by themselves."

It is hardly surprising, then, that most Germans were ignorant of basic Christian teachings. In Saxony: "In some villages one could not find a single person who knew the Ten Commandments." In Brandenburg: "A random group of men was . . . asked how they understood each of the Ten Commandments, but we found many who could give no answer at all. . . . None of them thought it a sin to get dead drunk and curse using the name of God." In Notenstein: "[Parishioners], including church elders, could remember none of the Ten Commandments." In Salzliebenhalle: "[No one knows] who their redeemer and savior is." In Nuremberg: Many could not name Good Friday as the day of the year when Jesus died. And the pastor at Graim summed up: "Since they never go to church, most of them cannot even say their prayers."

So much for claims that the Lutheran Reformation produced a revival among the general population.

Religious Freedom

So much, too, for the notion that the rise of Protestantism resulted in a new climate of religious freedom. Recall the measure Kim and Pfaff used to identify cities and towns that accepted the Reformation—the date when they outlawed saying the Catholic Mass. Luther's Reformation had nothing to do with religious freedom of choice; what took place was a switch from one monopoly church to another. Similarly, Henry VIII burned, beheaded, and hanged all sorts of dissenters from his newly imposed Anglican Church, including many Lutherans, and the English began a long era of searching out and executing priests. But nothing so testified to the religious intolerance of Europe as the series of brutal and bloody wars of religion.

First came the German Peasants' War, stirred up by Lutheran radicals in 1524. The war lasted a year and cost about one hundred thousand lives by the time it was suppressed. Then came the Schmalkaldic Wars, during which Charles V, Holy Roman Emperor, tried to reimpose Catholicism all across Germany, arousing the opposition of a group of princes who had adopted Lutheranism. The war was settled in 1555 by the Peace of Augsburg, which recognized Protestant principalities. This peace soon broke down, and the Thirty Years' War began in 1618. By war's end in 1648, Germany had been devastated—a third of the towns were wiped out, along with about a third of the population. But in the end, Protestant areas survived. In the Low Countries, the war to restore Catholicism lasted for eighty years, but the Dutch Protestants outlasted the Spanish (as seen in chapter 12). And, of course, religion was a central aspect of the English Revolution. Nor did peace bring much more than grudging toleration. For the most part, Catholics were unwelcome in Protestant areas and vice versa.

Nor is this a thing of the distant past. Recently, Brian Grim and Roger Finke created quantitative measures of government interference in religious life.[43] They based their coding on the highly respected annual *International Religious Freedom Report* produced by the U.S. Department of State. One of Grim and Finke's measures is the Government Favoritism

Index, which is based on "subsidies, privileges, support, or favorable sanctions provided by the state to a select religion or a small group of religions." This index varies from 0.0 (no favoritism) to 10.0 (extreme favoritism). The United States and Taiwan score 0.0, and Saudi Arabia and Iran each score 9.3. And while Afghanistan and the United Arab Emirates score 7.8, so too do Iceland, Spain, and Greece. Belgium scores 7.5, slightly higher than Bangladesh's 7.3 and India's 7.0. Morocco scores 6.3, while Denmark scores 6.7, Finland, 6.5, Austria 6.2, Switzerland 5.8, France 5.5, Italy, 5.3, and Norway, 5.2. Of course, these high scores reflect favoritism toward Protestantism (often the official state church) in northern Europe and toward Catholicism in southern Europe. Thus does the long tradition of religious inequality and intolerance survive!

Puritan "Achievements"

The most significant consequences claimed for the Reformations involve effects that supposedly arose when Puritan forms of Protestantism emerged. Perhaps the most widely circulated of these is that the Puritans initiated an era of extreme sexual repression that has lived on to disfigure modern life. As Bertrand Russell put it, Puritanism consisted of the "determination to avoid the pleasures of sex."[44] It turns out that this is a malicious myth: the Puritans were very frank and enlightened about sex![45]

For example, Puritan pastors and congregations in Massachusetts openly supported a wife's *right* to orgasms. During the seventeenth century, when James Mattock's wife complained first to her pastor and then to the entire congregation that her husband was not sexually responsive to her, the members of the First Church of Boston expelled him for denying conjugal "fellowship unto his wife for a space of two years together."[46] In fact, court records for the years 1639 to 1711 reveal that about one of every six divorce petitions filed by women "involved charges of male sexual incapacity."[47] Nor was impotence the only grounds for female dissatisfaction that the courts recognized. John Williams's wife was granted a divorce on her complaint of his "refuysing to perform marriage duty unto her."[48] Indeed, it was widely agreed that husbands who failed to sexually gratify their wives bore primary responsibility for the wife's extramarital affairs. Elizabeth Jerrad was granted a divorce and exonerated of adultery because of her husband's inattention, the court ruling to "release her from her matrimoniall tye to sayd Robert Jarrad that so she may allso be freed from such temptation as hath occasioned her gross & scandolouse fall into the sinn of uncleaness."[49] New England courts consistently "upheld the view that women had a right to expect 'content and satisfaction' in bed," according to the historian Richard Godbeer.[50]

Two other major claims about Puritan "achievements" are far more significant than—but just as ill founded as—the claims about Puritan sexual repression: that Puritans invented capitalism and that they produced the "Scientific Revolution" of the sixteenth century.

As mentioned in chapter 6, at the start of the twentieth century the German sociologist Max Weber published his immensely influential study *The Protestant Ethic and the Spirit of Capitalism*.[51] In it Weber proposed that capitalism originated only in Europe because, of all the world's religions, only Puritan Protestantism provided a moral vision that led people to restrain their material consumption while vigorously seeking wealth. Weber argued that prior to the Reformation, restraint on consumption was invariably linked to asceticism and hence to condemnations of commerce. Conversely, the pursuit of wealth was linked to profligate consumption. Either cultural pattern was inimical to capitalism. According to Weber, the Protestant ethic shattered these traditional linkages, creating a culture of frugal entrepreneurs content to systematically reinvest profits in pursuit of ever greater wealth, and therein lay the key to capitalism and the ascendancy of the West.

Perhaps because it was such an elegant thesis, it was widely embraced despite being so obviously wrong. Even today, *The Protestant Ethic* enjoys an almost sacred status among sociologists,[52] although economic historians quickly dismissed Weber's surprisingly undocumented[53] monograph on the irrefutable grounds that the rise of capitalism in Europe *preceded* the Reformation by centuries. As the historian Hugh Trevor-Roper explained, "The idea that large-scale industrial capitalism was ideologically impossible before the Reformation is exploded by the simple fact that it existed."[54] Only a decade after Weber published, the celebrated scholar Henri Pirenne noted a large literature that "established the fact that all of the essential features of capitalism—individual enterprise, advances in credit, commercial profits, speculation, etc.—are to be found from the twelfth century on, in the city republics of Italy—Venice, Genoa, or Florence."[55] As noted in chapter 6, the first examples of capitalism appeared in the great Catholic monasteries as early as the ninth century.[56]

As for Puritans as the leaders of the "Scientific Revolution," this claim will be disposed of in chapter 15. For now we can state simply that

Catholics played as important a role as Protestants in the great scientific achievements of the sixteenth and seventeenth centuries—and very few, if any, of the Protestant scientific stars of this era were Puritans.

The Catholic Reformation

Probably the most profound and lasting consequence of the Protestant Reformations was that they prompted the Catholic Reformation or Counter-Reformation. At the Council of Trent (1551–1552, 1562–1563), the Catholic Church ended simony (the sale of church offices), enforced priestly celibacy, and made available official, inexpensive Bibles in local languages (vulgates). In short, the Church of Piety permanently replaced the Church of Power. At Trent the Church also decided to establish a network of seminaries to train men for the local priesthood. No longer would there be priests who did not know the Seven Deadly Sins or who preached the Sermon on the Mount. By the eighteenth century, in most places the Church was staffed by literate men well versed in theology. Even more important, the seminaries produced priests whose vocations had been shaped and tested in a formal, institutional setting.[57]

But there was a dark side to the Catholic Reformation. The new spirit of strictness shifted the Church's economic and intellectual outlook. A reemphasis on asceticism set the Church against business and banking to such an extent that the false argument that Protestantism gave birth to capitalism could be taken seriously.[58] The same sort of thing happened with science. Although Western science is rooted in Christian theology and arose in the medieval universities, the Catholic Reformation imposed such severe intellectual restrictions that Catholic universities declined in scientific significance. By the latter part of the nineteenth century, therefore, there flourished the mistaken belief that the Reformation gave birth to a scientific evolution.

Organized Diversity

If the Reformation failed to result in an era of religious liberty, it did at least produce organized diversity within Christendom. There was, of course, the division between Catholics and Protestants, but just as important was the diversity *among* Protestants. In fact, from earliest days, the term *Protestant* was a somewhat misleading label, meaning little more than that a person was a Christian who was not a Roman Catholic. Toleration, not only across the Catholic/Protestant divide but also among Protestants, came only after centuries of bloodshed.

14

⟨⟩

Exposing Muslim Illusions

In 1520, four years after Charles V became king of Spain, and three years after Martin Luther posted his Ninety-Five Theses, Suleiman became the tenth sultan to rule the Ottoman Empire. Immediately, the twenty-six-year-old Turk began to pursue his boyhood dream of conquering the West and imposing the True Faith on the Christian infidel.[1] It would be a two-pronged attack: sending a huge army overland into Europe through the Balkans and taking control of the Mediterranean in order to land armies on the coasts of Italy, France, and Spain. The plan was so monumental that Suleiman continues to be known as "Suleiman the Magnificent"—even though, after he had scored a few unimportant victories, Europeans smashed his armies and sank his navy, just as they had done to his ancestors' forces centuries before during the Crusades.

Despite this record, far too many recent Western historians promulgate politically correct illusions about Islamic might, as well as spurious claims that once upon a time Islamic science and technology were far superior to that of a backward and intolerant Europe. But, as Suleiman discovered, wishing doesn't make it so.

Misleading Victories

Over the centuries Muslims had come to remember the conquest of the crusader kingdoms as a major demonstration of their superior military power. It was nothing of the sort. It hadn't taken much military might to overwhelm the few hundred Knights Templar and Knights Hospitallers left defending the crusader kingdoms after Europeans had decided, for financial reasons, to abandon the kingdoms to their fate. The notion of Muslim superiority over the crusaders also flies in the face of the fact that only sixteen years after the fall of the last crusader stronghold of Acre in 1291, a few of the surviving Knights Hospitallers seized Rhodes, an island barely eleven miles off the shores of Turkey, and held it for several centuries while they plundered and devastated Ottoman shipping. We will return to the case of Rhodes, but other bases for Muslim overconfidence must be treated first.

Constantinople Falls

The fall of Constantinople in 1453, which ended the existence of the Byzantine Empire, was the cause of wild celebrations across Islam and of great consternation in the West. Both reactions were unwarranted. By this time Byzantium consisted of little more than the capital city, and therefore its fall to the Ottomans was of little geopolitical significance. Similarly, its capture by Ottoman forces was an unimpressive military feat.[2]

Constantinople was defended by little more than its massive walls, which crusaders had easily scaled when they sacked the city in 1204. By the time the Ottoman sultan Mehmed II encircled Constantinople with an army of 80,000, including 10,000 members of the elite Janissary force, the Byzantines could man the walls with only about 7,000 defenders (2,000 of them volunteers sent from the West).[3] This meant that the Byzantine commander had at best only about 560 soldiers to defend each mile of the walls, or one defender about every ten feet.[4]

Even so, the sultan's forces did not scale the walls and sweep the defenders away as the crusaders had done so easily (despite their having a much smaller force than did the Byzantine defenders). Instead, the sultan counted on blasting huge gaps in the walls with gigantic cannons that a Hungarian engineer had cast for him.[5] The largest of these cannons came to be known as the Basilica. It was twenty-seven feet long and able to fire a thousand-pound ball. Several others were about twenty feet long. But the big guns did not live up to the sultan's expectations. First of all, to transport the Basilica to Constantinople had required seventy oxen and two hundred men.[6] Once on site, the Basilica took so long to reload and resight that it could be fired only seven times a day. The several other huge guns could not fire much faster. As a result, the Byzantines could plug up holes in the walls as quickly as the Ottoman guns could create them.[7] In addition, Byzantine troops took advantage of poor Ottoman security to kill the gun crews and disable several of the guns. Finally, after being fired for about a week, the Basilica exploded, killing the gun crew, its Hungarian creator, and many bystanders. The sultan barely escaped unharmed.

Although he ordered the lesser guns to continue firing, Mehmed decided to try other tactics. Among these was a massive effort by thousands of slave miners to dig tunnels under the walls of the city. But the Byzantines dug countertunnels that allowed them to enter the Ottoman tunnels and kill the miners. Mehmed then realized that to take Constantinople he would need to use his immensely superior numbers to fight his way over the walls. Shortly after midnight on May 29, 1453, the assault began. Ottoman casualties were so heavy that the sea surrounding three sides of the city was filled with bodies bobbing "like melons," in the words of one eyewitness.[8] Eventually, however, the Ottoman attackers captured several gates, whereupon tens of thousands of their comrades stormed into the city.

What followed was mass slaughter and enslavement. According to an Ottoman account, "They took captive the youths and maidens . . . and they slew the miserable common people." A Christian eyewitness wrote that the Ottomans "slew mercilessly all the elderly" and threw "newborn infants . . . into the streets."[9] The esteemed historian Steven Runciman, surely no enemy of Islam,[10] summed up: "They slew everyone that they met in the streets, men, women, and children without discrimination. . . . But soon the lust for slaughter was assuaged. The soldiers realized that captives . . . would bring them greater profit. . . . Many of the lovelier maidens and youths were almost torn to death as their captors quarreled over them. . . . Some of the younger nuns preferred martyrdom and flung themselves down well-shafts . . . [Prisoners destined for slavery] were about fifty thousand."[11] Constantinople was now an empty city, awaiting an Ottoman population.

Unfortunately for sultans to come, this victory inflated their belief in the invincibility of their armies—never mind that it was dearly won despite the Ottomans' having had an advantage in numbers of better than eleven to one.

The victory in Constantinople provided the Ottomans with prestige, a splendid new capital city, and a base on the European continent (barely) from which to launch attacks through the Balkans. But on the whole it mattered little. (It wasn't until 1930 that the Turks renamed the city Istanbul when they moved their capital back to Ankara, Turkey.)

Trying to make inroads through the Balkans proved difficult for the Ottomans. The Muslim armies that were dispatched to the northwest soon after the fall of Constantinople were turned back by Hungarian forces led by Vlad the Impaler (also known as Dracula), whose brutal executions of Ottoman prisoners were judged sadistic even by Turkish standards. Thus it was left to Suleiman to finally conquer the city of Belgrade in 1521. Suleiman reveled in his victory, writing: "Rejoice with me . . . that . . . I have captured that most powerful of fortresses, Belgrade . . . and destroyed most of the inhabitants."[12] In 1526 Suleiman also defeated a badly outnumbered Hungarian army at Mohács. But not even this victory resulted in an Ottoman breakthrough into Austria. What it did accomplish was to arouse the Habsburgs (including Charles V) to prepare for war.

Rhodes

The existence of Rhodes as a western outpost from which the Knights of St. John (as the Knights Hospitallers had renamed themselves) devastated Ottoman coastal shipping should have given pause to the Ottomans about their military capacities. Seized by the Knights in 1307, Rhodes stood for two centuries in defiance of Islam, despite being defended by only a tiny force. In 1480 the Ottomans sent 160 ships and a force of 70,000 troops under Mesih Pasha to put an end to this blatant affront. The Knights, numbering no more than 500 and supported by perhaps 2,000 mercenaries, repelled repeated attacks on the city's walls, turning the final Ottoman assault into a rout that ended with the sacking of the Muslim camp and the capture of the "holy standard of Islam."[13]

In 1522 Suleiman himself led an army of about 100,000 men (some sources say 200,000) to eliminate these "damnable workers of wickedness."[14] Once again Rhodes was defended by only about 500 knights; in addition to the knights were 1,500 mercenaries and a few local peasants-in-arms. The Knights had known for many years that the island would be attacked again and had used the time to perfect their fortifications, cleverly rebuilding the city's walls at angles to resist cannon fire and setting up devastating cross fires for their own artillery. Much of this redesign was done under the direction of Gabriele Tadino, who may have been the greatest military engineer of the era. Led by their brilliant grand master, Philippe Villiers de L'Isle-Adam, the Knights knew that their chances were slim. But they also knew that their ancestors had prevailed against similar odds.

Although Suleiman had brought a large battery of siege guns, he seemed aware that they might not be sufficient against the newly remodeled walls: he had brought thousands of miners to dig tunnels under the walls. When the miners went to work, they succeeded in blowing gaps in the fortress walls, but the narrowness of the gaps prevented Ottoman infantry from outnumbering the defenders at point of contact. One on one, the Ottomans were no match for the Knights. This was because the Knights, all being from noble backgrounds,[15] had been trained for combat from childhood and then had trained constantly once they joined the order. In contrast, most of the Ottoman troops were slaves or conscripts, and aside from the Janissaries (who were slaves seized from subject Christian populations as young boys), the average Ottoman soldier had very little training and less armor.[16] In addition, the Knights possessed individual firearms, so they could inflict heavy losses on Ottoman forces at a distance. In close combat, the Knights' far superior swordsmanship prevailed. Equally important, Tadino had adapted the Knights' artillery for close-range use against attacking troops. Instead of firing a single, large cannonball, the Knights loaded each cannon with dozens of small balls as well as scrap iron, bolts, nails, and pieces of chain to kill or wound many attackers with each shot. These small cannons could be quickly reloaded and resighted. Positioned to cross-fire at the most suitable approaches, they killed thousands. As time passed, the Ottoman troops became increasingly demoralized and reluctant to engage. Eventually their officers had to threaten them with drawn swords to drive them to the walls.[17]

Meanwhile, however, many Knights had been killed, many others had been wounded, and the survivors were growing short of food. On December 22, after six months of fighting, Suleiman was realistic enough to offer generous terms for the Knights' surrender. Grand Master L'Isle-Adam preferred to go down fighting, but he was brought around by concerns to spare the civilians on the island. According to the surrender terms, the Knights had twelve days to leave the island with all their belongings. No Christian church would be desecrated or turned into a mosque. Civilians could leave at will anytime during the next three years, and those who stayed would be exempt from all Ottoman taxes for the next five years. Unlike many other Islamic leaders, Suleiman kept his word.

Hence, on January 1, 1523, led by their grand master, about 180 surviving Knights of St. John—those who could walk wearing full battle armor—marched from the city to the harbor with their flags flying and drums beating. There they boarded Venetian ships and sailed away to Crete.[18] If more than half of the Knights had died, so had about half of Suleiman's huge army, an astounding casualty ratio of about 40,000 to 320. But the sultan had troops to spare, and he returned to Constantinople in triumph. Victory over the West seemed to beckon.

Suleiman may not have known for several years that, subsequent to their withdrawal to Crete, Charles V had ceded the island of Malta to the Knights of St. John in return for their sending one trained falcon annually to the viceroy of Sicily. (This inspired the plot of Dashiell Hammett's famous novel *The Maltese Falcon* and the classic Humphrey Bogart 1941 movie.) Renaming themselves the Knights of Malta, and still led by Grand Master L'Isle-Adam, they immediately set about fortifying this small, rocky island—eighteen miles long and nine miles wide, about one-fifth the size of Rhodes—and recruiting new Knights from the leading aristocratic families of Europe. To Charles V's delight, they soon resumed their raids on Muslim shipping.

Failure at Vienna

In 1529 Suleiman made his next move in pursuit of his dream: he laid siege to Vienna. In doing so he struck directly at the Habsburgs. Fortunately for the sultan, at that moment Charles V was pinned down by a war with France and could spare only a contingent of Spanish arquebusiers and some German mercenaries to aid his Austrian subjects. So, as usual, the Western defenders were greatly outnumbered: by at least five to one, and perhaps as high as ten to one, not counting thousands of slave miners the Ottomans brought.[19] Fortunately for Vienna, the Germans were led by the seventy-year-old Nicholas, Count of Salm, a distinguished veteran, who took command of all forces. He immediately had the walls strengthened, blocked the four city gates, and leveled buildings to create clear fields of fire at vital points.

The Ottoman invasion was hampered by unusually long and heavy spring rains and by bad planning. The flooding and the mire caused by the rains made the route barely passable, and impassable for the sultan's many big cannons, which had to be abandoned. Most of the large contingent of camels died, and their supply loads left along the way. At least a third of the Ottoman army was made up of light cavalry, useless for a siege or even for defending against sallies by the Austrian infantry, but a huge drain on supplies. Finally, sickness broke out among the troops during the march, especially among the elite Janissaries, and many died.

Suleiman and his army did not reach Vienna until late September—not long before cold weather arrived. The sultan immediately began a bombardment of Vienna with the light artillery that had been dragged through the muddy roads. But the balls bounced harmlessly off the walls. He also put his miners to work tunneling. But the Austrians dug counter-tunnels from which they killed all the Ottoman miners. Early in October it began to rain. By that point Suleiman's forces were short of food, sickness was still taking a toll, casualties were very high, and desertions were increasing rapidly.

On October 12 the sultan held a council with his commanders and decided to commit everything to a frontal attack on the walls. Although Count Salm was killed during the battle, the attack was a bloody failure and thousands of Ottoman troops died. Then it began to snow. It was time to quit.

The Ottoman retreat was a disaster. Austrian forces struck again and again at isolated units, killing or capturing thousands of stragglers. It was a small Ottoman force lacking all its baggage and artillery that finally made it back to Hungary.

But that wasn't to be the end of it. Six years later Suleiman tried again. This time the Ottoman forces were frequently and very effectively attacked on their march forward. When word reached Suleiman that Charles V, his conflict with France resolved for the moment, had dispatched 80,000 of his best troops to defend Vienna, the sultan turned back.

In 1682 Mehmed IV tried to take Vienna again, with a force of 120,000. Once again it was a bloody disaster—this time the Ottoman army was destroyed in the field by Polish knights sent to relieve the siege.[20]

The attacks on Vienna were the high-water mark of Islamic overland invasions of Europe. Amazingly, some recent historians cite the three attempts to take Vienna as evidence of the Ottomans' military superiority over Europeans. That's a bit like claiming that the defeat of the Armada demonstrated Spain's naval superiority.

The Siege of Malta

Having been defeated in eastern Europe, Suleiman ceased mounting major attacks on the West for about thirty years, during which he gained considerable fame by victories in the East. But then, in 1565, his attention was drawn to his enemies in the Mediterranean. The most vexing of these were those same Knights who had put up such a damaging fight at Rhodes: from their new fortress on Malta they were victimizing his merchant fleet. So Suleiman proclaimed: "Those sons of dogs whom I already have conquered and who were spared only by my clemency at Rhodes forty-three years ago—I say now that, for their continual raids and insults, they shall be finally crushed and destroyed."[21]

By now the sultan was seventy-one and in failing health, unable to serve as his own field commander. He assigned the task of conquering Malta to Mustafa Pasha, commander of the army, and Piyale Pasha, commander of the navy. A split command always entails risks.

An attack on Malta was far more challenging than the one against Rhodes. Rhodes is only eleven miles off the Turkish coast; Malta is eight hundred miles to the west. Rhodes is fertile and has rivers with abundant water, able to support an invading army; Malta is barren rock. If the attackers needed timbers for siege works, each timber had to be shipped. Because the invasion posed such enormous supply requirements, a huge task force had to be built. "The cost was phenomenal—perhaps 30 percent of the treasury income," author Roger Crowley noted.[22] Still, the sultan was very confident: two renegade Greek engineers who had visited Malta pretending to be fishermen assured Suleiman that the whole island could be taken in a few days.[23]

For the assault on Malta, Suleiman sent a fleet of 193 vessels with an army of about fifty thousand aboard. Included were about seven thousand arquebusiers and more than sixty cannons, including two giant guns.[24]

To meet this overwhelming force were about five hundred Knights led by Grand Master Jean Parisot de Valette, a seventy-year-old veteran of many battles who had spent a year as an Ottoman galley slave. In addition to his Knights, de Valette had about a thousand mercenaries recruited in Spain and Italy, and about three thousand men from the local population who had no training in the use of arms. Although even the pope had worked hard to rouse European kings to reinforce the Knights, nothing was sent; according to the pope, Philip II of Spain "has withdrawn into the woods, and France, England and Scotland [are] ruled by women and boys."[25] Malta was on its own. It would seem to have been no contest.

From the start, de Valette had known from his spies at the Ottoman court that the Turks planned first to take Fort St. Elmo, which guarded the entrance to the island's main harbor.[26] To meet the onslaught he stationed half his heavy artillery in Fort St. Elmo.[27] The Ottomans eventually reduced the fort to rubble, but they did so only after five weeks and the loss of at least six thousand men, including more than half of their elite Janissaries.[28] After taking the fort, Mustafa Pasha, the army commander, had the dead and wounded Knights beheaded, their bodies nailed to wooden crosses, and floated across the bay to taunt the Knights. De Valette responded by beheading his Ottoman prisoners and firing their heads back into the Turkish camp from his large cannons, which seems to have had a significant effect on Turkish morale. But what really mattered was that the Ottomans' decision to focus on Fort St. Elmo gave the Knights time to finish rebuilding their main defensive works.[29]

The Turks attacked these fortifications again and again, but all they accomplished was to incur heavy casualties and further depress morale. Where the fighting was hottest, Grand Master de Valette always appeared, setting a ferocious example for his younger Knights. The incredible superiority of the Knights is attested by engagements in which hundreds of Turks were killed and only one or two Knights.[30]

A rapidly growing sense of doom prevailed in the Ottoman camp. The invaders' daily casualties ran at a very high rate, and they were growing short of supplies—not only food and water but also powder and even cannonballs. By early September the Turks were preparing to reboard their galleys and go home, but then a force of Spaniards arrived to reinforce the Knights. The resulting attack on the dispirited Turkish forces was a huge massacre, with only scattered elements of the Ottoman force able to reach their ships. When the siege of Malta ended, two-thirds of the Knights were still alive. Ottoman casualties may have been as high as twenty thousand. Whatever the total, it was a resounding defeat.

As the news spread, there were celebrations across Europe. Suleiman, however, chose to dismiss the defeat at Malta as if it had never happened: he ordered that rewards be given to all who had taken part.

Disaster at Lepanto

A few months after the failure to take Malta, Suleiman died, a sad and lonely man. Only his least competent son, Selim, survived him. The others died in conflicts with one another—except, that is, for Mustafa, his most talented and most loved son: Suleiman had had one of his bodyguards strangle Mustafa, while he watched, for plotting against him, only to discover later that the charges had been false.

Selim was said to be lazy and something of a drunkard. Still, the Ottoman policies of conquest seem to have been self-perpetuating, and rumors circulated constantly that the Ottomans were going to attack again in Europe. Philip II, who commanded the major Christian forces in the Mediterranean, was too busy fighting elsewhere to give much attention to the Ottoman threats: he had to cope with English attacks on Spanish treasure fleets from the New World, ongoing battles with the rebellious Dutch, and never-ending French machinations. Nevertheless, Philip was sufficiently farsighted to have a hundred new galleys completed by 1567.[31] Pope Pius V had subsidized the Spanish naval construction program, because he was dedicated to creating a Holy League to defeat the Ottomans once and for all. Philip and the Venetians had resisted the pope's efforts until the Turks attacked Cyprus in 1570, committing a number of atrocities. This meant war.

Preparations to meet an Ottoman fleet began with the assembly of a naval force under the command of John of Austria, the bastard son of Charles V and therefore the half brother of Philip II. Don John turned out to be an excellent choice. He was only twenty-two but had already distinguished himself in battle, and he was intelligent and eager to fight. Moreover, he was given a fleet designed for victory.

Although the Holy League galleys came from many sources, including Spain, Venice, Genoa, the pope, Savoy, and the Knights of Malta, nearly all of them were of a new Venetian design that maximized firepower. The traditional ramming beak at the front of a galley was replaced by a low prow that facilitated forward firing by two huge cannons and up to six smaller cannons, and the stern of the new galley was weighted to balance the guns up front.[32] The new galleys needed no ramming beak because they meant to blow an enemy galley to kindling well before any ramming could occur. These galleys required about 300 rowers and 40 sailors, and they carried about 250 soldiers. The rowers aboard the Venetian galleys were mostly free citizens who could be depended on to take up arms when needed. Most of the other rowers in the Christian fleet were criminals sentenced to the galleys. In cases of dire necessity the criminal rowers could be motivated by promises of freedom at the end of the fighting.

In addition to the new forward-firing galleys, the Holy League fleet had a devastating new weapon: the galleass, which adapted to galley warfare aspects of the powerfully armed carracks and galleons sailing the Atlantic. The galleass carried three masts as well as oars, and it rode so high in the water that it could sustain a lower gun deck with broadsides of as many as ten heavy cannons per side.[33] Six of these new galleasses joined the Holy League navy, along with 202 galleys.

The Ottoman fleet that sailed forth to attack the Holy League consisted of 206 galleys and 45 galliots—smaller than a regular galley but faster. The Ottoman ships were copies of somewhat out-of-date European designs—the sultan hired shipbuilders from Venice and Naples—and they were built of inferior materials.[34] The Ottoman galleys also had far fewer, and much smaller-bore, cannons. All rowers in the Ottoman fleet were slaves, many of them Christian prisoners; during onboard fighting, therefore, they often rebelled and aided the attackers. Moreover, many of the Ottoman galley captains were Greek and Venetian mercenaries, some of them deserters.[35]

The Ottoman fleet gathered at Lepanto Bay, off the western coast of Greece, under the command of Ali Pasha, Sultan Selim's brother-in-law. The Christian fleet arrived on October 7, 1571, and immediately deployed for battle. By a swift and brilliant stroke, Don John's forces trapped the Ottoman fleet within the bay, limiting their ability to maneuver. As the battle began, the Turks mistook the galleasses, which were positioned about a half mile in front of the rest of Christian fleet, for merchant supply ships and launched an all-out attack on them. When the closely bunched Turkish galleys got within short range, the galleasses unleashed their broadsides with catastrophic results. The other Turkish galleys fared little better, being blasted apart by the forward-firing Christian guns and overrun by Spanish boarding parties. Spanish borders seized Ali Pasha's flagship, killed him, and then waved his head aloft from the end of a pike. By 4 p.m. it was over. The Ottomans had lost 210 ships, sunk or captured, whereas the Christians had lost 20.

Only seventeen years later, the Spanish Armada sailed against England—130 great ships, compared to which the galleys of Lepanto were quaint relics of a bygone age. But the Ottomans clung to galleys for many generations longer, although they had enough sense not to commit them against the West.

A bizarre footnote to the Battle of Lepanto: victorious Christian sailors looting Turkish vessels still afloat or gone aground discovered an enormous fortune in gold coins in *Sultana*, the captured flagship of Ali Pasha. Fortunes nearly as huge were found in the galleys of several other Muslim admirals. As Victor Davis Hanson explained, "Without a system of banking, fearful of confiscation should he displease the sultan, and always careful to keep his assets hidden from the tax collectors, Ali Pasha toted his huge personal fortune to Lepanto."[36] Ali Pasha was not a peasant hiding harvest surplus but a member of the upper elite. If such a person could find no safe investments and dared not leave his money at home, how could anyone else hope to do better? It was precisely this repressive command economy that explains the lack of progress in the Ottoman Empire and why, in order to compete with the West, the Ottomans had to buy military technology and experts from Europe.

Illusions about Islamic Culture

It has long been the received wisdom that while Europe slumbered through the "Dark Ages," science and learning flourished in Islam.[37] The well-known historian Bernard Lewis advanced this view when he wrote that Islam "had achieved the highest level so far in human history in the arts and sciences of civilization" and that, intellectually, "medieval Europe was a pupil and in a sense dependent on the Islamic world."[38] But then, Lewis argued, Europeans suddenly began to advance "by leaps and bounds, leaving the scientific and technological and eventually the cultural heritage of the Islamic world far behind them."[39] Hence the question Lewis posed in the title of his book: *What Went Wrong?*

Nothing went wrong. The belief that once upon a time Muslim culture was superior to that of Europe is at best an illusion. To ask what went wrong is the equivalent of asking why Spain fell, when in fact the collapse of the Spanish Empire revealed that Spain had never risen but had remained a backward medieval society. So too with Islam.

Dhimmi Culture

To the extent that Muslim elites acquired a sophisticated culture, they learned it from their subject peoples. As Lewis put it (without seeming to fully appreciate the implications), Arabs inherited "the knowledge and skills of the ancient Middle East, of Greece and of Persia."[40] That is, the sophisticated culture so often attributed to Muslims (more often referred to as "Arabic" culture) was actually the culture of the *dhimmis*, the conquered people. It was the Judeo-Christian/Greek culture of Byzantium, combined with the remarkable learning of heretical Christian groups such as the Copts and the Nestorians, plus extensive knowledge from Zoroastrian (Mazdean) Persia and the great mathematical achievements of the Hindus (keep in mind the early and extensive Muslim conquests in India). This legacy of learning, including much that had originated with the ancient Greeks, was translated into Arabic, and portions of it were somewhat assimilated into Muslim culture. But even after having been translated, this learning continued to be sustained primarily by the dhimmi populations living under Muslim regimes. For example, as the scholar Samuel H. Moffett observed, the "earliest scientific book in the language of Islam" was a "treatise on medicine by a Syrian Christian priest in Alexandria, translated into Arabic by a Persian Jewish physician."[41] As in this example, not only did dhimmis originate most "Arab" science and learning, but they even did most of the translating into Arabic.[42] That did not transform this body of knowledge into Arab culture. Rather, as the remarkable historian of Islam Marshall G. S. Hodgson noted, "those who pursued natural science tended to retain their older religious allegiances as dhimmis, even when doing their work in Arabic."[43]

The highly acclaimed Muslim architecture also turns out to have been mainly a dhimmi achievement, adapted from Persian and Byzantine origins. In 762, when the Caliph al-Mansūr founded Baghdad, he entrusted the design of the city to a Zoroastrian and a Jew.[44] One of the great masterpieces attributed to Islamic art is the Dome of the Rock in

Jerusalem. But when Caliph Abd al-Malik had the shrine built in the seventh century, he employed Byzantine architects and craftsmen, which is why it so closely resembled the Church of the Holy Sepulchre.[45] In fact, many famous Muslim mosques were originally built as Christian churches and converted by merely adding external minarets and redecorating the interiors. As an acknowledged authority on Islamic art and architecture put it, "The Dome of the Rock truly represents a work of what we understand today as Islamic art, that is, art not necessarily made by Muslims . . . but rather art made in societies where most people—or the most important people—were Muslims."[46]

Similar examples abound in the intellectual areas that have inspired so much admiration for Muslim learning. In his much-admired book written to acknowledge the Arabs' "enormous" contributions to science and engineering, Donald R. Hill admitted that very little could be traced to Arab origins and that most of these contributions originated with conquered populations. Many of the Muslim world's most famous scholars were Persians, not Arabs.[47] That includes Avicenna, whom the *Encyclopaedia Britannica* ranks as "the most influential of all Muslim philosopher-scientists," as well as Omar Khayyám, al-Bīrūnī, and Razi. Another Persian, al-Khwārizmī, is credited as the father of algebra. Al-Uqlidisi, who introduced fractions, was a Syrian. Bakht-Ishū' and ibn Ishaq, leading figures in "Muslim" medical knowledge, were Nestorian Christians. Masha'allah ibn Atharī, the famous astronomer-astrologer, was a Jew. This list could be extended for several pages. What may have misled so many historians is that most contributors to "Arabic science" were given Arabic names and their works were published in Arabic, that being the official language of the land.

Consider mathematics. The so-called Arabic numerals were entirely of Hindu origin. The splendid Hindu numbering system based on the concept of zero was, in fact, published in Arabic, but only mathematicians adopted it—other Muslims continued to use their cumbersome traditional system. Thābit ibn Qurra, noted for his many contributions to geometry and to number theory, is usually identified as an "Arab mathematician," but he was actually a member of the pagan Sabian sect. Of course, there were some fine Muslim mathematicians, perhaps because it is a subject so abstract as to insulate its practitioners from any possible religious criticism.

The same might be said for astronomy, although here, too, most of the credit should go not to Arabs but to Hindus and Persians. The "discovery" that the earth turns on its axis is often attributed to the Persian al-Bīrūnī, but he acknowledged having learned of it from Brahmagupta and other Indian astronomers.[48] Nor was al-Bīrūnī certain about the matter, remarking in his *Canon Masudicus* that "it is the same whether you take it that the Earth is in motion or the sky. For, in both cases, it does not affect the Astronomical Science."[49] Another famous "Arab" astronomer was al-Battānī, but like Thābit ibn Qurra, he was a member of the pagan Sabian sect (who were star worshippers, which explains their particular interest in astronomy).

The many claims that the Arabs achieved far more sophisticated medicine than had previous cultures are as mistaken as those regarding "Arabic" numerals.[50] "Muslim" or "Arab" medicine was in fact Nestorian Christian medicine; even the leading Muslim and Arab physicians were trained at the enormous Nestorian medical center at Nisibus in Syria. Nisibus offered not only medicine but the full range of advanced education, as did the other institutions of learning the Nestorians established, including the one at Jundishapur in Persia, which the distinguished historian of science George Sarton called "the greatest intellectual center of the time."[51]

The scholar Mark Dickens pointed out that the Nestorians "soon acquired a reputation with the Arabs for being excellent accountants, architects, astrologers, bankers, doctors, merchants, philosophers, scientists, scribes and teachers. In fact, prior to the ninth century, nearly all the learned scholars in the [Islamic area] were Nestorian Christians."[52] It was primarily the Nestorian Christian Hunayn ibn Ishaq al-'Ibadi (known in Latin as Johannitius) who "collected, translated, revised, and supervised the translation of Greek manuscripts, especially those of Hippocrates, Galen, Plato, and Aristotle into Syriac and Arabic," in the words of William W. Brickman.[53] As late as the middle of the eleventh century, the Muslim writer Nasir-i Khrusau reported, "Truly, the scribes here in Syria, as is the case of Egypt, are all Christians . . . [and] it is most usual for the physicians . . . to be Christians."[54] In Palestine under Muslim rule, according to the monumental history by Moshe Gil, "the Christians had immense influence and positions of power, chiefly because of the gifted administrators among them who occupied government posts despite the ban in Muslim law against employing Christians [in such positions] or who were part of the intelligentsia of the period owing to the fact that they were outstanding scientists, mathematicians, physicians and so on."[55] In the late tenth century Abd al-Jabbār also acknowledged the prominence of Christian officials, writing that "kings in Egypt, al-Shām, Iraq, Jazīra, Fāris, and in all their surroundings, rely on Christians in matters of officialdom, the central administration and the handling of funds."[56]

Even many of the most partisan Muslim historians, including the famous English convert to Islam and translator of the Qur'an Marmaduke Pickthall,[57] agree that sophisticated Muslim culture originated with the conquered populations. What has largely been ignored is that that culture could not keep up with the West because so-called Muslim culture was largely an illusion, resting on a complex mix of dhimmi cultures. As soon the dhimmis were repressed as heretical, that culture would be lost. Hence, when Muslims stamped out nearly all religious nonconformity in the fourteenth century, Muslim backwardness came to the fore.

Islam and Aristotle

Underlying the belief that the Muslims were more learned and sophisticated than the Christian West is the presumption that a society not steeped in Greek philosophy and literature was a society in the dark. Thus, for the past several centuries, many Western writers have stressed the Arab possession of the classical writers, assuming that by having access to the wisdom of the ancients, Islam was the much superior culture. True enough, because of the persistence of Byzantine/Greek culture in most of the conquered Arab societies, the most educated Arabs did have greater knowledge of the work of classical Greek authors such as Plato and Aristotle (although medieval European scholars were more familiar with these works than has been claimed). What is less known is that access to Greek scholarship had a *negative* impact on Arab scholarship.

The works of Plato and Aristotle reached the Arabs via translations into Syrian late in the seventh century and then into Arabic by Syrians in, perhaps, the ninth century. But rather than treating these works as *attempts* by Greek scholars to answer various questions, Muslim intellectuals read them the same way they read the Qur'an—as settled truths to be understood without question or contradiction. The respected Muslim historian Caesar Farah explained: "In Aristotle Muslim thinkers found the great guide; to them he became the 'first teacher.' Having accepted this *a priori*, Muslim philosophy as it evolved in subsequent centuries merely chose to *continue* in this vein and to enlarge on Aristotle rather than to innovate."[58] As such, the twelfth-century scholar Averroes and his followers imposed the position that Aristotle's physics was complete and infallible, and if actual observations were inconsistent with one of Aristotle's teachings, those observations were either in error or an illusion.[59]

Such attitudes prevented Islam from taking up where the Greeks had left off in their pursuit of knowledge. In contrast, knowledge of Aristotle's work prompted experimentation and discovery among the early Christian Scholastics. Then as now, a scholar enhanced his reputation by disagreeing with received knowledge, by innovation and correction. That motivated Scholastics to find fault with the Greeks—and there were many faults to be found.[60]

The "Tolerant" Muslims

A common refrain of both scholarly and popular histories is that, in contrast with Christian brutality against Jews and heretics, Islam showed remarkable tolerance for conquered people, treated them with respect, and allowed them to pursue their faiths without interference. Thus, Moorish Spain has been hailed as "a shining example of civilized enlightenment"[61] and the "ornament of the world."[62]

The truth about life under Muslim rule is quite different.

It is true that the Qur'an forbids forced conversions. But that recedes to an empty legalism given that many subject peoples often were allowed to "choose" conversion as an alternative to death or enslavement. That was the usual choice presented to pagans; Jews and Christians often faced that option, or one only somewhat less extreme.[63] In principle, as "People of the Book," Jews and Christians were supposed to be tolerated and permitted to follow their faiths. But only under quite repressive conditions: death was (and remains) the fate of any Muslim who converted to either faith. No new churches or synagogues could be built. Jews and Christians were prohibited from praying or reading their scriptures aloud, even in their homes or in churches or synagogues, lest Muslims should accidentally hear them. And as Marshall Hodgson pointed out, Muslim authorities went to great lengths to humiliate and punish Jews and Christians who refused to convert to Islam. It was official policy that dhimmis should "feel inferior and to know 'their place,'" Hodgson wrote. Muslim authorities imposed restrictive laws—"that Christians and Jews should not ride horses, for instance, but at most mules, or even that they should wear certain marks of their religion on their costume when among

Muslims."[64] In some places non-Muslims were prohibited from wearing clothing similar to that of Muslims and from being armed.[65] In addition, non-Muslims were invariably severely taxed compared with Muslims.[66]

And these were the *normal* circumstances of Jewish and Christian subjects of Muslim states. Conditions often were far worse.

Stamping Out the "Unbelievers"

The final destruction of the dhimmi communities of eastern Christians occurred in the fourteenth century.[67] Although the historical record lacks detail, apparently Muslim mobs in Cairo began destroying Coptic churches in 1321. According to the historian Donald P. Little, these anti-Christian riots "were carefully orchestrated throughout Egypt," destroying large numbers of churches and monasteries.[68] Although the ruling authorities eventually put down the mobs, small-scale anti-Christian attacks, arson, looting, and murder became chronic. In 1354 once again mobs "ran amok, destroying churches . . . and attacking Christians and Jews in the streets, and throwing them into bonfires if they refused to pronounce the *shadādatayn*" (to acknowledge Allah as the one true God).[69] Soon, according to the Egyptian historian Al-Maqrizi (1364–1442), in "all the provinces of Egypt, both north and south, no church remained that had not been razed. . . . Thus did Islam spread among the Christians of Egypt."[70]

The massacres of Christians and the destruction of churches and monasteries were not limited to Egypt. Having converted to Islam, the Mongol rulers of Mesopotamia, Armenia, and Syria took even more draconian measures. When Ghāzān took the Mongol throne of Iran in 1295, in pursuit of increased public support he converted to Islam (he had been raised a Christian and then became a Buddhist) and then, yielding to popular pressure, he began to persecute Christians.[71] According to an account written by the Nestorian patriarch Mar Yaballaha III (1245–1317), in keeping with his aim of forcing all Christians and Jews to become Muslims, Ghāzān issued this edict:

> The churches shall be uprooted, and the altars overturned, and the celebrations of the Eucharist shall cease, and the hymns of praise, and the sounds of calls to prayer shall be abolished; and the heads of the Christians, and the heads of the congregations of the Jews, and the great men among them, shall be killed.[72]

Within a year Ghāzān changed his mind and attempted to end the persecutions of Christians, but by now the mobs were out of control. It was widely accepted that (in the words of the historian of Islam Laurence E. Browne) "everyone who did not abandon Christianity and deny his faith should be killed."[73]

Meanwhile, in an effort to force Christians into Islam, Mongol Armenia forbade church services and imposed a crushing tax. In addition, local authorities were ordered to seize each Christian man, pluck out his beard, and tattoo a black mark on his shoulder. Still, few Christians defected, leading the Khan to order that all Christian men be castrated and have one eye put out—which caused many deaths in this era before antibiotics but did lead to many conversions.[74]

Similar atrocities occurred all across the East and North Africa.[75] In 1310 there was a massacre in Mesopotamia.[76] In 1317 the Syrian city of Āmid was the scene of an anti-Christian attack. The bishop was beaten to death; the churches were burned; the Christian men were all murdered; and twelve thousand women and children were sold into slavery.[77]

Then came Tamerlane.

A Muslim of Turkic-Mongol origins, Tamerlane (also known as Timur) was born near the Persian city of Samarkand in 1336. Seeking to restore the Mongol Empire, he conquered vast areas of Asia. Again and again Tamerlane perpetrated huge massacres—perhaps as many as two hundred thousand captives (men, women, and children) were slaughtered during his march on Delhi[78]—and had towering pyramids built from the heads of his victims. So barbaric were his conquests that he earned the sobriquet the "Scourge of God," as Christopher Marlowe put it in his great play (1587).[79] And while Tamerlane killed huge numbers of Muslims, Hindus, and Buddhists, he virtually wiped out the Christians and Jews in the East. In Georgia alone, Samuel H. Moffett reported, Tamerlane "destroyed seven hundred large villages, wiped out the inhabitants, and reduced all the Christian churches . . . to rubble."[80] Any Christian communities that survived Tamerlane were destroyed by his grandson, Ulugh Beg.[81]

Christians were the prominent targets of these attacks both because they were the most numerous dhimmi population and because anti-Christian sentiments were fueled by conflict with the West. But all nonbelievers were persecuted in this era, including Jews. The first massacre of Jews for *being* Jews was committed by Muhammad, who forced members of the last Jewish community in Mecca to dig a trench, along which from six to nine hundred Jewish men were lined up, beheaded, and pushed in.[82] The Jewish women and children were sold into slavery, and Muhammad took one of the Jewish women as a concubine.[83] Umar, Muhammad's second successor, expelled all Jews from the Arabian Peninsula.

As for "enlightened" Moorish Spain, about four thousand Jews were murdered there in 1066 and several thousand more in 1090.[84] Much is made of the fact that upon reconquering Moorish Spain, in 1492 Ferdinand and Isabella ordered all Jews to convert to Christianity or to leave. But almost nowhere is it mentioned that in doing so they merely repeated a prior Muslim policy: in 1148 all Christians and Jews were ordered to convert to Islam or leave Moorish Spain immediately, on pain of death.[85] Consequently, the great Jewish scholar Moses Maimonides (1135–1204) pretended to convert to Islam and lived many years in fear of being found out, even after having fled to Egypt.[86]

By the end of the fourteenth century only tiny remnants of Christianity and Judaism remained scattered in the Middle East and North Africa, having been almost completely destroyed by Muslim persecution. And as the dhimmis disappeared, they took the "advanced" Muslim culture with them. What they left behind was a culture so backward that it couldn't even copy Western technology but had to buy it and often even had to hire Westerners to use it.

Illusions

So much, then, for the "mystery" of how Muslim culture was somehow lost or left behind. The notion that in the medieval era Islamic culture was advanced well beyond Europe is as much an illusion as recent ones about an "Arab Spring." The Islamic world was backward then, and so it remains.

Science Comes of Age

Isaac Newton (1642–1727) famously remarked, "If I have seen further it is by standing on the shoulders of giants." Unfortunately, too few who quote this line realize that Newton was not only quite serious but also quite correct. Science did not suddenly erupt in a great intellectual revolution during Newton's time; this era of superb achievements was the culmination of centuries of sustained, normal scientific progress. After all, Newton's First Law of Motion[1] was simply an expansion of William of Ockham's (1295–1349) insight that once a body is in motion, it will remain so unless some force, such as friction, acts upon it. This was refined by Jean Buridan (1300–1358), who developed the principle of *inertia* (that unless acted upon by an external force, bodies at rest will stay at rest and bodies in motion will stay in motion). Inertia was further refined by Galileo (1564–1642), who, characteristically, claimed more credit than he deserved. Of course, Newton's First Law was merely the starting point for his magnificent system of physics, but, contrary to claims made on his behalf by the philosophers of the so-called Enlightenment, Newton didn't have to start from scratch. Rather, as chapter 8 demonstrated, the glorious scientific breakthroughs of the sixteenth and seventeenth centuries were based on the work of a long line of natural philosophers.

Nevertheless, the notion that a scientific revolution erupted in the sixteenth century is so ingrained in our intellectual culture that the historian of science Steven Shapin began his study with the charming line: "There was no such thing as the Scientific Revolution, and this is a book about it."[2] It seems more accurate to identify what occurred in this era as the *coming of age* of Western science. I have written at length on this era in three previous books,[3] but there is little repetition in what follows, for I have discovered important new questions to address.

In particular, I will dispel several widely advocated but spurious claims, each of them a variation on the theme that science could arise only during the "Enlightenment" because by that point the churches, sufficiently weakened, could no longer suppress science. Since this is an obvious falsehood, so too are claims derived from it. The first of these claims is that most of the great scientific stars of this time had freed themselves from the confines of supernaturalism and faith. The second is that the Protestant Reformation had freed England and many parts of the Continent from "the dead hand of the Catholic Church,"[4] thereby making real scientific thinking possible—or, in the case of Puritanism, a moral duty. The third claim is that science arose outside the universities because they were controlled by the churches and therefore were inhospitable to new ideas. Finally, all these factors are said to have combined to explain why England was the center of it all.

Overwhelming evidence falsifies each of these claims. Indeed, Christianity was *essential* to the rise of science, which is why science was a purely Western phenomenon.

What Is Science?

Aristotle was not a scientist. It is true that he attempted to explain many natural phenomena. It also is true that his explanations usually took the form of abstract generalizations, as do scientific theories. But none of Aristotle's work constituted science because his explanations were not linked to systematic observations. It wasn't merely that he didn't make the obvious tests of his claims; he failed to recognize that such tests were relevant. He assumed that because his explanations were based on reason, their truth was not in doubt. This was the typical view taken by Greek philosophers—Plato even believed that reality was an inferior representation of the abstract, and hence empirical observations were not to be trusted. In contrast, recall from chapter 8 that Roger Bacon disproved Aristotle's generalization that hot water freezes faster than does cold water by putting out a container of cold water and one of hot water on a cold day and *seeing* which froze first. By the same token, had Aristotle been a scientist he would have at least recognized the need to test his assertion in *On the Heavens* that heavy objects fall faster than light ones in the way Galileo claimed to have done (never mind that Galileo probably made up the story about dropping two stones from the Tower of Pisa). Aristotle was not a scientist because he based his "theories" on logic without any concern for testing them through appropriate observations. Consequently, as James Hannam wrote in *The Genesis of Science*, "not even Aristotle's powers of reason could prevent blunders in his arguments."[5]

Science must not be confused with philosophy—big ideas may or may not be scientific. Nor must science be confused with technology. Ancient China had no science despite knowing how to smelt iron, make firecrackers, and manufacture porcelain plates.

Science is best defined as *a method* used in *organized efforts* to formulate *explanations of nature*, always subject to modification and correction through *systematic observations*. Put another way, science consists of two parts: *theory* and *research*. Scientific theories are *abstract statements* about *how* and *why* some portion of nature (including human social life) fits together and works. But not all abstract statements about nature, even those offering explanations, qualify as scientific theories. Rather, abstract statements are scientific *only* if it is possible to deduce from them some definite predictions and prohibitions about what will be observed. And that's where research comes in. It consists of making those observations that are relevant to the theory's empirical prohibitions and predictions.

Given the linkage between theory and research, science is limited to statements about natural and material reality—about things that are at least in principle observable. Hence, there are entire realms of discourse that science is unable even to address, including such matters as the existence of God. So much, then, for notions that science refutes religion.

Defining science as an *organized effort* is to note that science is not random discovery but involves intentional and sustained actions and that it seldom, if ever, is pursued in solitude. Granted, some scientists have worked alone, but not in isolation. From earliest days, scientists have constituted networks and have been very communicative. As noted in chapter 8, that was true even in medieval times, and by the sixteenth century communication among scientists was well organized. Although there were no journals to publish and circulate scientific findings, scientists were active correspondents. The University of Paris initiated a private mail system as early as the thirteenth century. Early in the seventeenth century the French friar and brilliant mathematician Marin Mersenne (1588–1648) sustained a large network of correspondence for the specific purpose of informing scientists of one another's work; among his correspondents were René Descartes and Galileo. Scientists also formed learned societies to meet regularly and share knowledge: the Royal Society of London began gathering in about 1645 and the Parisian Académie Royale in 1666.

Consistent with the views of most contemporary historians of science, the above definition of science excludes the efforts through most of human history to explain and control the material world, even those efforts not involving supernatural means. That is because until recent times "technical progress—sometimes considerable—was mere empiricism," as the historian Marc Bloch put it.[6] In other words, progress was the product of observation and trial and error but was lacking in explanations, in theorizing. Unlike Aristotle and his Greek colleagues, many ancients knew that under normal conditions cold water froze faster than hot water, but they had no theories about why anything froze. Their achievements are better described as techniques, crafts, technologies, lore, skills, wisdom, engineering, or even knowledge. But not as science.

It is now the consensus among historians, philosophers, and even sociologists of science that real science arose only once: in Europe. In this regard it is instructive that China, Islam, India, and ancient Greece and Rome had a highly developed alchemy, but only in Europe did alchemy develop into chemistry. By the same token, many societies developed elaborate systems of astrology, but only in Europe did astrology lead to astronomy.

Scientific Stars: 1543–1680

Historians often are misled (and mislead) by relying on atypical examples. This problem can be solved by proper use of quantitative methods. Rather than citing examples of famous early scientists who were Protestants, or irreligious, or ordained clergy, or affiliated with a university, we can achieve far more trustworthy results based on analysis of *all* the famous scientists of this era.

Hence, I identified all the significant scientific stars of the era beginning with the publication of Copernicus's *De revolutionibus* in 1543 and including all born prior to 1680. I based my selections on study of the rosters provided in a number of specialized encyclopedias and biographical dictionaries, among which Isaac Asimov's *Encyclopedia of Science and Technology* (1982) was especially useful and reliable. I limited my selections to *active scientists*, thereby excluding some well-known intellectual figures of the day, such as Francis Bacon and Joseph Scaliger. Having assembled a list, I then consulted various sources, including individual biographies, to determine the facts I wished to code for each case. In the end I had a data set consisting of fifty-two scientists:[7]

1. Brayer, Johann (1572–1625)
2. Borelli, Giovanni (1608–1679)
3. Boyle, Robert (1627–1691)
4. Brahe, Tycho (1546–1601)
5. Briggs, Henry (1561–1630)
6. Cassini, Giovanni (1625–1712)
7. Copernicus, Nicolaus (1473–1543)
8. Descartes, René (1596–1650)
9. Fabricius, Hieronymus (1537–1619)
10. Fallopius, Gabriel (1523–1562)
11. Fermat, Pierre (1601–1665)
12. Flamsteed, John (1646–1719)
13. Galilei, Galileo (1564–1642)
14. Gassendi, Pierre (1592–1655)
15. Gellibrand, Henry (1597–ca. 1637)
16. Gilbert, William (1544–1603)
17. Glauber, Johann (1604–1668)
18. Graaf, Regnier de (1641–1673)
19. Grew, Nehemiah (1641–1712)
20. Grimaldi, Francesco (1618–1663)
21. Guericke, Otto (1602–1686)
22. Halley, Edmond (1656–1742)
23. Harvey, William (1578–1657)
24. Helmont, Jan Baptista van (1579/80–1644)
25. Hevelius, Johannes (1611–1687)
26. Hooke, Robert (1635–1703)
27. Horrocks, Jeremiah (1619–1641)

28. Huygens, Christiaan (1629–1695)
29. Kepler, Johannes (1571–1630)
30. Kircher, Athanasius (1601–1680)
31. Leeuwenhoek, Anton (1632–1723)
32. Leibniz, Gottfried (1646–1716)
33. Malpighi, Marcello (1628–1694)
34. Mariotte, Edme (1620–1684)
35. Mersenne, Marin (1588–1648)
36. Napier, John (1550–1617)
37. Newton, Isaac (1642–1727)
38. Oughtred, William (1574–1660)
39. Papin, Denis (1647–1712)
40. Pascal, Blaise (1623–1662)
41. Picard, Jean (1620–1682)
42. Ray, John (1628–1705)
43. Redi, Francesco (1626–1697)
44. Riccioli, Giovanni (1598–1671)
45. Roemer, Olaus (1644–1710)
46. Scheiner, Christoph (1573–1650)
47. Steno, Nicolaus (1638–1686)
48. Stevinus, Simon (1548–1620)
49. Torricelli, Evangelista (1608–1647)
50. Vesalius, Andreas (1514–1564)
51. Vieta, Franciscus (1540–1603)
52. Wallis, John (1616–1703)

Table 14–1 shows the distribution of scientific fields pursued by these fifty-two stars.

Table 14–1: Scientific Fields

Field	Number	Percent
Physics	15	29%
Astronomy	13	25%
Biology/physiology	13	25%
Mathematics	11	21%
Total	52	100%

What is most striking about these data is the even distribution across fields. That held among both Protestants and Catholics and for both Continental and English stars.

"Enlightened" Scientists

Just as a group of eighteenth-century philosophers invented the notion of the "Dark Ages" to discredit Christianity, they labeled their own era the "Enlightenment" on grounds that religious darkness had finally been dispelled by secular humanism. As Bertrand Russell later explained, the "Enlightenment was essentially a revaluation of independent intellectual activity, aimed quite literally at spreading light where hitherto darkness had prevailed."[8] Thus did Voltaire, Rousseau, Locke, Hume, and others wrap themselves in the achievements of the "Scientific Revolution" as they celebrated the victory of secularism, eventuating in the Marquis Laplace's claim that God was now an unnecessary hypothesis.

Of course, not one of these "Enlightened" figures played *any* part in the scientific enterprise. What about those who did? Were they a bunch of skeptics too? Hardly.

First of all, thirteen of the scientific stars (25 percent) were members of the clergy, nine of them Roman Catholics. In addition, I coded each of the fifty-two stars as to their personal piety. To code someone as *devout*, I required clear evidence of especially deep religious involvement. For example, Robert Boyle spent a great deal of money on translations of the Bible into non-Western languages. Isaac Newton wrote far more on theology than he did on physics—he even calculated a date for the Second Coming (1948). Johannes Kepler was deeply interested in mysticism and in biblical questions: he devoted great effort to working out the date of the Creation, settling for 3992 BC.

I used the code *conventionally religious* to identify those whose biography offers no evidence of skepticism but whose piety does not stand out as other than satisfactory to their associates. An example is Marcello Malpighi, whose observations of a chick's heart are regarded as one of the most remarkable achievements of seventeenth-century biology. Malpighi's biography offers no direct evidence of concerns about God similar to Boyle's or Newton's. On the other hand, he did retire to Rome to serve as the personal physician of Pope Innocent XII, a very pious Counter-

Reformation pontiff, who surely expected a similar level of piety from those around him. If anything, then, I have underrated Malpighi's level of personal piety, and I may well have done so in other cases, but I have not overstated anyone's level of piety.

Finally, I reserved the label *skeptic* for anyone about whom I could infer disbelief, or at least profound doubt, in the existence of a conscious God. Only one of the fifty-two qualified: Edmond Halley—he was rejected for a professorship at Oxford on grounds of his "atheism."

Table 14–2 displays the religious profile of these fifty-two scientific stars.

Table 14–2: Personal Piety

Piety	Number	Percent
Devout	31	60%
Conventional	20	38%
Skeptic	1	2%
Total	52	100%

Clearly, the superb scientific achievements of the sixteenth and seventeenth centuries were the work not of skeptics but of Christian men—at least 60 percent of whom were devout. The era of the "Enlightenment" is as imaginary as the era of the "Dark Ages," both myths perpetrated by the same people for the same reasons.

A Protestant Revolution?

In 1938 Robert K. Merton, soon to become one of America's most influential sociologists, published a lengthy study in the history-of-science journal *Osiris*: "Science, Technology, and Society in Seventeenth-Century England." Rejecting the Marxist and secularist orthodoxies of the day, Merton proposed that Protestant Puritanism had given birth to the "Scientific Revolution." According to Merton, this occurred because the Puritans had reasoned (and, presumably, they were the first Christians to do so) that since the world was God's handiwork, it was their duty to study and understand this handiwork as a means of glorifying God. Thus, Merton argued, among Puritan intellectuals in seventeenth-century England, science was defined as a religious calling.

Merton's whole argument was merely an extension of Max Weber's claims about the role of the Protestant ethic in the rise of capitalism. And, like Weber's, Merton's position is untenable. Merton was certainly correct about the personal piety of the scientists he cited (despite claims of his early critics that those scientists must have faked their piety). But he went wrong in two ways. First, by keeping a narrow focus on England, he ignored the substantial Catholic participation in science at this time. Second, he misidentified English Protestant scientists as Puritans when most of them were conventional Anglicans.[9] Indeed, Merton's definition of "Puritan" was so broad that essentially no Christian was excluded, not even Catholics.[10] In Barbara J. Shapiro's pithy summation, "What [Merton] is essentially saying is that Englishmen contributed to English science."[11]

The claim that the "Scientific Revolution" was the work of Protestants (let alone Puritans specifically) is clearly undermined by the data in table 14–3. Only half of the fifty-two stars were Protestants, and with the English removed, Catholics outnumbered Protestants by twenty-six to eleven, which approximates the distribution of Protestants and Catholics on the Continent in this era. As the scholar Paul J. Kocher aptly observed, "There was nothing in the dogmas of Catholicism, Anglicanism, or Puritanism which made any one of them more or less favorable to science in general than any of the others. . . . [In each, the majority held] that science should be welcomed as a faithful handmaid of theology."[12]

Table 14–3: Religious Affiliation

	All	Continent Only
Protestants	26	11
Catholic	26	26
Total	52	37

Escape from the University

Perhaps because Roger Bacon attacked universities as "adverse to the progress of science," most modern historians of the rise of science have condemned the universities, especially since doing so provided additional grounds to attack religion.[13] Typical of this view was Richard S. Westfall, who in 1971 wrote, "Not only were the universities of Europe not the foci of scientific activity, not only did science have to develop its own centers of activity independent of universities, but the universities were the principal centers of opposition for the new conceptions of nature which modern science constructed."[14]

In light of chapter 8, this seems very surprising; at the very least it requires an account of how the universities turned against science and became bastions of the received wisdom, having previously sustained generations of distinguished scientific progress. No such accounts have been offered. That's because it never happened! The universities remained the primary institutional base for science in this glorious era, just as they had through the prior centuries.

For example, what eventually became the celebrated Royal Society for Improving Natural Knowledge, later known simply as the Royal Society of London, began when a group of scientists started holding regular meetings at the University of Oxford in the 1640s.[15] The move to London coincided with the rise to prominence of Gresham College, located in London; a number of English scientists held joint appointments at Gresham and at Oxford or Cambridge.

In addition, 48 of the 52 stars (92 percent) were, as historian Hugh F. Kearney pointed out, "university educated, not in the conventional sense of two or three years, but over an extended period [often] of ten years or more."[16] Put in modern terms, these stars attended graduate school. For example, after four years at the University of Krakow, Copernicus went to Italy, where he spent six more years at the Universities of Bologna, Padua, and Ferrara. Had he not been trained in Italy, it is inconceivable that Copernicus would have made substantial contributions to astronomy. These findings are supported by an analysis of the careers of all 720 known scientists from 1550 to 1650, 87 percent of whom were university educated.[17] Moreover, 24 of the stars—nearly half—served as professors for at least a period of their careers.

This is as it should have been because, rather than being opposed to science, the universities in this era were especially committed to it. As the distinguished historian of science Edward Grant put it, "The medieval university laid far greater emphasis on science than does its modern counterpart."[18]

Why England?

Many have claimed that England was the primary setting for this scientific era. Merton focused exclusively on England in pushing his Puritan explanation, and the prominence of nonacademics among the London scientific set encouraged many to disdain the role of the universities. Although both of these interpretations are false, there is some basis for the view that England was exceptionally productive of scientists, as can be seen in table 14–4.

Table 14–4: Nationality

Nationality	Number	Percent
English	14	27%
French	11	21%
Italian	9	17%
German	8	15%
Dutch	4	8%
Danish	3	6%
Flemish	1	2%
Polish	1	2%
Scottish	1	2%
Total	52	100%

In fact, England does stand out, especially when we consider that in this era Italy had about twice the population of England.[19] It is legitimate to ask, why England? My explanation is that England led the way in science for the same reasons that it led the way in the Industrial Revolution—its substantially greater political and economic liberty had produced a relatively open class system that enabled the emergence of an ambitious and creative upper middle class, sometimes called the bourgeoisie. Although the rise of the bourgeoisie occurred all across western Europe, it did so earlier and to a far greater degree in England (and the Netherlands). These matters will be pursued at great length in chapter 17; here it is sufficient to establish a few preliminary points.

The first is that from earliest days the pursuit of knowledge was the work of persons whose status was less than aristocratic. Aristotle tutored future kings, but he was the son of a physician. Recall, from chapter 8, historian Hastings Rashdall's observation that most students at medieval universities "were of a social position intermediate between the highest and the very lowest—sons of knights and yeomen, merchants, tradesmen or thrifty artisans."[20] Although there were universities all across western Europe, in the seventeenth century more students enrolled in "the English universities than at any time until the nineteenth century," as Kearney pointed out.[21] In fact, beginning in the 1540s England saw a remarkable explosion of education at all levels, resulting in a huge increase in literacy and a corresponding leap in the sale of books.[22] This was fully consistent with the Elizabethan court, where "commoners" such as John Hawkins and Francis Drake played prominent roles in the queen's service.

Something else equally remarkable was taking place in England at this time: lesser aristocrats were, in effect, joining the bourgeoisie from above. As the historian Lawrence Stone reported, "They were pouring into the universities and the Inns of Court."[23] For that reason, perhaps, English scientific stars in the era were far more likely to have been of bourgeois origins than were Continental scientists, as can be seen in table 14–5.

Table 14–5: Class Origins

	England	Continent
Nobility	7%	14%
Gentry	7%	38%
Bourgeois	79%	43%
Lower	7%	5%
Total	100%	100%

These codes apply to each scientist's family. *Nobility* means one's father had a title. *Gentry* includes people of high social status but no title, such as government officials, large landowners, and, as Deirdre McCloskey put it, "any dignified people just below the aristocracy."[24] *Bourgeois* fathers were in business or were members of the professions, clergy, professors, and the like. *Lower* refers to those who rose from peasant or laboring backgrounds, there being only three among these stars—Marin Mersenne's parents were peasants, Johann Glauber's father was a barber, and John Ray was the son of a blacksmith.

But even though England produced more scientists, the principal fact about this wonderful era of science is that it was spread across all of western Europe. And for good reason: it was the normal result of the organized pursuit of knowledge that was fundamental to Christianity.

The Christian Basis of Science

Science arose only in Christian Europe because only medieval Europeans believed that science was *possible* and *desirable*. And the basis of their belief was their image of God and his creation. This was dramatically asserted to a distinguished audience of scholars attending the 1925 Lowell Lectures at Harvard by the great English philosopher and mathematician Alfred North Whitehead, who explained that science developed in Europe because of the widespread "faith in the possibility of science . . . derivative from medieval theology."[25] This claim shocked not only his audience but Western intellectuals in general when his lectures were published. How could this world-famous thinker, coauthor with Bertrand Russell of the landmark *Principia Mathematica* (1910–13), not know that religion is the unrelenting enemy of science?

Whitehead had recognized that Christian theology was essential for the rise of science, just as non-Christian theologies had stifled the scientific enterprise everywhere else. He explained:

> The greatest contribution of medievalism to the formation of the scientific movement [was] the inexpugnable belief . . . that there was a secret, a secret which can be unveiled. How has this conviction been so vividly implanted in the European mind? . . . It must come from the medieval insistence on the rationality of God, conceived as with the personal energy of Jehovah and with the rationality of a Greek philosopher. Every detail was supervised and ordered: the search into nature could only result in the vindication of faith in rationality.[26]

Whitehead was, of course, merely summarizing what so many of the great early scientists had said. René Descartes justified his search for the "laws" of nature on grounds that such laws must exist because God is perfect and therefore "acts in a manner as constant and immutable as possible."[27] That is, the universe functions according to rational rules or laws. The great medieval Scholastic Nicole d'Oresme said that God's creation "is much like that of a man making a clock and letting it run and continue its own motion by itself."[28] Furthermore, because God has given humans the power of reason, it ought to be possible for us to discover the rules established by God.

Many of the early scientists felt morally obliged to pursue these secrets, just as Whitehead had noted. The great British philosopher concluded his remarks by pointing out that the images of God and creation found in the non-European faiths, especially those in Asia, are too impersonal or too irrational to have sustained science. Any particular natural "occurrence might be due to the fiat of an irrational despot" god, or might be produced by "some impersonal, inscrutable origin of things. There is not the same confidence as in the intelligible rationality of a personal being."[29] It should be noted that given Judaism and Christianity's common roots, the Jewish conception of God is as suitable to sustaining science as is the Christian conception. But Jews were a small, scattered, and often repressed minority in Europe during this era and took no part in the rise of science—although Jews have excelled as scientists since their emancipation in the nineteenth century.

In contrast, most religions outside the Judeo-Christian tradition do not posit a creation at all. The universe is said to be eternal, without beginning or purpose; never having been created, it has no Creator. From this view, the universe is a supreme mystery, inconsistent, unpredictable, and (perhaps) arbitrary. For those holding this view, the only paths to wisdom are meditation or inspiration—there being nothing to reason about. But if the universe was created in accord with rational rules by a perfect, rational creator, then it ought to yield its secrets to reason and observation. Hence the scientific truism that nature is a *book* meant to be read.

Of course, the Chinese "would have scorned such an idea as being too naive for the subtlety and complexity of the universe as they intuited it,"[30] as the esteemed Oxford historian of Chinese technology Joseph Needham explained. As for the Greeks, many of them also regarded the universe as eternal and uncreated—recall that Aristotle condemned the idea "that the universe came into being at some point in time . . . as unthinkable."[31] And as seen in chapter 2, the Greeks treated the cosmos, and inanimate objects more generally, as living things, and as a result they attributed many natural phenomena—such as the movement of heavenly bodies—to *motives*, not to inanimate forces. As for Islam, the orthodox conception of Allah is hostile to the scientific quest. There is no suggestion in the Qur'an that Allah set his creation in motion and then let it run. Rather, it is assumed that he often intrudes in the world and changes things as it pleases him. Through the centuries, therefore, many influential Muslim scholars have held that efforts to formulate natural laws are blasphemy because they would seem to deny Allah's freedom to act. Thus did the Chinese, Greek, and Muslim images of God and the universe deflect scientific efforts.[32]

It was only because Europeans believed in God as the Intelligent Designer of a rational universe that they pursued the secrets of creation. Johannes Kepler stated, "The chief aim of all investigations of the external world should be to discover the rational order and harmony imposed on it by God and which he revealed to us in the language of mathematics."[33] In his last will and testament, the great seventeenth-century chemist Robert Boyle wished the members of the Royal Society of London continued success is "their laudable attempts to discover the true Nature of the Works of God."[34]

Perhaps the most remarkable aspect of the rise of science is not that the early scientists searched for natural laws, confident that they existed, but that *they found them*. It thus could be said that the proposition that the universe had an Intelligent Designer is the most fundamental of all scientific theories and that it has been successfully put to empirical tests again and again. For, as Albert Einstein once remarked, the most incomprehensible thing about the universe is that it is comprehensible: *"A priori* one should expect a chaotic world which cannot be grasped by the mind in any way. . . . That is the 'miracle' which is constantly being reinforced as our knowledge expands."[35] And that is the "miracle" that testifies to a creation guided by intention and rationality.

Of course, the rise of science did engender some conflicts with the Catholic Church, as well as with the early Protestants. That in no way diminishes the essential role of the Christian conception of God in justifying and motivating science; it merely reflects that many Christian leaders failed to grasp the important differences between science and theology. Christian theologians attempt to deduce God's nature and intentions from scripture; scientists attempt to discover the nature of God's creation by empirical means. In principle, the two efforts do not overlap, but in practice theologians have sometimes felt that a scientific position was an attack on faith (and some modern scientists have in fact attacked religion, albeit on spurious grounds). In early days, a major dispute took place because both Catholic and Protestant theologians were reluctant to accept that the earth was not the center of the universe, let alone not the center of the solar system. Both Luther and the pope opposed the Copernican claim, but their efforts to defeat it had little impact and were never very vigorous.

What about Galileo?

Unfortunately, this modest conflict has been blown into a monumental event by those determined to show that religion is the bitter enemy of science. They have turned Galileo Galilei into a heroic martyr to blind faith. Voltaire reported: "The great Galileo, at the age of fourscore, groaned away his days in the dungeons of the Inquisition, because he had demonstrated by irrefutable proofs the motion of the earth."[36] The Italian gadfly Giuseppe Baretti (1719–1789) added that Galileo was "put to the torture, for saying that *the earth moved*."[37]

It is true that Galileo was called before the Roman Inquisition and charged with the heretical teaching that the earth moves—around the sun or otherwise. And he was forced to recant. But he was neither imprisoned nor tortured; he was sentenced to a comfortable house arrest, during which he died at age seventy-eight. More important, what got Galileo in trouble with the Church were not his scientific convictions nearly as much as his arrogant duplicity. It happened this way.

Long before he became Pope Urban VIII (reigned 1623–44), while still a cardinal, Maffeo Barberini knew and liked Galileo. In 1623, when he published *Assayer*, Galileo dedicated the book to Barberini (the Barberini family crest appeared on the title page of the book), and the new pope was said to have been delighted by the many nasty insults it directed against various Jesuit scholars. *Assayer* was mainly an attack on Orazio Grassi, a Jesuit mathematician, who had published a study that (correctly) treated comets as small heavenly bodies; Galileo ridiculed this claim, arguing (wrongly) that comets were but reflections on vapors arising from the earth.[38] In any event, *Assayer* prompted Pope Urban to write an adulatory poem on the glory of astronomy. So what went wrong?

It is important to put the Galileo affair in historical context. At this time, the Reformation stood defiant in northern Europe, the Thirty Years' War raged, and the Catholic Counter-Reformation was in full bloom. Partly in response to Protestant charges that the Catholic Church was not faithful to the Bible, the limits of acceptable theology were being narrowed, and this led to increasing church interference in scholarly and scientific discussions. Urban and other leading officials were not, however, ready to clamp down on scientists; instead they proposed ways to avoid conflicts between science and theology by separating their domains. Thus, Friar Marin Mersenne advised his network of leading scientific correspondents to defend their studies on grounds that God was free to place the earth anywhere he liked, and it was the duty of scientists to find out where he had put it.[39] More-cautious early scientists adopted the tactic of identifying scientific conclusions as hypothetical or mathematical, hence being without direct theological implications.

And that was what the pope asked Galileo to do. Urban wanted Galileo to acknowledge in his publications that (in John Hedley Brooke and Geoffrey Cantor's words) "definitive conclusions could not be reached in the natural sciences. God in his omnipotence could produce a natural phenomenon in any number of ways and it therefore was presumptuous for any philosopher to claim that he had determined a unique solution."[40] That seemed an easy evasion. And given Galileo's propensity to claim false credit for others' inventions, such as the telescope, and for empirical research he probably did not perform, such as dropping weights from the Tower of Pisa, it would not seem to have stretched his ethical standards to have gone along with the pope. But to defy the pope in a rather offensive way was quite consistent with Galileo's ego.

In 1632 Galileo published his awaited *Dialogue Concerning the Two Chief World Systems*. Although the ostensible purpose of the book was to present an explanation of tidal phenomena, the two systems involved were Ptolemy's, in which the sun circles the earth, and Copernicus's, wherein the earth circles the sun. The dialogue involved three speakers, two of them philosophers and the third a layman. It was the layman, Simplicio, who presented the traditional views in support of Ptolemy—the name's resemblance to "simpleton" was obvious to all. This allowed Galileo to exploit the traditional straw-man technique to ridicule his opponents. Although Galileo did include the pope's suggested disclaimer, he put it in the mouth of Simplicio, thereby disowning it.

The book caused an immense stir and, understandably, the pope felt betrayed—although Galileo never seemed to have grasped that fact and continued to blame the Jesuits and university professors for his troubles.

Despite that, the pope used his power to protect Galileo from any serious punishment. Unfortunately, Galileo's defiant action stimulated a general crackdown by the Counter-Reformation Church on intellectual freedom.

Ironically, much that Galileo presented in the book as correct science was not; his theory of the tides, for example, was nonsense, as Albert Einstein pointed out in his foreword to a 1953 translation of Galileo's notorious book. Equally ironic is the fact that the judgment against Galileo was partly motivated by efforts to suppress *astrologers*, as some theologians mistakenly equated the claim that the earth moved with doctrines that fate was ruled by the motion of heavenly bodies.

So what does the case of Galileo reveal? It surely demonstrates that powerful groups and organizations often will abuse their power to impose their beliefs, a shortcoming certainly not limited to religious organizations—the Communist regime in the Soviet Union outlawed Mendelian genetics on grounds that all characteristics are caused by the environment. But it also shows that Galileo was not some naive scholar who fell victim to a bunch of ignorant bigots; these same "bigots" ignored dozens of other prominent scientists—many of them resident in Italy.

In any event, this celebrated case does nothing to alter the fact that the rise of science was rooted in Christian theology. Indeed, for all his posturing, Galileo remained deeply religious. As the historian William Shea noted, "Had Galileo been less devout, he could have refused to go to Rome [when summoned by the Inquisition]; Venice offered him asylum."[41] But he did not flee to Venice and often expressed his personal faith to his daughter and friends after his trial was over.

Of course, although Christianity was essential for the development of Western science, that dependency no longer exists. Once properly launched, science has been able to stand on its own, and the conviction that the secrets of nature will yield to prolonged inquiry is now as much a secular article of faith as it originally was Christian. The rise of an independent scientific establishment has given birth to new tensions between theology and science. If the church fathers were leery of the implications of science for theology, there now exists a militant group of atheists, only some of them actually scientists, who attack religion as superstitious nonsense and claim that science refutes the existence of God and the possibility of miracles. Amazingly, several of the most prominent of these are confident that godlike beings have evolved on distant planets.

Progress in Separate Spheres

Some have argued that the scientific enterprise was motivated by and sustained by concerns for practical advances in technology, especially in England.[42] The problem with this view is that during the sixteenth and seventeenth centuries few if any technological applications developed from the most significant scientific achievements. The lack of scientific applications was true not only of the more theoretical sciences, such as physics and astronomy, but even in more nearly applied sciences such as physiology. For example, it was several more centuries before Gabriel Fallopius's identification of the tubes leading from the ovary, named after him, was of any medical significance. Nor did it matter, either to physicians or to lovers, that he coined the term *vagina*.

True, this glorious era of scientific achievements also was marked by a great deal of technological progress. But the inventors and the scientists seem to have pretty much inhabited separate worlds. An example involves Denis Papin, one of the scientific stars. Papin claimed to have invented a better pump than the one Thomas Savery designed to drain British mines. To prove his point, Papin urged the Royal Society to test his pump against Savery's, but the members did not find it a matter of interest.[43] It seems not to have occurred to Papin to take his pump and go demonstrate it to mine owners.

Although there was not a direct linkage between innovations in science and technology, both stemmed from and reflected the aggressive pursuit of progress by a rapidly growing, increasingly educated, and achievement-oriented bourgeoisie.

And, of course, advances in both science and technology occurred not in spite of Christianity but because of it. Contrary to the conventional narrative, science did not suddenly flourish once Europe cast aside religious "superstitions" during the so-called Enlightenment. Science arose in the West—and only in the West—precisely because the Judeo-Christian conception of God encouraged and even demanded this pursuit.

Part V

Modernity
(1750–)

The Industrial Revolution

The most significant changes in the quality of human life were the result of the domestication of some plants and animals during the Stone Age. No longer were humans entirely dependent on whatever food they could find growing wild or on whatever game they could catch and kill. But following these Stone Age discoveries, progress was slow. It is estimated that in terms of the standard of living, things were pretty much the same for the next seven thousand years.[1] People ate about the same amount, lived about the same lifespan, and buried about the same high percentage of their children. Even in the West, as recently as the seventeenth century life was hard and short.

But then an era of immense and stunningly rapid progress began in Britain, with a wave of inventions and innovations transforming nearly every aspect of life. From 1750 to 1850 the standard of living of the average person in Britain doubled. And that was just the start. What soon became known as the Industrial Revolution continued and spread, so that today the average person in a Western nation enjoys a standard of living sixteen times as high as in 1700,[2] and lives nearly three times as long.[3] In fact, an infant born today in the Republic of the Congo can expect to live twenty-five years longer than a baby born in France in 1800.[4] Welcome to modernity.

The reason for this extraordinary increase in the quality of life was simple: suddenly people were able to produce far more goods, including food, for far less labor. This "miracle" took place because machines—

tireless, accurate, and uncomplaining—replaced humans as the primary means of production, resulting in extraordinary gains in speed and performance. To use a simple example, the Scott and Chisholm mechanical pea sheller could equal the output of six hundred workers shelling by hand.[5]

Unfortunately, with all this progress came new concerns and disenchantments. Machines freed humans from backbreaking labor, but by becoming machine operators, people fell subject to a uniformity and discipline that was often resented and sometimes bitterly condemned (particularly by intellectuals who had never done any physical labor). The first factories were powered by coal and, lacking modern filter systems, they caused severe pollution. Greatly increased life expectancy created problems of supporting an elderly population that places heavy demands on health-care facilities. And so it has gone. But only the ignorant propose turning back to a "simpler time," when half of those born died in childhood; when large families lived in smoky, one-room huts; and when few people ever journeyed more than ten miles from home.

In any event, the changes in production that took place during the Industrial Revolution make a fascinating tale to which this chapter primarily is devoted. *Why* it occurred at this time and place will be the subject of chapter 17.

The Industrial Revolution occurred so rapidly, and involved so many inventions and innovations in so many different industries, that even many long books cannot do it full justice.[6] What follows is a mere sketch intended only to give a valid sense of what took place. Because the most dramatic leap in productivity during the Industrial Revolution occurred in the cotton industry, that is where it is best to begin.

A Revolution in Cotton

In 1760 the British imported 2.5 million pounds of raw cotton, which was spun into thread and woven into cloth by hand, mostly at home or by a few weavers in master weavers' shops. By 1787 cotton imports had increased to 22 million pounds of raw cotton per year; machines had begun handling some steps in the manufacturing process, but the bulk of the work still took place in homes and small shops. Then came cotton mills, where people used machines in large plants to produce cotton cloth. Raw cotton imports increased to 366 million pounds by the 1830s.[7]

The total value of British cotton cloth jumped from about £600,000 in 1770 to £10.5 million by 1805. In the city of Manchester alone, the number of cotton mills grew from two in 1790 to sixty-six in 1821. By 1830 cotton manufacturing had become Britain's leading industry in terms of the value of the product and the number of people employed. All this was due to the rapid invention and improvement of technology, which enabled weaving machines to replace hand labor.[8]

Across the Atlantic, in 1793 the American Eli Whitney developed the cotton gin to quickly remove the seeds from cotton pods, which had been a slow and tedious process when done by hand. Cotton production in the American South expanded from 750,000 bales of cotton in 1830 (each bale weighing five hundred pounds) to 2.85 million bales in 1850.[9] This made it possible to meet the British mills' rapidly growing demand for raw cotton.

As the machines involved in producing cotton cloth became more complex, it was necessary to locate the mills along a stream sufficient to turn waterwheels. But then, in the 1770s, came the invention that was fundamental to everything else: the steam engine.

Steam

The single individual who contributed most to the Industrial Revolution was James Watt (1736–1819).[10] Watt was born in Scotland of bourgeois parents. He became an instrument maker at the University of Glasgow. There he became interested in Thomas Newcomen's primitive and inefficient steam engine, which was being used to pump the water from mines. Newcomen's engine was large and not very powerful, was hard to maintain, and wasted more than 80 percent of its steam. Using quite different principles, Watt designed a far superior engine in 1765.

Watt's engine and all its successors work this way. Water is heated by a wood, coal, or oil fire in a boiler—an enclosed vessel. When the water reaches 212 degrees Fahrenheit (100 degrees Celsius), it begins to turn into steam, thereby greatly increasing in volume and putting pressure on the boiler. Were the boiler to remain shut up, eventually the pressure of the steam would burst it open—that is the basic power source involved in the steam engine. But instead of allowing the boiler to explode, the engine harnesses the power of the expanding steam by means of a valve that opens to allow steam to escape from the boiler into a cylinder. The cylinder contains a piston, and the entering steam forces the piston to the end of the cylinder, at which point the steam is allowed to escape. When the spent steam is released, the piston returns to the other end of the cylinder, whereupon a new blast of steam is admitted to the cylinder and the power cycle is repeated. The piston is connected to a cam shaft that turns whatever the engine is being used to power—the wheels of a locomotive or an industrial machine such as a power loom. Thus, the movement of the piston up and down in the cylinder provides the power.

Watt tried to market his invention but lacked the necessary finances. So in 1775 he entered into a partnership with the wealthy Matthew Boulton, and the next year they introduced the revolutionary Boulton and Watt engine. Watt continued to make significant improvements to the engine, which soon spread far and wide with many applications.

The steam engine changed everything. First of all, there soon were engines far more powerful than any waterwheel (to assess power, Watt invented the horsepower metric: 1 hp equals the pulling power of one horse). Second, mills no longer needed to be located on rivers and streams; powered by steam, they could be placed anywhere convenient. Moreover, there was no limit to the number of steam engines that could be built and utilized. With virtually unlimited power now readily available, even cumbersome manufacturing machinery became practical. Perhaps the most important and immediate effect was to create a new era in the smelting of iron.

The New Iron Age

As noted in chapter 9, the blast furnace was one of the great medieval inventions. What the blast furnace did was to smelt iron ore at a far higher temperature than had been possible previously, allowing better iron to be produced less expensively and in larger quantities. It was named after the reason for its superiority: blasts of air were introduced into the firebox, thereby increasing the intensity of the blaze. For small blast furnaces this was accomplished by use of a hand-operated bellows. For larger furnaces, the bellows was operated by a waterwheel. But there turned out to be a severe limit on the size of the bellows that a waterwheel could power. Watt's steam engine overcame this limit in 1776.

That alone was not enough to usher in the new iron age, however. Most of the iron produced was cast iron, which is brittle and lacks tensile strength, meaning it cannot bend and is easily broken. Wrought iron (or bar iron) overcomes this shortcoming (as does steel), but it was very difficult to produce in this era. The only known method required repeated heating with charcoal. Transforming iron into steel posed still another problem: even when waterwheel-powered hammers were used, the process of pounding on and repeatedly heating a piece of iron was slow and only moderately effective. Both of these problems were solved by a remarkable Englishman, whose wife inherited a small ironworks.

Henry Cort (1740–1800) invented the *puddling* technique for producing wrought iron and the *rolling mill* to replace hammering to produce steel. Puddling involved stirring molten iron with rods that were consumed during the process. This reduced the carbon in the iron and increased its tensile strength. To turn that wrought iron into steel, which has even more tensile strength, Cort hit upon the technique of passing iron bars through a series of grooved rollers that pressed the metal into steel. His first rolling mill produced fifteen times as much steel per day as could have been produced with hammers.[11] These immense gains in metallurgy prompted many other improvements, including the coking of coal to make it burn hotter and to use less fuel.

Consequently, at the start of the Industrial Revolution, better, stronger iron and steel were readily available in Britain, which made it possible to build more powerful but smaller and lighter steam engines. This had the truly revolutionary effect of providing *portable* power: steam engines became powerful and small enough to move themselves as well as things to which they were attached—such as railroads and steamboats.

Railroads

As noted in chapter 9, rail transportation long preceded the steam engine. Because rails so greatly reduce friction, horses could pull much greater loads more rapidly when hooked to carts that ran on rails. This proved especially vital for moving heavy materials such as coal and iron ore. Consequently, many miles of rail were laid down during the reign of Queen Elizabeth. By the time the steam engine was invented, a number of significant rail lines already existed. Because it was unnecessary to lay track to demonstrate the utility of railroads, there was considerable competition among inventors to produce a successful railroad using the steam engine.

The earliest attempt was made by Richard Trevithick (1771–1833) in 1804. His steam-powered locomotive used an existing track in Wales and pulled five cars holding seventy passengers and ten tons of iron ingots nine miles. But Trevithick's train proved too heavy for the existing cast-iron rails and was abandoned after three trips.[12] The first successful railroad venture was by Matthew Murray (1765–1826) in 1812, whose locomotive, the *Salamanca*, was much lighter and did not damage the rails. Even so, railroading did not take off until 1825, when a truly self-made young man perfected both rails and engines.

George Stephenson (1781–1848) was born in poverty and grew up without any education. At seventeen he began to attend night school, where he learned to read and write. Initially he was employed to help operate the pumping engine at a coal mine, and he taught himself to fix clocks to earn money on the side.[13] In 1814 Stephenson built a locomotive he named the *Blücher* after the famous Prussian general, and it was the first to have sufficient traction between the wheels and the rails to allow it to pull loads uphill. But rails were still a problem, being too brittle and apt to break under the weight of a train. Stephenson improved the design of rails and constructed them from the newly available supply of wrought iron, eventually using them to construct the Stockton and Darlington Railway. This consisted of twenty-five miles of track that connected various coal mines to the River Tees, where the coal was loaded on barges. Using Stephenson's newly designed *Locomotion*, this became the first public steam-driven railroad. But Stephenson's ultimate success, the one that earned him the title "Father of Railways," came with his construction of the *Rocket*.

The *Rocket* was built to win a competition held by the Liverpool and Manchester Railway in 1829 (Stephenson had played the major role in designing its route and roadbed). The rules of the contest were quite strict. To compete, a locomotive could weigh no more than six tons (including water) if on six wheels and four and a half tons if on four wheels. It must be able to pull a load of twenty tons, at no less than ten miles an hour, forty times over a mile-and-a-half course.[14] Stephenson's *Rocket* easily won the competition and made him a major figure in this, the first intercity passenger railroad, which covered a distance of thirty-five miles.

The *Rocket* had a tall smokestack at the front, which prevented the smoke from the coal fire from engulfing the passenger cars; a round boiler section; and the firebox in the rear so that it could be constantly fueled with coal carried in a car directly behind the engine cabin. This became the standard design of steam locomotives, still unchanged when they were replaced by diesel units in the 1950s. The successful operation of the Liverpool and Manchester Railway prompted an outburst of railroad construction. By 1830 there were 98 miles of railroad in Britain. By 1840 this had grown to 1,498 miles. This doubled by 1845 and doubled again by 1850. In 1860 Britain had 10,433 miles of railroads.[15]

A similar pattern occurred in the United States. The Baltimore and Ohio Railroad began in 1830; initially it was only 40 miles long. The first locomotives were imported from Britain, but American-built engines soon took over—the first being the *DeWitt Clinton*, perfected in the early 1830s. By 1840 Americans had laid more railroad track (2,755 miles) than had the British—not surprising since distances were far longer in America. By 1860 American railroads rolled over nearly 30,000 miles of track. And the lonesome whistle of trains passing through became a staple of life as well as poetry.

Although getting a later start than Britain or the United States, Europe soon joined the rush for rails. But with some typically European flaws, especially in France. The French railroad system radiated from Paris. Built by six private companies, nonetheless it was tightly controlled by the government, with each company having a government monopoly on a particular area. Rather than develop any domestic technology, the French government directed that all the locomotives and cars be purchased from Britain. From the start the government set fares, freight charges, and schedules. Inefficiency was the inevitable result, since routes and schedules often were determined by political rather than economic factors.[16] The French also designed their rail system at least partly to serve military objectives, such as troop movements to the frontier with Germany.

The Germans quickly noted the developments in Britain, and several private companies built lines, using locomotives Stephenson built in Britain. The first to operate was the Bavarian Ludwig Railway, which began running trains in December 1835. It was only four miles long. Then, in 1839, came the Leipzig-Dresden railway, which was seventy-five miles long and passed through the world's first railroad tunnel. But the Germans were not content to keep relying on the British for locomotives and

cars. They began to design their own and by 1850 were entirely independent of British imports. After this flying start, the various governments
involved (Germany was not united until 1871) took over. Unlike the
French, however, these governments recognized the economic importance of railroads and focused construction efforts on linking industrializing cities and the major seaports. The Germans soon pulled far ahead
of France in terms of both miles of track and number of trains. Only
somewhat later did the Germans expand their rail system to support
troop movements and to deliver military supplies to both the western
front (facing France) and the eastern front (facing Russia).

A major consequence of railroads was to create national, and in
Europe, international economies. Before railroads it was too costly and
slow to transport anything but light goods such as luxuries or textiles very
far by horse-drawn wagons; shipments of grain, for example, were feasible
only by water. Therefore, only seaports or places on navigable rivers could
obtain bulky goods from afar. For the most part this meant that economies
were local and thereby limited in available goods and commodities. For
example, before railroads it would have been pointless to establish large
cattle ranches in the American West, because there was no way to send
cattle or meat to customers in the East. Railroads overcame these limits.
Long trainloads of western cattle could now reach the eastern markets in
several days. Steel made in Pittsburgh could be shipped to Atlanta at an
acceptable cost. In Europe, Danish farm products could be eaten in Ber-
lin. And, of course, trains were also people movers: the age of travel began.

Steamboats

To use Watt's steam engine to power a boat was an obvious application,
since no rails were required and there was no need for the engine to be
light. Consequently, efforts to build a steamboat began nearly at once
(these followed a number of not very satisfactory attempts to use the inefficient Newcomen engine to power a boat). A number of the early boats—
in France, Italy, Scotland, and the United States—seem to have performed
adequately but were not pursued. Then came Robert Fulton (1765–1815).

Fulton was an American, but he began his illustrious career in France,
where he built the first successful submarine, the *Nautilus*, under a commission from Napoleon Bonaparte. He then built a large steamboat,

sixty-six feet long, and tested it on the River Seine in 1803. It performed well and even achieved a speed of three to four miles an hour against the current. During a subsequent test, however, it sank. At that point Fulton broke off with Napoleon and moved to London, where he helped the British prepare to resist a threatened invasion by the French. To this end, he designed and successfully tested the first naval torpedoes. But after the British fleet destroyed the French fleet in 1806 at the Battle of Trafalgar (without using torpedoes), the British lost interest in the new weapons. So Fulton decided to go home.

As he prepared to return to the United States, Fulton ordered the latest steam engine model from Boulton and Watt. He had it shipped to the United States (by sailboat, of course) and used it in 1807 to power a steamboat that eventually became known as the *Clermont*. The boat was 150 feet long and 16 feet wide and had a paddle wheel on each side—this came to be a classic steamboat design. It could sustain a speed of about five miles an hour. The *Clermont* was an immediate commercial success, carrying passengers on the Hudson River between New York City and the state capital at Albany. The boat could make this 150-mile trip in about thirty hours, far faster than any other means of travel. And it was much cheaper—to haul freight the same distance by wagon cost hundreds of times more.[17]

Once the *Clermont* had shown the way, steamboats soon crowded the American waterways, especially the Ohio, the Mississippi, and the Great Lakes. Nor were steamboats limited to America. Soon western Europe's rivers were crowded with steamboats, too. Eventually oceangoing steamboats were constructed.

Urbanization and Agriculture

The rapidly growing demand for factory workers drew large numbers of people from rural areas to the cities. Here, too, Britain led the world. In 1700 about 13 percent of England's residents lived in towns having populations of 10,000 or more. A century later 24 percent did so. In 1600 the population of London was about 200,000; by 1700 it had increased to 575,000; and by 1800 about 960,000 lived in London.[18] Early in the twentieth century Britain became the first nation wherein the majority of people lived in urban areas.

The early and rapid migration of workers from rural areas to the cities was possible only because of corresponding increases in the productivity of agriculture: between 1700 and 1850 British agricultural output more than trebled.[19] By the early eighteenth century—even before machines played a major role in replacing agricultural labor—British farms had become more productive than those in western Europe. For one thing, as is discussed in the next chapter, British taxes were so low that farmers were not discouraged from investing in improvements, as they were in Europe. In addition, urbanization raised the prices for farm products, and many farmers used their increased incomes to buy more land. The average size of British farms greatly increased, making for savings in scale. British agriculture, moreover, was no longer mired in traditional peasant-landlord relations, which discouraged progress in Europe. Instead, landlords were free to pursue new methods and new crops.

Even as farm technology produced its immense benefits, however, Britain's population grew so much that the nation came to rely on imported food. Of course, given Britain's large volume of manufactured exports, this was a favorable exchange.

Modernity and Its Discontents

From the start, the Industrial Revolution has been denounced as a catastrophe that devastated the quality of life. Critics have imagined a now-lost bucolic utopia wherein no one hungered or shivered, and everyone enjoyed doing creative work, with short hours, allowing ample time to tend their vegetable gardens and enjoy an intimate family life. In truth, life in preindustrial rural villages was, as Thomas Hobbes put it, "solitary, poor, nasty, brutish, and short." Most people had little or no conception of the world more than five miles beyond their village. Most families lived without any privacy in one-room hovels. In winter they often shared their dwelling with their livestock. No one ever bathed. From time to time most people went to bed hungry. Seldom did anyone have more than two sets of clothes and often not even that. Most lived by doing backbreaking labor. Half the children did not live to the age of five. And people were old, and often toothless, by forty.

With this reality in mind, we now turn to examining some of the "evils" of industrialization.

Child Labor

Without a doubt, in its early days the Industrial Revolution exploited children to labor in the factories. In 1788 two-thirds of the workers in 143 water-powered cotton mills in England and Scotland were children, some of them younger than twelve.[20] Hours were long—twelve hours a day was not unusual. Pay was low. Conditions often were dangerous and even debilitating.

But before joining the chorus that condemns the evils of capitalism, consider this: the Industrial Revolution did not initiate child labor, it *ended* it. From earliest times most children had labored long and hard. But by gathering child laborers into factories, industrialization made them visible. This shocked genteel sensibilities to such an extent that governments began to pass laws to reform and subsequently to end these practices. The British Parliament passed Factory Acts in 1833 and 1844 that imposed age limits, reduced the number of hours children could work, and initiated government inspections to enforce these rules. The United States soon began to limit child labor as well. Over the years the rules have been made progressively more restrictive. Throughout the Western world it has become very difficult for anyone under age sixteen to hold any sort of employment.

Technophobia

The technological basis of the Industrial Revolution has always inspired fear and antagonism, especially among urban intellectuals. The romantic movement in art, music, and especially literature was partly a reaction against the rationality embodied in the new technology and against the "pollution" of nature and of spontaneous feelings by the rise of the mechanical. Technophobia began with poets such as Wordsworth and Blake, was celebrated in Mary Shelley's *Frankenstein* (1818), and launched a whole series of movies in which technology dehumanizes or even attacks people—from Charlie Chaplin's *Modern Times* (1936) to *The Day the Earth Stood Still* (1951) to *The Terminator* (1984) and on to *Avatar* (2009). In the political sphere, technophobia propels many so-called green proposals, such as allowing all the agricultural land in the Midwest to return to a state of nature and outlawing most forms of electrical generation—not only fossil and atomic fuels but even dams.[21]

This hatred and fear of technology can be traced back to intellectuals who visited the earliest factories and were revolted by the way the fast-moving machines restricted human action. They found it dehumanizing for people to work in coordination with machines. But many of these critics had never done physical labor and therefore failed to comprehend that factory work was less physically demanding than the traditional forms of labor they deemed to be more natural and humane. The truth is that field hands flocked to the factories not only because they paid much better but also because the work was less grueling. Sadly, too many of the critics' intellectual descendants have failed to catch on.

Luddite Fantasies

In November 1811 a group of weavers of hosiery and lace destroyed several mechanical looms in Nottinghamshire, England, motivated by fears that they would be reduced to unskilled laborers as machines took over the skilled craft of weaving. These machine smashers came to be known as Luddites. Although their activities soon ended, they remain celebrated among left-wing historians and others who not only accept the premise that the Industrial Revolution displaced many skilled craftsmen but also proclaim that technology today is eliminating workers. Economists have demonstrated both claims to be fallacies.

As to the first, it is true that technology replaced some skilled occupations, but it created many more skilled jobs than it eliminated. Granted, the demand for skilled hand weavers almost vanished as power looms became capable of matching them in quality. But many new highly skilled jobs were created by the need to design, build, install, and repair power looms. Thus, although the Luddites and their intellectual supporters charged that industrialization would lower the standard of living of workers, the opposite happened.

As for the second claim, every several years new alarms are raised that computers, robots, and other advanced technologies will replace human labor, leaving millions permanently unemployed.[22] In 1961 Walter Buckingham claimed in his well-received book *Automation: Its Impact on Business and People* that "there are about 160,000 unemployed in Detroit who will probably never go back to making automobiles—partly because automation has taken their jobs."[23] In fact, 300,000 new jobs opened up in Detroit's auto plants during the next four years.[24] In 1965 John Snyder claimed that automation was destroying 40,000 American jobs a week, with no end in sight.[25] By now that should have amounted to about 100 million lost jobs. What these experts missed is that although technology eliminates some jobs, it creates others. Ditchdiggers with shovels were replaced by various machines. But these machines generate jobs—directly, because they need operators and mechanics, as well as workers to build them, design them, and even sell them; indirectly, because they increase construction and other economic activities. The critics also have gone wrong by assuming that demand is fixed, when in fact new wants constantly arise to create new jobs. These alarmists missed the enormous expansion of the service sector, for example.

A Straight Line through the Centuries

The Industrial Revolution was the culmination of the rise of Western civilization that began in Greece twenty-seven centuries ago. It was the product of human freedom and the pursuit of knowledge, which is precisely why it happened where and when it did.

17

17

⌘

Liberty and Prosperity

K arl Marx got very little right in his explanations of history and social structure. But he got some things half-right. Among them was the claim that the bourgeoisie played the leading role in the Industrial Revolution.

Marx borrowed the term *bourgeoisie* from the French, who used it to identify wealthy, urban commoners. He distorted the term to identify the bourgeoisie as the capitalist ruling class. In the *Communist Manifesto* (1848), Marx and Engels credited this group with having produced the Industrial Revolution: "The bourgeoisie, during its rule of scarce one hundred years, has created more massive and more colossal productive forces than have all preceding generations together." The wealth the bourgeoisie had produced, they said, would be sufficient to fund the coming communist state—although, to achieve this state, the people (the proletariat) must destroy the bourgeoisie. According to Marx, this was inevitable: "What the bourgeoisie . . . produces, above all, are its own grave-diggers. Its fall and the victory of the proletariat are equally inevitable."

Of course, when Marxist regimes appeared in the world, they turned out to be nothing more than the same old command economies. The only difference was that, in comparison with Joseph Stalin and Mao Tse-tung, the Ottoman sultans and the Egyptian pharaohs seemed enlightened and restrained tyrants.

Still, Marx was correct to credit the bourgeoisie—that is, a newly respectable upper middle class—with the Industrial Revolution. The singular aspect of bourgeois societies is the belief that status and power should be achieved through merit rather than through inheritance. Innovation is valued and rewarded. Consequently, the two primary supports of bourgeois societies are education and liberty.

Bourgeois societies did not rise everywhere at the same time. Initially this class emerged only in the Netherlands and, especially, Britain. In his famous study *The Wealth of Nations*, Adam Smith (1723–1790) referred to Britain as "a nation of shopkeepers." [1] Therein lies the answer to the question of why Britain led the way in the Industrial Revolution as well as being unusually prolific in science. In Britain there was sufficient liberty for merit and ambition to prevail, creating a society dominated not by a hereditary nobility but by "strivers" and "achievers." The rise of the bourgeoisie in Britain was accelerated and solidified by a flood of younger sons of the nobility into its ranks.

Compared with Britain, the Continental nations lagged in liberty and education—and achieved modernity later and less fully. Across the Atlantic, the United States was a bourgeois society from the beginning, and it quickly caught up with and then surpassed Britain in industrial and economic development.

To fully explain why the Industrial Revolution began in Britain, it is necessary to explain why it became a bourgeois society.

Liberty and Property Rights

When property rights are not secure, it may be pointless to be more productive. If, for example, the lord leaves the peasant the same bare minimum no matter how good the crop, it is better for the peasant to conceal some of the crop than to improve the yield. That has been the state of affairs in most societies throughout history—not just for the peasantry but for nearly everyone else as well. Recall from chapter 14 that Ali Pasha, the Ottoman commander at the Battle of Lepanto, was afraid to leave his fortune at home, even though he was the sultan's brother-in-law. The Ottoman sultan, like the emperor of China, claimed ownership of everything; whenever either of them needed funds, "confiscation of the property of wealthy subjects was entirely in order," as the economist William K. Baumol observed. [2] And that is precisely why the rulers of the great empires were rich but their societies were poor and unproductive. It also is precisely why the Industrial Revolution took place in Britain, not in China or even in France.

Recall from chapter 9 that the Magna Carta guaranteed the property rights not only of British citizens but even of foreign merchants. Hence, unlike their counterparts in China, iron industrialists in England were secure against government seizure. Writing in 1776, the same year that James Watt perfected his steam engine, Adam Smith explained why liberty and secure property rights produce progress:

> That security which the laws of Great Britain give to every man that he shall enjoy the fruits of his own labour, is alone sufficient to make any country flourish. . . . The natural effort of every individual is to better his own condition, when suffered to exert itself with freedom and security, is so powerful a principle, that it is alone, and without any assistance, . . . capable of carrying on the society to wealth and prosperity. . . . In Great Britain industry is perfectly secure; and though it is far from being perfectly free, it is as free or freer than in any other part of Europe.[3]

In contrast, taxes were so confiscatory in France that, as Smith pointed out, the French farmer "was afraid to have a good team of horses or oxen, but endeavors to cultivate with the meanest and most wretched instruments of husbandry that he can," so that he will appear poor to the tax collector.[4] Writing to a friend back in France during a visit to England, Voltaire expressed his surprise that the British farmer "is not afraid to increase the number of his cattle, or to cover his roof with tile, lest his taxes be raised next year."[5]

High Labor Costs

An essential element in the Industrial Revolution was the productivity of the British farmer, which freed more well-fed laborers for industrial employment. French farmers, for example, were less productive—to the point that during the eighteenth century as many as 20 percent of the French were so poorly fed that they couldn't do even light work for more three hours a day.[6] In the late 1700s the average British soldier was four inches taller than the average French soldier.[7]

A related factor was the high cost of labor in Britain. Recall that although the Romans were fully aware of water power, they made almost no use of it. Why not? Because it was cheaper to buy slaves to do such tasks as grinding grain than to invest in building and maintaining water-wheels.

British firms, in contrast, often found it cheaper to invest in machines to reduce the need for labor than to pay laborers to do what the machines could do. In 1775 laborers in London earned about twelve times as much as did laborers in Delhi, four times as much as in Beijing, Florence, or Vienna, and a third higher than in Amsterdam.[8]

The elevated cost of British labor began with the industrial and economic developments of the thirteenth and fourteenth centuries (discussed in chapter 9). These developments created high demand for British products, especially its woolens, on the international market. The British quickly realized that while their luxury woolens were popular with wealthy Europeans, there was far more money to be made in high-volume, inexpensive goods sold to the mass market. As a French nobleman noted, "The English have the wit to make things for the people, rather than for the rich."[9] By successfully developing a mass market, the British faced the constant need to expand production, and that created competition for workers among British firms. Wages were further raised by the "putting-out" system in the woolen industry (the major British industry in this era), which allowed work to be performed in the home rather than by a gathered labor force. Management saved on the costs of providing the facilities and supervising a workforce, and it passed on part of these savings to workers to attract good laborers.

High wages begat even higher wages because they led to lower fertility rates prior to 1700—and where fertility rates are low, the demand for potential workers tends to exceed the supply. As Robert C. Allen wrote in his economic history of the British Industrial Revolution, the high wages permitted "young people—and young women in particular—[to] support themselves apart from their parents and control their lives and marriages. Women put off marriage until it suited them, and they found the right partner."[10] The average British woman married at about twenty-six, compared with the prevalence of teenage marriages elsewhere in Europe.[11] While wages in Britain increased, prices remained about the same as elsewhere, which made British workers better consumers than their counterparts on the Continent.[12]

For all these reasons, high wages made it profitable for British industries to invest in labor-saving devices, which helped spur the Industrial Revolution.

Cheap Energy

As noted in chapter 9, Britain was well ahead of the rest of the world in switching from wood to coal as its primary fuel. Because coal generated much higher temperatures than wood, the transition had many important consequences for the metal industries. Britain's adoption of coal also prompted innovations in mining technology and in transportation that made Britain by far the world's leading producer of coal.[13] In the 1560s Britain produced 227,000 tons of coal per year; by 1750 that had risen to 5.2 million tons per year; by 1800 coal production exceeded 15 million tons a year.[14] Consequently, coal was far cheaper in Britain than anywhere else. This, quite literally, fueled the Industrial Revolution.[15]

Embracing Commerce

In addition to having secure property, high wages, and cheap energy, British culture was favorable to commerce. That made Britain different from most other societies throughout history, which generally regarded commercial activities as degrading.

In his *Politics*, Aristotle noted that although it might be useful to explore "the various forms of acquisition" of wealth, it "would be in poor taste" to do so. He condemned commerce as unnatural, unnecessary, and inconsistent with "human virtue."[16] Plutarch thought it especially virtuous that Archimedes, one of the shining lights of ancient inventiveness, regarded all practical enterprises "as ignoble and vulgar."[17] Cicero wrote with contempt that "there is nothing noble about a workshop."[18]

As for the Romans, they were especially acquisitive but considered participation in industry or commerce to be degrading.[19] The Emperor Constantius declared, "Let no one aspire to enjoy any standing or rank who is of the lowest merchants, money-changers, lowly officers or foul agents of . . . assorted disgraceful professions."[20] Freedmen were largely responsible for commercial and industrial activities in Rome. Having been slaves, they were already stigmatized and had no status at risk in such enterprises.[21] Freedmen were, of course, at the mercy of the state, and their property was insecure.

Things were not much different in Byzantium. In 829 Emperor Theophilus watched a beautiful merchant ship sail into the harbor of Constantinople. When he asked who owned the ship, he was enraged to learn that it belonged to his wife. He snarled at her, "God made me an emperor and you would make me a ship captain!" He had the ship burned at once.[22]

In China, as seen in previous chapters, the Mandarins held commerce in such contempt that they outlawed significant commercial enterprises.

Similar attitudes prevailed in many parts of Europe. In 1756 the Abbé Coyer wrote: "The Merchant perceives no luster in his career, & if he wants to succeed in what is called in France *being something*, he must give it up. This . . . does a lot of damage. In order to be *something*, a large part of the Nobility remains nothing."[23]

Contrast all this with the frequent joint financial ventures Queen Elizabeth entered into with merchant voyagers and privateers. Elizabeth reigned during a major transformation of the British class system—a transformation that supplied the innovators, inventors, and managers who produced the Industrial Revolution.

This transformation resulted in part because the British embraced trade with the New World. Sophisticated recent research has validated the traditional view that the rise of the bourgeoisie occurred first in those European nations most involved in Atlantic trade *and* having relatively free (nonabsolutist) political institutions.[24] That is why Britain and the Netherlands emerged as the first bourgeois societies, while absolutist monarchies prevailed in the other Atlantic trading nations: Spain, Portugal, and France. Why absolutist states limited the rise of the bourgeois is not difficult to explain. By imposing a command economy, the state also sustained the nobility's status and power—and their contempt for commerce. Moreover, these states actually impeded commerce. In France, for example, nearly every commercial enterprise operated under a monopoly license purchased from the state; there was no competition.[25]

But why should Atlantic trade have spurred the rise of the bourgeoisie in nonabsolutist nations? Three factors were involved. First, vigorous Atlantic trade expanded and strengthened those merchant groups involved directly or indirectly in this trade. Second, as these groups grew and became rich, they gathered sufficient power to demand changes, including even more secure property rights, that expanded their ranks. The third factor might have been the most important one: by virtue of their success and influence, the bourgeois earned respect and dignity.[26]

Claims[27] that the rise of the West was funded by the profits of trade with the New World—from colonialism and slavery—are refuted by the simple fact that these profits were too small to have made a substantial contribution to the economic growth of western Europe.[28] These profits were, however, sufficient to make groups of merchants "very rich by the standards of seventeenth- and eighteenth-century Europe, and typically politically and socially very powerful," in the words of the historian J. V. Beckett.[29]

MIT economist Daron Acemoglu and his colleagues empirically confirmed an immense historical literature proposing that from 1500 through 1800:

- All Atlantic port cities grew much faster than did inland cities or ports on the Mediterranean. These cities were dominated by merchants engaged in import-export trading with the New World.
- Rapid urbanization took place in Britain and the Netherlands but much less so in France and Spain, and there was a strong correlation between urbanization and per capita income, for in cities commerce was king.
- Legal changes that greatly improved property rights (including patent laws) took place in Britain and the Netherlands but much less so or not at all elsewhere.
- Merchants came to dominate the Parliament in Britain and the Dutch States-General.

But in Britain, it was not just the rising bourgeoisie that proved open to commerce. The nobility displayed little of the contempt for commercial activities that their peers on the Continent did. For one thing, British nobles were much less inclined to live in London and spend their days at court (in part because several sixteenth-century kings had taken measures to deter the aristocracy from spending time at court).[30] In contrast, most of the French nobility lived in Paris and seldom visited their estates. Therefore, rather than being absent landlords, most of the British nobility took an active role in administering their lands. In this sense they actually "worked" for their livings. Moreover, they were fully involved in the market economy, their incomes being governed by prices for their crops, livestock, wool, and other products such as minerals. In fact, according to scholar Colin Mooers, an estimated "two-thirds of the peerage, in the period 1560–1640, was engaged in colonial, trading or industrial enterprises."[31]

An equally important aspect of the British nobility was that younger sons "automatically descended into the gentry," as Beckett pointed out. They could use the "courtesy title 'lord,'" but only for themselves, not for their children."[32] For example, Winston Churchill's father was Lord Randolph Churchill because he was the third son of the 7th Duke of Marlborough, but his son Winston could not call himself a lord. Thus did the overwhelming number of noble English offspring "disappear" into the population of commoners. Nor could younger sons expect to live off the family lands (as was typical on the Continent). Rather, as Beckett noted, many younger sons received a "cash payment to set themselves up as best they could."[33] In each generation, then, a large number of younger sons of the nobility were forced to find gainful occupations and professions. They not only staffed the church and the officer corps but also were active in law, academia, banking, mining, manufacturing, and other forms of commerce. The flood of well-educated and well-connected young men into these occupations brought with them substantial prestige and power.

The Expansion of British Education

The rise of the bourgeoisie was accompanied by what Lawrence Stone called an "educational revolution in England."[34]

As noted in chapter 15, massive educational changes began in the mid-sixteenth century. First was the establishment of thousands of "petty schools" for the purpose of teaching "basic literacy to the bulk of the population."[35] Nothing like this had ever been attempted before, anywhere. These efforts were financed not by the government but by a huge number of private bequests for the establishment of local schools to provide free instruction. By about 1640 England had a petty school for every 4,400 people, or "one approximately every twelve miles."[36] Also free were schools that taught not only reading but also grammar, writing, arithmetic, and bookkeeping. And, of course, there were the sophisticated "grammar schools," meant to prepare students for entry into the universities and the Inns of Court (law school). Perhaps surprisingly, the grammar schools were not limited to the children of the aristocracy. For example, from 1636 to 1639 Norwich grammar school sent on to the University of Cambridge the sons of "one esquire, four gentlemen, two clergymen, a doctor, a merchant, an attorney, a weaver, a carpenter, a fishmonger, two staymakers and two drapers."[37]

As that list attests, in this era many from humble origins went to the great universities of Oxford and Cambridge. In fact, at no time between 1560 and 1629 were the majority of university students classified as "gentlemen."[38] This era saw a dramatic expansion in the enrollment of sons of the bourgeoisie. For example, the sons of merchants and tradesmen accounted for 6 percent of the students at Caius College, Cambridge, in 1580–90; by 1620–29 the figure had increased to 23 percent. Similarly, enrollment by the sons of clergy and the professions grew from 5 percent to 19 percent. Hence, by 1620–29, nearly half (42 percent) of the students were from the bourgeoisie.[39]

By 1630, well before the takeoff of the Industrial Revolution, Britain had by far the best-educated population in the world. Furthermore, large numbers of those involved in industry and commerce had attended the elite universities, forming a critical mass of educated leaders to launch the Industrial Revolution. A remarkable study by the historian François Crouzet, based on 226 founders of large industrial firms in Britain from 1750 to 1850, revealed that 9 percent were the sons of aristocrats and 60 percent were the sons of the bourgeoisie. A similar study by the sociologist Reinhard Bendix, based on 132 leading industrialists from 1750 to 1850, reported that two-thirds were from families already well established in business.[40]

The American "Miracle"

When the Industrial Revolution began in Britain in about 1750, North America had hardly any manufacturing, aside from a large shipbuilding industry based on plentiful local supplies of timber and other materials (in 1773 American shipyards built 638 oceangoing vessels).[41] Ships aside, manufacturing in America was limited to small workshops making items such as shoes, horse harnesses, nails, pails, and simple hand tools for the local market. Only the many little gunsmith shops, dedicated to fabricating the newly invented rifle, could compete with British goods in terms of quality. Nearly everything else in the way of manufactured goods was imported from England.

A century later the United States was catching up with Britain as a manufacturing power, and in fact the Americans soon surpassed the British and everyone else, as can be seen in table 17–1. In 1870 Great Britain produced about a third (31.8 percent) of all the world's manufactured goods and the United States produced about a quarter (23.3 percent). By 1900 the United States was producing more than a third (35.3 percent) of all the world's manufacturing output, compared with 14.7 percent produced by Great Britain and 15.9 percent by Germany. By 1929 the United States dwarfed the world as a manufacturing power, producing 42.2 percent of all goods, compared with Germany's 11.6 percent and Britain's 9.4.

This "miracle" of production was possible only because America had also forged ahead in the Industrial Revolution. Indeed, during the nineteenth century it seemed as if all the inventors lived in the United States.[42]

Why had this occurred? For all the same reasons that the Industrial Revolution had originated in Britain—political freedom, secure property rights, high wages, cheap energy, and a highly educated population—plus a plenitude of resources and raw materials and a huge, rapidly growing domestic market. In fact, by early in the nineteenth century, the United States surpassed Britain in all these crucial factors.

Property and Patents

The early American colonies came under English common law. Therefore individuals had an unlimited right to property that they had legally obtained, and not even the state could abridge that right without adequate compensation. Eventually that became the basis of American property law as well. Thus, the state could not seize iron foundries as had taken place in China, although it could purchase them should that seem desirable—as the socialist government of Britain did when it nationalized most basic industries right after World War II (until government control of these industries proved so unprofitable that they were transformed back into private companies).

Table 17–1: Percentage Shares of the
World's Manufacturing Output

Nation	Percentage of World's Manufacturing Output		
	1870	1900	1929
Great Britain	31.8	14.7	9.4
United States	23.3	35.3	42.2
Germany	13.2	15.9	11.6
France	10.3	6.4	6.6
Russia	3.7	5.0	4.3
Belgium	2.9	2.2	1.9
Italy	2.4	3.1	3.3
Canada	1.0	2.0	2.4
Sweden	0.4	1.1	1.0
India	-	1.1	1.2
Japan	-	0.6	2.5
Finland	-	0.3	0.4
Latin America	-	-	2.0
China	-	-	0.5
All others	11.0	12.3	10.7

Source: League of Nations, 1945

But this approach to property law was inadequate for protecting inventions and other forms of intellectual property. Consider the steam engine. Obviously, James Watt owned the steam engine he had constructed—it was his personal property and to steal it would have been a crime. But what if someone made an exact copy? Was it that person's? If so, then how could Watt or any other inventor benefit from inventing? The solution was to grant a *patent* on inventions. Watt, for example, secured the exclusive right to ownership of all steam engines based on his principles for a number of years, including the right to sell, rent, license, or otherwise exploit that invention. The British Crown had initially granted patents, but the government formalized the process during the reign of Queen Anne (1702–1714), requiring applicants to submit a full description of their invention.

The American Founders regarded patent rights as so important that they wrote them into the Constitution: Article I, Section 8, states: "The Congress shall have power . . . to promote the progress of science and useful arts, by securing for limited times to authors and inventors the exclusive right to their respective writings and discoveries." In keeping with this mandate, in 1790 Congress passed the U.S. Patent Act, which gave inventors an exclusive right to their inventions for a period of fourteen years. This was later amended to twenty-one years. Initially few applied for patents—only fifty-five were issued between 1790 and 1793. But by 1836 ten thousand patents had been registered. Then came an inventive explosion, and by 1911 one million patents had been granted. Among them were patents covering the invention of electric lightbulbs, movies, sound recordings, telephones, and the zipper.

Although it has often been overlooked, American laws concerning bankruptcy also facilitated industrial development. In Britain and most of Europe, laws concerning debts were brutal: in Britain those unable to pay their debts were sentenced to debtors' prison, from where "they could scarcely repay their obligations let alone start new careers," the historian Maury Klein noted. But America had no debtors' prisons, and the law limited legal liabilities sufficiently "to give debtors enough breathing space to survive their downfall and get back into the game."[43] Many famous American industrialists and inventors survived early failures. More than that, entrepreneurs dared to take risks.

High Wages

If wages were high in Britain, they were towering in America. American wages were so high because employers had to compete with the exceptional opportunities of self-employment in order to attract adequate numbers of qualified workers. Alexander Hamilton explained shortly after the American Revolution, "The facility with which the less independent condition of an artisan can be exchanged for the more independent condition of a farmer . . . conspire[s] to produce, and, for a length of time, must continue to occasion, a scarcity of hands for manufacturing occupation, and dearness of labour generally."[44] Good farmland was so abundant and so cheap that even those who arrived in America without any funds could, in several years, save enough to buy and stock a good farm. Consider that in the 1820s the federal government sold good land for $1.25 an acre while wages for skilled labor amounted to between $1.25 and $2 a day.[45] Consider, too, that in America there were no mandatory church tithes, and taxes were low.

Given higher labor costs, how could American manufacturers possibly compete on price? Through better technology. American industrialists eagerly embraced promising new technology if they anticipated a sufficient increase in worker productivity. For if workers equipped with a new technology could produce a sufficient amount more than could less mechanized workers in Europe, this reduced the relative cost of American labor *per item*. Technology made it irrelevant that American workers were paid, say, three times as much per hour as European workers (as they often were), when they produced five or six times as much per hour. That increased productivity offset both their own higher wages and the capital investments their employers made in new technology. Throughout the nineteenth century Americans led the way in developing and adopting new techniques and technologies. And they did so without provoking the reactionary labor opposition to innovation that nineteenth-century British capitalists so often faced—no Luddites smashed machines in the United States. Why not? Because, given the constant shortage of labor, American manufacturers competed with one another for workers and used a significant portion of their productivity gains to increase wages and to offer more attractive conditions.

Worker productivity was the basis for the incredible growth of American manufacturing shown in table 17–1, and why it came largely at the expense of the British. Americans were not more humane employers. They were more sophisticated capitalists who recognized that satisfied, productive workers are the greatest asset of all. This attitude toward labor brought many skilled and motivated British and European workers to America, and the expanded labor force sustained ever more industrial growth. Too many published discussions of the rise of American industry (especially in textbooks) denounce the "robber barons" and "plutocrats" for supposedly exploiting labor, and especially for abusing immigrants. Such tracts are anachronistic, comparing labor practices back then with those of today, almost as if factory latrines in 1850 should have had flush toilets. The proper comparison is between the situation of American labor and labor in the other industrializing nations in the same era.

In addition to being highly paid and equipped with the latest technology, American workers were notable in another way. They were far better educated than workers anywhere else in the world (excluding Canada).

Educating a Nation

During his 1818 visit to America, the English intellectual William Cobbett wrote home: "There are very few really *ignorant* men in America. . . . They have all been *readers* from their youth up" (his italics).[46] From the earliest days of settlement the American colonists invested heavily in "human capital," as modern economists would put it. And in this, religion played a primary role.

A major point of contention during the Reformation had to do with reading the Bible. For centuries the Church had thought the best way to avoid endless bickering about God's Word was to encourage only well-trained theologians to read the Bible. To this end, the Church discouraged translations of the Bible into contemporary languages, thus tending to limit readership to those proficient in Latin or Greek, which even most clergy were not. In the days before the printing press there were so very few copies of the Bible that even most bishops did not have access to one. Consequently, the clergy learned about the Bible from secondary sources written to edify them and to provide them with suitable quotations for preaching. What the public knew about the Bible was only what their priests told them.

Then came the printing press. The Bible was the first book Gutenberg published. It was written in Latin, but soon Bibles were being printed in all the major "vulgar" languages (hence "vulgate" Bibles), making the Bible the first bestseller. As had been feared, conflict quickly arose as one reformer after another denounced various church teachings and activities as unbiblical. And the one doctrine most widely shared among the various dissenting Protestant movements was that everyone must consult scripture for themselves. So when the Pilgrims arrived in America in 1620, one of the first things they did was to concern themselves with educating their children.

In 1647 the Massachusetts Colony enacted a law asserting that all children must attend school.[47] It required that in any township having fifty households, one person must be appointed to teach the children to read and write, with the teacher's wages to be paid either by parents or by the inhabitants in general. In any township having a hundred or more households, a school must be established, "the master thereof being able to instruct youth so far as they may be fitted for the university." Any community that failed to provide these educational services was to be fined "till they shall perform this order." Other states followed suit, and free public schools became a fixture of American life. As the nation spread west, one-room schoolhouses were among the first things the settlers constructed (along with saloons, jails, and churches). Much the same took place in Canada, and by the end of the eighteenth century North America had by far the world's most literate population.[48]

Notice that the Massachusetts law required that schoolmasters be qualified to prepare students for college. This was not as unreasonable as it might appear. A decade before they passed this law and only sixteen years after landing at Plymouth Rock, the Puritans had founded Harvard. This initiated three centuries of intense competition among the religious denominations to found their own colleges and universities. Prior to the Revolution ten institutions of higher learning had begun operating in the American colonies (compared with two in England). Of these, only the University of Pennsylvania, instituted by Benjamin Franklin to train businessmen, was not affiliated with a denomination. At least twenty more colleges were founded before 1800, including Georgetown University, founded by Jesuit scholars in 1789. During the next century literally hundreds of colleges and universities arose in the United States, and most of these also were of denominational origin (although many abandoned their denominational ties during the twentieth century). In 1890 two out of every hundred Americans age eighteen to twenty-four were enrolled in college; by 1920 this had risen to five of each hundred.[49] At the time, nothing like this was going on anywhere else in the world.

Immigration

British North America grew at a remarkable rate from the very start. An estimated total of 600,000 people came from Britain between 1640 and 1760,[50] and many others came from the Netherlands, France, Germany and other parts of Europe. The thirteen colonies had 1.6 million residents by 1760, more than 2.1 million in 1770, nearly 3 million by 1780, and 4 million by 1790.[51] Given that Britain had a population of only about 8 million in the 1770s,[52] the Revolutionary War was not as unequal as is often supposed. Moreover, by 1830 the United States population (13 million) was equal to that of Britain, and by 1850 it was far larger (23 million versus 17 million). In 1900 there were 76 million Americans and 32 million British.[53] Hence, the American domestic market far surpassed that of Britain.

It also seems obvious that there was a powerful selective factor in who chose to come to America—the most ambitious and alert. In fact, immigrants were more likely to have come in pursuit of opportunity than to escape poverty. In his remarkable study based on immigration records, the celebrated historian Bernard Bailyn found that only 23 percent of immigrants from Britain from 1773 to 1776 were classified as laborers (most of them as servants), while half were classified as skilled craftsmen and another 20 percent as independent farmers. Aristocrats made up 2 percent of the British immigrants.[54] This is consistent with the fact that younger sons of the nobility flocked to America.[55] For example, during the last half of the nineteenth century membership in the Wyoming Stock Growers' Association and its famous Cheyenne Club was dominated by younger sons of the British nobility as well as some titled Frenchmen and Germans.[56] In the 1880s the largest ranch in the New Mexico Territory was owned by the youngest son of the 4th Marquis of Waterford.[57]

It seems significant that many of those involved in the explosion of American invention were immigrants. Alexander Graham Bell, inventor of the telephone, was an immigrant from Scotland. Nikola Tesla, inventor of fluorescent lighting and of the alternating current (AC) electrical system, was raised in what is now Croatia. Thomas Edison's two most important assistants were immigrants, one from Switzerland, the other from England.

Organized Invention

Accidental inventions are the stuff of dreams. Almost always, an inventor has set about trying to meet a significant need—often with a pretty good notion of how to do so. In fact, most "inventions" are actually *improvements*, and therefore the goal is well defined. In the wake of the Industrial Revolution, however, the flood of inventions gave rise to a new approach—a general commitment to invention and discovery per se. Leading this movement was Thomas Alva Edison (1847–1931). It could be said that Edison invented modern life, as he was responsible for the electric lightbulb, recorded sound, movies, the fluoroscope, great improvements to the telephone and telegraph, and basic research on electric railroads—a total of 1,093 patents.

But his most important contribution was to invent the research laboratory, with the primary mission of discovering that some new technology was needed and then launching research efforts to invent it. Edison's laboratory in Menlo Park, New Jersey, was so successful at discovering needs and solutions that it became known as the "invention factory." Today we take such an approach for granted. Most major companies survive by sustaining effective research and development divisions. Consumers expect new products and the constant improvement of old ones. That expectation, and the reality it reflects, is the epitome of modernity.

From Freedom to Prosperity

From early days, the rise of Western modernity was a function of freedom—freedom to innovate and freedom from confiscation of the fruits of one's labors. When the Greeks were free they created a civilization advanced beyond anything else in the world. When Rome imposed its imperial rule all across the West, progress ceased for a millennium. The fall of Rome once again unleashed creativity and, for good and for ill, the fragmented and competing Europeans soon outdistanced the rest of the world, possessed not only of invincible military and naval might but also of superior economies and standards of living. All these factors combined to produce the Industrial Revolution, which subsequently changed life everywhere on earth.

18

Globalization and Colonialism

W ith all the elements of Western modernity in place, this chapter turns to the ways by which it spread around the world.

The primary means of cultural transmission was colonialism. In 1800 Europeans controlled 35 percent of the land surface of the globe. By 1878 this figure had risen to 67 percent. Then, in the next two decades, Europeans seized control of nearly all of Africa, so that in 1914, on the eve of World War I, Europeans dominated 84 percent of the world's land area.[1] The British Empire alone ruled about 25 percent of the earth's inhabitants.[2] Everywhere Europeans ruled, Western culture quickly penetrated, aided by the fact that most colonial regimes established a substantial number of local schools.

Nearly all modern accounts stress greed and racism as the basis for Europe's colonial expansion. Granted, both were significant factors, but so too were idealism and charity, especially on the part of Christian missionaries, who often were at least as concerned to educate and modernize foreign lands as to convert the world to Christ. For example, by 1910 British and American overseas mission organizations had established 86 colleges and universities, 522 teachers colleges (often referred to as *normal schools*), and thousands of elementary schools in Asia and Africa.[3] Nor were missionaries the only idealists involved. The earliest British military intrusions into Africa were devoted mainly to stamping out the slave trade.[4] During 1840 alone the British navy intercepted 425 slave ships off the West African coast, hanged the slavers, returned the slaves to Sierra Leone, and set them free.[5]

Of course, some instances of European colonialism were brutal and entirely exploitative—Belgian king Leopold II's rule of the Congo being the most notorious example. But while some individuals and companies profited greatly from colonialism, they usually did so at the expense of their fellow countrymen, since when government expenses are taken into account, European nations typically lost money on their colonial empires.[6] It is worth remembering that the American Revolution was fought largely because the British Parliament, tired of losing money on the thirteen colonies, tried to impose taxes sufficient to cover the costs of administering and defending them.

Why, then, did Europeans establish colonies and try so hard to preserve them? Partly it was a matter of prestige. Many European leaders sought to expand their empires to qualify as "world powers." And everyone cited the economic benefits of colonies, for the fact that most, if not all, colonies were money-losing operations was not obvious and often required complex calculations. For example, the huge British Empire could not have existed without the superiority of the British navy—but no naval costs were charged against the colonies. Nor did anyone seem concerned about the costs to taxpayers of maintaining the huge number of British civil servants needed to rule and run the many colonies. These officials were drawn overwhelmingly from among the privileged, their ranks abounding in those with "firsts" from Oxford and Cambridge.[7] Meanwhile, many powerful British families and firms grew rich from colonial commerce; they not only served as "proof" that colonies were a national asset but also formed a potent lobby on behalf of imperial policies. It was the same in other European nations. Nevertheless, for the average European, colonialism was a losing proposition.[8]

Unfortunately, many social scientists remain convinced that colonialism was mainly responsible for the wealth of the West while causing "underdevelopment" or even substantial economic decline in the non-Western world.[9] The facts are otherwise. Indeed, it is clear that the major impact of the West has been to immensely *improve* the quality of life in other parts of the world.

Imperial Technology

Economic and prestige motives aside, perhaps the key factor in the nine-teenth century's massive wave of European colonialism was that never before had the subjugation of other societies been so easy to accomplish. Because of revolutionary developments in medicine, ships, firearms, and communications, the Western advantage over the rest of the world was even greater than the one Cortés and Pizarro had enjoyed over the Aztecs and the Mayans. And, once again, the temptations of such superiority were irresistible.[10]

Medicine

For centuries, sub-Saharan Africa was superbly defended against Western intruders by a microorganism to which native-born Africans were largely immune. Beginning with a Portuguese expedition to explore the Congo River in 1485, Westerners had to abandon one exploration of Africa after another because of appalling death rates from malaria. For example, in 1832 the British merchant-adventurer Macgregor Laird sailed a steam-boat up the Niger River. Of the forty-eight Europeans aboard, only nine returned—the rest having died of disease, mainly of malaria.[11] Of eighty-nine English missionaries who went to West Africa between 1804 and 1825, fifty-four died and fourteen went home in ill health.[12] The historian Philip Curtin reported staggering death rates of 48 percent for British mil-itary personnel stationed in Sierra Leone between 1817 and 1836 and 67 percent for troops assigned to the British installation on the Gold Coast.[13] No African military defenders, no matter how well armed and trained, could have imposed such losses. Africa was effectively invulnerable.

Then came quinine. During the seventeenth century Jesuits in Peru had discovered the effectiveness of the bark of the cinchona tree for treat-ing malaria (the bark is a natural source of quinine). But few European physicians accepted claims made for the effectiveness of the ground bark, and for many years an amazing array of quack treatments were preferred. Only in the 1830s did clinical tests by French army doctors demonstrate quinine's effectiveness. Soon cinchona bark became a major export from Latin America, rising from two million pounds in 1860 to twenty mil-lion in 1881.[14] With the widespread use of quinine, sub-Saharan Africa no longer was the "white man's grave," and the rush to colonize the entire region began.

There were, of course, a number of other diseases that deterred Western colonialism in Africa and Asia—sleeping sickness and yellow fever among them. These, too, were overcome by Western medicine.

Steamships

To colonize the world, Westerners needed to be able to get there and back in some reasonable time—and usually by sea. In the days of Francis Drake, it took a long time to sail anywhere. Galleons such as Drake's *Golden Hind* were doing very well to attain speeds of five miles per hour. Even then, sailing ships could not sail directly toward their destination but had to keep tacking owing to the direction of the wind. They also could expect to be delayed by periods without wind, or to be blown off course by gales. In this era, a trip from England to India took from six to eight months. Worse yet, even the largest sailing ships were relatively small—the *Golden Hind* was only a hundred feet long.

Although the British and the Portuguese managed to sustain colonies in that era, colonization became far easier when steam engines began to power oceangoing ships. Even more important was the introduction of the screw propeller to replace paddle wheels. This revolution in voyaging began in 1843 with the launching of the SS *Great Britain*. That steamship not only featured a screw propeller but also was built of iron and was 322 feet long. The *Great Britain* could steam at twelve to thirteen miles per hour and sail directly toward her destination. In 1845 she crossed the Atlantic in fourteen days (compared with about sixty-five days for sailing ships). The globe was now much smaller.

Although private entrepreneurs were responsible for these innovations, Western navies soon joined in. In 1869 the British Admiralty launched HMS *Devastation*, an ironclad ship that was 307 feet long and was powered by two steam engines turning two screw propellers. It had an armor belt twenty inches thick around its waterline. *Devastation* mounted two heavily armored turrets, each housing two twelve-inch guns firing six-hundred-pound shells, as well as many smaller guns. This heavyweight could achieve a speed of sixteen miles per hour.[15]

Devastation was only the start of what became a frantic arms race. Britain, France, Germany, and Russia constructed fleets of battleships, as did the United States and, to everyone's surprise, Japan. The ships rapidly got bigger, faster, and more heavily armed. On May 27, 1905, the Russian fleet, having sailed halfway around the world, gave battle to the Japanese fleet off the Pacific coast of Siberia. All ten of the Russian battleships were sunk or surrendered, while no Japanese ship was even badly damaged.

The very next year, however, the British made all other navies obsolete as they launched the HMS *Dreadnought*.[16] She was 527 feet long, built entirely of steel. Propelled by four screws, each driven by a steam turbine, *Dreadnought* could reach a top speed of twenty-four miles per hour. Her battery of ten twelve-inch guns had an effective range of more than three miles. By the outbreak of World War I in 1914, Britain had twenty-nine battleships of the *Dreadnought* class. The Germans had sixteen. But the only sea battle to take place—off the coast of Denmark, near Jutland—was inconclusive as neither the Germans nor the British were willing to commit to a full-scale fight.[17]

Of course, World War I was not a colonial war but a war among European nations (partly over which ones would have the better colonial empires—the Versailles Treaty stripped Germany of its colonies). Battleships were built for such a war, but for gaining and dominating colonies, much smaller vessels able to sail up rivers played the critical role.

Gunboats

China had long imposed severe limits on Western trade and contact, restricting Western merchants to small areas in a few port cities. In fact, Westerners might have been excluded even from these ports had it not been for the Europeans' overwhelming naval power. Eventually some British officials realized that steam power held the key to penetrating China's major rivers. With their fleet of large sailing ships unable to navigate rivers well, the British in 1839 began construction of a revolutionary ship called the *Nemesis*. The Scottish shipbuilder John Laird had developed a new technique to bend iron plates and rivet them together to build iron ships (as opposed to ironclad ships, which were built of wood and then armored). The *Nemesis* was the first iron ship to carry guns. Powered by two steam engines, she was 184 feet long and 29 feet wide but had a draft of less than 5 feet, even when fully loaded, making her ideal for navigating on rivers.[18] In January 1841 the *Nemesis* went up the Pearl River, just below Canton, and laid waste to a whole series of Chinese forts, sank a number of Chinese war junks, and asserted British invincibility. When the Chinese refused to sue for peace, the British brought in more gunboats modeled on the *Nemesis*. This flotilla sailed up the Yangtze River in 1842, devastated Chinese opposition, and imposed a peace treaty on the Chinese court.[19]

Western gunboats, including several American vessels, patrolled the Yangtze for the next century: in 1937 Japanese planes bombed the American gunboat USS *Panay*, which was anchored near Nanking. Gunboats also played an important role in penetrating Africa and on the Ganges River in India.

Rapid-Fire Small Arms

In 1898 the British writer Hilaire Belloc summed up Europe's immense military superiority over the rest of the world:

> Whatever happens we have got
> The Maxim gun, and they have not.

The Maxim gun was the first modern machine gun. Invented in 1884 by Hiram Maxim, an American who emigrated to Britain, it was water-cooled, belt-fed, and capable of firing six hundred rounds per minute. In the Battle of Shangani in southeastern Africa in 1894, fifty British soldiers with four Maxim guns mowed down five thousand Matabele warriors armed only with muzzle-loading rifles and spears. Even so, the Maxim gun and other advanced weapons played a secondary role in the spread of European colonialism. A tiny company of British troops armed only with single-shot rifles had been almost equally lethal against the Zulus fifteen years before.

The real breakthrough had come with the invention of the breech-loading rifle in the 1820s. Rather than pouring powder down the barrel of a musket, followed by a paper wad jammed in with a ramrod, then a lead bullet, and then another wad, the soldier loaded the new rifle by opening the breech (the rear portion of the barrel) and inserting a paper cartridge containing both powder and bullet. This dramatically reduced reloading time and allowed the soldier to reload while kneeling or even lying prone. Breech-loading rifles could produce many volleys while muzzle loaders produced one. According to the social scientist Daniel Headrick, the breech-loading rifle was as superior to the musket as the musket was to the bow and arrow.[20]

Then, with the invention of the brass cartridge in 1866, repeating and rapid-fire weapons became possible. One Maxim gun was the equivalent of three hundred riflemen firing twice a minute.

Telegraphs and Cables

Until modern times, slow communications were the bane of organized social life. Word of an invading army often did not arrive much before that army marched over the horizon—messengers not being able to greatly outpace the invaders. It is worth noting that modern marathon races are 26 miles and 385 yards long because that is the estimated distance covered by the Greek messenger Pheidippides in 490 BC when he ran to Athens to bring word that the Greek army had defeated the Persians in the Battle of Marathon. It is said that he gasped out "victory" and then collapsed and died.

Slow communications long hindered colonialism. British officials in India could expect to wait at least a year for an answer to a letter sent to London. In the United States, during the War of 1812 fighting continued in Louisiana for some weeks before the combatants received word that a peace treaty had been signed. Then, in 1837, the American Samuel F. B. Morse (1791–1872) invented the telegraph.

It was already well known that an electrical signal could be sent over a wire when Morse, a Yale graduate and successful portrait painter, became interested in this phenomenon. The problem was that a signal could not be sent very far over a wire—only a few hundred yards—before it dissipated. Morse invented the relay, a mechanism that repeated the signal. With repeaters inserted along the wire, there was no longer any limit on the distance a message could be sent. As for the message, this was no telephone wire—you couldn't talk over it. All you could do was interrupt the electrical charge sent along the wire. Morse turned this into a message-transmitting signal by using shorter and longer interruptions of the electrical charge—the famous dits and dahs of the Morse code. For each letter of the alphabet, Morse designated a code group: A = dit, dah; B = dah, dit, dit, dit; and so on to Z = dah, dah, dit, dit. With this code, it was possible to spell out any message. Soon operators became so skilled that they could send messages at a rate of about forty words per minute—the record is seventy-five words. Morse named his system the telegraph. Soon telegraph lines stretched from one major city to another, in Europe as well as the United States, and messages were flowing, each for a modest charge.

But that did nothing to speed up communications across the oceans—messages between London and India still took six months or more each way. Then, in 1850, the Brett brothers laid a cable across the English

Channel. Highly insulated to protect against water damage, it continued to work until well into the twentieth century.[21] A rush to lay submarine cables began: one was laid across the Atlantic from Britain to America in 1857–58, and an incredibly long series of cables was laid from Britain to India in 1859, at the staggering cost of £800,000. But when the cables to America and to India failed, the British government appointed a committee to solve the problems of submarine cables. Headed by the illustrious physicist Lord Kelvin (1824–1907), the committee quickly overcame the difficulties involved, and the rush to lay submarine cables resumed. By 1865 London was linked by cable with both India and the United States. Soon thereafter Britain was linked to every outpost of its huge and rapidly growing empire.

The Age of Imperialism

The Age of Imperialism was shorter and more recent than many realize, coming to full flower from 1870 to 1914.[22] As for the extent of Western imperialism, the prominent historian D. K. Fieldhouse observed that it is "easier to list the few places which were not and had never been under European domination than to name those which were. Turkey, parts of Arabia, Persia, Afghanistan, Tibet, China, Mongolia, Siam, Japan, a number of small islands, the Arctic and the Antarctic."[23] Everything else was either part of the West or a colony. Even some of the places that weren't actual colonies were subject to a considerable degree of Western control—China being a good example.

By the nineteenth century few European nations actually qualified as colonial powers. Spain's once-immense holdings in Latin America were long gone. Having lost Brazil in 1822, Portugal had only a few bits of Africa, and Belgium had just one colony, the Congo. Germany and Italy did not acquire their colonies until the 1880s, most of them gained during the partition of Africa. In contrast, the Dutch colonies were spread around the world, their most important ones being in Asia. The French Empire came to be second only to the British in terms of area, even though the French had lost or sold all their North American possessions. The French held Indochina, invaded Algiers in 1830, and during the 1880s gained most of northwest Africa. And then there was the enormous British Empire.

There were substantial differences in how various European nations treated their colonies. No colony was mistreated as badly as the Belgian Congo.[24] Initially the Congo was the personal possession of King Leopold II, who sent in military forces that imposed a brutal, murderous regime on the population, forcing the men to work deep in the jungle to tap wild rubber trees, and mutilating and killing those who complained. In 1904 the British consul Roger Casement issued a report estimating that several million Africans had perished, many from starvation as the forced labor had prevented the locals from farming. Prompted by both Catholic and Protestant missionaries, an international commission investigated conditions in the Congo and confirmed that crimes against humanity were routinely taking place. The Belgian government took over the Congo from the king. But dreadful abuses continued. In 1960 the Congo gained its independence from Belgium, but sad to say, self-rule did not bring a better life to the people—a series of African tyrants have enriched themselves and imposed harsh repression.

At the other end of the spectrum were the British colonies. Granted, the British sometimes were oppressive and ruthless, but they also were concerned to improve the circumstances of their colonial subjects. This sense of obligation was expressed in Rudyard Kipling's phrase "the white man's burden." Today that phrase is uniformly condemned as unmitigated racism, and without a doubt it reflected the routine racism of the day. But for many British civil servants as well as missionaries serving abroad, it also reflected their conviction that those enjoying the benefits of modernity had an obligation to share it with those less fortunate.

Interestingly enough, two of the darkest blots on the British colonial record involve the brutal mistreatment of *white* subjects. The first occurred with the potato famine in Ireland (1845–51), when the Irish starved while the English landlords obeyed the Corn Laws and exported grain to England. The second happened in South Africa, where the British conducted a long and bloody war (1899–1902) against Dutch settlers to take over the Boer republics. In most other incidents involving British colonial military forces, they protected not only British interests but also colonial subjects. For example, the 1885 Mahdi Revolt in the Sudan took the city of Khartoum and was responsible for the death of the famous British general Charles "Chinese" Gordon; the British response relieved substantial numbers of Egyptian and Sudanese residents from the threat of massacre.

The most admirable aspects of British colonialism involved the immense efforts devoted to education and health.[25] Colonial administrators and the educators they hired were responsible for some of these achievements.[26] But just as important were the thousands of missionaries (Americans as well as British) who flocked to the colonies.

Missionary Effects

Perhaps the most bizarre of all the charges leveled against Christian missionaries (along with colonialists in general) is that they "imposed modernity" on much of the non-Western world. It has long been the received wisdom among anthropologists and other cultural relativists that by bringing Western technology and learning to "native peoples," the missionaries corrupted their cultures, which were as valid as those of the West. This "cultural imperialism" is defined as imposing Western tastes, beliefs, and practices upon non-Western cultures. Admittedly, the English may have committed an abomination when they converted so many colonials to the game of cricket, and the worldwide popularity of Coca-Cola may not have made the world a better place. But to embrace the fundamental message of cultural imperialism requires that one be comfortable with such crimes against women as foot binding, female circumcision, the custom of Sati (which caused widows to be burned to death, tied to their husbands' funeral pyres), and the stoning to death of rape victims on grounds of *their* adultery. It also requires one to agree that tyranny is every bit as desirable as democracy and that slavery should be tolerated if it is in accord with local customs. Similarly, one must classify high infant-mortality rates, toothlessness in early adulthood, and the castration of young boys as valid parts of local cultures, to be cherished along with illiteracy. For it was especially on these aspects of non-Western cultures that modernity was "imposed," both by missionaries and by other colonialists.

Moreover, missionaries undertook many aggressive actions to defend local peoples against undue exploitation by colonial officials. In the mid-1700s, for example, the Jesuits tried to protect the Indians in Latin America from European efforts to enslave them; Portuguese and Spanish colonial officials brutally ejected the Jesuits for interfering.[27] Protestant missionaries frequently became involved in bitter conflicts with commercial and colonial leaders in support of local populations, particularly in India and Africa.[28]

But perhaps the best approach to assessing missionary effects is to follow the biblical injunction (Matthew 7:16) to know them by their fruits. Data show that Christian missionaries' efforts from a century ago or more are still bearing fruit today.

A remarkable new study by Robert D. Woodberry has demonstrated conclusively that Protestant missionaries can take most of the credit for the rise and spread of stable democracies in the non-Western world.[29] That is, the greater the number of Protestant missionaries per ten thousand local population in 1923, the higher the probability that by now a nation has achieved a stable democracy. The missionary effect is far greater than that of fifty other pertinent control variables, including gross domestic product (GDP) and whether or not a nation was a British colony.

Woodberry not only identified this missionary effect but also gained important insights into why it occurred. Missionaries, he showed, contributed to the rise of stable democracies because they sponsored mass education, local printing and newspapers, and local voluntary organizations, including those having a nationalist and anticolonial orientation.

These results so surprised social scientists that perhaps no study ever has been subjected to such intensive prepublication vetting. Woodberry was required to turn over his entire database to editors of the *American Political Science Review*, who subjected it to extensive, independent reanalysis. But after this vetting, the editors were satisfied that the robust statistical results were correct; in fact, they gave Woodberry considerably more space than the usual maximum to present his findings in detail.

Protestant missionaries did more than advance democracy in non-Western societies. The local schools and colleges they established had a profound impact on these societies. The schools they started even sent some students off to study in Britain and America. It is amazing how many leaders of successful anticolonial movements in British colonies received university degrees in England—among them Mahatma Gandhi and Jawaharlal Nehru of India and Jomo Kenyatta of Kenya, who led the Mau Mau Rebellion and ended up as the first president of independent Kenya.

Less recognized are the lasting benefits of the missionary commitment to medicine and health. American and British Protestant missionaries made incredible investments in medical facilities in non-Western nations. As of 1910 they had established 111 medical schools, more than 1,000 dispensaries, and 576 hospitals.[30] To sustain these massive efforts, the missionaries recruited and trained local doctors and nurses, who soon greatly outnumbered the Western missionaries. These efforts made a great difference in places that otherwise would have lacked access to modern medicine. And the benefits have lived on.

Once again, it is research by Robert Woodberry that reveals the long-term influence.[31] His study showed that the higher the number of Protestant missionaries per one thousand population in a nation in 1923, the lower that nation's infant-mortality rate in 2000—an effect more than nine times as large as the effect of current GDP per capita. Similarly, the 1923 missionary rate was strongly positively correlated with a nation's life expectancy in 2000.

If these effects constitute "cultural imperialism," so be it.

Colonialism and "Underdevelopment"

In 1902 the English economist J. A. Hobson published *Imperialism*, a book in which he charged that the industrial European nations looted their colonies by forcing them to sell their raw materials too cheaply and to buy manufactured goods at too high a price. In 1915 V. I. Lenin, soon to lead the Russian Revolution, essentially plagiarized Hobson's book (including his statistics) for a book he titled *Imperialism, the Highest Stage of Capitalism*. Ever since, it has been an article of faith on the extreme Left that Western nations stole their wealth from the non-Western nations and, in doing so, prevented them from modernizing. This line has, of course, been popular in the less-developed nations. It tells them that their lack of progress is not their fault but is imposed upon them by the developed world.

Unfortunately, this claim also proved to be popular among Western social scientists. During the 1970s there arose a group of social scientists who identified themselves as "world systems" theorists. Led by Immanuel Wallerstein, Andre Gunder Frank, and a cast of supporting players, world-systems theory was, for several decades, the prevailing view in academia, despite its obvious incompatibility with basic facts.

For example, echoing Hobson, world-systems theorists divide the world into poor nations that export raw materials and rich nations that export manufactured goods, and they explain at length how this arrangement must keep poor nations poor. This claim is immediately challenged by the fact that Canada and the United States, two highly developed nations, export more raw foodstuffs than the rest of the world combined and that during its rapid period of industrialization during the nineteenth century, the United States exported huge amounts of raw cotton, tobacco, timber, fur, and coal. More damaging to this claim was a careful analysis of world trade statistics for fifty-nine nations that revealed no correlation between growth of per capita GDP and the proportion of a nation's exports that are raw materials.[32] World-systems proponents responded that increases in the GDP of less-developed nations benefited only the rich in those societies.[33] That also turned out not to be so.[34]

The Oxford economic historian Patrick O'Brien offered perhaps the most devastating refutation of the world-systems perspective.[35] Drawing on a large body of trade statistics going back to 1750, O'Brien demonstrated that the advanced nations could not have extracted their wealth from the poor nations because the volume of trade between them was trivial. The error of world-systems analysts, beginning with Hobson, is that they have focused on the obvious facts that some Europeans made fortunes from trade with the non-Western world and that some port cities also prospered, and from these points they generalized to the national economies. But this wealth was too little to have had a significant impact on national economies. Indeed, it is clear that during the Age of Imperialism European nations as a whole *lost* money on their colonies.[36]

The obvious exception is Spain, which enjoyed an era of great prosperity from importing gold and silver from its New World colonies. But this spurt of wealth had no long-term benefits, Spain having remained backward and poor. Nor did this "outflow" of precious metals have any significant impact on the economic development of Latin America.[37]

Another bizarre proposition of the world-systems school was Andre Gunder Frank's claim that the greater the contact between a less-developed society and the industrial nations, the more retarded the less-developed society's economic development.[38] My colleague Arthur Stinchcomb often amused his graduate classes at Berkeley by pointing out that if this were true, then groups in Latin America that live farthest from the coast would be more economically developed than those on the coast—as clearly demonstrated by the Indians living far up the Amazon who have yet to have contact with anyone.

Of course, as is typical in such matters, a pile of negative evidence has not converted the world-systems proponents. But they lost much of their appeal when the demise of Soviet Union took them by surprise and deprived them of the exemplary society toward which they held that social change was inexorably moving. As Daniel Chirot noted, "Because world-system theory ultimately shut out those who did not agree with its political objectives, it lost a lot of its credibility."[39]

Partial Modernity

Although modernity has spread around the globe, in many places what has arisen is not *Western* modernity. Instead, technological aspects of modernity have been grafted onto non-Western cultural systems that still lack many of the basic political and moral aspects of Western civilization. As Samuel P. Huntington noted so perceptively, many observers mistakenly see the worldwide popularity of Western consumer products such as Coke and Levi's as reflecting the development of a "universal civilization." But to do so "trivializes Western culture."[40]

In Arab societies many people own cell phones and drive automobiles, and the armies have an abundance of modern weapons. But to the extent that this reflects modernity, it is modernity by purchase and import—these are not industrial societies. Nor are they modern in most other respects. There are no Arab democracies. Women have few rights, and religious intolerance is the rule.

Even successfully building an industrialized society is not tantamount to becoming modern in the Western sense, as the case of China illustrates. To use the classic phrase the scholar Karl A. Wittfogel coined more than a half century ago, modern China remains an "Oriental despotism."[41]

A substantial degree of individual freedom is inseparable from Western modernity, and this still is lacking in much of the non-Western world.

No doubt Western modernity has its limitations and discontents. Still, it is far better than the known alternatives—not only, or even primarily, because of its advanced technology but because of its fundamental commitment to freedom, reason, and human dignity.

Notes

Introduction: What You *Don't* Know about the Rise of the West

1. Ricketts et al., 2011. On September 21, 2008, the *New York Times* ran a long article on efforts to restore "Western Civilization" courses, headlined "Conservatives Try New Tack on Campuses." This article prompted renewed efforts at the University of Texas that culminated in the elimination of the "Western Civilization" course.
2. Thornton, 2000 (he rejects that position).
3. Shaw, 2012; Kimball, 2008: 56.
4. Bernal, 1987.
5. Goldstone, 2009; Nasr, 1968; Saliba, 2007.
6. Frank, 2011; Wallerstein, 1974, 2004.
7. Frank, 1998; Hobson, 2004; Pomeranz, 2000.
8. Stark, 2009. When the Turks took Constantinople in 1453, they breached the walls with cannons cast for them by Hungarian craftsmen. (See McNeill, 1982.)
9. Most recently Ian Morris, 2010.
10. Hanson, 2001: 16.
11. Diamond, 1998; Cipolla, 1965.
12. Mendelssohn, 1976.
13. Marx and Engels, *The Communist Manifesto*.
14. McCloskey, 2010: 6, 8.
15. Marx [1845] 1998: 61.
16. Mornet, 1947 (translation by Christopher Hill, 1980: 2–3).
17. Osborne, 2006: 60.

Chapter 1: Stagnant Empires and the Greek "Miracle"

1. Taagepera, 1978, 1979.
2. Oppenheim, 1977; Saggs, 1989.

3. Harris [1977] 1991: 235.
4. Wilkinson, 2010: 37–38.
5. Harris [1977] 1991: 172–73.
6. Ghirshman, 1955.
7. Jones, 1987: xxiii–xxiv.
8. Harris [1977] 1991: 234.
9. Jones, 1987: 5.
10. See: Wittfogel [1957] 1981: 71–72.
11. Quoted in Wilkinson, 2010: 342.
12. Grossman, 1963.
13. Wilkinson, 2010: 344.
14. Russell, 1967: 99.
15. Dawson, 1972: 62.
16. Hartwell, 1966, 1967, 1971; McNeill, 1982.
17. Reade, 125: 108.
18. McNeill, 1963: 40.
19. Finley, 1965: 29.
20. Moritz, 1958.
21. Lewis, 2002: 118; Gimple, 1976.
22. I see no need to refute the nonsense that the Greeks stole it all from Africa: Bernal, 1987.
23. Hamilton [1930] 1993: 24–25.
24. Herodotus, *The History*, bk. 8; Hansen, 2006b.
25. Grant, 1988: xiii.
26. Hansen, 2006b.
27. Chandler, 1987: 461.
28. Lacey, 2011: 125.
29. Migeotte, 2009: 16.
30. Ibid.
31. Hanson, 2001: 17.
32. Chirot, 1985.
33. Grant, 1988: 28.
34. Jones [1987] 2003: 2.
35. Lacey, 2011: 136.
36. Quote in Lacey, 2011: 135.
37. Herodotus based his account on conversations with Athenian veterans of the battle. We can be certain about the number of Athenian dead, since they were buried in a common grave mound and the name of each was inscribed on one of three small marble monuments placed at the site. The mound can still be visited; two of the monuments have disappeared, the third is now in the Athens Museum.
38. Hanson, 2001, 2009.
39. Lacey, 2011: 189.
40. Although Greek armies consisted of citizen volunteers, during peacetime some adventuresome souls were always willing to fight elsewhere for pay.
41. Hanson, 2001: 2.
42. Ibid., 279–333.
43. Plato, *Laches*.
44. Tod, 1948: 2:204.

45. Hanson, 2001: 329.
46. Josephus, *Jewish War* 3:107
47. Austin and Vidal-Naquet, 1972: 107.
48. Johnson, 2003: 48.
49. Austin and Vidal-Naquet, 1972; French, 1964; Finley, 1973, 1981; Migeotte, 2009; Scheidel, Morris, and Saller, 2007.
50. Migeotte, 2009; Scheidel, Morris, and Saller, 2007.
51. Morris, 2009: 113.
52. Migeotte, 2009: 21; Scheidel, Morris, and Saller, 2007: 42.
53. Scheidel, Morris, and Saller, 2007: 11.
54. Reden, 2007: 400.
55. Cohen, 1992: 3.
56. Ibid., 61.
57. Harris, 1989: 329.
58. Harris, 1989; Thomas, 1992.
59. Lyons, 2010: 13.
60. Harris, 1989: 58–59.
61. As quoted by Xenophon, *Memorabilia of Socrates*, 1:6:14.
62. Spoken by Prometheus in Aeschylus's *Prometheus Unbound* (ca. 442 BC).
63. Boardman, 1988; Johnson, 2003.
64. Johnson, 2003: 60–64.
65. Brockett and Hildy, 2007.
66. Ulrich and Pisk, 1963.
67. Williams, 1903.
68. Beye, 1987; Whitmarsh, 2004.
69. Cuomo, 2007; Finley, 1959; Major, 1996; Moritz, 1958; White, 1984; Wilson, 2002.
70. Cuomo, 2007.
71. Ibid.
72. West, 2001: 140.
73. Needham, 1956: 581.
74. Herodotus, *The History*, 2:19
75. Freeman, 1999: 150.
76. Anaxagoras, *Fragments of Anaxagoras*, frag. 12.
77. Whitehead [1929] 1979: 39.
78. Plato, *Phaedo*, 95.
79. McLendon, 1959: 90.
80. Wild, 1949: 8.
81. Caird, 1904; McLendon, 1959; Wolfson, 1947.
82. Plato, *Laws*, bk. 10.
83. Plato, *Republic*.
84. Plato, *Laws*.
85. In Lindberg, 1992: 54.
86. See: Aristotle, *On the Heavens* and *Metaphysics*.
87. Aristotle, *Eudemian Ethics*.
88. Aristotle, *Metaphysics*.
89. Stark, 2005.
90. Freeman, 1999: 6.

91. Westermann, 1941.
92. Freeman, 1999: 121.
93. For a summary, see Finley, 1980.
94. Vogt, 1974: 25.
95. Freeman, 1999: 3.
96. Aristotle, *Constitution of Athens*, 24.
97. Kroeber's findings were replicated by Gray, 1958.
98. Roberts, 1998: 38.

Chapter 2: Jerusalem's Rational God

1. See Cohen, 1975; Kadushin, 1965; Urbach, 1975. Quotation from Fuller, 2003: 27.
2. Smith, 1956: 71.
3. Meeks, 1983: 34.
4. Tcherikover [1959] 1999: 353.
5. Finegan, 1992: 325–26.
6. Tcherikover [1959] 1999: 346.
7. Hengel, 1974, 1989; Levine, 1998; Smith, 1987.
8. Batey, 1991.
9. Feldman, 1981: 310.
10. Ibid.
11. Chadwick, 1966: 6.
12. Frend, 1984: 35.
13. Corrigan et al., 1998: 88.
14. Goodenough, 1962: 10.
15. Clement of Alexandria, *The Stromata*: 1:5.
16. Chadwick, 1966: 10–11.
17. In Chadwick, 1966: 15.
18. Ibid., 16.
19. Saint Augustine, *The City of God*, 8:11.
20. In Chadwick, 1966: 16.
21. Ibid., 19.
22. Ibid., 17.
23. Lindberg, 1992. Many scholars doubt that Plato really meant for his postulated demiurge to be taken literally. But whether real creator or metaphor, the demiurge is nothing like the Christian conception of a Creator.
24. Mason, 1962.
25. In Jaki, 1986: 114.
26. Full text in Danielson, 2000: 14–15.
27. In Plato, *Timaeus*.
28. Jaki, 1986: 105.
29. Clark, 1989; Nash, 1992.
30. Grant, 1994, 1996; Jaki, 1986; Lindberg, 1992; Mason, 1962, as well as the cited original sources.
31. For this section, I draw extensively on my own research and writing for *The Victory of Reason*. See Stark, 2005: ch. 1.
32. 1 Corinthians 13:9, RSV.

33. Tertullian, *On Repentance*: ch. 1.

34. Recognitions of Clement: 2: 69.

35. In Lindberg and Numbers, 1986: 27–28.

36. Saint Augustine, *The City of God*, 8: 4; Wild, 1949: 8.

37. Edelstein, 1967.

38. Nisbet, 1980: 4.

39. Marjorie Reeves, *The Influence of Prophecy in the Latter Middle Ages*, quoted in Nisbet, 1980: 49.

40. For this section, too, I draw extensively on my own research and writing for *The Victory of Reason*. See Stark, 2005: ch. 1.

41. In Lindberg, 1986: 27.

42. Saint Augustine, *The City of God*, 22: 24.

43. In Gimpel, 1961: 165.

44. Ibid., 149.

45. Grant, 1996; Meyer, 1944; Southern, 1970a: 50.

46. Benin, 1993.

47. In Benin, 1993: 68.

48. In Lindberg, 1986: 27–28.

49. Finley, 1965: 147.

50. Macmurray, 1938: 115.

51. White, 1975: 527.

52. Khalidi, 1975: 279.

53. Reilly, 2011.

54. Reilly, 2011: 6; see also Stark, 2009: ch. 3.

55. Gimpel, 1976: 13.

56. Ibid.

57. In Hartwell, 1971: 691.

58. Dreyer, 2007; Jung-Pang Lo, 1955; Levathes, 1994; McNeill, 1982

59. Claims that some of Zheng He's ships exceeded four hundred feet in length seem unlikely—imagine a flat-bottomed, wooden Chinese junk nearly half the length of the *Titanic* or of the largest World War II battleships. (See Dreyer, 2007.) Notions that Zheng He's fleet would have crushed any Western navy are also absurd (see chapter 11). The recent sensational assertion that Zheng He and his fleet beat Columbus to America is equally fatuous. (See Menzies, 2002; Finlay, 2004.)

60. Lilley, 1966: 45.

Chapter 3: The Roman Interlude

1. Hanson, 2002.

2. Quoted in Osborne, 2006: 97.

3. Heather, 2006: 15.

4. Fox, 2008: 323.

5. Osborne, 2006: 100.

6. Stark, 2011.

7. Liebeschuetz, 1979: 3.

8. MacMullen, 1981: 109.

9. Gombrich, 1978.

10. Clarke, 1998.
11. Smith, 1867.
12. Morford, 2002; Saunders, 1997.
13. Lilley, 1966: 40.
14. White, 1984.
15. Lilley, 1966: 40.
16. Carcopino, 1940.
17. Leighton, 1972: 59.
18. Lilley, 1966: 39.
19. Quoted in Heather, 2006: 68.
20. Barton, 1993: 63.
21. Baker, 2000.
22. Wiedmann, 1992: 38–39; Zoll, 2002.
23. Futrell, 1997; Golvin, 1988.
24. Futrell, 1997.
25. Stark, 2006.
26. Heather, 2006: 68.
27. Hamilton [1930] 1993: 25.
28. Ferrill, 1986; Heather, 2006; Luttwak, 1976.
29. Ferrill, 1986: 29.
30. Heather, 2006: 7.
31. Luttwak, 1976: 16; Ferrill, 1986; Osborne, 2006.
32. Stark, 1996, 2006, 2011.
33. Hvalvik, 2007: 191.
34. Harnack, 1905: 382; Sordi, 1986: 28.
35. Stark, 1996, 2011.
36. Mattingly, 1967: 54.
37. Barnes, 1981: 19; Mattingly, 1967: 56.
38. Stark, 2011: ch. 10.
39. Heather, 2006: 126.
40. Often called the Visigoths—the western Goths, in contrast with the Ostrogoths, or eastern Goths.
41. Saint Jerome, *Commentary on Ezekiel*, preface.
42. Ward-Perkins, 2006: 183.
43. Goffart, 1971: 413.
44. Demandt, 1984.
45. Gilfillan, 1965.
46. Sale, 1990: 82.
47. Jones, 1964, 2:1027.
48. Toynbee, 1936.
49. Rostovtzeff, 1926: 453–54.
50. Heather, 2006: 114; Ward-Perkins, 2006: 42.
51. Luttwak, 1976.
52. Ferrill, 1986.
53. Quoted in Ferrill, 1986: 25.
54. Ferrill, 1986: 46.
55. Ibid., 47.
56. Quoted in Ferrill, 1986: 129.

57. Jones, 1964, 2:1038.
58. Heather, 1998: 139.
59. Ferrill, 1986: 102.
60. Wolfram, 1997: 77.
61. Ibid., 76.
62. Mokyr, 1992: 26.
63. Heather, 2006: 87.
64. Jones, 1988: 57.
65. Musset [1965] 1993: 203.
66. Ferrill, 1986: 103.
67. Manchester, 1993: 5.
68. Heather, 2006: 228.

Chapter 4: The Blessings of Disunity

1. Brown [1971] 1989.
2. Brown, 1997: 14–15.
3. Hayek, 1988: 33.
4. Privat et al., 2002; Wells, 2008: 139–40.
5. For this section and later sections in this chapter, I draw on my own research and writing for *The Triumph of Christianity*. See Stark, 2011.
6. Fremantle, 1954: ix.
7. Voltaire, *Works*, vol. 12.
8. Quoted in Gay, 1966.
9. Gibbon, *The History of the Decline and Fall*, 6:71.
10. Russell, 1959: 142.
11. Van Doren, 1991: 89.
12. Ibid., 95–97.
13. Manchester, 1993: 3.
14. Osborne, 2006: 163.
15. Ibid., 165.
16. Ibid., 163.
17. Ibid.
18. Bridbury, 1969: 533.
19. Van Doren, 1991: 91.
20. Williams-McClanahan, 2006: 2.
21. Bridbury, 1969: 532.
22. Jankuhn, 1982; Wells, 2008.
23. Hodges, 1989b; McCormick, 2001.
24. Harris, 1989: 272.
25. Singman, 1999: 54–55; Wells, 2008: 139.
26. Dopsch, 1969; the quotation is a summary of Dopsch's conclusions in Postan, 1952: 158.
27. Manchester, 1993: 3.
28. Pyle, 1888: 1.
29. See Waterbolk, 1968: 1099.
30. Jones, 1987: 105.

31. Ibid., 106.
32. Jones, 2003: 227.
33. Arnold, 1984; Burmeister, 2000; Hamerow, 1997; Hodges, 1989a.
34. Wells, 2008: 33, 31.
35. Arnold, 1984; Burmeister, 2000; Hamerow, 1997; Hodges, 1989a; Wells, 2008.
36. Chirot, 1985: 183.
37. Gimpel, 1976: viii, 1.
38. White, 1962: 151.
39. Duby, 1974: 4.
40. Heather, 2006: 87.
41. White, 1962: 43.
42. McNeil, 1996: 21.
43. Russell, 1958.
44. For this section, I draw on my own research and writing for *The Victory of Reason*. See Stark, 2005: 38–40.
45. Lopez, 1976: 43.
46. Holt, 1988: 7–8. This is an undercount, since the book is known to be incomplete. See Gies and Gies, 1994: 113.
47. Gimpel, 1976: 13.
48. Ibid., 16.
49. Gies and Gies, 1994: 117.
50. Landes, 1998: 46.
51. Gimpel, 1976: 14.
52. Ibid., 25–27.
53. Leighton, 1972: 74–75.
54. Postan, 1952: 148.
55. Haywood, 1999.
56. Ibid., 32–33.
57. Ibid., 36–37.
58. Unger and Gardiner, 2000.
59. Gilfillan, 1945: 66.
60. Tacitus, *Germany and Its Tribes*: 5–6.
61. Musset [1965] 1993: 203.
62. The recently deciphered second-century map of Germania created by Ptolemy reveals that there were many cities in this era (Kleineberg et al., 2011).
63. Holmqvist, 1979.
64. Wells, 2008: 143–44.
65. Holmqvist, 1979; Jankuhn, 1982; Wells, 2008.
66. Jankuhn, 1982.
67. Pirenne [1927] 1939.
68. Bridbury, 1969: 527.
69. Lopez, 1952: 261.
70. Wells, 2008: 154.
71. Wells, 2008.
72. Bridbury, 1969: 533.
73. Daniel, 1981: 705.
74. Gardner and Crosby, 1959: 236.
75. Johnson, 2003: 190.

76. Stark, 2009: 3–4.
77. Wigelsworth, 2006: 89.
78. Smail, 1995: 81.
79. Ayton, 1999: 188.
80. Many have suggested that the high cost of medieval arms and armor led to the feudal system, because a lord, rather than equipping and supporting his men-at-arms, assigned land to each of them that would provide sufficient rents to arm and support them. Recently, however, historians have mostly dispensed with the whole notion of feudalism on grounds that the relationships that have defined it seldom if ever really existed in medieval Europe. See Brown, 1974; Reynolds, 1994.
81. White, 1962: 35.
82. Payne-Gallwey, 2007.
83. Boutell [1907] 1996: 105–6.
84. Oakeshott [1960] 1996: 83.
85. Lewis, 1969: 56–57.
86. White, 1962: 30.
87. Ayton, 1999: 193.
88. Quoted in Karsh, 2007: 4.
89. Davis, 2001: 105.
90. Quoted in Mitchell and Creasy, 1964: 111.
91. Hanson, 2001; Montgomery, 1968.
92. Both quotations from Mitchell and Creasy, 1964: 110–11.
93. Davis, 1913: 363.
94. White, 1962, 1940.
95. Mitchell and Creasy, 1964.
96. Gibbon [1776–88] 1994: 5:52:336.
97. Delbrück [1920] 1990: 441.
98. Hitti, 2002: 469.
99. Cardini, 2001: 9
100. Lewis [1982] 2002: 19.
101. Ibid., 59–60.
102. Hanson, 2001.
103. Barbero, 2004: 118.

Chapter 5: Northern Lights over Christendom

1. Bohemond of Taranto and Robert, Duke of Normandy.
2. Stark, 2009
3. It is true, of course, that the name "Europe" originated with the ancient Greeks and that the term *Europa* was sometimes used in the Middle Ages. But "Europe" was rather nonexistent much before the eighteenth century.
4. Cantor, 1993: 193–94.
5. Ferguson, 2009: 114.
6. Ibid., 60.
7. Ibid., 61.
8. Jones, 1984: 192–94.
9. Ropars et. al, 2011.

10. Quoted in Ferguson, 2009: 42.
11. In Ferguson, 2009: 54.
12. Bauer, 2010: 468.
13. Carpenter, 2004: 82–83.
14. Thomas, 2003: 105–37.
15. Daniell, 2003: 13–14.
16. Ibid.
17. Russell, 1987: 138.
18. For this section, I draw on my own research and writing for *God's Battalions: The Case for the Crusades*. See Stark, 2009: ch. 2.
19. Brown, 2003: 36.
20. Brown, 2003: 37.
21. Norwich, 1991: 285.
22. Ibid.
23. Brown, 2003: 42.
24. In Van Houts, 2000: 243.
25. Matthew, 1992.
26. See Stark, 2009.
27. Both examples from Riley-Smith, 1997: 37–38. There were many similar incidents; see Runciman, 1969: 78.
28. Runciman, 1969: 78.
29. Duncalf, 1969: 276.
30. Ibid., 267.
31. Riley-Smith, 1997.
32. Ibid.
33. A fifth, led by Hugh of Vermandois, was largely destroyed by a disaster at sea.
34. Comnena [ca. 1148] 1969: 422.
35. France, 1994: 116.
36. Anonymous [ca. 1102] 1962: 6, 10.
37. France, 1994: 118.
38. Ibid., 279.
39. Anonymous [ca. 1102] 1962: 69.
40. Runciman, 1951, 1:279.
41. Fulcher of Chartres [ca. 1127] 1969: 150.
42. Hamilton, 2000; LaMonte, 1932; Prawer, 1972; Riley-Smith, 1973; Runciman, 1951; Tyerman, 2006. For this section, I draw on my own research and writing for *The Triumph of Christianity*. See Stark, 2011: ch. 13.
43. Madden, 1999: 49.
44. Tyerman, 2006: 179; Issawi, 1957: 272.
45. *New York Times*, June 20, 1999, sec. 4, p. 15.
46. Carroll, 2004: 5.
47. Armstrong, 2001: 4.
48. Irwin, 2006: 213.
49. Tyerman, 2006: 351.
50. Siberry, 1995: 368.
51. Ibid., 115.
52. Quoted in Madden, 1999: 78.
53. Madden, 1999: 181.

54. Ibid.
55. Ibid., 181–82.
56. Duffy, 1997: 27.
57. Fletcher, 1997: 38.
58. Cheetham, 1983; Duffy, 1997; McBrien, 2000.
59. Stark, 2004: 56.
60. Fletcher, 1997: 236.
61. For this section, I draw on my own research and writing for *Cities of God and The Triumph of Christianity*. See Stark, 2006; Stark, 2011.
62. Lofland and Stark, 1965.
63. Stark and Finke, 2000.
64. Kox, Meeus, and t'Hart, 1991; Smilde, 2005; Stark and Finke, 2000.
65. Turner and Killian, 1987: 5.
66. Brøndsted, 1965; Mayr-Harting, 1993; Sawyer, 1982; Sawyer and Sawyer, 1993; Stark, 2001.
67. Sawyer, 1982: 134.
68. Brøndsted, 1965: 312.
69. Ibid., 306.
70. Ibid., 307.
71. Nickerson, 1999; Stark, Hamberg, and Miller, 2005; Swatos and Gissurarson, 1997.
72. Mayr-Harting, 1993: 109.
73. Erdoes, 1988: 26.
74. Ibid.
75. Lopez, 1969: 61.
76. Davis, 1970: 137.

Chapter 6: Freedom and Capitalism

1. For this comparison, I am indebted to Colin Morris [1972] 2000: 4.
2. *Julius Caesar*, act 1, scene 2.
3. For this section and certain sections that follow, I draw on my own research and writing for *The Victory of Reason*. See Stark, 2005.
4. Saint Augustine, *De libero arbitrio* bk. 3: ch.1, translated and quoted in Kehr, 1916: 602.
5. Saint Augustine, *The City of God*, bk. 5, ch. 9.
6. Aquinas, *Summa Contra Gentiles*, bk. 3, cap. 113.
7. Henry, 1927.
8. Donald, 1997.
9. U.S. State Department, *2013 Trafficking in Persons Report*, June 19, 2013.
10. Finley, 1980: 67.
11. Bensch, 1998: 231.
12. Fogel, 1989: 25.
13. Bloch, 1961, 1975; Davis, 1966.
14. In Bonnassie, 1991: 6.
15. Duby, 1974: 32.
16. For a summary of these views, see Bonnassie, 1991; Dockès, 1982.

17. Lopez, 1979: 138.
18. Conrade and Meyer, 1958; Easterlin, 1961; Fogel and Engerman, 1974; Stark, 2003a.
19. Bloch, 1975: 13.
20. Bonnassie, 1991: 30.
21. Bloch, 1975: 14.
22. In Bonnassie, 1991: 54.
23. Smaragde, *Via Regia*, my translation.
24. Bloch, 1975: 11.
25. Bloch 1975: 30.
26. Lopez, 1952: 353.
27. Stark, 2003.
28. Berman, 2008; Stark, 2003.
29. Benedict, 1946.
30. Finley, 1973: 28.
31. Lewis, 1990; Watt, 1961, 1965.
32. In Gordon, 1989: 19.
33. Lopez, 1976: 99.
34. Lopez, 1967: 129. Venice was populated with an abundance of families who had legitimate claims to noble status but who no longer had rural estates to support them with rents; they therefore had seized the opportunity to engage in commerce.
35. Wickham, 1989: 90.
36. Waley, 1988: 35.
37. Lane, 1973: 95–101; Nicholas, 1997: 248–55.
38. Bairoch, 1988.
39. Epstein, 1996: 14.
40. Greif, 1994: 280.
41. Greif, 1994: 282.
42. Waley, 1988.
43. Russell, 1972a; Chandler, 1987.
44. Braudel, 1977: 66–67.
45. For this section and sections that follow, I draw on my own research and writing for *The Victory of Reason*. See Stark, 2005.
46. Some authors, however, actually remark that "everyone knows" what capitalism is—see, e.g., Rosenberg and Birdzell, 1986: vi.
47. The orthodox Marxist definition is plain and simple: capitalism exists where the actual producers are wage laborers who do not own their tools, and these, as well as the raw materials and finished products, are owned by their employer. (See Sombart, 1902, as well as Hilton, 1952.) Taken seriously, this definition would make capitalists out of all owners of small craft shops such as potteries and metal smithies in ancient times. That seems especially odd since Marxists cling to their belief that capitalism first appeared during (and caused) the Industrial Revolution, a necessary assumption for those who accept Marx's theory of social change wherein all history rests on changes in modes of production. Thus, Marxists condemn all "talk about capitalism before the end of the eighteenth century" (Braudel, vol. 2, 1979: 238), equating capitalism with "the modern industrial system" (Gerschenkron, 1970: 4). But for those of us who associate capitalism with particular kinds of firms and markets, the Marxist definition is not useful.

48. Stark, 2005: 56.
49. For all of his fulminating about "wage slavery," Marx opened his study *Pre-Capitalist Economic Formations* with the statement that "one of the historic conditions for capital is free labour."
50. 1 Timothy 6:10.
51. Little, 1978: 38.
52. Baldwin, 1959: 15.
53. Mumford, 1967: 266.
54. Hayes, 1917; Herlihy, 1957; Ozment, 1975.
55. Little, 1978: 62.
56. Gilchrist, 1969; Russell, 1958, 1972a.
57. Little, 1978: 93.
58. Dawson, 1957: 63.
59. Duby, 1974: 218.
60. Little, 1978: 65.
61. Ibid.
62. Fryde, 1963: 441–43.
63. de Roover, 1948: 9.
64. Collins, 1986: 47, 55, 52.
65. Duby, 1974: 91.
66. Gimpel, 1976: 47.
67. Mumford, 1967: 1:272.
68. Dawson, 1957; Hickey, 1987; King, 1999; Mayr-Harting, 1993; Stark, 2003.
69. Collins, 1986: 54.
70. Ch. 40, *The Daily Manual Labor.*
71. Hilton, 1985: 3.
72. That interest could be charged of foreigners explains the role of Jews as money lenders in Christian societies, a role Christians in need of funds sometimes imposed on them. Historians usually ignore another consequence: medieval Christians with money to lend often masqueraded as Jews. See Nelson, 1969: 11; Little, 1978: 56–57.
73. Nelson, 1969: 9.
74. Olsen, 1969: 53.
75. In his *Commentary on the Sentences of Peter Lombard*, quoted in de Roover, 1958: 422.
76. Little, 1978: 181.
77. Gilchrist, 1969; Little, 1978; Raftus, 1958.
78. Gilchrist, 1969: 67.
79. Hunt and Murray, 1999: 73.
80. Dempsey, 1943: 155, 160.
81. de Roover, 1946: 154.
82. Little, 1978: 181.
83. Southern, 1970b: 40.
84. Rodinson, 1978: 139.
85. Maxime Rodinson suggests that Islam did not reconsider its economic rules because the elite held commerce in contempt and because state interference so limited and distorted the economy that nothing like the pressure for theological change that built up in Europe ever developed in Islam. Indeed, the elite no doubt favored

keeping their creditors in potential religious jeopardy and having a "legitimate" basis for settling their debts by usurpation. In any event, even today banks exist in Islamic societies only by means of extremely cumbersome "workarounds" of the absolute prohibition of usury, which remains defined as any compensation given in return for a loan. A frequent modern solution to the prohibition of interest involves banks going into business partnership with those to whom they advance commercial loans. This allows loans to be repaid for no more than the sum borrowed, while the reward for lending (the "interest") comes from shared profits. Another ploy is to charge extensive fees for servicing loans. Even so, the huge fortunes produced by petroleum have mostly taken refuge in Western investments, rather than to finance domestic economic development. See Rodinson, 1978.

86. For a summary, see Stark 2003.
87. Lopez, 1952: 289; 1976.
88. Gies and Gies, 1969.
89. De Roover, 1963: 75–76.
90. De Roover, 1963; Hunt, 1994; Lloyd, 1982.

Chapter 7: Climate, Plague, and Social Change

1. Lamb, 1965.
2. Benedictow, 2004: 5–6.
3. Fagan, 2000.
4. Fagan, 2008.
5. Ferguson, 2009; Jones, 1986
6. Ferguson, 2009: 283.
7. Ingstad and Ingstad, 2001.
8. Ziegler, 1971: 31.
9. Gottfried, 1985: 17; Russell, 1972b.
10. Metcalf, 1967: 357.
11. Fagan, 2000: 21.
12. Bennett and Hollister, 2006: 326.
13. Gottfried, 1985; Postan, 1973.
14. Issawi, 1980: 490.
15. Aberth, 2005; Cantor, 2002; Cartwright, 1972; Gottfried, 1985; Herlihy, 1997; Ziegler, 1971; Zinsser, 1963.
16. Haensch et al., 2010.
17. Ziegler, 1971: 15.
18. Gottfried, 1985: 77.
19. Benedictow, 2004.
20. Aberth, 2005: 72.
21. Gottfried, 1985: 54.
22. Quoted in Benedictow, 2004: 91.
23. Gottfried, 1985: 58.
24. Ibid., 78–80.
25. Stark, 2011: ch. 15.
26. Benedictow, 2004: 166; Gottfried, 1985: 56.
27. Quoted in Gottfried, 1985: 57.

28. A few Flagellant companies included women, imposing strict sex segregation and limiting women's acts of penance.
29. Leff [1967] 1999: 488.
30. Ziegler, 1971: 96.
31. Ibid., 92.
32. Stark, 2001: 131.
33. In Aberth, 2005: 158–59.
34. See, e.g., Gottfried, 1985: 52–53.
35. Stark, 2001: 132.
36. Stark, 2009.
37. Graetz, 1894: 3: 611.
38. Magnus, 1997: 18.
39. Bolton, 1996: 29–33.
40. For an excellent summary, see Herlihy, 1997: 31–33.
41. Ziegler, 1971: 131.
42. Ibid., 133.
43. Bolton, 1996: 34–39.
44. Blum, 1978.
45. McGarry, 1976: 242.
46. Hilton [1973] 2003, 1969; Gottfried, 1985.
47. Gottfried, 1985: 94.
48. Hilton, 1969: 55.
49. Phelps Brown and Hopkins, 1962: 179–96.
50. Bridbury, 1962; Stark, 2005.
51. Bridbury, 1962: 85.
52. Gottfried, 1985: 95.
53. Bolton, 1996: 49.
54. Herlihy, 1997.
55. Ibid., 50.
56. Carus-Wilson, 1941, 1952.
57. Dresbeck, 1976: 181.
58. See, e.g., Rodney Hilton, 1969: 98.
59. Dresbeck, 1976: 184.
60. Ibid., 186.
61. That was true only for the somewhat affluent. For those with one-room houses, nothing changed, except, of course, that their room was warmer and not smoky.
62. In Stark, 2007b: 527.

Chapter 8: The Pursuit of Knowledge

1. For this section and later sections of this chapter, I draw on my own research and writing for *The Victory of Reason*. See Stark, 2005: ch. 1.
2. John Locke, *Essay Concerning Human Understanding*, 3:9.
3. Quoted in Dales [1973] 1994: 170.
4. Rahner, 1975: 1687.
5. Stark, 2007a.
6. Clough, 1997: 57.

7.   Saint Augustine, *The City of God*, 5:1
8.   Tertullian, *On Repentance*, 1.
9.   *Recognitions of Clement*, 2:69.
10. Southern, 1970a: 49.
11. Grant, 1996: 182.
12. Ibid., 183.
13. Ibid., 184.
14. Haskins [1923] 2002: 3.
15. Colish, 1997: 266.
16. For this section and later sections of this chapter, I draw on my own research and writing for *For the Glory of God*. See Stark, 2003.
17. Grant, 1996; Porter, 1998.
18. Porter, 1998: 56.
19. Mason, 1962.
20. Porter, 1998.
21. Grant, 1996: 205.
22. Schachner, 1938: 3.
23. Quoted in Grant, 2007: 148–49.
24. Chandler, 1987.
25. Grant, 1996; Haskins [1923] 2002; Janin, 2008; Rashdall [1936] 1977.
26. Janin, 2008: 73.
27. Rashdall [1936] 1977: 3:408.
28. Ibid., 3:407.
29. Stark, 2011: 258.
30. Grant, 1996: 38.
31. Quoted in Janin, 2008: 77.
32. Rait, 1918: 63–64.
33. Janin, 2008: 79.
34. Haskins [1923] 2002: 41.
35. Ibid., 46.
36. Janin, 2008: 76.
37. Ibid., 81.
38. Haskins [1923] 2002: 69.
39. Ibid., 60–61.
40. I have written on this at length on this in Stark, 2003: ch. 2.
41. Dales [1973] 1994: 83–86.
42. Ibid., 64. See also Crombie, 1953.
43. Pederson, 1985.
44. Lindberg, 1992: 230.
45. Crombie, 1953; Evans, 2002; Grant, 1996.
46. Clegg, 2004: 99.
47. Quoted in Fisher and Unguru, 1971: 358.
48. Bridges, 1914: 162. See also Clegg, 2004; Easton, 1952.
49. Benjamin and Toomer, 1971.
50. Grant, 1974: 864.
51. Crombie, 1953: 236–37.
52. Quoted in Truesdell, 1968: 82.
53. Adams, 1987; Panaccio, 2004.

54. Glick, Livesey, and Wallis, 2005: 107.
55. Klima, 2008; Zupko, 2003.
56. Clagett, 1968; Grant, 1971.
57. Moody, 1970.
58. Grant, 1994: 620–21.
59. Smoller, 1994.
60. Danielson, 2000: 98; Mason, 1962: 120–21.
61. Evans, 2002: 173. See also Bellitto, 2004; Yamaki, 2001.
62. Crosby, 1997: 104.
63. Cohen, 1985: 107.
64. Jaki, 2000; Rosen, 1971.
65. Cohen, 1985; Jaki, 2000.

Chapter 9: Industry, Trade, and Technology

1. Frank, 1998; Pomeranz, 2000.
2. Frank, 1998.
3. Ibid., 10.
4. Cantor, 2002: 178–83.
5. Rose, 2002.
6. Chase, 2003; Norris, 2003; Parker [1988] 2010.
7. Fleming, 1960.
8. Carus-Wilson, 1952: 389–90.
9. Ibid., 386.
10. Ibid., 1952: 392.
11. Lloyd, 1982.
12. Carus-Wilson and Colman, 1963: 13.
13. Constructed from Carus-Wilson and Coleman, 1963.
14. Gray, 1924.
15. Carus-Wilson, 1952: 374.
16. Ibid., 415.
17. For this and later sections, I draw on my own research and writing for *The Victory of Reason*. See Stark, 2005.
18. Carus-Wilson, 1941: 40.
19. It has been estimated that without fulling mills, firms needed nearly half as many fullers as weavers, "whereas one fuller working at a mill would be able to finish the product of 40 to 60 weavers." See Usher, 1966: 269.
20. Carus-Wilson, 1952: 409.
21. Usher, 1966: 270.
22. Bridbury, 1982; Gray, 1924; Miller, 1965.
23. Carus-Wilson, 1952: 422.
24. Bridbury, 1982: 103.
25. Galloway, Keene, and Murphy, 1996: 449.
26. Nef, 1934: 102.
27. Reynolds, 1983: 77–79.
28. Shedd, 1981: 477.
29. Postan, 1952: 224.

30. Pounds, 1974: 382.
31. Chandler, 1987.
32. Findlay and O'Rourke, 2009: 120–21.
33. Ibid., 121.
34. Phillips, 1998: 96.
35. Wood, 1995.
36. For a fine account of the whole controversy, see Larner, 1999.
37. Phillips, 1998: 193.
38. Ibid., 97.
39. Lopez,1976: 111.
40. Phillips, 1998: 104.
41. Bjökenstam, 1995.
42. King, 1973.
43. Pirenne [1927] 1939: 25.
44. Stark, 2009: 36–39.
45. Bridbury, 1969: 527.
46. Lewis, 1951: 242.
47. Stark, 2009.
48. Rose, 2002; Stark, 2009.
49. Konstam, 2008: 25–28.
50. Walton, 2002.
51. Konstam, 2008: 40–41.
52. Messenger, 1996.
53. Quoted in Norris, 2003: 15.
54. Ibid., 19.
55. Ibid., 52.
56. Parker, 1972: 274.
57. Ames, 2005.
58. Lopez, 1976: 111.

Chapter 10: Discovering the World

1. Burman, 1989: 10.
2. Quoted in Burman, 1989: 13.
3. Burman, 1989; Phillips, 1998.
4. Ibid.
5. Ibid.
6. Skelton, Marston, and Painter, 1995.
7. Luce, 1971: 53.
8. Aczel, 2000; Gurney, 2004; Hitchins and May, 1951; Kreutz, 1973; May and Howard, 1981.
9. Evans, 1998; Morrison, 2007.
10. Chabas and Goldstein, 2000.
11. Watkins, 2004: 161–62.
12. Ibid.
13. Kemp, 1976.
14. Fritze, 2002: 64.

15. Russell, 2000.
16. A nasty backstage fight took place among contributors to Wikipedia over whether to identify Prince Henry as a homosexual. There is no evidence of his homosexuality, it being entirely deduced from his celibacy. It must be noted that in this era, many men, especially among the nobility, chose celibacy despite being obvious heterosexuals—consider Saint Augustine. To me, it is unimportant whether Henry was homosexual, but I do think it important not to substitute wishful thinking for facts.
17. Fernández-Armesto, 1987: 152.
18. Ibid.
19. In *Sertorius*.
20. Babcock, 1922; Russell, 2000.
21. Ponting, 2000: 482.
22. Diffie and Winius, 1977: 61–62; Fernández-Armesto, 1987: 197.
23. Panzer, 1996: 8.
24. Fritze, 2002: 81.
25. Ibid.
26. His year of birth is disputed: some say 1460 and others say 1469. The former seems more likely, since the king of Portugal probably would not have called on a twenty-three-year-old to command a force to seize French ships in the major Portuguese harbors.
27. Subrahmanyam, 1997: 62.
28. Cliff, 2011.
29. Ibid.
30. Russell, 1991.
31. Morison, 1974.
32. Ibid., 45.
33. Columbus [1492–93] 2005: 123.
34. Ibid., 114, 138.
35. Morison, 1974: 106.
36. Arens, 1979.
37. After I had written this paragraph, I discovered Jared Diamond's similar argument (1998: 412–13).
38. Fritze, 2002: 125.
39. Ibid., 126.
40. Jones and Ruddock, 2008.

Chapter 11: New World Conquests and Colonies

1. Morison, 1972: 71.
2. Keegan, 1993.
3. Windschuttle, 1996: 56.
4. Hanson, 2001: 171.
5. Ibid.
6. Thomas, 1994.
7. Díaz [ca. 1555] 1996: 119.
8. Carrasco, 1999: 2.

9.   Ibid., 3.
10. Ibid., 83.
11. Ibid., 192.
12. Clendinnen, 1991: 91.
13. Carrasco, 1999: 76, 81.
14. Hemming, 1970; MacQuarrie, 2008.
15. MacQuarrie, 2008: 79.
16. Hemming, 1970: 39.
17. MacQuarrie, 2008: 84.
18. Ibid.
19. Morison, 1971: 315; Wroth, 1970: 237.
20. Cook, 1993; Morison, 1971.
21. Bishop, 1948.
22. Trevelyan, 2002.
23. Bawlf, 2004; Kelsey, 1998.
24. I have written at length on slavery in *For the Glory of God: How Monotheism Led to Reformations, Science, Witch-Hunts, and the End of Slavery* (2003).
25. Rodney, 1984.
26. Thornton, 1998: 27.
27. Curtin, 1969.
28. Bean, 1975; Thomas, 1997.
29. Hurbon, 1992; Noonan, 1993.
30. Brett, 1994; Panzer, 1996.
31. Latourette, 1975: 944.
32. Davis, 1966: 228–29.
33. Harris, 1963, 1964.
34. For this section, I draw on my own research and writing for *Exploring the Religious Life*. See Stark, 2004.
35. Gay, 1969: 411.
36. Davis, 1966: 258.
37. Goveia, 1969: 132.
38. Schafer, 1994: 2–3.
39. Tannenbaum [1946] 1992.
40. Klein, 1969: 145.
41. Klein, 1967; Meltzer, 1993; Thomas, 1997.
42. Fogel, 1989: 36.
43. Dunn, 1972: 243.
44. Davis, 1966: 243.
45. Beckles, 1989; Curtin, 1969; Dunn, 1972.
46. Stark, 2003: 322.
47. In the first printing of Stark, 2003, this figure was misprinted as 31.2 percent.
48. Quoted in Himmelfarb, 2005: 20.
49. Stannard, 1993: 52.
50. Quoted in Sale, 1990: 319.
51. Washburn, 1975: 56.
52. Sale, 1990: 318.
53. Arens, 1979: 182.
54. Ibid., 45.

55. Sale, 1990: 131.
56. The distinguished David Carrasco had to confront rude demonstrators when he gave lectures on Aztec human sacrifices. See Carrasco, 1999: 4.
57. Abler, 1980; Carrasco, 1999; Culotta, 1999; Gibbons, 1997; Mead et al., 2003; Turner, 2011.
58. Díaz [ca. 1555] 1996: 102.
59. Ibid., 436–37.
60. For an extensive summary, see Axtell, 1981: 18–21.
61. Deloria, 1969: 6–7.
62. *Hec Ramsey* starring Richard Boone.
63. Axtell, 1981.
64. Haines and Steckel, 2000: 68.
65. McNickle, 1975.
66. Sale, 1990: 318.
67. Arkush and Allen, 2008; Chacon and Mendoza, 2007.
68. LeBlanc, 2007; Turner, 2011.
69. Sale, 1990: 322.
70. Butzer, 1992: 348.
71. Medina-Elizalde and Rohling, 2012.
72. Schele and Freidel, 1990.
73. Fried, 1967.
74. Ruby and Brown, 1993; Ruyle, 1973.
75. Donald, 1997: 33–34.
76. Suttles and Jonaitis, 1990: 87.
77. Jahoda, 1975.
78. Quoted in Royal, 1992: 19.
79. Cook, 1998: 214.
80. Quoted in Royal, 1992: 62–63.
81. Sale, 1990: 322.
82. Diamond, 1998: 79.
83. Sowell, 1998: 251.
84. Diamond, 1998: 355.
85. Ibid., 357.
86. Sowell, 1998: 253.

Chapter 12: The Golden Empire

1. Kamen, 2002; Maltby, 2009; Thomas, 2010.
2. Hamilton, 1929; Sluiter, 1998.
3. Elliot, 1966: 180.
4. Maltby, 2002.
5. Kamen, 2002: 61.
6. Charles V proudly exhibited the treasure from the third ship in Brussels, just after his coronation as Holy Roman Emperor (Thomas, 2005: 444.)
7. Ronald, 2008.
8. Bawlf, 2003: 27.
9. Ibid., 34.

10. Ibid., 35.
11. Ibid., 67–68.
12. Ibid., 191.
13. Maltby, 2009: 86.
14. Ibid., 85.
15. Alvarez, Cebellos, and Quinteiro, 2009.
16. Maltby, 2009: 104–5.
17. Israel, 1998: 148.
18. Ibid.
19. Kamen, 2002: 178.
20. Israel, 1998: 156–57.
21. Wegg, 1924: 202–3.
22. Ibid.
23. Williams, 1975: 86.
24. Mattingly, 1962: 88.
25. Barbour, 1930: 263.
26. Mattingly, 1962: 88.
27. Marcus, 1961: 89.
28. Quoted in Mattingly, 1962: 109.
29. Marcus, 1961: 84.
30. Landes, 1998: 151.
31. Ibid.
32. Kamen, 2002: 89.
33. North and Thomas, 1973: 129.
34. Parker, 1970: 75.
35. Ibid., 85.
36. Ibid., 86.
37. Read, 1933.
38. Quoted in Kamen, 1978: 26.
39. Quoted in Cipolla, 1994: 238.
40. Both quotations from Kamen, 1978: 24–28.
41. Kamen, 1978, 2002.
42. Elliot, 1966: 33.
43. North and Thomas, 1973: 130.
44. Elliot, 1966: 120.
45. Cipolla, 1994: 239.
46. Kamen, 2002: 169.
47. Elliot, 1966: 289.
48. Kamen, 2002: 130.
49. Engerman and Sokoloff, 1997: 264; Jacobs, in Kamen, 2002: 130.
50. Thomas, 2010: 199.
51. Engerman and Sokoloff, 1997: 264.
52. Breen, 1986.
53. North and Thomas, 1973: 131.
54. Parker [1988] 2010.

Chapter 13: The Lutheran Reformation: Myths and Realities

1. For this section and later sections of this chapter, I draw on my own research and writing for *The Triumph of Christianity* and *For the Glory of God*. See Stark, 2003, and Stark, 2011.
2. Bainton, 1995; Kittelson, 1986; Marty, 2004; McNally, 1969; Oberman, 1992; Schweibert, 1950.
3. Oberman, 1992: 149.
4. Ibid.
5. Chadwick, 1972: 42.
6. In Oberman, 1992: 188.
7. Schwiebert, 1950: 314.
8. Eisenstein, 1979.
9. Luther [1520] 1915: 84.
10. Ibid., 139.
11. Rupp, 1981: 192.
12. In Strauss, 1975: 32.
13. Brady, 1978; Durant, 1957; Engels, [1873] 1964; Grimm, 1969, 1962; Ozment, 1980; Swanson, 1967; Tracy, 1999; Weber [1904–5] 1958; Wuthnow, 1989.
14. Coulton, 1930; Gottfried, 1985.
15. MacCulloch, 2004.
16. Holborn, 1942: 129.
17. Ibid., 130.
18. Ibid., 131.
19. Kim and Pfaff, 2012.
20. Cole, 1984; Edwards, 1994; Gilmont, 1998; Holborn, 1942.
21. Holborn, 1942: 134.
22. Stone, 1987: 102.
23. Edwards, 1994; Ozment, 1980: 201.
24. Grendler, 2004: 18.
25. Schwiebert, 1996: 471.
26. Grendler, 2004: 19.
27. Brady, 1985; Grimm, 1962; Strauss, 1988, 1978.
28. Moeller, 1972.
29. Rörig, 1969.
30. Stark, 2003: 111.
31. Chadwick, 1972: 26.
32. Bush, 1967; Hill, 1967; Latourette, 1975.
33. Latourette, 1975: 735.
34. Ibid., 737.
35. Roberts, 1968.
36. Johnson, 1976: 267.
37. Belloc [1928] 1975: 172.
38. Berger, 2002; Michael, 2006; Wiener, 1944.
39. MacCulloch, 2010: 664–73.
40. Stone, 1987: 102–3.
41. Luther's preface to his *Kleine Catechismus*, translated in Parker, 1992: 45.
42. Strauss, 1975: 49.

43. Grim and Finke, 2010.

44. Russell, 1970: 287–88.

45. For this section, I draw on my own research and writing for *America's Blessings* and *The Victory of Reason*. See Stark, 2012, and Stark, 2005.

46. Godbeer, 2002: 59; Morgan, 1942: 593; Smith, 1954: 11.

47. Foster, 1999: 727.

48. Ibid., 741.

49. Ibid., 742.

50. Godbeer, 2002: 60.

51. Weber [1904–5] 1958.

52. See Lenski, Nolan, and Lenski, 1995; Smelser, 1994. See also the summary in Hamilton, 1996.

53. With one minor exception, Weber took it as self-evident that throughout Europe Protestants far surpassed Catholics in educational and occupational achievement and that Protestant areas were, and had been, well ahead in the Industrial Revolution. The exception was his rather offhand citation of a study by his student Martin Offenbacher of educational attainment in Baden that purported to show that Protestant students were more likely to enroll in schools offering mathematics and science than in schools specializing in the classics. Not only is this astonishingly slim evidence for a thesis of immense historical scope, but it wasn't even correct—the shortcomings of Offenbacher's "findings" have been fully exposed (see Becker, 2000, 1997; Hamilton, 1996). In any event, Weber's starting point seems to have reflected nothing more scholarly than the smug anti-Catholicism of his time and place. Daniel Chirot has suggested to me that Weber's deep anti-Catholicism also explains his disregard for French scholarship.

54. Trevor-Roper [1969] 2001: 20–21.

55. Pirenne was refuting not Weber, whom he may not yet have read, but Sombart, 1902, and other Marxists who equated capitalism with the Industrial Revolution.

56. Gilchrist, 1969: 1.

57. Mullett, 1999.

58. Stark, 2005.

Chapter 14: Exposing Muslim Illusions

1.   Ahmed, 2006; Bridge, 1983; Crowley, 2005, 2008; Greenblatt, 2003; Palmer, 1994.

2.   Nicolle, 2000; Norwich, 1995; Runciman, 1965: 85.

3.   Nicolle, 2000.

4.   Turnbull, 2004.

5.   Crowley, 2005; Norwich, 1997: 374; Runciman, 1965: 77.

6.   Crowley, 2005: 94.

7.   Crowley, 2005; Norwich, 1997: 376.

8.   As described by Nicolò Barbaro, 1969.

9.   In Bostom, 2005: 616–17.

10. He spent four years as a professor at Istanbul University.

11. Runciman, 1965: 145–48.

12. Quoted in Crowley, 2008: 3.

13. Crowley, 2008.
14. Quoted in Crowley, 2008: 11.
15. To join, a man had to prove that he was from the nobility for at least four generations, on both sides of the family.
16. Murphey, 1999.
17. Crowley, 2008: 15.
18. Ibid., 21.
19. Turnbull, 2003.
20. Millar, 2008; Stoye, 2007.
21. Bradford, 1961: 13.
22. Crowley, 2008: 95.
23. Bradford, 1961: 37.
24. Crowley, 2008: 96.
25. Ibid., 102.
26. Braudel, 1976: 2:1017.
27. Sire, 1993: 68.
28. Ibid., 70.
29. Braudel, 1976: 2:1017.
30. See Beeching, 1982: 85.
31. Crowley, 2008: 196.
32. Bicheno, 2004: 44–45.
33. The gun deck was generally below the rowers, but in some models it sat above.
34. Beeching, 1982: 192; Hanson, 2001: 260.
35. Beeching, 1982: 192.
36. Hanson, 2001: 262.
37. Goldstone, 2009; Saliba, 2007.
38. Lewis, 2002: 6.
39. Ibid., 7.
40. Ibid., 6.
41. Moffett, 1992: 344.
42. Hodgson, 1974: 1:298.
43. Ibid.
44. Hill, 1993: 10.
45. Kollek and Pearlman, 1970: 59; Gil, 1992: 94.
46. Bloom, 2007: 7.
47. Hill, 1993.
48. Nasr, 1993: 135–36.
49. Ibid., 136.
50. For examples of such claims, see Ajram, 1992.
51. Quoted in Brickman, 1961: 85.
52. Dickens, 1999: 8.
53. Brickman, 1961: 84.
54. In Peters, 1993: 90.
55. Gil, 1992: 470.
56. Quoted in Gil, 1992: 470.
57. Pickthall, 1927.
58. Farah, 1994: 199.
59. Jaki, 1986: 208.

60. See Colish, 1997; Stark, 2003: ch. 2.
61. Stanley Lane-Pool, quoted in Fletcher, 1992: 172.
62. Menocal, 2002.
63. Hodgson, 1974: vol. 1.
64. Ibid., 1:268.
65. Payne [1959] 1995: 105.
66. Hodgson, 1974; Payne [1959] 1995.
67. For this section, I draw on my own research and writing for *The Triumph of Christianity*. See Stark, 2011.
68. Little, 1976: 563.
69. Ibid., 567.
70. Quoted in Little, 1976: 568.
71. Browne [1933] 1967: 163.
72. In Foltz, 2000: 129.
73. Browne [1933] 1967: 167.
74. Ibid., 169.
75. Jenkins, 2008.
76. Browne [1933] 1967: 170.
77. Ibid., 171.
78. Marozzi, 2004: 264.
79. Hookham, 1981: 424.
80. Moffett, 1992: 485.
81. Jenkins, 2008: 138.
82. Hodgson, 1974; Kister, 1986; Rodinson, 1980.
83. Rodinson, 1980: 213.
84. Stark, 2001.
85. Ibid.
86. Alroy, 1975.

Chapter 15: Science Comes of Age

1. "Every body persists in its state of being at rest or of moving straight forward, except insofar as it is compelled to change its state by force impressed." Newton [1687] 1971: 13.
2. Shapin, 1996: 1.
3. Stark, 2003, 2005, 2011.
4. Gribbin, 2005: xiv.
5. Hannam, 2011b: 48.
6. Bloch [1940] 1961: 83.
7. This data set differs slightly from the version that appeared in my earlier version. See Stark, 2003.
8. Russell, 1959: 232.
9. Kearney, 1964: especially 95.
10. Kearney, 1964; Rabb, 1965
11. Shapiro, 1968: 288.
12. Kocher, 1953: 4.
13. Gascoigne, 1990.

14. Westfall, 1971: 105.
15. Gribben, 2005: 125.
16. Kearney, 1964: 94.
17. Gascoigne, 1990: table 5.1.
18. Grant, 1984: 68.
19. Ozment, 1980: 191.
20. Rashdall [1936] 1977: 3:408.
21. Kearney, 1964: 100.
22. Stone, 1964.
23. Stone, 1972: 75.
24. McCloskey, 2010: 403.
25. Whitehead [1925] 1967: 13.
26. Ibid., 12.
27. René Descartes, *Oeuvres*: book 8, ch. 61.
28. In Crosby, 1997: 83.
29. Whitehead [1925] 1967: 13.
30. Needham, 1954: 581.
31. Lindberg, 1992: 54.
32. I have written extensively on this in Stark, 2003: ch. 2.
33. In Bradley, 2001: 160.
34. In Merton, 1938: 447.
35. Einstein, 1987, 131.
36. Quoted in Finocchiaro, 2009: 68.
37. Ibid.
38. Drake and O'Malley, 1960.
39. Brooke and Cantor, 1998: 20.
40. Ibid., 110.
41. Shea, 1986: 132.
42. Mason, 1950.
43. Landes, 1994: 649.

Chapter 16: The Industrial Revolution

1. Rosen, 2010: xvi.
2. McCloskey, 2010: 48.
3. Fogel, 2004.
4. Rosen, 2010: xvii.
5. Klein, 2007: 28.
6. Some of the very best books on the subject are: Ashton, 1955; Landes, 2003; Mokyr, 2009; Rosen, 2010; Wrigley, 2010.
7. Landes, 2003.
8. So many inventors and so many separate inventions were involved that the interested reader should consult specialized sources.
9. Smith, 2009: 82.
10. Dickinson, 1935; Rosen, 2010.
11. Roberts, 1978: 6.
12. Ellis, 1968.

13. Davies, 1975.
14. Rosen, 2010: 304–5.
15. Wikipedia, "History of Rail Transport." http://en.wikipedia.org/wiki/History_of_ rail_transport, accessed January 11, 2014.
16. O'Brien, 1983.
17. North, 1982: 103.
18. Wrigley, 2010: 59–61.
19. Allen, 1997.
20. Galbi, 1997.
21. Rirdan, 2012.
22. For a summary, Ford, 2009.
23. Buckingham, 1961: 17.
24. Mabry and Sharplin, 1986.
25. Quoted in Mangum, 1965: 56.

Chapter 17: Liberty and Prosperity

1. Smith [1776] 1981: 2:613. This characterization was later repeated by Napoleon Bonaparte.
2. Baumol, 1990: 901.
3. Smith [1776] 1981: 1:540.
4. Root, 1994: 62.
5. Ibid.
6. Fogel, 1991: 46.
7. Allen, 2009: 48.
8. Ibid., 34.
9. In Landes, 1998: 222.
10. Allen, 2009: 14.
11. For a good discussion, see Mokyr, 2009.
12. Allen, 2009: 33, 49.
13. Ibid., 82.
14. Wrigley, 2010: 37.
15. Nef, 1932; Wrigley, 2010.
16. In Lewis, 2002: 69.
17. In Finley, 1965: 32–33.
18. In Childe, 1952: 53.
19. Baumol, 1990: 899.
20. In MacMullen, 1988: 61.
21. Veyne, 1961.
22. Lopez, 1976: 65–66.
23. In Stark, 2005: 193.
24. Acemoglu, Johnson, and Robinson, 2005.
25. Stark, 2005: 188–89. See also McCloskey, 2010: 395.
26. See McCloskey, 2010.
27. Frank, 2011; Wallerstein, 1974, 2004.
28. Engerman, 1972; Inikori, 2002; O'Brien, 1982.
29. Acemoglu, Johnson, and Robinson, 2005: 550.

30. Beckett, 1988: 325.
31. Mooers, 1991: 157.
32. Beckett, 1988: 23.
33. Ibid.
34. Stone, 1964: "The Educational Revolution in England, 1560–1640."
35. Ibid., 42.
36. Ibid., 44.
37. Ibid., 45.
38. Simon, 1963.
39. Ibid.
40. Bendix, 1956.
41. Bureau of the Census, 1955: vol. 2: table Z 294.
42. Byrn [1900] 2010.
43. Klein, 2007: 24.
44. Ibid.
45. In Habakkuk, 1967: 11–12.
46. Ibid., 12–13.
47. Cobbett [1818] 1967: 195–96.
48. Mariscal and Sokoloff, 2000: 161.
49. Bureau of the Census, 1955: vol. 1: table H 700–715.
50. Engerman and Sokoloff, 1997: 254.
51. Bureau of the Census, 1955: vol. 2: table Z 1–19; Bureau of the Census, 1955: vol. 1: table A 1–5.
52. Mitchell, 1962: table 2.
53. Bureau of the Census, 1955: vol. 1: table A 1–5; Mitchell, 1962: table 2.
54. Bailyn, 1986: table 5.11.
55. Pagnamenta, 2012.
56. Griske, 2005.
57. Rickards, 1966.

Chapter 18: Globalization and Colonialism

1. Fieldhouse, 1973: 3.
2. Ferguson, 2004.
3. Dennis, Beach, and Fahs, 1911: 83–84.
4. Trench, 1979.
5. Ferguson, 2004: 139.
6. Fieldhouse, 1973; McCloskey, 2010; O'Brien, 1982.
7. Whitehead, 2003.
8. McCloskey, 2010: 231–38.
9. Frank, 1998, 2011; Hobson, 2004; Wallerstein, 1974, 2004.
10. Let me fully acknowledge my debt in this section to Daniel R. Headrick and his wonderful book *The Tools of Empire* (1981).
11. Lloyd, 1973.
12. Headrick, 1981: 63.
13. Curtin, 1964: 483–87.
14. Headrick, 1981: 71.

15. Brown, 2011.
16. Massie, 1992.
17. Massie, 2003.
18. Brown, 1978.
19. Headrick, 1981: 51–54.
20. Ibid., 84.
21. Ibid., 158.
22. Wesseling, 2004: x.
23. Fieldhouse, 1973: 3.
24. Fieldhouse, 1973; Wesseling, 2004.
25. Windel, 2009.
26. Whitehead, 2003.
27. Stark, 2003: 336.
28. Hiney, 2000.
29. Woodberry, 2012.
30. Dennis, Beach, and Fahs, 1911.
31. Woodberry, 2007a.
32. Delacroix, 1977.
33. Wimberly and Bello, 1992.
34. Firebaugh and Beck, 1994.
35. O'Brien, 1982, 1983a.
36. Fieldhouse, 1973; McCloskey, 2010.
37. Stark, 2005: ch. 7.
38. Frank, 1966, 1967.
39. Chirot, 2012: 15.
40. Huntington, 1997: 58.
41. Wittfogel [1957] 1981

Bibliography

Aberth, John. 2005. *The Black Death: The Great Mortality of 1348–1350: A Brief History with Documents*. Boston: Bedford/St. Martin's.

Abler, Thomas S. 1980. "Iroquois Cannabalism: Fact Not Fiction." *Ethnohistory* 27: 309–16.

Acemoglu, Daron, Simon Johnson, and James Robinson. 2005. "The Rise of Europe: Atlantic Trade, Institutional Change, and Economic Growth." *American Economic Review* 95: 546–79.

Aczel, Amir D. 2002. *The Riddle of the Compass*. New York: Mariner Books.

Adams, Marilyn. 1987. *William of Ockham*. Notre Dame, IN: University of Notre Dame Press.

Africa, Thomas W. 1969. *The Ancient World*. Boston: Houghton Mifflin.

———. 1974. *The Immense Majesty: A History of Rome and the Roman Empire*. New York: Crowell.

Ahmed, Syed Z. 2006. *The Zenith of an Empire: The Glory of Suleiman the Magnificent and the Law Giver*. West Conshohocken, PA: Infinity Publications.

Ajram, K. 1992. *The Miracle of Islamic Science*. Cedar Rapids, IA: Knowledge House.

Allen, Robert C. 2009. *The British Industrial Revolution in Global Perspective*. Cambridge: Cambridge University Press.

———. 1997. "Agriculture During the Industrial Revolution." In Roderick Floud and D. N. McClosky, *The Economic History of Britain Since 1700*, 96–122. Cambridge: Cambridge University Press.

Alroy, Gil Carl. 1975. *Behind the Middle East Conflict*. New York: G. P. Putnam's Sons.

Alvarez, Gonzalo, Francisco C. Ceballos, and Clesa Quinteiro. 2009. "The Role of Inbreeding in the Extinction of a European Royal Dynasty." *Plos ONE* (April 15, 2009). http://www.plosone.org/article/info%3Adoi%2F10.1371%2Fjournal.pone.0005174. Accessed January 14, 2014.

Ames, Glenn J. 2005. *Vasco da Gama*. New York: Pearson.

Anonymous (translation by Rosalind Hill). [ca. 1102] 1962. *Gesta Francorum: The Deeds of the Franks and Other Pilgrims to Jerusalem*. Oxford: Clarendon Press.

Arens, William. 1979. *The Man-Eating Myth*. New York: Oxford University Press.

Arkush, Elizabeth N., and Mark W. Allen, eds. 2008. *The Archaeology of Warfare: Prehistories of Raiding and Conquest*. Gainesville: University of Florida Press.

Armstrong, Karen. 2001. *Holy War: The Crusades and Their Impact on Today's World*. 2nd ed. New York: Random House.

Arnold, Christopher J. 1984. *Roman Britain to Saxon England*. London: Croom Helm.

Ashton, T. S. 1955. *The Industrial Revolution, 1760–1830*. Oxford: Oxford University Press.

Asimov, Isaac. 1982. *Asimov's Biographical Encyclopedia of Science and Technology*. Rev. 2nd ed. New York: Doubleday

Austin, M. M., and P. Vidal-Naquet. 1972. *Economic and Social History of Ancient Greece: An Introduction*. Berkeley: University of California Press.

Ayton, Andrew. 1999. "Arms, Armour, and Horses." In Maurice Keen, ed., *Medieval Warfare*, 186–208. Oxford: Oxford University Press.

Axtell, James. 1981. *The European and the Indian*. Oxford: Oxford University Press.

Babcock, W. H. 1922. *Legendary Islands of the Atlantic: A Study of Medieval Geography*. New York: American Geographical Society.

Bailyn, Bernard. 1986. *Voyagers to the West*. New York: Knopf.

Bainton, Roland H. [1950] 1995. *Here I Stand*. New York: Meridian.

Bairoch, Paul. 1988. *Cities and Economic Development: From the Dawn of History to the Present*. Chicago: University of Chicago Press.

———. 1993. *Economics and World History: Myths and Paradoxes*. Chicago: University of Chicago Press.

Baker, Alan. 2000. *The Gladiator: The Secret History of Rome's Warrior Slaves*. New York: Thomas Dunne.

Baldwin, John W. 1959. *The Medieval Theories of the Just Price*. Philadelphia: American Philosophical Society.

Baldwin, Marshall W., ed. 1969. *A History of the Crusades*. Vol. 1. *The First Hundred Years*. Madison: University of Wisconsin Press.

Barbaro, Nicolò. 1969. *Diary of the Siege of Constantinople, 1453*. New York: Exposition Press.

Barbero, Alessandro. 2004. *Charlemagne: Father of a Continent*. Berkeley: University of California Press.

Barbour, Violet. 1930. "Dutch and English Merchant Shipping in the Seventeenth Century." *Economic History Review* 2: 261–90.

Barnes, Timothy D. 1981. *Constantine and Eusebius*. Cambridge: Harvard University Press.

Barton, Carlin A. 1993. *The Sorrows of the Romans: The Gladiator and the Monster*. Princeton: Princeton University Press.

Batey, Richard A. 1991. *Jesus and the Forgotten City*. Grand Rapids, MI: Baker Book House.

Bauer, Susan Wise. 2010. *The History of the Medieval World*. New York: W. W. Norton.

Baumol, William J. 1990. "Entrepreneurship: Productive, Unproductive, and Destructive." *Journal of Political Economy* 98: 893–921.

Bawlf, Samuel. 2004. *The Secret Voyage of Sir Francis Drake*. New York: Penguin.

Beacham, Richard C. 1999. *Spectacle Entertainments of Early Imperial Rome*. New Haven: Yale University Press.

Bean, Richard N. 1975. "British-American and West African Slave Prices." In *Historical Statistics of the United States*, 1174. Washington, DC: Bureau of the Census.

Beckett, J. V. 1988. *The Aristocracy in England 1660–1914*. Oxford: Basil Blackwell.

Beckles, Hilary. 1989. *White Servitude and Black Slavery in Barbados, 1627–1715*. Knoxville: University of Tennessee Press.

Beeching, Jack. 1982. *The Galleys at Lepanto*. New York: Charles Scribner's Sons.

Bellitto, Christopher. 2004. *Introducing Nicholas of Cusa*. Mahwah, NJ: Paulist Press.

Belloc, Hilaire. [1928] 1975. *How the Reformation Happened*. Rockford, IL: Tan Books and Publishers.

Bendix, Reinhard. 1956. *Work and Authority in Industry*. New York: Harper and Row.

Benedict, Ruth. 1946. *The Chrysanthemum and the Sword: Patterns of Japanese Culture*. Cambridge: Houghton Mifflin.

Benedictow, Ole J. 2004. *The Black Death 1346–1353: The Complete History*. Rochester, NY: Boydell Press.

Benin, Stephen D. 1993. *The Footprints of God: Divine Accommodation in Jewish and Christian Thought*. Albany: State University of New York Press.

Benjamin, Francis S. Jr., and G. J. Toomer. 1971. *Campanus of Novara and Medieval Planetary Theory*. Madison: University of Wisconsin Press.

Bennett, Judith, and C. Warren Hollister. 2006. *Medieval Europe: A Short History*. New York: McGraw-Hill.

Bensch, Stephen P. 1998. "Historiography: Medieval European and Mediterranean Slavery." In Seymour Drescher and Stanley L. Engerman, eds., *A Historical Guide to World Slavery*, 229–31. New York: Oxford University Press.

Berger, Ronald. 2002. *Fathoming the Holocaust: A Social Problems Approach*. New York: Aldine De Gruyter.

Berman, Joshua A. 2008. *Created Equal: How the Bible Broke with Ancient Political Thought*. Oxford: Oxford University Press.

Bernal, Martin. 1987. *Black Athena: The Afroasiatic Roots of Classical Civilization*. New Brunswick, NJ: Rutgers University Press.

Beye, Charles Rowan. 1987. *Ancient Greek Literature and Society*. Ithaca, NY: Cornell University Press.

Bicheno, Hugh. 2004. *Crescent and Cross: The Battle of Lepanto 1571*. London: Phoenix.

Bickerman, Elias. 1979. *The God of the Maccabees*. Leiden: Brill.

Bishop, Morris. 1948. *Champlain: The Life of Fortitude*. New York: Knopf.

Björkenstam, N. 1995. "The Blast Furnace in Europe During the Middle Ages." In G. Magnusson, ed., *The Importance of Ironmaking*, 143–53. Stockholm: Jernkontoret.

Black, Jeremy. 1998. *War and the World*. New Haven: Yale University Press.

Bloch, Marc. [1940] 1961. *Feudal Society*. 2 vols. Chicago: University of Chicago Press.

———. 1975. *Slavery and Serfdom in the Middle Ages*. Berkeley: University of California Press.

Bloom, Jonathan. 2007. "Islam on the Temple." *Times Literary Supplement*, December 7, 7–8.

Blum, Jerome. 1978. *The End of the Old Order in Rural Europe*. Princeton: Princeton University Press.

Boardman, John. 1988. "Greek Art and Architecture." In John Boardman, Jasper Griggin, and Oswyn Murray, eds., *The Oxford History of Greece and the Hellenistic World*, 330–61. Oxford: Oxford University Press.

Bolton, Jim. 1996. "'The World Upside Down': Plague as an Agent of Economic and Social Change." In W. M. Ormrod, and P. G. Lindley, eds., *The Black Death in England*, 17–78. Stamford, UK: Paul Watkins.

Bonnassie, Pierre. 1991. *From Slavery to Feudalism in South-Western Europe*. Cambridge: Cambridge University Press.

Bostom, Andrew G. 2005. *The Legacy of Jihad*. Amherst, NY: Prometheus Books.

Boutell, Charles. [1907] 1996. *Arms and Armour in Antiquity and the Middle Ages*. Conshohocken, PA: Combined Books.

Bowersock, G. W. 1996. *Hellenism in Late Antiquity*. Ann Arbor: University of Michigan Press.

Bradford, Ernle. 1961. *The Great Siege, Malta 1565*. New York: E-Reads.

Bradley, Walter I. 2001. "The 'Just So' Universe: The Fine-Tuning of Constants and Conditions in the Cosmos." In William A. Dembski and James M. Kushiner, eds., *Signs of Intelligence: Understanding Intelligent Design*. Grand Rapids: Brazos Press: 157–70.

Brady, Thomas. 1978. *Ruling Class, Regime, and Reformation at Strasbourg, 1529–1555*. Leiden, Brill.

Braudel, Fernand. 1977. *Afterthoughts on Material Civilization and Capitalism*. Baltimore: Johns Hopkins University Press.

———. 1979. *Civilization and Capitalism, 15th–18th Century*. Vol. 1, *The Wheels of Commerce*; Vol. 2, *The Perspective of the World*; Vol. 3, *The Structures of Everyday Life*. New York: Harper and Row.

———. 1976. *The Mediterranean and the Mediterranean World in the Age of Philip II*. 2 vols. New York: Harper and Row.

Breen, T. H. 1986. "An Empire of Goods: The Anglicization of Colonial America, 1690–1776." *Journal of British Studies* 25: 467–99.

Brett, Stephen F. 1994. *Slavery and the Catholic Tradition*. New York: Peter Lang.

Brickman, William W. 1961. "The Meeting of East and West in Educational History." *Comparative Education Review* 5: 82–98.

Bridbury, A.R. 1969. "The Dark Ages." *The Economic History Review* 22: 526–37.

———. 1962. *Economic Growth: England in the Later Middle Ages*. London: George Allen and Unwin.

———. 1982. *Medieval English Clothmaking: An Economic Survey*. London: Heinemann Educational Books.

Bridge, Anthony. 1983. *Suleiman the Magnificent, Scourge of Heaven*. New York: F. Watts.

Bridges, John Henry. 1914. *The Life and Work of Roger Bacon*. London: Williams and Norgate.

Brockett, Oscar G., and Franklin J. Hildy. 2007. *History of Theater* 10th ed. Upper Saddle River, NJ: Allyn and Bacon.

Brøndsted, Johannes. 1965. *The Vikings*. Baltimore: Penguin Books.

Brooke, John, and Geoffrey Cantor. 1998. *Restructuring Nature*. Oxford: Oxford University Press.

Brown, David K. 1978. "Nemesis, The First Iron Warship." *Warship* 8: 283–85.

———. 2011. *Warrior to Dreadnought: Warship Development 1860–1905*. Annapolis, MD: Naval Institute Press.

Browne, Laurence E. [1933] 1967. *The Eclipse of Christianity in Asia*. New York: Howard Fertig.

Brown, Elizabeth A. R. 1974. "The Tyranny of a Concept: Feudalism and Historians of Medieval Europe." *American Historical Review*. 70: 1063–88.

Brown, Gordon S. 2003. *The Norman Conquest of Southern Italy and Sicily*. Jefferson, NC: McFarland.

Brown, Peter. 1996. *The Rise of Western Christendom*. Oxford: Blackwell.

———. [1971] 1989. *The World of Late Antiquity, AD 150–750*. New York: W. W. Norton.

———. 1997. "The World of Late Antiquity Revisited." *Symbolae Oslosenses* 72: 5–30.

Brueggemann, Walter. 2009. *An Unsettling God: The Heart of the Hebrew Bible*. Minneapolis: Fortress Press.

Buckingham, Walter. 1961. *Automation: Its Impact on Business and People*. New York: Harper and Row.

Bureau of the Census. 1975. *Historical Statistics of the United States*. 2 vols. Washington, DC: U.S. Government Printing Office.

Burman, Edward. 1989. *The World Before Columbus 1100–1492*. London: W. H. Allen.

Burmeister, Stefan. 2000. "Archaeology of Migration: Approaches to an Archaeological Proof of Migration." *Current Anthropology* 41: 539–67.

Burtt, Edwin A. 1951. *Types of Religious Philosophy*. Rev. ed. New York: Harper.

Bush, M. L. 1967. *Renaissance, Reformation, and the Outer World, 1450–1660*. London: Blandford.

Butzer, Karl W. 1992. "The Americas Before and After 1492: An Introduction to Current Geographical Research." *Annals of the Association of American Geographers* 82: 345–68.

Byrn, Edward W. [1900] 2010. *The Progress of Invention in the Nineteenth Century*. Charleston, SC: Nabu Press, 2010.

Caird, Edward. 1904. *The Evolution of Theology in the Greek Philosophers*. Glasgow: James MacLehose and Sons.

Calvin, John. [ca. 1555] 1980. *John Calvin's Sermons on the Ten Commandments*. Grand Rapids, MI: Baker Bookhouse.

Cantor, Norman F. 1993. *The Civilization of the Middle Ages*. New York: HarperCollins.

———. 2002. *In the Wake of the Plague: The Black Death and the World It Made*. New York; Harper Perennial.

Carcopino, Jerome. 1940. *Daily Life in Ancient Rome*. New Haven: Yale University Press.

Cardini, Franco. 2002. *Europe and Islam*. Oxford: Blackwell.

Carpenter, David. 2004. *The Struggle for Mastery: The Penguin History of Britain 1066–1284*. New York: Penguin.

Carrasco, David. 1999. *City of Sacrifice: The Aztec Empire and the Role of Violence in Civilization*. Boston: Beacon Press.

Carroll, James. 2004. *Crusade: Chronicles of an Unjust War*. New York: Metropolitan Books.

Cartwright, Frederick E. 1972. *Disease and History*. New York: Dorset Press.

Carus-Wilson, Eleanora. 1941. "An Industrial Revolution of the Thirteenth Century." *Economic History Review* 11: 39–60.

———. 1950. "Trends in the Export of English Woollens in the Fourteenth Century." *Economic History Review* 3: 162–79.

———. 1952. "The Woollen Industry." In *The Cambridge Economic History of Europe*. Vol. 2, *Trade and Industry in the Middle Ages*, 355–428. Cambridge: Cambridge University Press.

Carus-Wilson, Eleanora, and Olive Coleman. 1963. *England's Export Trade, 1275–1547*. Oxford: Clarendon Press.

Chabas, Jose, and Bernard R. Goldstein. 2000. *Abraham Zacut*. Darby, PA: Diane Publishing.

Chacon, Richard J., and Ruben G. Mendoza, eds. 2007. *North American Indigenous War-fare and Ritual Violence*. Tucson: University of Arizona Press.

Chadwick, Henry. 1966. *Early Christian Thought and the Classical Tradition*. Oxford: Oxford University Press.

———. 1972. *The Reformation*. Rev. ed. London: Penguin.

Chandler, Tertius. 1987. *Four Thousand Years of Urban Growth: An Historical Census*. Lewiston, NY: Edwin Mellen Press.

Chase, Kenneth. 2003. *Gunpowder: A Global History to 1700*. Cambridge: Cambridge University Press.

Cheetham, Nicholas. 1983. *Keeper of the Keys: A History of Popes from St. Peter to John Paul II*. New York: Scribner's.

Chibnall, Majorie. 2000. *The Normans*. Oxford: Blackwell.

Childe, Gordon. 1958. *The Prehistory of European Society*. Baltimore: Pelican.

———. 1952. "Trade and Industry in Barbarian Europe till Roman Times." In *The Cambridge Economic History of Europe*. Vol. 3, *Trade and Industry in the Middle Ages*, 1–32. Cambridge: Cambridge University Press.

Chirot, Daniel. 2012. "Revisiting the Rise of the West." *Contemporary Sociology* 41: 12–15.

———. 1985. "The Rise of the West." *American Sociological Review* 50: 181–95.

Cipolla, Carlo M. 1994. *Before the Industrial Revolution: European Society and Economy, 1000–1700*. 3rd ed. New York: W. W. Norton.

———. 1965. *Guns, Sails and Empires: Technological Innovation in the Early Phases of European Expansion, 1400–1700*. New York: Minerva Press.

Clagett, Marshall. 1968. *Nicole Oresme and the Medieval Geometry of Qualities and Motions*. Madison: University of Wisconsin Press.

Clark, Gordon H. 1989. *Thales to Dewey*. Jefferson, MD: Trinity Foundation.

Clarke, H. B. 1999. "The Vikings." In Maurice Keen, ed., *Medieval Warfare*, 36–58. Oxford: Oxford University Press.

Clarke, John R. 1998. *Looking at Lovemaking: Constructions of Sexuality in Roman Art, 100 BC–AD 250*. Berkeley: University of California Press.

Clegg, Brian. 2004. *The First Scientist: A Life of Roger Bacon*. Cambridge, MA: Da Capo Press.

Clendinnen, Inga. 1991. *Aztecs: An Interpretation*. Cambridge: Cambridge University Press.

Cliff, Nigel. 2011. *Holy War: How Vasco Da Gama's Epic Voyages Turned the Tide in a Centuries-Old Clash of Civilizations*. New York: Harper Collins.

Clough, Bradley S. 1997. "Buddhism." In Jacon Neusner, ed., *God*, 56–84. Cleveland: Pilgrim Press.

Cobbett, William. [1818] 1967. *Journal of a Year's Residence in the United States of America*. Excerpted in Milton B. Powell, ed., *The Voluntary Church*. New York: Macmillan.

Cohen, Abraham. 1975. *Everyman's Talmud*. New York: Schocken.

Cohen, Edward E. 1992. *Athenian Economy and Society: A Banking Perspective*. Princeton: Princeton University Press.

Cohen, J. Bernard. 1985. *Revolution in Science*. Cambridge: Belknap Press of Harvard University Press.

Cole, Richard G. 1984. "Reformation Printers: Unsung Heroes." *Sixteenth Century Journal* 15: 327–39.

Colish, Marcia L. 1997. *Medieval Foundations of the Western Intellectual Tradition, 400–1400*. New Haven: Yale University Press.

Collins, Randall. 1998. *The Sociology of Philosophies: A Global Theory of Intellectual Change.* Cambridge: Harvard University Press.

———. 1986. *Weberian Sociological Theory.* Cambridge: Cambridge University Press.

Columbus, Christopher. [1492–93] 2005. *The Journal of Christopher Columbus during His First Voyage.* Boston: Adamant Media.

Comnena, Anna. [ca. 1148] 1969. *The Alexiad.* London: Penguin Classics.

Conrad, Alfred H., and John R. Meyer. 1958. *The Economics of Slavery and Other Studies in Econometric History.* Chicago: Aldine.

Cook, Nobel David. 1998. *Born to Die: Disease and the New World Conquest, 1492–1650.* Cambridge: Cambridge University Press.

Cook, Ramsay. 1993. *The Voyages of Jacques Cartier.* Toronto: University of Toronto Press.

Corrigan, John A., Carlos M. N. Eire, Frederick M. Denny, and Martin S. Jaffee. 1998. *Readings in Judaism, Christianity, and Islam.* Upper Saddle River, NJ: Prentice-Hall.

Coulton, G. G. 1930. *The Black Death.* New York: Cope and Smith.

Crombie, A. C. 1953. *Robert Grosseteste and the Origins of Experimental Science.* Oxford: Clarendon Press.

Crosby, Alfred W. 1997. *The Measure of Reality.* Cambridge: Cambridge University Press.

Crouzet, Françis. 1985. *The First Industrialists.* Cambridge: Cambridge University Press.

Crowley, Roger. 2008. *Empires of the Sea.* New York: Random House.

———. 2005. *1453: The Holy War for Constantinople and the Clash of Islam and the West.* New York: Hyperion.

Culotta, Elizabeth. 1999. "Neanderthals Were Cannibals, Bones Show." *Science Magazine* 286 (October 1): 18–19.

Cuomo, S. 2007. *Technology and Culture in Greek and Roman Antiquity.* Cambridge: Cambridge University Press.

Curtin, Philip D. 1969. *The Atlantic Slave Trade: A Census.* Madison: University of Wisconsin Press.

———. 1964. *The Image of Africa: British Ideas and Actions 1780–1850.* Madison: University of Wisconsin Press.

Dales, Richard C. [1973] 1994. *The Scientific Achievement of the Middle Ages.* Philadelphia: University of Pennsylvania Press.

Daniel, Ralph Thomas. 1981. "Music, Western." *Encyclopaedia Britannica*, vol. 12, 704–15. Chicago: University of Chicago Press.

Daniell, Christopher. 2003. *From Norman Conquest to the Magna Carta: England 1066–1215.* London: Routledge.

Danielson, Dennis Richard. 2000. *The Book of the Cosmos: Imagining the Universe from Heraclitus to Hawking.* Cambridge, MA: Perseus.

Davies, Hunter. 1975. *George Stevenson.* London: Weidenfeld and Nicolson.

Davis, David Brion. 1966. *The Problem of Slavery in Western Culture.* Ithaca, NY: Cornell University Press.

Davis, Paul K. 2001. *Besieged: An Encyclopaedia of Great Sieges from Ancient Times to the Present.* Santa Barbara, CA: ABC-CLIO.

Davis, R. H. C. 1970. *A History of Medieval Europe.* Rev. ed. London: Longman.

Dawson, Christopher. [1929] 2001. *Progress and Religion: An Historical Enquiry.* Washington, DC: Catholic University of America Press.

———. 1957. *Religion and the Rise of Western Culture.* New York: Doubleday Image Books.

Dawson, Raymond. 1972. *Imperial China*. Harmondsworth, Middlesex: Penguin Books.

Delacroix, Jacques. 1977. "The Export of Raw Materials and Economic Growth: A Cross-National Study." *American Sociological Review* 18: 795–808.

Delbrück, Hans. [1920] 1990. *The Barbarian Invasions: History of the Art of War*. Vol. 2. Lincoln: University of Nebraska Press.

Deloria, Vine. 1969. *Custer Died for Your Sins*. New York: Macmillan.

Demandt, Alexander. 1984. *Der Fall Roms*. München: C. H. Beck.

Dempsey, Bernard W. 1943. *Interest and Usury*. Washington, DC: American Council on Public Affairs.

Dennis, James S., Harlan P. Beach, and Charles H. Fahs. 1911. *World Atlas of Christian Missions*. New York: Student Volunteer Movement for Foreign Missions.

de Roover, Raymond. 1958. "The Concept of the Just Price: Theory and Economic Policy." *Journal of Economic History* 18: 418–34.

———. 1946. "The Medici Bank Financial and Commercial Operations." *Journal of Economic History* 6: 153–72.

———. 1948. *Money, Banking, and Credit in Bruges*. Cambridge, MA: Medieval Academy of America.

———. 1963. "The Organization of Trade." In M. M. Postan, E. E. Rich, and Edward Miller, eds., *The Cambridge Economic History of Europe*. Vol. 3, *Economic Organization and Policies in the Middle Ages*, 42–118. Cambridge: Cambridge University Press.

———. 1966. *The Rise and Decline of the Medici Bank, 1397–1494*. New York: W. W. Norton.

Diamond, Jared. 1998. *Guns, Germs, and Steel*. New York: W. W. Norton.

Díaz, Bernal del Castillo. [ca. 1555] 1996. *The Discovery and Conquest of Mexico*. New York: Da Capo Press.

Dickens, A. G. 1991. *The English Reformation*. University Park: Pennsylvania State University Press.

Dickens, Mark. 1999. "The Church in the East." Accessed January 16, 2014. http://www.oxuscom.com/ch-of-east.htm.

Dickinson, H. W. 1935. *James Watt: Craftsman and Engineer*. Cambridge: Cambridge University Press,

Diffie, Bailey W., and George D. Winius. 1977. *Foundations of the Portuguese Empire 1415–1580*. Minneapolis: University of Minnesota Press.

Dockès, Pierre. 1982. *Medieval Slavery and Liberation*. Chicago: University of Chicago Press.

Donald, Leland. 1997. *Aboriginal Slavery on the Northwest Coast of North America*. Berkeley: University of California Press.

Dopsch, Alfons. 1969 *The Economic and Social Conditions of European Civilization*. New York: H. Fertig.

Drake, Stillman, and C. D. O'Malley. 1960. *The Controversy of the Comets of 1618*. Philadelphia: University of Pennsylvania Press.

Dresbeck, LeRoy. 1976. "Winter Climate and Society in the Northern Middle Ages: The Technological Impact." In Bert S. Hall and Delno C. West, eds., *On Pre-Modern Technology and Science: Studies in Honor of Lynn White, Jr.*, 177–199. Malibu, CA: Undena Publications.

Dreyer, Edward L. 2007. *Zheng He: China and the Oceans in the Early Ming Dynasty, 1405–1433*. New York: Pearson Longman.

Duby, Georges. 1974. *The Early Growth of the European Economy*. Ithaca, NY: Cornell University Press.

Duffy, Eamon. 1997. *Saints and Sinners: A History of Popes*. New Haven: Yale University Press.

Duncalf, Frederic. 1969. "The First Crusade: Clermont to Constantinople." In Baldwin, 1969, 253–79.

Dunn, Richard S. *Sugar and Slaves: The Rise of the Planter Class in the English West Indies, 1624–1713*. New York: Norton, 1972.

Durant, Will. 1957. *The Reformation*. New York: Simon and Schuster.

Easterlin, Richard A. 1961. "Regional Income Trends, 1840–1850." In Seymour Harris, ed., *American Economic History*, 525–47. New York: McGraw-Hill.

Easton, Stewart C. 1952. *Roger Bacon and the Search for a Universal Science*. New York: Columbia University Press.

Edelstein, Ludwig. 1967. *The Idea of Progress in Classical Antiquity*. Baltimore: Johns Hopkins University Press.

Edwards, Mark U., Jr. 1994. *Printing, Propaganda, and Martin Luther*. Minneapolis: Fortress Press.

Einstein, Albert. 1987. *Letters to Solovine*. New York: Philosophical Library.

Elliot, J. H. 1966. *Imperial Spain 1469–1716*. New York: Mentor Books.

Ellis, Hamilton, 1968. *The Pictorial Encyclopedia of Railways*. London: Hamlyn.

Engerman, Stanley L. 1972. "The Slave Trade and British Capital Formation in the Eighteenth Century. *Business History Review* 46: 430–43.

Engerman, Stanley L., and Kenneth L. Sokoloff. 1997. "Factor Endowments, Institutions, and Differential Paths of Growth Among the New World Economies." In Stephen Haber, ed., *How Latin America Fell Behind*, 260–304. Stanford: Stanford University Press.

Engels, Friedrich. [1873] 1964. "Dialectics of Nature." Reprinted in Karl Marx and Friedrich Engels, *On Religion*, 152–93. Atlanta, GA: Scholars Press.

Epstein, Steven A. 1996. *Genoa and the Genoese, 958–1528*. Chapel Hill, NC: University of North Carolina Press.

Erdoes, Richard. 1988. *A.D. 1000: Living on the Brink of the Apocalypse*. New York: Harper and Row.

Esposito, John, ed. 1980. *Islam and Development: Religion and Sociopolitical Change*. Syracuse, NY: Syracuse University Press.

Evans, James. 1998. *The History and Practice of Ancient Astronomy*. Oxford: Oxford University Press.

Fagan, Brian. 2008. *The Great Warming: Climate Change and the Rise and Fall of Civilizations*. New York. Bloomsbury Press.

———. 2000. *The Little Ice Age. How Climate Made History, 1300–1850*. New York: Basic Books.

———. 2004. *The Long Summer: How Climate Changed Civilization*. New York: Basic Books.

Fairweather, William. 1924. *Jesus and the Greeks*. Edinburgh: T&T Clark.

Farah, Caesar E. 1994. *Islam: Beliefs and Observances*. 5th ed. Hauppauge, NY: Barron's.

Febvre, Lucien, and Henri-Jean Martin. [1958] 2010. *The Coming of the Book: The Impact of Printing 1450–1800*. London: Verso (New Left Books).

Feldman, Louis H. 1981. "Judaism, History of, III, Hellenic Judaism." *Encyclopaedia Britannica*. Chicago: University of Chicago Press.

Ferguson, Niall. 2004. *Empire: The Rise and Demise of the British World Order and the Lessons for Global Power*. New York: Basic Books.

Ferguson, Robert. 2009. *The Vikings: A History*. New York: Viking.

Fernandez-Armesto, Felipe. 1987. *Before Columbus: Exploration and Colonisation from the Mediterranean to the Atlantic 1229–1492*. Philadelphia: University of Pennsylvania Press.

———. 1999. "Naval Warfare After the Viking Age ca. 1100–1500." In Maurice Keen, ed., *Medieval Warfare*, 230–72. Oxford: Oxford University Press.

Ferrill, Arther. 1986. *The Fall of the Roman Empire: The Military Explanation*. London: Thames and Hudson.

Fieldhouse, D. K. 1973. *Economics and Empire 1830–1914*. Ithaca, NY: Cornell University Press.

Findlay, Ronald, and Kevin H. O'Rourke. 2009. *Power and Plenty: Trade, War, and the World Economy in the Second Millennium*. Princeton: Princeton University Press.

Finegan, Jack. 1992. *The Archeology of the New Testament*. Rev. ed. Princeton: Princeton University Press.

Finlay, Robert. 2004. "How Not to (Re)Write Wold History: Gavin Menzies and the Chinese Discovery of America." *Journal of World History* 15: 229–42.

Finley, M. I. 1973. *The Ancient Economy*. Berkeley: University of California Press.

———. 1980. *Ancient Slavery and Modern Ideology*. New York: Viking Press.

———. 1981. *Economy and Society in Ancient Greece*. New York: Viking Press.

———. 1965. "Technical Innovation and Economic Progress in the Ancient World." *Economic History Review* 18: 29–45.

———. 1959. "Technology in the Ancient World." *Economic History Review* 12: 120–35.

Firebaugh, Glenn, and Frank D. Beck. 1994. "Does Economic Growth Benefit the Masses? Growth, Dependence, and Welfare in the Third World." *American Sociological Review* 59: 631–53.

Fisher, N. W., and Sabetai Unguru. 1971. "Experimental Science and Mathematics in Roger Bacon's Thought." *Traditio* 27: 353–78.

Fleming, Peter. 1960. *The Siege at Peking*. London: Readers Union.

Fletcher, Richard. 1997. *The Barbarian Conversion: From Paganism to Christianity*. New York: Henry Holt.

———. 1992. *Moorish Spain*. Berkeley: University of California Press.

Finocchiaro, Maurice A. 2009. "Myth 8: That Galileo Was Imprisoned and Tortured for Advocating Copernicanism." In Ronald L. Numbers, ed., *Galileo Goes to Jail: And Other Myths About Science and Religion*, 68–78. Cambridge: Harvard University Press.

Fogel, Robert William. 1991. "The Conquest of High Mortality and Hunger in Europe and America: Timing and Mechanisms." In Patrice Higonnet, David S. Landes, and Henry Rosovsky, eds., *Favorites of Fortune*, 33–71. Cambridge: Harvard University Press.

———. 2004. *The Escape from Hunger and Premature Death, 1700–2100*. Cambridge: Cambridge University Press.

———. 1989. *Without Consent or Contract: The Rise and Fall of American Slavery*. New York: W. W. Norton.

Fogel, Robert William, and Stanley L. Engerman. 1974. *Time on the Cross: The Economics of American Negro Slavery*, 2 vols. Boston: Little, Brown.

Ford, Martin R. 2009. *The Lights in the Tunnel: Automation, Accelerating Technology and the Economy of the Future*. Sunnyvale, CA: Acculant Press.

Forsythe, Gary. 2005. *A Critical History of Early Rome*. Berkeley: University of California Press.

Foster, Thomas A. 1999. "Deficient Husbands: Manhood, Sexual Incapacity, and Marital Sexuality in Seventeenth Century New England." *William and Mary Quarterly* 56: 723-74.

Fox, Robin Lane. 2008. *The Classical World*. New York: Basic Books.

France, John. 1994. *Victory in the East*. Cambridge: Cambridge University Press.

Frank, Andre Gunder. 1967. *Capitalism and Underdevelopment in Latin America*. New York: Monthly Review Press.

———. 1966. *The Development of Underdevelopment*. New York: Monthly Review Press.

———. 1998. *ReOrient: Global Economy in the Asian Age*. Berkeley: University of California Press.

———. 2011. *World Accumulation*. New York: Monthly Review Press.

Freeman, Charles. 1999. *The Greek Achievement: The Foundation of the Western World*. New York: Penguin Books.

Fremantle, Anne, ed. 1954. *The Age of Belief: The Medieval Philosophers*. New York: New Amsterdam Library.

French, A. 1964. *The Growth of the Athenian Economy*. New York: Barnes and Noble.

Frend, W. H. C. 1984. *The Rise of Christianity*. Philadelphia: Fortress Press.

Fried, Morton H. 1967. *The Evolution of Political Society: An Essay in Political Anthropology*. New York: Random House.

Fritze, Ronald H. 2002. *New Worlds: The Great Voyages of Discovery 1400–1600*. Westport, CT: Praeger.

Fryde, E. B. 1963. "Public Credit, with Special Reference to North-Western Europe." In *The Cambridge Economic History of Europe*. Vol. 3, *Economic Organization and Policies in the Middle Ages*, 430–553. Cambridge: Cambridge University Press.

Fulcher of Chartres. [ca. 1127] 1969. *A History of the Expedition to Jerusalem 1095–1127*. Knoxville: University of Tennessee Press.

Fuller, Russell. 2003. "The Rabbis and the Claims of the Openness Advocates." In John Piper, Justine Taylor, and Paul Kjoss Helseth, eds., *Beyond the Bounds*, 23–41. Wheaton, IL: Crossway Books.

Futrell, Alison. 1997. *Blood in the Arena*. Austin: University of Texas Press.

Galbi, Douglas A. 1997. "Child Labor and the Division of Labor in the Early English Cotton Mills." *Journal of Population Economics* 10: 357–75.

Galloway, James A., Derek Keene, and Margaret Murphy. 1996. "Fuelling the City: Production and Distribution of Firewood and Fuel in London's Region, 1290–1400." *Economic History Review* 49: 447–72.

Gardiner, Helen, and Sumner Crosby. 1959. *Art through the Ages*. New York: Harcourt, Brace, and World.

Garnsey, Peter, and Richard Saller. 1987. *The Roman Empire: Economy, Society, and Culture*. London: Duckworth.

Gascoigne, John. 1990. " A Reappraisal of the Role of the Universities in the Scientific Revolution." In Lindberg and Westman, 1990, 207–60.

Gay, Peter. 1969. *Enlightenment: An Interpretation*. New York: W. W. Norton.

Gerschenkron, Alexander. 1970. *Europe in the Russian Mirror: Four Lectures in Economic History*. Cambridge: Cambridge University Press.

Ghirshman, Roman. 1955. "The Ziggurat of Choga-Zanbil." *Archaeology* 8: 260–63.

Gibbons, A. "Archaeologists Rediscover Cannibals." *Science* 277: 635–37.

Gies, Frances, and Joseph Gies. 1994. *Cathedral, Forge, and Waterwheel: Technology and Invention in the Middle Ages*. New York: HarperCollins.

Gies, Joseph, and Frances Gies. 1969. *Leonard of Pisa and the New Mathematics of the Middle Ages*. New York: Crowell.

Gilchrist, John. 1969. *The Church and Economic Activity in the Middle Ages*. New York: St. Martin's Press.

Gilfillan, S. C. 1945. "Invention as a Factor in Economic History." *Journal of Economic History* 5: 66–85.

———. 1965. "Lead Poisoning and the Fall of Rome." *Journal of Occupational Medicine* 7: 53–60.

Gilmont, Jean-Francois. 1998. *The Reformation and the Book*. Aldershot, UK: Ashgate.

Gil, Moshe. 1992. *A History of Palestine, 634–1099*. Cambridge: Cambridge University Press.

Gimpel, Jean. 1961. *The Cathedral Builders*. New York: Grove Press.

———. 1976. *The Medieval Machine: The Industrial Revolution of the Middle Ages*. New York: Penguin Books.

Goffart, Walter. 1971. "Zosimus: The First Historian of Rome's Fall." *American Historical Review*. 76: 412–41.

Glick, Thomas F., Steven Livesey, and Faith Wallis. 2005. *Medieval Science, Technology and Medicine: An Encyclopedia*. London: Routledge.

Godbeer, Richard. 2002. *Sexual Revolution in Early America*. Baltimore: Johns Hopkins University Press.

Goldstone, Jack. 2009. *Why Europe? The Rise of the West in World History, 1500–1850*. New York: McGraw-Hill.

Golvin, Jean-Clause. 1988. *L'Amphithéâtre romain*. Paris: E. de Boccard.

Gombrich, E. H. 1978. *The Story of Art*. New York: E. P. Dutton.

Goodenough, Erwin Ramsdell. 1962. *An Introduction to Philo Judaeus*. 2nd ed. Oxford: Blackwell.

Gordon, Murray. 1989. *Slavery in the Arab World*. New York: New Amsterdam Books.

Gottfried, Robert S. 1985. *The Black Death*. New York: The Free Press.

Goveia, Elsa V. 1969. "The West Indian Slave Laws of the Eighteenth Century." In Laura Foner and Eugene D. Genovese, eds., *Slavery in the New World: A Reader in Comparative History*, 113–37. Englewood Cliffs, NJ: Prentice-Hall.

Graetz, Heinrich Hirsh. 1894. *History of the Jews*. Vol. 3. Philadelphia: Jewish Publication Society of America.

Graham, Loren. 1993. *Science in Russia and the Soviet Union*. New York: Cambridge University Press.

Grant, Edward. 1996. *The Foundations of Modern Science in the Middle Ages*. Cambridge: Cambridge University Press.

———. 2007. *A History of Natural Philosophy: From the Ancient World to the Nineteenth Century*. Cambridge: Cambridge University Press.

———. 1971. *Nicole Oreseme and the Kinematics of Circular Motion*. Madison: University of Wisconsin Press.

———. 1994. *Planets, Stars, and Orbs: The Medieval Cosmos, 1200–1687*. New York: Cambridge University Press.

———. 1984. "Science and the Medieval University." In James M. Kittekson and Pamela J. Transue, eds., *Rebirth, Reform, and Resilience: Universities in Transition, 1300–1700*. Columbus: Ohio State University Press.

———. 1974. *A Sourcebook in Medieval Science*. Cambridge: Harvard University Press.

Grant, Michael. 1988. *The Rise of the Greeks*. New York: Charles Scribner's Sons.

Gray, Charles Edward. 1958. "An Analysis of Greco-Roman Development." *American Anthropologist* 60: 13–31.

———. 1966. "A Measurement of Creativity in Western Civilization." *American Anthropologist* 68: 1384–417.

Gray, H. L. 1924. "The Production and Exportation of English Woollens in the Fourteenth Century." *English Historical Review* 39: 13–35.

Greenblatt, Miriam. 2003. *Sülyman the Magnificent and the Ottoman Empire*. New York: Benchmark Books.

Greif, Avner. 1994. "On the Political Foundations of the Late Medieval Commercial Revolution: Genoa During the Twelfth and Thirteenth Centuries." *Journal of Economic History*. 54: 271–87.

Grendler, Paul F. "The Universities of the Renaissance and Reformation." *Renaissance Quarterly* 57: 1–42.

Gribbin, John. 2005. *The Fellowship: Gilbert, Bacon, Harvey, Wren, Newton, and the Story of a Scientific Revolution*. New York: Overlook Press.

Grim, Brian J., and Roger Finke. 2010. *The Price of Freedom Denied*. New York: Cambridge University Press.

Grimm, Harold J. 1969. "The Reformation and the Urban Social Classes in Germany." In John C. Olin, James D. Smart, and Robert E. McNally, SJ, eds., *Luther, Erasmus, and the Reformation*, 75–86. New York: Fordham University Press.

Griske, Michael. 2005. *The Diaries of John Hunton*. New York: Heritage Books.

Grossman, Gregory. 1963. "Notes for a Theory of the Command Economy." *Soviet Studies* 15: 101–23.

Gurney, Alan. 2004. *Compass: A Story of Exploration and Innovation*. London: Norton.

Habakkuk, H. J. 1967. *American and British Technology in the Nineteenth Century*. Cambridge: Cambridge University Press.

Haensch, S., R. Bianucci, M. Signoli, M. Rajerison, M. Schultz, et al. 2010. "Distinct Clones of *Yersinia pestis* Caused the Black Death." *PLoS Pathog* 6, no. 10. http://www.plospathogens.org/article/info%3Adoi%2F10.1371%2Fjournal. ppat.1001134. Accessed January 13, 2014.

Haines, Michael R., and Richard H. Steckel. 2000. *A Population History of North America*. New York: Cambridge University Press.

Halpern, Louis. 1924. "The Church from Charlemagne to Sylvester II." *The Cambridge Medieval History*. Vol. 3, 443–57. New York: Macmillan.

Hamerow, Helena. 1997. "Migration Theory and the Anglo-Saxon 'Identity Crisis'." In John Chapman and Helena Hamerow, eds., *Migrations and Invasions in Archaeological Explanation. British Archaeological Reports International Series* 664: 33–44.

Hamilton, Bernard. 2000. *The Leper King and His Heirs: Baldwin IV and the Crusader Kingdom of Jerusalem*. Cambridge: Cambridge University Press.

Hamilton, Earl J. 1929. "Imports of American Gold and Silver Into Spain, 1503–1660." *Quarterly Journal of Economics* 43: 436–72.

Hamilton, Edith. [1930] 1993. *The Greek Way*. New York: W. W. Norton.

Hamilton, Richard F. 1996. *The Social Misconstruction of Reality*. New Haven: Yale University Press.

Hannam, James, 2011a. *The Genesis of Science: How the Christian Middle Ages Launched the Scientific Revolution*. Washington, DC: Regnery.

———. 2011b. "Modern Science's Christian Origins." *First Things* (October): 47–51.

Hansen, Mogens Herman. 2006a. *Polis: An Introduction to the Ancient Greek City-State.* Oxford: Oxford University Press.

———. 2006b. *The Shotgun Method: The Demography of the Ancient City-State Culture.* Columbia, MO: University of Missouri Press.

Hanson, Victor Davis. 2001. *Carnage and Culture: Landmark Battles in the Rise of Western Power.* New York: Doubleday.

———. [1994] 2009. *The Western Way of War.* Berkeley: University of California Press.

———. 2002. *Why the West Has Won.* London: Faber and Faber.

Hanson, Victor Davis, and John Heath. 2001. *Who Killed Homer?* New York: Encounter Books.

Harkness, Deborah E. 2007. *The Jewel House: Elizabethan London and the Scientific Revolution.* New Haven: Yale University Press.

Harnack, Adolf von. 1905. *The Expansion of Christianity in the First Three Centuries.* Vol. 2. New York: G. P. Putnam's Sons.

Harris, Marvin. [1977] 1991. *Cannibals and Kings.* New York: Vantage.

———. 1964. *Patterns of Race in America.* New York: Walker.

———. 1963. *The Nature of Cultural Things.* New York: Random House.

Harris, William V. 1989. *Ancient Literacy.* Cambridge: Harvard University Press.

Hartwell, Robert. 1971. "Historical Analogism, Public Policy, and Social Science in Eleventh- and Twelfth-Century China." *American Historical Review.* 76: 690–727.

———. 1966. "Markets, Technology, and the Structure of Enterprise in the Development of the Eleventh-Century Chinese Iron and Steel Industry." *Journal of Economic History* 26: 29–58.

Haskins, Charles Homer. [1923] 2002. *The Rise of Universities.* New Brunswick, NJ: Transaction.

Hatch, Edwin. [1888] 1957. *The Influence of Greek Ideas on Christianity.* New York: Harper and Brothers.

Hayek, F. A. 1988. *The Fatal Conceit: The Errors of Socialism.* Chicago: University of Chicago Press.

Hayes, Carlton J. H. 1917. *Political and Social History of Modern Europe.* 2 vols. New York: Macmillan.

Haywood, John. 1999. *Dark Age Naval Power.* 2nd ed. Norfolk, GB: Anglo-Saxon Books.

Headrick, Daniel R. 1981. *The Tools of Empire: Technology and European Imperialism in the Nineteenth Century.* New York: Oxford University Press.

Heather, Peter. 2010. *Empires and Barbarians: The Fall of Rome and the Birth of Europe.* Oxford: Oxford University Press.

———. 2006. *The Fall of the Roman Empire: A New History of Rome and the Barbarians.* Oxford: Oxford University Press.

———. 1998. *The Goths.* Oxford: Blackwell.

———. 1999. *The Visigoths.* Rochester, NY: Boydell Press.

Hemming, John. 1970. *The Conquest of the Incas.* Boston: Houghton Mifflin.

Hengel, Martin. 1989. The 'Hellenization' of Judea in the First Century After Christ. London. SCM Press.

———. 1974. *Judaism and Hellenism: Studies in their Encounter in Palestine during the Early Hellenistic Period.* 2 vols. Philadelphia: Fortress Press.

Henige, David. 1998. *The American Indian Contact Population Debate.* Norman: University of Oklahoma Press.

Henry, Margaret Y. 1927. *Cicero's Treatment of the Free Will Problem*. Transactions and Proceedings of the American Philological Association 58: 32–42.

Herlihy, David. 1997. *The Black Death and the Transformation of the West*. Cambridge: Harvard University Press.

———. 1957. "Church Property on the European Continent, 701–1200." *Speculum* 18: 89–113.

———. 1989. "Demography." In Joseph R. Strayer, *Dictionary of the Middle Ages*. New York: Scribner.

Hickey, Anne Ewing. 1987. *Women of the Roman Aristocracy as Christian Monastics*. Ann Arbor, MI: UMI Research Press.

Hill, Donald Routledge. 1993. *Islamic Science and Engineering*. Edinburgh: Edinburgh University Press.

Hilton, Rodney (also R. H.) [1973] 2003. *Bond Men Made Free: Medieval Peasant Movements and the English Rising of 1381*. London: Routledge.

———. 1952. "Capitalism—What's in a Name?" *Past and Present* 1: 32–43.

———. 1969. *The Decline of Serfdom in Medieval England*. London: Macmillan.

———. 1967. *A Medieval Society*. London: Weidenfeld and Nicholson.

Hilton, Walter. 1985. *Toward a Perfect Love*. Translated by David L. Jeffrey. Portland, OR: Multnomah Press.

Himmelfarb, Gertrude. 2005. *The Roads to Modernity*. New York; Vintage Books.

Hiney, Tom. 2000. *On the Missionary Trail*. New York: Atlantic Monthly Press.

Hitchins, H. L., and William E. May. 1951. *From Lodestone to Gyro-Compass*. London: Hutchinson's Scientific and Technical Publications.

Hitti, Philip K. 2002. *History of the Arabs: From the Earliest Times to the Present*. New York: Palgrave Macmillan.

Hobhouse, Henry. 2005. *Seeds of Change: Six Plants that Transformed Mankind*. Berkeley, CA: Counterpoint.

Hobson, J. A. [1902] 1938. *Imperialism: A Study*. London: Allen and Unwin.

Hobson, John M. 2004. *The Eastern Origins of Western Civilization*. Cambridge: Cambridge University Press.

Hodges, Richard. 1989a. *The Anglo-Saxon Achievement: Archaeology and the Beginnings of English Society*. London: Duckworth.

———. 1989b. *Dark Age Economics: The Origins of Towns and Trade AD 600–1000*. 2nd ed. London: Duckworth.

Hodgson, Marshall G. S. 1974. *The Venture of Islam*. 3 vols. Chicago: University of Chicago Press.

Holborn, Louise W. 1942. "Printing and the Growth of the Protestant Movement in Germany from 1517 to 1524." *Church History* 11: 123-37.

Holmqvist, Wilhelm. 1979. *Swedish Vikings on Helgö and Birka*. Stockholm: Swedish Booksellers' Association.

Holt, Richard. 1988. *The Mills of Medieval England*. Oxford: Blackwell.

Hookham, Hilda. 1981. "Timur." *Encyclopedia Britannica*. Chicago: University of Chicago Press.

Hopkins, Keith. [1978] 2007. *Conquerors and Slaves*. Cambridge: Cambridge University Press.

Hunt, Edwin S. 1994. *The Medieval Super-Companies: A Study of the Peruzzi Company of Florence*. Cambridge. Cambridge University Press.

Hunt, Edwin S., and James M. Murray. 1999. *A History of Business in Medieval Europe, 1200–1550*. Cambridge: Cambridge University Press.

Huntington, Samuel P. 1997. *The Clash of Civilizations and the Remaking of the World Order*. New York: Touchstone Book.

Hurbon, Laennec. 1992. "The Church and Afro-American Slavery." In Enrique Dussell, ed., *The Church in Latin America*. Maryknoll: Orbis Books.

Hvalvik, Reidar. 2007. "Jewish Believers and Jewish Influence in the Roman Church until the Early Second Century." In Oskar Skarsaune and Reidar Hvalik, eds., *Jewish Believers in Jesus: The Early Centuries*, 179–216. Peabody, MA: Hendrickson Publishers.

Ingstad, Helge, and Anne Stine Ingstad. 2001. *The Viking Discovery of America*. New Tork: Checkmark Books.

Inikori, Joseph E. 2002. *Africans and the Industrial Revolution in England: A Study in International Trade and Economic Development*. Cambridge: Cambridge University Press.

Irwin, Robert. 2006. *Dangerous Knowledge: Orientalism and Its Discontents*. Woodstock and New York: Overlook Press.

Israel, Jonathan L. 1998. *The Dutch Republic: Its Rise, Greatness, and Fall, 1477–1806*. Corrected paperback ed. Oxford: Clarendon Press.

Issawi, Charles. 1957. "Crusades and Current Crisis in the Near East: A Historical Parallel." *International Affairs* 33: 269–79.

———. 1980. "Europe, the Middle East, and the Shift in Power: Reflections on a Theme by Marshall Hodgson." *Comparative Studies in Society and History* 22: 487–504.

Jahoda, Gloria. 1975. *Trail of Tears*. New York: Holt, Rhinehart and Wilson.

Jaki, Stanley L. 2000. *The Savior of Science*. Grand Rapids, MI: Eerdmans.

———. 1986. *Science and Creation*. Edinburgh: Scottish Academic Press.

Janin, Hunt. 2008. *The University in Medieval Life, 1170–1499*. Jefferson, NC: McFarkand.

Jankuhn, Herbert. 1982. "Trade and Settlement in Central and Northern Europe up to and during the Viking Period." *Journal of the Royal Society of Antiquaries of Ireland* 112: 18–50.

Janson, H. W. 1986. *The History of Art*. New York: Harry N. Abrams.

Jenkins, Philip. 2008. *The Lost History of Christianity*. San Francisco: HarperOne.

Johnson, Paul. 2003. *Art: A New History*. New York: Harper Collins.

———. 1976. *A History of Christianity*. New York: Atheneum.

Jones, A. H. M. 1964. *The Later Roman Empire, 284–602: A Social, Economic, and Administrative Survey*. 2 vols. Norman, OK: University of Oklahoma Press.

Jones, Archer. 2001. *The Art of War in the Western World*. Urbana: University of Illinois Press.

Jones, E. L. 1987. *The European Miracle*. 2nd ed. Cambridge: Cambridge University Press.

———. 2003. *The European Miracle*. 3rd ed. Cambridge: Cambridge University Press.

———. 1988. *Growth Recurring: Economic Growth in World History*. 2nd ed. Ann Arbor: University of Michigan Press.

Jones, Evan T., and Alwyn Ruddock. 2008. "John Cabot and the Discovery of America." *Historical Research* 81: 224–54.

Jones, Gwyn. 1986. *The Norse Atlantic Saga: Being the Norse Voyages of Discovery and Settlement to Iceland, Greenland, and North America*. Oxford: Oxford University Press.

———. 1984. *A History of the Vikings*. 2nd edition. Oxford: Oxford University Press.

Jones, W. T. 1969. *The Medieval Mind*. New York: Harcourt, Brace, and World.

Joravsky, David. *The Lysenko Affair*. Chicago: University of Chicago Press.

Jung-Pang Lo. 1955. "The Emergence of China as a Sea Power during the Late Sung and Early Yuan Periods." *Far Eastern Quarterly* 14: 489–503.

Kaelber, Lutz. 1998. *Schools of Asceticism: Ideology and Organization in Medieval Religious Communities*. University Park, PA: Pennsylvania State University Press.

Kadushin, Max. 1965. *The Rabbinic Mind*. 2nd ed. New York: Blaisdell.

Kamen, Henry. 1978. "The Decline of Spain: A Historical Myth." *Past and Present* 1: 24–50.

———. 2002. *Spain's Road to Empire: The Making of a World Power, 1492–1763*. London: Allen Kane.

Karsh, Efraim. 2007. *Islamic Imperialism: A History*. New Haven: Yale University Press.

Kearney, H. F. 1964. "Puritanism, Capitalism, and the Scientific Revolution." *Past and Present* 28: 81–101.

Keegan, John. 1993. *A History of Warfare*. London: Hutchinson.

Keen, Maurice. 1999. "The Changing Scene: Guns, Gunpowder, and Permanent Armies." In Maurice Keen, ed., *Medieval Warfare*, 273–91. Oxford: Oxford University Press.

Kehr, Marguerite Witmer. 1916. "The Doctrine of the Self in St. Augustine and in Descartes." *Philosophical Review* 25: 5687–615.

Kelsey, Harry. 1998. *Sir Francis Drake, the Queen's Pirate*. New Haven: Yale University Press.

Kemp, Peter, ed. 1976. *The Oxford Companion to Ships and the Sea*. Oxford: Oxford University Press.

Khalidi, Tarif. 1975. *Islamic Historiography*. Albany, NY: State University of New York Press.

Kimball, Roger. 2008. *Tenured Radicals*. 3rd ed. Chicago: Ivan R. Dee.

Kim, Hyojoung, and Steven Pfaff. 2012. "Structure and Dynamics of Religious Insurgency: Students and the Spread of the Reformation." *American Sociological Review* 77: 188–215.

King, Peter. 1999. *Western Monasticism: A History of the Monastic Movement in the Latin Church*. Kalamazoo, MI: Cistercian Publications.

King, P. W. 1973. "The Production and Consumption of Iron in Early Modern England and Wales." *Economic History Review* 57: 1–33.

Kister, James. 1986. "The Massacre of the Banu Qurayza: A Re-examination of a Tradition." *Jerusalem Studies of Arabic and Islam* 8: 61–96.

Kittleson, James. 1986. *Luther the Reformer*. Minneapolis: Augsburg Fortress.

Klein, Herbert S. 1969. "Anglicanism, Catholicism, and the Negro Slave." In Laura Foner and Eugene D. Genovese, eds., *Slavery in the New World: A Reader in Comparative History*, 138–69. Englewood Cliffs, NJ: Prentice-Hall.

———. 1967. *Slavery in the Americas: A Comparative Study of Virginia and Cuba*. Chicago: University of Chicago Press.

Klein, Maury. 2007. *The Genesis of Industrial America, 1870–1920*. Cambridge: Cambridge University Press.

Kleinberg, Andreas, Christian Marx, Eberhard Knobloch, and Dieter Leigemann. 2011. *Germania und die Isle Thule*. Darmstadt: WBG.

Klima, Gyula. 2008. *John Buridan*. New York: Oxford University Press.

Kocher, Paul H. 1953. *Science and Religion in Elizabethan England*. San Marino, CA: The Huntington Library.

Kollek, Teddy, and Moshe Pearlman. 1970. *Pilgrims in the Holy Land*. New York: Harper and Row.

Kollias, Elias. 2003. *The Knights of Rhodes—the Palace and the City*. Athens: Ekdotike Athenon.

Konstam, Angus. 2003. *Lepanto 1571*. Oxford: Osprey.

———. 2008. *Sovereigns of the Sea: The Quest to Build the Perfect Renaissance Battleship*. New York: Wiley.

Kox, Willem, Wim Meeus, and Harm t'Hart. 1991. "Religious Conversion of Adolescents: Testing the Lofland and Stark Model of Religious Conversion." *Sociological Analysis* 52: 227–40.

Kreutz, Barbara M. 1973. "Mediterranean Contributions to the Medieval Mariner's Compass." *Technology and Culture* 14: 367–83.

Kroeber, A. L. 1944. *Configurations of Culture Growth*. Berkeley: University of California Press.

Lacey, Jim. 2011. *The First Clash: The Miraculous Greek Victory at Marathon and Its Impact on Western Civilization*. New York: Bantam Books.

Lamb, Hubert. 1965. "The Early Medieval Warm Epoch and its Sequel." *Palaeography, Palaeoclimatology, Palaeoecology* 1: 13–37.

LaMonte, John L. 1932. *Feudal Monarchy in the Latin Kingdom of Jerusalem, 1100–1291*. Cambridge, MA: Harvard University Press.

Landes, David S. 2003. *The Unbound Prometheus*. 2nd ed. Cambridge: Cambridge University Press.

———. 1998. *The Wealth and Poverty of Nations*. New York: W. W. Norton.

———. 1994. "What Room for Accident in History? Explaining Big Changes by Small Events." *Economic History Review* 47: 637–56.

Lane, Frederic Chopin. 1973. *Venice: A Maritime Republic*. Baltimore: Johns Hopkins University Press.

Larner, John. 1999. *Marco Polo and the Discovery of the World*. New Haven: Yale University Press.

Latouche, Robert. 1961. *The Birth of Western Economy*. London: Methuen.

Latourette, Kenneth Scott. 1975. *A History of Christianity*. Vol. 2. Rev. ed. San Francisco: HarperSanFrancisco.

LeBlanc, Steven A. 2007. *Prehistoric Warfare in the American Southwest*. Salt Lake City: University of Utah Press.

League of Nations. 1945. *Industrialization and Foreign Trade*. Geneva: League of Nations.

Leff, Gordon. [1969] 1999. *Heresy in the Later Middle Ages*. London: Sandpiper Books.

Leighton, Albert C. 1972. *Transport and Communication in Early Medieval Europe, A.D. 500–1100*. Newton Abbot, UK: David and Charles.

Lenski, Gerhard, Patrick Nolan, and Jean Lenski. 1995. *Human Societies: An Introduction to Macrosociology*. 7th ed. New York: McGraw-Hill.

Lester, Toby. 2009. *The Fourth Part of the World*. New York: Free Press.

Levathes, Louise. 1994. *When China Ruled the Seas: The Treasure Fleet of the Dragon Throne*. New York: Simon and Schuster.

Levine, Lee I. 1998. *Judaism and Hellenism in Antiquity*. Seattle: University of Washington Press.

Lewis, Archibald R. 1969. *Emerging Medieval Europe, AD 400–1000*. New York: Knopf.

———. 1951. *Naval Power and Trade in the Mediterranean, A.D. 500–1100*. Princeton: Princeton University Press.

Lewis, Bernard. 1990. *Race and Slavery in the Middle East*. Oxford: Oxford University Press.

———. 2002. *What Went Wrong?* Oxford: Oxford University Press.

Lewis, M. J. T. 1997. *Millstone and Hammer: The Origins of Water Power*. Hull, UK: University of Hull Press.

Lieberman, Saul. 1945. *Greek in Jewish Palestine*. New York: Jewish Theological Seminary of America.

———. 1962. *Hellenism in Jewish Palestine*. 2nd ed. New York: Jewish Theological Seminary of America.

Liebeschuetz, J. H. W. G. 1979. *Continuity and Change in Roman Religion*. Oxford: Clarendon.

Lilley, Samuel. 1966. *Men, Machines, and History*. New York: International Publishers.

Lindberg, David C. 1992. *The Beginnings of Western Science*. Chicago: University of Chicago Press.

———. 1986. "Science and the Early Church." In David C. Lindberg and Ronald L. Numbers, eds. *God and Nature: Historical Essays on the Encounter between Christianity and Science*, 19–48. Berkeley: University of California Press.

———. 1978. *Science in the Middle Ages*. Chicago: University of Chicago Press.

Lindberg, David C., and Ronald L. Numbers, eds. 1986. *God and Nature: Historical Essays on the Encounter between Christianity and Science*. Berkeley: University of California Press.

Lindberg, David C., and Robert S. Westman, eds. 1990. *Reappraisals of the Scientific Revolution*. Cambridge: Cambridge University Press.

Little, Donald P. 1976. "Coptic Conversion to Islam under the Mahri Mamluks, 692–755/1293–1354." *Bulletin of the School of Oriental and African Studies*, University of London 39: 552–69.

Little, Lester K. 1978. *Religious Poverty and the Profit Economy in Medieval Europe*. Ithaca, NY: Cornell University Press.

Lloyd, Christopher. 1973. *The Search for the Niger*. London: Collins.

Lloyd, T. H. 1982. *Alien Merchants in England in the High Middle Ages*. New York: St. Martin's Press.

Lofland, John, and Rodney Stark. 1965. "Becoming a World-Saver: A Theory of Conversion to a Deviant Perspective." *American Sociological Review* 30: 862–75.

Lopez, Robert S. 1967. *The Birth of Europe*. New York: M. Evans.

———. 1976. *The Commercial Revolution of the Middle Ages, 950–1350*. Cambridge: Cambridge University Press.

———. 1969. "The Norman Conquest of Sicily." In Baldwin, 1969, 54–67.

———. 1979. "The Practical Transmission of Medieval Culture." In David Lyle Jeffrey, ed., *By Things Seen: Reference and Recognition in Medieval Thought*, 125–42. Ottawa: University of Ottawa Press.

———. 1952. "The Trade of Medieval Europe: The South." In Michael Postan and E. E. Rich, eds., *The Cambridge Economic History of Europe*. Vol. 2, *Trade and Industry in the Middle Ages*, 257–354. Cambridge: Cambridge University Press.

Luther, Martin. [1520] 1915. *Works*. Vol. 2. Philadelphia: Muhlenberg Press.

Luce, J. V. 1971. "Ancient Explorers." In Geoffrey Ashe, et al., eds. *The Quest for America*, 53–95. New York: Praeger.

Luttwak, Edward N. 1976. *The Grand Strategy of the Roman Empire*. Baltimore: Johns Hopkins University Press.

Lyons, Martyn. 2010. *A History of Reading and Writing: In the Western World*. New York: Palgrave Macmillan.

Mabry, R. H., and A. D. Sharplin. 1986. "Does More Technology Create Unemployment?" *Policy Analysis* 68 (March 18, 1986).

MacCulloch, Diarmaid. 2010. "Evil Is Just." *London Review of Books* 32 (May 13): 23–24.

———. 2004. *Reformation*. New York: Viking.

Mackensen, Ruth Stellhorn. 1935. "Background of the History of Moslem Libraries." *American Journal of Semitic Languages and Literature* 51: 114–25.

MacMullen, Ramsay. 1988. *Corruption and the Decline of Rome*. New Haven: Yale University Press.

———. 1981. *Paganism in the Roman Empire*. New Haven: Yale University Press.

Macmurray, John. 1938. *The Clue to History*. London: Student Christian Movement Press.

MacQuarrie, Kim. 2008. *The Last Days of the Incas*. New York: Simon and Schuster.

Madden, Thomas F. 1999. *A Concise History of the Crusades*. Lanham, MD: Rowman and Littlefield.

Magnus, Shulamit S. 1997. *Jewish Emancipation in a German City, Cologne, 1798–1871*. Stanford, CA: Stanford University Press.

Major, J. Kenneth. 1996. "Water, Wind and Animal Power." In Ian McNeil, ed., *An Encyclopedia of the History of Technology*, 229–71. London: Routledge.

Maltby, William S. 2002. *The Reign of Charles V*. New York: St. Martin's Press.

———. 2009. *The Rise and Fall of the Spanish Empire*. New York: Palgrave/Macmillan.

Man, John. 2000. *Alpha Beta: How 26 Letters Shaped the Western World*. New York: John Wiley and Sons.

Manchester, William. 1993. *A World Lit Only by Fire*. New York: Little, Brown.

Mangum, Garth L. 1965. *The Manpower Revolution: Its Policy Consequences*. New York: Doubleday.

Marcus, G. J. 1961. *A Naval History of England I: The Formative Centuries*. Boston: Little, Brown.

Mariscal, Elisa, and Kenneth L. Sokoloff. 2000. "Schooling, Suffrage, and the Persistence of Inequality in the Americas, 1800–1945." In Stephen Haber, ed., *Political Institutions and Economic Growth in Latin America*, 159–217. Stanford, CA: Hoover Institution Press.

Marozzi, Justin. 2004. *Tamerlane: Sword of Islam, Conqueror of the World*. Cambridge, MA: De Capo Books.

Marty, Martin. 2004. *Martin Luther*. New York: Viking.

Marx, Karl. [1845] 1998. *The German Ideology*. Amherst: Prometheus Books.

Mason, Stephen F. 1962. *A History of the Sciences*. Rev. ed. New York: Macmillan.

———. 1950. "Some Historical Roots of the Scientific Revolution." *Science and Society* 14: 237–64.

Massie, Robert K. 2003. *Castles of Steel: Britain, Germany, and the Winning of the Great War at Sea*. New York: Random House.

———. 1992. *Dreadnought: Britain, Germany, and the Coming of the Great War*. New York: Ballantine Books.

Matthew, Donald. 1992. *The Norman Kingdom of Sicily*. Cambridge: Cambridge University Press.

Mattingly, Garrett. 1962. *The Armada*. Boston: Houghton Mifflin.

Mattingly, Harold. 1967. *Christianity in the Roman Empire*. New York: W. W. Norton.

Mawer, Allen. 1924. "The Vikings." *The Cambridge Medieval History*, vol. 3, 309–39. New York: Macmillan.

May, William E., and John L. Howard. 1981. "Compass." *Encyclopedia Britannica*. 15th ed.

Mayr-Harting, Henry. 1993. "The West: The Age of Conversion (700–1050)." In John McManners, ed., *The Oxford History of Christianity*. Oxford: Oxford University Press: 101–29.

McBrien, Richard P. 2000. *Lives of the Popes*. San Francisco: HarperSanFrancisco.

McCloskey, Deirdre N. 2010. *Bourgeois Dignity: Why Economics Can't Explain the Modern World*. Chicago: University of Chicago Press.

———. 2007. *The Bourgeois Virtues: Ethics for an Age of Commerce*. Chicago: University of Chicago Press.

———. 1994. "The Industrial Revolution, 1780–1860: a Survey." In Roderick Floud and Deirdre McCloskey, eds., *The Economic History of Britain Since 1700*, vol. 1, 242–73. New York: Cambridge University Press.

McCormick, Michael. 2001. *Origins of the European Economy: Commerce and Communication A.D. 300–900*. Cambridge: Harvard University Press.

McGarry, Daniel D. 1976. *Medieval History and Civilization*. New York: Macmillan.

McLendon, Hiram J. 1959. "Plato without God." *Journal of Religion* 39: 88–102.

McNeil, Ian, ed. 1996. *An Encyclopedia of the History of Technology*. London: Routledge.

McNeill, William H. 1972. *Plagues and Peoples*. Garden City, NY: Doubleday.

———. 1982. *The Pursuit of Power: Technology, Armed Force, and Society Since A.D. 1000*. Chicago: University of Chicago Press.

———. 1963. *The Rise of the West*. Chicago: University of Chicago Press.

McNickle, D'Arcy. 1975. *They Came First: the Epic of the American Indian*. New York; Harper and Row.

Mead, Simon, Michael P. H. Stumpf, Jerome Whitfield, Jonathan A. Beck, Mark Poulter, Tracy Campbell, James B. Uphill, David Goldstein, Michael Alpers, Elizabeth M. C. Fisher, and John Collinge. 2003. "Balancing Selection at the Prion Protein Gene Consistent with Prehistoric Kurulike Epidemics." *Science* 25 (April): 640–43.

Medina-Elizalde, Martin, and Eelco J. Rohling, 2012. "Collapse of Classic Maya Civilization Related to Modest Reduction in Precipitation." *Science* 24: 956–59.

Meeks, Wayne A. 1983. *The First Urban Christians*. New Haven: Yale University Press.

Meltzer, Milton. 1993. *Slavery: A World History*. New York: Da Capo Press.

Mendelsson, Kurt. 1976. *The Secret of Western Domination*. New York: Praeger.

Menocal, Maria Rosa. 2002. *The Ornament of the World: How Muslims, Jews, and Christians Created a Culture of Tolerance in Medieval Spain*. Boston: Little, Brown and Company.

Menzies, Gavin. 2002. *1421: The Year China Discovered America*. New York: Harper Perennial.

Merton, Robert K. 1938. "Science, Technology and Society in Seventeenth Century England." *Osiris* 4 (1938): 360–632.

Messenger, Charles. 1996. "Weapons and Armour." In Ian McNeil, ed., *An Encyclopedia of the History of Technology*. London: Routledge: 967–1011.

Metcalf, D. M. 1967. "The Prosperity of North-Western Europe in the Eighth and Ninth Centuries." *Economic History Review*. 20: 344–57.

Meyer, Hans. 1994. *The Philosophy of St. Thomas Aquinas*. St. Louis: B. Herder.

Michael, Robert. 2006. *Holy Hatred: Christianity, Antisemitism, and the Holocaust*. New York: Palgrave Macmillan.

Migeotte, Leopold. 2009. *The Economy of Greek Cities*. Berkeley: University of California Press.

Millar, Simon. 2008. *Vienna 1683: Christian Europe Repels the Ottomans*. New York: Osprey.

Miller, Edward. 1965. "The Fortunes of the English Textile Industry during the Thirteenth Century." *Economic History Review* 18: 64–82.

Mitchell, B. R. 1962. *Abstract of British Historical Statistics*. Cambridge: Cambridge University Press.

Mitchell, Joseph B., and Edward S. Creasy. 1964. *Twenty Decisive Battles of the World*. New York: Macmillan.

Moeller, Bernd. 1972. *Imperial Cities and the Reformation: Three Essays*. Philadelphia: Fortress Press.

Moffett, Samuel Hugh. 1992. *A History of Christianity in Asia*. Vol. 1. San Francisco: HarperSanFrancisco.

Mokyr, Joel. 2009. *The Enlightened Economy: An Economic History of Britain 1700–1850*. New Haven: Yale University Press.

———. 1992. *The Lever of Riches: Technological Creativity and Economic Progress*. Oxford: oxford University Press.

———. 2003. "Why Was the Industrial Revolution a European Phenomenon?" *Supreme Court Economic Review* 10: 27–63.

Monroe, Arthus Eli. 1975. *Early Economic Thought: Selections from Economic Literature Prior to Adam Smith*. New York: Gordon Press.

Montgomery, Field-Marshal Viscount (Bernard). 1968. *A History of Warfare*. New York: World.

Moody, Ernest A. 1970. "Albert of Saxony." *Dictionary of Scientific Biography*, vol. 1, 93–95. New York: Charles Scribner's Sons.

Mooers, Colin, 1991. *The Making of Bourgeois Europe*. London: Verso (New Left Books).

Morford, Mark. 2002. *Roman Philosophers*. New York: Routledge.

Morgan, Edmund S. 1942. "The Puritans and Sex." *New England Quarterly* 15: 591–607.

Morison, Samuel Eliot. 1971. *The European Discovery of America: The Northern Voyages*. New York: Oxford University Press.

———. 1974. *The European Discovery of America: The Southern Voyages*. New York: Oxford University Press.

———. 1972. *The Oxford History of the American People*. New York: Mentor.

Moritz, Ludwig Alfred. 1958. *Grain-Mills and Flour in Classical Antiquity*. Oxford: Oxford University Press.

Mornet, Daniel. 1947. *Les origines intellectuelles de la Révolution française 1715-1787*. Paris: Librairie Armand Olin.

Morris, Colin. 1993. "Christian Civilization (1050–1400)." In John McManners, ed., *The Oxford History of Christianity*, 205–42. Oxford: Oxford University Press.

———. [1972] 2000. *The Discovery of the Individual, 1050–1200*. Toronto: University of Toronto Press.

Morris, Ian. 2010. *Why the West Rules—For Now*. New York: Farrar, Straus and Giroux.

———. 2009. "The Greater Athenian State." In Ian Morris and Walter Scheidel. eds., *The Dynamics of Ancient Empires*, 99–177. Oxford: Oxford University Press.

Morris, Ian, and Walter Scheidel. eds. 2009. *The Dynamics of Ancient Empires*. Oxford: Oxford University Press.

Morrison, James E. 2007. *The Astrolabe*. London: Janus.

Mullett, Michael A. 1999. *The Catholic Reformation*. New York and Oxford: Routledge.

Mumford, Lewis. 1967. *The Myth of the Machine*. Vol. 1. New York: Harcourt Brace Jovanovich.

———. 1939. *Technics and Civilization*. New York: Harcourt Brace.

Murphey, Rhoads. 1999. *Ottoman Warfare 1500–1700*. New Brunswick, NJ: Rutgers University Press.

Musset, Lucien. [1965] 1993. *The Germanic Invasions: The Making of Europe AD 400–600*. New York: Barnes and Noble.

Nafzinger, George F., and Mark W. Walton. *Islam at War*. Westport: Praeger.

Nash, Ronald H. 1992. *The Gospel and the Greeks*. Richardson, TX: Probe Books.

Nasr, Seyyed Hossein. 1993. *An Introduction to Islamic Cosmological Doctrines*. Albany: State University of New York Press.

———. 1968. *Science and Civilization in Islam*. Cambridge: Harvard University Press.

McNally, Robert E., SJ. 1969. "The Reformation: A Catholic Reappraisal." In John C. Olin, James D. Smart, and Robert E. McNally, SJ, eds., *Luther, Erasmus, and the Reformation*, 26–47. New York: Fordham University Press.

Needham, Joseph. 1954. *Science and Civilization in China*. Vol. 1. Cambridge: Cambridge University Press.

———. 1956. *Science and Civilization in China*. Vol. 2. Cambridge: Cambridge University Press.

Nef, John. 1932. *The Rise of the British Coal Industry*. London: Routledge.

Nelson, Benjamin. 1969. *The Idea of Usury: From Tribal Brotherhood to Universal Otherhood*. 2nd ed. Chicago: University of Chicago Press.

Newton, Isaac. [1687] 1971. *The Motion of Bodies*. Vol. 1 of *Principia*. Berkeley: University of California Press.

Nicholas, David. 1997. *The Growth of the Medieval City: From Late Antiquity to the Early Fourteenth Century*. London: Longman.

———. 1991. "Of Poverty and Primacy: Demand, Liquidity, and the Flemish Economic Miracle, 1050–1200." *American Historical Review* 96: 17–41.

Nickerson, Colin. 1999. "In Iceland, Spirits Are in the Material World." *Seattle Post-Intelligencer*, December 25, A12.

Nicolle, David. 2000. *Constantinople 1453: The End of Byzantium*. Oxford: Osprey Publishing.

———. 1964. "Byzantium and the Papacy in the Eleventh Century." *Journal of Ecclesiastical History* 13: 1–20.

———. 1999. *Medieval Warfare Sourcebook: Warfare in Western Christendom*. London: Brockhampton Press.

Nisbet, Robert. 1980. *History of the Idea of Progress*. New York: Basic Books.

———. 1973. "The Myth of the Renaissance." *Comparative Studies in History of Society* 15: 473–92.

Norris, John. 2003. *Early Gunpowder Artillery, ca. 1300–1600*. Ramsbury, UK: Crowood Press.

North, Douglass C. 1982. *Growth and Welfare in the American Past*. Englewood Cliffs, NJ: Prentice-Hall.

North, Douglass C., and Robert Paul Thomas. 1973. *The Rise of the Western World: A New Economic History*. Cambridge: Cambridge University Press.

Norwich, John Julius. 1991. *Byzantium: The Apogee*. New York: Alfred A. Knopf.

————. 1995. *Byzantium: The Decline and Fall*. New York: Alfred A. Knopf.

————. 1997. *A Short History of Byzantium*. New York: Vintage Books.

Oakeshott, R. Ewart. [1960] 1996. *The Archaeology of Weapons*. Mineola, NY: Dover.

Oberman, Heiko. 1992. *Luther: Man between God and the Devil*. New York: Doubleday.

O'Brien, Patrick. 1982. "European Economic Development: The Contribution of the Periphery." *Economic History Review* 35: 1–18.

————. 1983a. "European Economic Development: A Reply." *Economic History Review* 36: 584–85.

————. 1983b. *Railways and the Economic Development of Western Europe, 1830–1914*. London: Palgrave Macmillan.

O'Donnell, James J. 2009. *The Ruin of the Roman Empire*. New York: Ecco.

Olsen, Glenn. 1969. "Italian Merchants and the Performance of Papal Banking Functions in the Early Thirteenth Century." In David Herlihy, Robert S. Lopez, and Vsevold Slessarev, *Economy, Society, and Government in Medieval Italy: Essays in Memory of Robert L. Reynolds*. Kent, OH: Kent State University Press.

Oppenheim, A. Leo. 1977. *Ancient Mesopotamia*. Rev. ed. Chicago: University of Chicago Press.

Osborne, Roger. 2006. *Civilization: A New History of the Western World*. New York: Pegasus Books.

Ozment, Stephen. 1980. *The Age of Reform 1250–1550: An Intellectual and Religious History of Late Medieval and Reformation Europe*. New Haven: Yale University Press.

————. 1975. *The Reformation in the Cities*. New Haven: Yale University Press.

Pagnamenta, Peter. 2012. *Prairie Fever*. New York: Norton.

Palmer, Alan. 1994. *The Decline and Fall of the Ottoman Empire*. New York: Barnes and Noble.

Panaccio, Claude. 2004. *Ockham on Concepts*. Aldershot, UK: Ashgate.

Panzer, Joel S. 996. *The Popes and Slavery*. New York: Alba House.

Parker, Geoffrey. 1972. *The Army of Flanders and the Spanish Road*. Cambridge: Cambridge University Press.

————. [1988] 2010. *The Military Revolution: Military Innovation and the Rise of the West, 1500–1800*. Cambridge: Cambridge University Press.

————. 1970. "Spain, Her Enemies, and the Revolt of the Netherlands 1559–1648" *Past and Present* 49: 72–95.

————. 1992. "Success and Failure during the First Century of the Reformation." *Past and Present* 136: 43–82.

Payne-Gallwey, Ralph. 2007. *The Crossbow: Its Military and Sporting History, Construction, and Use*. New York: Skyhorse Press.

Payne, Robert. [1959] 1995. T*he History of Islam*. New York: Barnes and Noble.

Pederson, Olaf. 1985. "In Quest of Sacrobosco." *Journal for the History of Astronomy* 16: 175–221.

Peters, F. E. 1993. *The Distant Shrine: The Islamic Centuries in Jerusalem*. New York: A.M.S. Press.

Phelps Brown, E. H., and S. V. Hopkins. 1962. "Seven Centuries of prices of Consumables, compared with Builders' Wage-Rates." In E. M. Carus-Wilson, ed., *Essays in Economic History*, vol. 2, 179–96.

Phillips, Jonathan. 1995. "The Latin East 1098–1291." In Jonathan Riley-Smith, ed., *The Oxford Illustrated History of the Crusades*, 112–40. Oxford: Oxford University Press.

Phillips, J. R. S. 1998. *The Medieval Expansion of Europe*. Oxford: Clarendon Press.

Pickthall, M. M. 1927. *The Cultural Side of Islam*. New Delhi: Kitab Bhanan.

Pirenne, Henri. [1927] 1939. *Medieval Cities: Their Origins and the Revival of Trade*. Princeton: Princeton University Press.

Pomeranz, Kenneth. 2000. *The Great Divergence: China, Europe, and the Making of the Modern World Economy*. Princeton: Princeton University Press.

Ponting, Clive. 2000. *World History: A New Perspective*. London: Chatto and Windus.

Porter, Roy. 1998. *The Greatest Benefit to Mankind: A Medical History of Humanity*. New York: W. W. Norton.

Pounds, N. J. G. 1974. *An Economic History of Medieval Europe*. London: Longman.

Prawer, Joshua. 1972. *The Crusaders' Kingdom: European Colonialism in the Middle Ages*. New York: Praeger.

Privat, Karen L., Tamsin C. O'Connell, and Michael P. Richards. 2002. "Stable Isotope Analysis of Human and Faunal Remains from the Anglo-Saxon Cemetery at Berinsfield, Oxfordshire: Dietary and Social Implcations." *Journal of Archaeological Science* 29: 779–90.

Postan, Michael. 1973. *Medieval Agriculture and General Problems*. Cambridge: Cambridge University Press.

———. 1952. "The Trade of Medieval Europe: The North." In Michael Postan and E. E. Rich, eds., *The Cambridge Economic History of Europe*. Vol. 2, *Trade and Industry in the Middle Ages*, 119–256. Cambridge: Cambridge University Press.

Pyle, Howard. 1888. *Otto of the Silver Hand*. New York: Charles Scribner's Sons.

Rabb, Theodore K. 1965. "Religion and the Rise of Modern Science." *Past and Present* 31: 111–26.

Raftus, J. A. 1958. "The Concept of Just Price: Theory and Economic Policy: Discussion." *Journal of Economic History* 18: 435–37.

Rahner, Karl. 1975. *Encyclopedia of Theology*. New York: Seabury Press.

Rait, Robert S. 1918. *Life in the Medieval University*. Cambridge: Cambridge University Press.

Randall, John Herman, Jr. 1970. *Hellenistic Ways of Deliverance and the Making of the Christian Synthesis*. New York: Columbia University Press.

Rashdall, Hastings. [1936] 1977. *The Universities of Europe in the Middle Ages*. 3 vols. Oxford: Oxford University Press.

Read, Conyers. 1933. "Queen Elizabeth's Seizure of the Duke of Alva's Pay-Ships." *Journal of Modern History* 5: 443–64.

Reden, Sitta von. 2007. "Classical Greece: Consumption." In Walter Scheidel, Ian Morris, and Richard Saller, 2007, 385–406.

Reilly, Robert R. 2011. *The Closing of the Muslim Mind*. Wilmington: ISI Books.

Reuter, Timothy. 1999. "Carolingian and Ottonian Warfare." In Maurice Keen, ed., *Medieval Warfare*, 13–35. Oxford: Oxford University Press.

Reynolds, John Mark. 2009. *When Athens Met Jerusalem*. Downers Grove, IL: IVP Academic.

Reynolds, Susan. 1994. *Fiefs and Vassals: The Medieval Evidence Reinterpreted*. Oxford: Oxford University Press.

Reynolds, Terry S. 1983. *Stronger than a Hundred Men: A History of the Vertical Water Wheel*. Baltimore: Johns Hopkins University Press.

Rickards, Colin. 1966. *Bowler Hats and Stetsons: Stories of Englishmen in the Wild West*. Woodinville, WA: Bonanza Press.

Ricketts, Glenn, Peter W. Wood, Stephen H. Balch, and Ashley Thorne. 2011. *The Vanishing American West: 1964–2010: The Disappearance of Western Civilization from the American Undergraduate Curriculum*. Princeton: National Association of Scholars.

Riley-Smith, Jonathan. 1973. *The Feudal Nobility and the Kingdom of Jerusalem, 1174–1277*. New York: Macmillan.

———. 1997. *The First Crusaders, 1095–1131*. Cambridge: Cambridge University Press.

Rirdan, Daniel. 2012. *The Blueprint: Averting Global Collapse*. Louisville, CO: Corinno Press.

Roberts, J. M. 1998. *The Triumph of the West*. New York: Barnes and Noble.

Roberts, Michael. 1968. *The Early Vasas: A History of Sweden, 1523–1611*. Cambridge: Cambridge University Press.

Roberts, William L. 1978. *Cold Rolling of Steel*. Boca Raton: CRC Press.

Rodinson, Maxime. 1978. *Islam and Capitalism*. Austin: University of Texas Press.

———. 1980. *Muhammad*. New York: Random House.

Rodney, Walter. 1984. *How Europe Underdeveloped Africa*. Washington, DC: Howard University Press.

Rogers, Clifford. 1999. "The Age of the Hundred Years War." In Maurice Keen, ed., *Medieval Warfare*, 136–60. Oxford: Oxford University Press.

Ronald, Susan. 2008. *The Pirate Queen: Queen Elizabeth I, Her Pirate Adventurers, and the Dawn of Empire*. New York: Harper Collins.

Root, Hilton L. 1994. *The Fountain of Privilege*. Berkeley: University of California Press.

Ropars, Guy, Gabriel Gorre, Albert Le Floch, Jay Enoch, and Vasudevan Lakshminarayanan. 2011. "A Depolarizer as a Possible Precise Sunstone for Viking Navigation by Polarized Skylight." *Proceedings of the Royal Society: A Mathematical, Physical, and Engineering Science*. http://rspa.royalsocietypublishing.org/content/468/2139/671. Accessed January 14, 2014.

Rorig, Fritz. 1969. *The Medieval Town*. Berkeley: University of California Press.

Rose, Susan. 2002. *Medieval Naval Warfare 1000–1500*. London: Routledge.

Rosen, Edward. 1971. *Three Copernican Treatises*. 3rd ed. New York: Octagon Books.

Rosen, William. 2010. *The Most Powerful Idea in the World: A Story of Steam, Industry, and Invention*. Chicago: University of Chicago Press.

Rosenberg, Nathan, and L. E. Birdzell Jr. 1986. *How the West Grew Rich: The Economic Transformation of the Industrial World*. New York: Basic Books.

Rostovtzeff, Michael. 1926. *The Social and Economic History of the Roman Empire*. Oxford: Clarendon Press.

Royal, Robert. 1992. *1492 And All That*. Washington, DC: Ethics and Public Policy Center.

Ruby, Robert H., and John A. Brown. 1993. *Indian Slavery in the Pacific Northwest*. Spoke, WA: Clark.

Runciman, Sir Steven. 1965. *The Fall of Constantinople 1453*. Cambridge: Cambridge University Press.

———. 1951. *A History of the Crusades*. 3 vols. Cambridge: Cambridge University Press.

———. 1969. "The Pilgrimages to Palestine Before 1095." In Baldwin, 1969: 68–78.

Rupp, Ernest Gordon. 1981. "Luther, Martin." *Encyclopaedia Britannica*. 15th ed. Chicago: University of Chicago Press.

Russell, Bertrand. 1970. *Marriage and Morals*. New York: Liveright.

———. 1959. *Wisdom of the West*. New York: Doubleday.

Russell, Josiah Cox. 1958. *Late Ancient and Medieval Population*. Transactions of the

American Philosophical Society, n.s., 48, no. 3: 3–152. Philadelphia: American Philosophical Society.

———. 1987. *Medieval Demography*. New York: AMS Press.

———. 1972a. *Medieval Regions and Their Cities*. Newton Abbot, UK: David and Charles.

———. 1972b. "Population in Europe." In Carlo M. Cipolla, ed., *The Fontana Economic History of Europe*. Vol. 1, *The Middle Ages*. Glasgow: Collins/Fontana: 25–71.

Russell, Jeffrey Burton. 1991. *Inventing the Flat Earth: Columbus and Modern Historians*. New York: Praeger.

Russell, Peter. 2000. *Prince Henry "the Navigator": A Life*. New Haven: Yale University Press.

Russell, W. M. S. 1967. *Man, Nature, and History*, London: Aldus Books.

Russell-Wood, A. J. R. 1998. *The Portuguese Empire 1415–1808*. Baltimore: Johns Hopkins University Press.

Ruyle, Eugene R. 1973. "Slavery, Surplus, and Stratification on the Northwest Coast." *Current Anthropology* 14: 603–31.

Saeed, Abdullah. 1996. *Islamic Banking and Interest*. Leiden: E. J. Brill.

Saggs, H. W. F. 1989. *Civilization Before Greece and Rome*. New Haven: Yale University Press.

Sale, Kirkpatrick. 1990. *The Conquest of Paradise: Christopher Columbus and the Columbian Legacy*. New York: Knopf.

Saliba, George. 2007. *Islamic Science and the Making of the European Renaissance*. Cambridge: MIT Press.

Sanders, Jason L. 1997. *Greek and Roman Philosophy After Aristotle*. New York: The Free Press.

Sanders, John. 1994. "Historical Considerations." In Clark Pinnock, Richard Rice, John Sanders, William Hasker, and David Basinger, eds., *The Openness of God*, 59–100. Downer's Grove, IL: InterVarsity Press.

Sawyer, P. H. 1982. *Kings and Vikings*. London: Methuen.

Sawyer, P. H., and Birgit Sawyer. 1993. *Medieval Scandinavia*. Minneapolis: University of Minnesota Press.

Schachner, Nathan. 1938. *The Medieval Universities*. New York: Frederick A. Stokes.

Scheidel, Walter. 2007. "Demography." In Walter Scheidel, Ian Morris, and Richard Saller, eds. 2007. *The Cambridge Economic History of the Greco-Roman World*. Cambridge: Cambridge University Press: 38–86.

Scheidel, Walter, Ian Morris, and Richard Saller, eds. 2007. *The Cambridge Economic History of the Greco-Roman World*. Cambridge: Cambridge University Press.

Schele, Linda, and David Freidel. 1990. *A Forest of Kings: The Untold Story of the Ancient Maya*. New York: William Morrow.

Schlaifer, Robert. 1936. "Greek Theories of Slavery from Homer to Aristotle." *Harvard Studies in Classical Philology* 47: 165–204.

Schwiebert, Ernest. 1950. *Luther and His Times*. St. Louis: Concordia.

———. 1996. *The Reformation*. Vol. 2, *The Reformation as a University Movement*. Minneapolis: Fortress.

Schafer, Judith Kelleher. 1994. *Slavery, the Civil Law, and the Supreme Court of Louisiana*. Baton Rouge: Louisiana State University Press.

Shapin, Steven. 1996. *The Scientific Revolution*. Chicago: University of Chicago Press.

Shapiro, Barbara J. 1968. "Latitudinarism and Science in Seventeenth-Century England." *Past and Present* 40: 16–41.

Shaw, Jane S. 2012. "Study of 'Western Civ' Essential Here and Now." *Albuquerque Journal*, May 19, A7.

Shaw, Stanford. 1971. *Between Old and New: The Ottoman Empire under Selim III: 1789–1807*. Cambridge, MA: Harvard University Press.

Shea, William R. 1886. "Galileo and the Church." In Lindberg and Numbers, 1986, 114–135.

Shedd, Thomas Clark. 1981. "Railroads and Locomotives." *Encyclopaedia Britannica*. Chicago: University of Chicago Press.

Siberry, Elizabeth. 1995. "Images of the Crusades in the Nineteenth and Twentieth Centuries." In Jonathan Riley-Smith, ed., *The Oxford Illustrated History of the Crusades*, 365–385. Oxford: Oxford University Press.

Simon, Joan. 1963. "The Social Origins of Cambridge Students, 1603–1640." *Past and Present* 26: 58–67.

Singman, Jeffrey L. 1999. *Daily Life in Medieval Europe*. Westport, CT: Greenwood Press.

Sire, H. J. A. 1993. *The Knights of Malta*. New Haven: Yale University Press.

Skelton, R. A., Thomas E. Marston, and George D. Painter. 1995. *The Vinland Map and the Tarter Relation*. New ed. New Haven: Yale University Press.

Sluiter, Engel. 1998. *The Gold and Silver of Spanish America*. Berkeley: University of California Press.

Smail, R. C. 1995. *Crusading Warfare, 1097–1193*. Cambridge: Cambridge University Press.

Smelser, Neil. 1994. *Sociology*. Cambridge, MA: Blackwell-UNESCO.

Smilde, David. 2005. "A Qualitative Comparative Analysis of Conversion to Venezuelan Evangelicalism: How Networks Matter." *American Journal of Sociology* 111: 757–96.

Smith, Adam. [1776] 1981. *An Inquiry into the Nature and Causes of the Wealth of Nations*. Glasgow ed. 2 vols. Indianapolis: Liberty Fund.

Smith, Chad Powers. 1954. *Yankees and God*. New York: Heritage House.

Smith, Morton. 1956. "Palestinian Judaism in the First Century." In Moshe Davis, *Israel: Its Role in Civilization*, 67–81. New York: Harper and Brothers.

———. 1987. *Palestinian Parties and Politics that Shaped the Old Testament*. 2nd ed. London: SCM Press.

Smith, N. Jeremy. 2009. "Making Cotton King." *World Trade* 22 (July 2009): 82.

Smith, William. 1867. *Dictionary of Greek and Roman Biography and Mythology*. 3 vols. Boston: Little, Brown.

Smoller, Laura A. 1994. *History, Prophesy, and the Stars: The Christian Astrology of Pierre D'Ailly, 1350–1420*. Princeton: Princeton University Press.

Sombart, Werner. 1902. *Der moderne Kapitalismus*. Leipzig: Duncker and Humblot.

Sordi, Marta. 1986. *The Christians and the Roman Empire*. Norman, OK: University of Oklahoma Press.

Southern, R. W. 1953. *The Making of the Middle Ages*. New Haven: Yale University Press.

———. 1970a. *Medieval Humanism and Other Studies*. New York: Harper Torchbooks.

———. 1970b. *Western Society and the Church in the Middle Ages*. London: Penguin Books.

Sowell, Thomas. 1998. *Conquests and Cultures: An International History*. New York: Basic Books.

Stannard, David E. 1993. *American Holocaust*. New York: Oxford University Press.

Stark, Rodney. 2006. *Cities of God*. San Francisco: HarperSanFrancisco.

———. 2007a. *Discovering God: The Origins of the Great Religions and the Evolution of Faith*. San Francisco: HarperOne.

———. 2004. *Exploring the Religious Life*. Baltimore: Johns Hopkins University Press.

———. 2003. *For the Glory of God: How Monotheism Led to Reformations, Science, Witch-Hunts, and the End of Slavery*. Princeton: Princeton University Press.

———. 2009. *God's Battalions: The Case for the Crusades*. San Francisco: HarperOne.

———. 2001. *One True God: Historical Consequence of Monotheism*. Princeton: Princeton University Press.

———. 2007b. Sociology. 10th ed. Belmont, CA: Wadsworth.

———. 2011. *The Triumph of Christianity: How the Jesus Movement Became the World's Largest Religion*. San Francisco: HarperOne.

———. 2005. *The Victory of Reason: How Christianity Led to Freedom, Capitalism, and Western Success*. New York: Random House.

Stark, Rodney, and Roger Finke. 2000. *Acts of Faith: Explaining the Human Side of Religion*. Berkeley: University of California Press.

Stark, Rodney, Eva Hamberg, and Alan S. Miller. 2005. "Exploring Spirituality and Unchurched Religions in America, Sweden, and Japan." *Journal of Contemporary Religion* 20: 1–21.

Stone, Lawrence. 1972. *The Causes of the English Revolution*. New York: Harper and Row.

———. 1964. "The Educational Revolution in England, 1560–1640." *Past and Present* 28: 41–80.

———. 1987. *The Past and the Present Revisited*. Rev. ed. New York: Routledge.

Stoye, John. 2007. *The Siege of Vienna*. New York: Pegasus Books.

Strauss, Gerald. 1978. *Luther's House of Learning: Introducing the Young in the German Reformation*. Baltimore: Johns Hopkins University Press

———. 1988. "The Reformation and Its Public in an Age of Orthodoxy." In *The German People and the Reformation*, 194–214. Ithaca, NY: Cornell University Press.

———. 1975. "Success and Failure in the German Reformation." *Past and Present* 67: 3063.

Subrahmanyam, Sanjay. 1997. *The Career and Legend of Vasco da Gamma*. Cambridge: Cambridge University Press.

Suttles, Wayne, and Aldona Jonaitis. 1990. "History of Research in Ethnology." In Wayne Suttles, ed., *Handbook of North American Indians*, vol. 7, 73–87. Washington, DC: Smithsonian Institution.

Swanson, Guy E. 1967. *Religion and Regime: A Sociological Account of the Reformation*. Ann Arbor, MI: University of Michigan Press.

Swatos, William II., Jr., and Loftur Reimar Gissurarson. 1997. *Icelandic Spiritualism*. New Brunswick, NJ: Transaction.

Taagepera, Rein. 1978. "Size and Duration of Empires: Growth and Decline Curves, 3000 to 600 BC." *Social Science Research* 7: 180–96.

———. 1979. "Size and Duration of Empires: Growth and Decline Curves, 600 BC to 600 AD." *Social Science History* 3: 115–38.

Tcherikover, Victor. [1959] 1999. *Hellenistic Civilization and the Jews*. Peabody, MA: Hendrickson.

Thomas, Hugh M. 1994. *Cortés and the Downfall of the Aztec Empire*. New York: Simon and Schuster.

———. 2003. *English and Normans*. Oxford: Oxford University Press.

————. 2010. *The Golden Empire*. New York: Random House.

————. 2005. *Rivers of Gold*. New York: Random House.

————. 1997. *The Slave Trade: The Story of the Atlantic Slave Trade, 1440–1870*. New York: Simon and Schuster.

Thomas, Rosalind. 1992. *Literacy and Orality in Ancient Greece*. Cambridge: Cambridge University Press.

Thornton, Bruce. 2000. *Greek Ways: How the Greeks Created Western Civilization*. San Francisco: Encounter Books.

Thornton, John. 1998. *Africa and Africans in Making the Atlantic World, 1400–1800*. 2nd ed. Cambridge: Cambridge University Press.

Tod, M. N. 1948. *Greek Historical Inscriptions*. 2 vols. Oxford: Oxford University Press.

Toynbee, Arnold J. 1936. *A Study of History*. Vol. 4, *The Breakdown of Civilizations*. London: George Allen and Unwin.

Tracy, James D. 1999. *Europe's Reformations, 1450–1650*. Lanham, MD: Rowman and Littlefield.

Trench, Chales Chenevix. 1979. *The Road to Khartoum: A Life of General Charles Gordon*. New York: Doreset Press.

Trevelyan, Raleigh. 2002. *Sir Walter Raleigh*. New York: Henry Holt.

Trevor-Roper, H. R. [1969] 2001. *The Crisis of the Seventeenth Century: Religion, the Reformation, and Social Change*. Indianapolis: Liberty Fund.

Truesdell, Clifford. 1968. *Essays in the History of Mechanics*. New York: Springer-Verlag.

Turnbull, Stephen. 2003. *The Ottoman Empire 1326–1699*. New York: Osprey.

————. 2004. *The Walls of Constantinople AD 324–1453*. New York: Osprey.

Turner, Christy G., II. 2011. *Man Corn: Cannibalism and Violence in the Prehistoric American Southwest*. Salt Lake City: University of Utah Press.

Turner, Ralph H., and Lewis M. Killian. 1987. *Collective Behavior*. 3rd ed. Englewood Ciffs, NJ: Prenstice-Hall.

Turney-High, Harry. 1971. *Primitive War: Its Practice and Concepts*. 2nd ed. New York: Columbia University Press.

Tyerman, Christopher. 2006. *God's War: A New History of the Crusades*. Cambridge: Belknap Press.

Udovitch, Abraham L. 1970. *Partnership and Profit in Medieval Islam*. Princeton: Princeton University Press.

Ulrich, Homer, and Paul Pisk. 1963. *A History of Music and Musical Style*. New York: Harcourt Brace Jovanovich.

Unger, Richard W., and Robert Gardiner. 2000. *Cogs, Caravals, and Galleons*. New York: Chartwell Books.

Urbach, Efraim. 1975. *The Sages: Their Concepts and Beliefs*. Jerusalem: Magnes.

Usher, Abbott Payson. 1966. *A History of Mechanical Inventions*. Cambridge, MA: Harvard University Press.

Van Doren, Charles. 1991. *A History of Knowledge*. New York: Ballantine.

Van Houts, Elisabeth. 2000. *The Normans in Europe*. Manchester: Manchester University Press.

Verhulst, Adriaan. 1994. "The Origins and Early Development of Medieval Towns in Northern Europe." *Economic History Review* 47: 362–73.

Veyne, Paul. 1961. "Vie de trimalcion." *Annales: Économies, Societés, Civilisations* 16: 213–47.

Voigtländer, Nic. and Hans-Joachim Voth. 2006. "Why England? Demographic Factors, Structural Change. and Physical Capital Accumulation during the Industrial Revolution." *Journal of Economic Growth* 11: 319–61.

Vries, P. H. H. 2001. "Are Coal and Colonies Really Crucial?" *Journal of World History* 12: 407–46.

Waley, Daniel. 1988. *The Italian City-Republics*. 3rd ed. London: Longman.

Wallerstein, Immanuel. 1974. *The Modern World-System*. Vol. 1. New York: Academic Press.

———. 2011. *The Modern World-System*. Vol. 2. Berkeley: University of California Press.

———. 2004. *World-System Analysis: An Introduction*. Durham, NC: Duke University Press.

Walton, Timothy R. 2002. *The Spanish Treasure Fleets*. Sarasota, FL: Pineapple Press.

Walzer, Michael. 1985. *Exodus and Revolution*. New York: Basic Books.

Ward-Perkins, Bryan. 2006. *The Fall of Rome and the End of Civilization*. Oxford: Oxford University Press.

Washburn, Wilcomb. 1975. *The Indian in America*. 6th ed. New York: Harper-Collins.

Waterbolk, H. T. 1968. "Food Production in Prehistoric Europe." *Science* 162: 1093–1102.

Watkins, Ronald. 2004. *Unknown Seas: How Vasco da Gama Opened the East*. London: John Murray.

Watt, W. Montgomery. 1965. *Muhammad at Medina*. London: Oxford University Press.

———. 1961. *Muhammad: Prophet and Statesman*. London: Oxford University Press.

Weber, Max. [1904–5] 1958. *The Protestant Ethic and the Spirit of Capitalism*. London: Routledge.

Wegg, Jervis. 1924. *The Decline of Atwerp under Philip of Spain*. London: Methuen.

Wells, Peter S. 1999. *The Barbarians Speak*. Princeton: Princeton University Press.

———. 2008. *Barbarians to Angels: The Dark Ages Reconsidered*. New York: W. W. Norton.

Wesseling, H. L. *The European Colonial Empires, 1815–1919*. Harlow, UK: Pearson.

West, Martin. 1988. "Early Greek Philosophy." In John Boardman, Jasper Griggin, and Oswyn Murray, eds., *The Oxford History of Greece and the Hellenistic World*, 126–141. Oxford: Oxford University Press.

Westermann, William Linn. 1941. "Athenaeus and the Slaves of Athens." *Harvard Studies in Classical Philology*, supplemental volume, 451–70.

Westfall, Richard S. 1971. *The Construction of Modern Science*. New York: Wiley.

Whitehead, Alfred North. [1929] 1979. *Process and Reality*. New York: The Free Press.

———. [1925] 1967. *Science and the Modern World*. New York: Free Press.

Whitehead, Clive. 2003. *Colonial Educators: The British and Indian Colonial Educational Service 1858–1983*. London: I. B. Tauris.

White, K. D. 1984. *Greek and Roman Technology*. Ithaca, NY: Cornell University Press.

White, Lynn, Jr. 1962. *Medieval Technology and Social Change*. London: Oxford University Press.

———. 1975. "The Study of Medieval Technology, 1924–1974: Personal Reflections." *Technology and Culture* 16: 519–30.

Whitmarsh, Tim. 2004. *Ancient Greek Literature*. Cambridge: Polity Press.

Wickham, Chris. 1989. *Early Medieval Italy: Central Power and Local Society 400–1000*. Ann Arbor: University of Michigan Press.

Wiedemann, Thomas. 1992. *Emperors and Gladiators*. London: Routledge.

Wiener, Peter F. 1944. *Martin Luther: Hitler's Spiritual Ancestor*. London: Hutchinson.

Wigelsworth, Jeffrey R. 2006. *Science and Technology in Medieval European Life*. Westport, CT: Greenwood Press.

Wild, John. 1949. "Plato and Christianity: A Philosophical Comparison." *Journal of Bible and Religion* 17: 3–16.

Wilford, John Noble. 2000. *The Mapmakers*. Rev. ed. New York: Vintage Books.

Wilkinson, Toby. 2010. *The Rise and Fall of Ancient Egypt*. New York: Random House.

Williams, C. F. 1903. *The Story of the Organ*. New York: Charles Scribner and Sons.

Williams-McClanahan, Robin. 2006. *Out of the Ashes: The Rise of Towns and Trade in the Early Medieval West*. New York: iUniverse, Inc.

Williams, Neville. 1975. *The Sea Dogs*. New York: Macmillan.

Wilson, Andrew. 2002. "Machines, Power and the Ancient Economy." *Journal of Roman Studies* 92: 1–32.

Wimberly, Dale, and Rosaria Bello. 1992. "Effects of Foreign Investment, Exports, and Economic Growth on Third World Food Consumption." *Social Forces* 70: 895–921.

Windel, Aaron. 2009. "British Colonial Education in Africa: Policy and Practice in the Era of Trusteeship." *History Compass* 7: 1–21.

Windschuttle, Keith. 1996. *The Killing of History*. San Francisco: Encounter Books.

Wittfogel, Karl A. [1957] 1981. *Oriental Despotism*. New York: Vintage Books.

Wolfram, Herwig. 1988. *History of the Goths*. Berkeley: University of California Press.

———. 1997. *The Roman Empire and Its Germanic Peoples*. Berkeley: University of California Press.

Wolfson, Harry Austryn. 1947. "The Knowability and Describability of God in Plato and Aristotle." *Harvard Studies in Classical Philology* 56: 233–49.

Wood, Frances. 1995. *Did Marco Polo Go to China?* London: Secker and Warburg.

Woodberry, Robert D. 2007a. "The Medical Impact of Missions." Paper presented at the American Society for Church History, Atlanta, January 5.

———. "The Missionary Roots of Liberal Democracy." *American Political Science Review* 106: 1–30.

———. 2006. "Reclaiming the M-Word: The Legacy of Missions in Nonwestern Societies." *Reveiw of Faith and International Affairs* 4, no. 1: 3–12.

———. 2011. "Religion and the Spread of Human Capital and Poltiical Institutions." In Rachel M. McCleary, ed. *The Oxford Handbook of the Economics of Religion*, 111–31. New York: Oxford University Press.

———. 2007b. "The Social Impact of Missionary Higher Education." In Philip Yuen Sang Leung and Peter Tze Ming Ng, eds., *Christian Responses to Asian Challenges*, 99–120. Hong Kong: Centre for the Study of Religion and Chinese Society, the Chinese University of Hong Cong.

Wrigley, E. A. 2010. *Energy and the English Industrial Revolution*. Cambridge: Cambridge University Press.

Wroth, Lawrence C. 1970. *The Voyages of Giovanni de Verrazzano, 1524–1528*. New Haven: Yale University Press.

Wuthnow, Robert. 1989. *Communities of Discourse*. Cambridge: Harvard University Press.

Yamaki, Kazuhiko. 2001. *Nicholas of Cusa: A Medieval Thinker for a Modern Age*. New York: Routledge.

Ziegler, Philip. 1971. *The Black Death*. New York: Harper Torchbooks.

Zinsser, Hans. 1963. *Rats, Lice, and History*. New York: Black Dog and Leventhal.

Zoll, Amy. 2002. *Gladiatrix: The True Story of History's Unknown Woman Warrior*. New York: Berkley.

Zupko, Jack. 2003. *John Buridan: Portrait of a Fourteenth-Century Arts Master*. Notre Dame, IN: University of Notre Dame Press.

Index